**John
DOS PASSOS**

John DOS PASSOS

The Major Nonfictional Prose

Edited by
DONALD PIZER

Wayne State University Press

Detroit 1988

92 91 90 89 88   5 4 3 2 1

Library of Congress Cataloging-in-Publication Data

Dos Passos, John, 1896–1970.
  [Prose works. Selections]
  John Dos Passos : the major nonfictional prose / edited by Donald
Pizer.
      p.   cm.
  Includes index.
  ISBN 0–8143–2057–0 (alk. paper).   ISBN 0–8143–2058–9 (pbk. : alk.
paper)
  I. Pizer, Donald.   II. Title.
PS3507.O743A6 1988
818'.5408--dc19   88–18090
                                                        CIP

Contents

88-6788

Preface

John Dos Passos is one of the giants of twentieth-century American literature. His experimental modernistic novels *Three Soldiers* (1921), *Manhattan Transfer* (1925), and *U.S.A.* (1938) made him—along with Hemingway and Faulkner—one of the most widely discussed American writers of the 1920s and 1930s. And his lifelong commitment to an exploration of the basic issues of American life—what kind of nation are we and what kind should we be?—established his permanent centrality in early twentieth-century American intellectual and cultural history. As Edmund Wilson noted as early as 1930, Dos Passos, more than any other novelist of his generation, "is concerned with the larger questions of politics and society."

This concern is reflected both in the nature and the extent of the nonfictional prose that Dos Passos produced during his lifetime. Dos Passos' first work of this kind, *Rosinante to the Road Again*, appeared in 1922; his last, an account of Easter Island, in 1971, the year following his death. In between, he published some seventeen volumes that were neither fiction nor poetry nor drama. These books divide roughly into travel writing, historical accounts of the origin and nature of the American republic, patriotic reportage on American participation in the Second World War, one autobiography, and two miscellanies. This large body of descriptive, historical, and polemical prose is of course important for an understanding of Dos Passos' career and beliefs, but it is also limited and misleading in a number of ways. The great majority of these works were written after Dos Passos' shift to the right in the late 1930s and thus reflect principally that phase of his career and thought. (Even his two miscellanies—*The Theme Is Freedom* (1956) and *Occasions and Protests* (1964)—collect pre-1937 writing in the context of Dos Passos' polemical editorial commentary on this earlier work.) In addition, there exists a great deal of material—much of it from Dos Passos' early career—that he never collected. This writing—reviews, travel accounts, and argumentative reportage of every kind—offers a striking insight into Dos Passos' beliefs and activities during the period of his greatest vitality and centrality as a commentator on the American scene. Finally, his collections omit the frequently trenchant interviews, introductions, and published addresses of his later career, writings in which the usually reticent Dos Passos often commented openly and fully on the events of his career and on his literary motives.

The intent of this edition is to present in a single volume the best of Dos Passos' nonfictional prose from the beginning to the end of his career. By *best*, or *major*, I mean both the intrinsic quality of a selection and the light it casts on Dos Passos' beliefs and life. I have sought above all to present Dos Passos by the selection of previously uncollected material, both to make this material more generally available and because it frequently is the best representative of Dos Passos' activities and ideas at specific phases of his career. But I have also included a number of previously republished selections—Dos Passos' early "Young Spain" essay, for example, and his articles on Sacco and Vanzetti and on the Harlan County coal strike—when these can best serve the function of powerfully exemplifying a major moment in his life and thought. *John Dos Passos: The Major Nonfictional Prose* should thus provide the reader both with a general overview of Dos Passos' career and beliefs as expressed in his own writing and with an introduction to Dos Passos' writing at its most cogent and vital.

Permission to reprint has been granted by the American Academy and Institute of Arts and Letters ("Acceptance by John Dos Passos"); American Labor Conference on International Affairs, Inc. ("Conversation with Dos Passos"); *The Carleton Miscellany* ("Contemporary Chronicles"); Century Hutchinson Limited ("The Duty of the Writer"); Mrs. Elizabeth Dos Passos ("Translator's Foreword to *Panama*," "Introduction to *Three Soldiers*," "Introductory Note to *The 42nd Parallel*," "A Preface Twenty-Five Years Later," and "The American Cause"); Harvard University Press ("PS to Dean Briggs"); International Publishers Company ("The Writer As Technician"); Condé Nast Publications ("Is the 'Realistic' Theatre Obsolete?"); *The Nation* ("America and the Pursuit of Happiness," "Building Lots," "An Open Letter to President Lowell," and "To a Liberal in Office"); National Review, Inc. ("Faulkner," "The Battle of San Francisco," "What Hope for Maintaining a Conservative Opposition?" "The New Left," "What Makes a Novelist," and "On the Way to the Moon Shot"); the *New York Times* ("Mr. Dos Passos on *Him*," "An Interview with Mr. John Dos Passos," and "Looking Back on *U.S.A.*"); *Partisan Review* ("The Situation in American Writing"); Reader's Digest Association ("What Union Members Have Been Writing Senator McClellan"); *Saturday Review* ("Mr. Chambers's Descent into Hell"); Union College Press ("An Interview with John Dos Passos"); Viking Penguin, Inc. ("John Dos Passos"); and the *Washington Post* ("Portrait of a Man Reading").

A Note on the Text

Dos Passos often cut or otherwise revised material for republication. Since I wish in this edition to preserve his original expression rather than his later recasting, I have reprinted, except when otherwise noted, the text of first periodical appearance. A textual note at the foot of the first page of each selection cites the initial periodical appearance of the selection and the first book collection by Dos Passos. The absence of the second kind of information means that the selection is here collected for the first time. All selections are reprinted in full. (Ellipses and bracketed material in the text are in the original.) With the exception of titles of selections, I have not regularized or normalized punctuation or spelling. I have, however, corrected obvious typographical errors; these corrections are noted in the list of emendations following this note. In instances of the misspelling of a proper name, some (*Master's* for *Masters*, for example) are considered typographical errors, while others—especially of foreign names—remain uncorrected in the text, with the correct spelling cited in a note.

I have attempted to keep annotation to a minimum. But given the wide range of Dos Passos' activities and interests, it has been necessary to supply information in a good many instances. Headnotes provide the historical or personal context of a selection when this is deemed necessary, and footnotes identify obscure events or persons. Commonly known events or readily identifiable figures are not annotated, but the full name of each person mentioned in the text can be found in the index.

The following page and line numbers locate words and punctuation in this edition that are corrected from their form in the original publication; the word or punctuation following page and line numbers is that of the original: 23:21 famed; 23:36 enough the; 28:25 Master's; 28:37 Grey; 33:43 tentactular; 44:27, 44:30, 44:35 Barroja; 45:28 Fallo; 46:21 tradition"; 52:32 respons. . . ; 59:36 farded; 65:39 spluter; 72:12 Du; 72:25 O'Neil; 76:33 Gorelick; 85:34 hilling; 87:43 fast; 92:12 Rotonde Zelli's; 92:28 its; 103:4 connates; 106:10 baloon; 106:16 habor; 106:17 author; 107:35 thinest; 111:21 1927; 112:28 its; 112:31 utterer; 113:1 confused bullied; 114:28 Coolidge, meanheartedness; 114:33 resistence; 116:31 Its; 117:16 bleeched; 117:22 fullfil; 119:41 exciting tragic; 121:8 Goritzia; 122:6 its; 122:8 its; 122:26 is was; 134:9 Wyndham's; 134:17 Sandberg; 134:27 Cendrars'; 146:31 asperin; 152:24 Eight; 153:3 bretheren; 208:38 Providence; 236:1 Goncharova; 239:22 Marryatt's; 243:17 twenty hours off; 264:13 nineteenth; 265:43 kind; 272:39 Conrad; 274:7 his sort; 294:14 Ungharetti; 298:46 of blackboards.

Introduction

Whether Dos Passos' life and work constitute an "odyssey" in the sense of a quest, as is implied in the subtitle of one of his major biographies,[1] may be open to question. But there is little doubt that movement and change characterize most of his career both in his physical restlessness—his constant travel—and in the shift of his beliefs from one extreme of the political spectrum to the other. As several recent commentators have suggested, the roots of this basic cast of mind may lie in Dos Passos' unsettled childhood. Dos Passos' father, a hard-driving successful Wall Street lawyer, was already married when he met, and began living with, Lucy Madison, herself a widow. John Madison (he was not to take his father's name until he was sixteen) was born illegitimately in Chicago in 1896 and was to spend most of his childhood with his mother in various European and American cities awaiting the occasional visits of his father.

Dos Passos' parents were married in 1910, and Dos Passos himself—after over four years at Choate—appeared to be little different from most young men of his wealth and class when he entered Harvard in 1912. But there were significant signs—the slightly foreign accent and southern European surname, the stammer, and above all the preoccupation with books—that the tall myopic young man was indeed an outsider and that he would soon become less a participant in his world than a judge of it. Dos Passos' journal of his Harvard years reveals an amazing range of reading, much of it in contemporary literature.[2] By his junior year he had become active in a group of young aesthetes centered around the *Harvard Monthly*. The largely derivative and slight poems and stories he contributed to the journal suggest indirectly in their frequently exotic settings Dos Passos' restlessness within what he was later to call the "bellglass" or "ethercone" of Harvard.[3] Dos Passos' articles and reviews in the *Monthly*,[4] though of course miscellaneous in subject matter and tentative in belief, reflect a similar attitude. Running through these pieces is an enthusiasm for the new and unconventional: a new literary subject here, a new technique there. And above all there occurred during these last years at Harvard the gradual hardening of Dos Passos' rejection of America as a business and industrial civilization because of his belief that these aspects of American society were allied with the stifling and the repressive in life.

Dos Passos' mindset at this phase of his life—before he joined the ambulance service in the summer of 1917—is best revealed in the three most important essays of his early career: "A Humble Protest," "Against American Literature," and

12

"Young Spain." "Industrialism" to Dos Passos in these essays is not merely a technological process but—as to Emerson and Melville—a force in society comprising the mechanical, the materialistic, and the destructively competitive and thus a force restricting the freedom of the human spirit both to feel and to express its feelings. Spain, however, with its still living tradition of a "strong anarchistic reliance on the individual man," offered to Dos Passos a refuge and an alternative to the modern Western "industrial world of joyless enforced labor and incessant goading war."[5]

Dos Passos' first-hand experience of the war, initially as an ambulance driver and then as an enlisted man, confirmed in his mind the validity of the mythic construct of a worldwide conflict between a destructive industrialism and a liberating anarchism. But his experience of war also, as dramatized in *Three Soldiers*, led him to one of the central themes in all of his work, that of the capacity of the institution, and especially the state, to control belief and action through the manipulation of language. The duty of the writer, Dos Passos realized at this point and expressed fully and frequently throughout the late 1920s and early 1930s, was to attempt to preserve the integrity of language and especially the integrity of the "old words"— the heritage of democratic idealism encapsulated in such terms as *freedom, justice,* and *opportunity.*

With the success of *Three Soldiers* in 1921, Dos Passos was firmly established in a literary career. For Dos Passos in the early 1920s, being a writer meant foreign travel (a six months' journey to south Russia and the Near East during 1921–22, for example) and involvement at home in the avant garde and bohemian worlds of New York. He was especially intrigued by the experimental literary forms emerging out of cubism, film montage, and theatrical expressionism as these had applicability to the depiction of the helter-skelter of modern American urban life. Out of this enthusiasm was to come both his own experimental novel, *Manhattan Transfer* (1925), and his increasing interest in the kind of expressionist drama being devised by his friend John Howard Lawson.

Dos Passos was in Europe and North Africa from mid-1925 to early 1926, but on his return to New York his career took a number of new directions; or, perhaps more accurately, it moved more fully and openly in directions anticipated by his earlier interests and activities. Dos Passos' resentment toward the excesses and injustices of the industrial system in America was now prodded into overt political expression by the increasing prominence of the far Left in American life and by the seemingly successful example of a proletarian state offered at the time by the Soviet Union. More specifically, the growing significance of the Sacco-Vanzetti case in early 1926 (they were to be executed the following year) and the founding of the radical monthly the *New Masses* provided Dos Passos with both a vital cause and an important new outlet. Dos Passos also discovered on his return from abroad that Lawson and a number of other "advanced" playwrights were about to organize the New Playwrights Theatre in order to encourage the production of radical and experimental drama. Dos Passos' enthusiasm for Lawson's ideas about the theatre and his interest in a forum for his own plays led him to join the group and to take an active role in its affairs for almost three years.

As early as 1927 Dos Passos had begun to plan a panoramic novel about modern American life, a work that would fulfill his own prescription of 1928 that the novelist be "a sort of second-class historian of the age he lives in."[6] But it was principally after his lengthy trip to Russia in 1928 and the collapse of the New Play-

wrights Theatre in early 1929 that he fully committed himself to a trilogy of experimental novels in which he would attempt an epic portrait of twentieth-century
American life. During the late 1920s and early 1930s, while he was writing *U.S.A.*,
Dos Passos' involvement in left-wing causes, as reflected in his *New Masses* and
New Republic articles and reviews, continued unabated. But he was also becoming,
as he later recalled, increasingly suspicious of Communist methods and goals within
the activities of the far Left. A number of encounters with doctrinaire party beliefs
and procedures[7] finally led him, within the hostile context of the Communist-
controlled American Writers' Congress of 1935, to state a kind of declaration of independence. The principal purpose of art is to aid in the achievement of humanistic
goals, he wrote in "The Writer As Technician." Therefore, "a writer . . . must never
. . . no matter how much he is carried away by even the noblest political partisanship in the fight for social justice, allow himself to forget that his real political aim,
for himself and his fellows, is liberty."[8]

There thus runs through Dos Passos' writing and correspondence of the early
1930s (especially in his letters to Edmund Wilson)[9] a kind of debate in which his
recognition of the continuing role of the Left in combatting both social injustice at
home and fascism abroad argues with his growing dismay over the threat to freedom of belief and action represented by the authoritarianism of the Communist
party and its adherents. By the mid-1930s Dos Passos' antagonism toward Party
control of the Left surfaced clearly in his withdrawal from the now fully doctrinaire
New Masses in favor of the anti-Communist (though still radical) *Common Sense*,
and by the powerful strain of distrust present in his depiction of the Communist
Don Stevens in *The Big Money* (1936), the concluding novel of *U.S.A.*

Dos Passos broke fully and openly with the Left in 1937. Appropriately for
Dos Passos, who was a man of strong personal loyalties throughout his life, the
break arose out of the death of his old friend José Robles during the Spanish Civil
War. The quasi-judicial murder of Robles by a Communist firing squad convinced
Dos Passos that the party was essentially a "tremendously efficient and ruthless
machine for power"[10] and was therefore a danger to individual liberty both in Spain
and America. By the time he returned to the United States from Spain in mid-1937,
Dos Passos was committed—at considerable cost to himself, given the strongly pro-
loyalist sympathies of most American intellectuals of the time—to exposing this
danger. His essays of this period caused him to lose two of his closest friends, Hemingway and Lawson, and antagonized such influential critics and reviewers as Malcolm Cowley. But far more significantly for his career as a whole, Dos Passos' rejection of the Left moved him to devote much of his energy as a writer both to
defending his political beliefs in a series of autobiographical novels and to demon-
strating the roots of these beliefs in native American institutions and values in a series of historical and biographical studies. The first series began with *Adventures of a
Young Man* (1939) and continued with *Chosen Country* (1951) and *Most Likely To
Succeed* (1954); the second began with *The Ground We Stand On* (1941) and continued for the remainder of Dos Passos' life.

"The Atlantic is a good wide ocean," Dos Passos wrote in 1937 on his return
from Spain.[11] In our distance from foreign ideologies, he was increasingly to affirm,
and in our commitment to the fundamental liberties institutionalized in our constitution and laws, lay our strength. As early as 1941 he sounded the note that was to
run, in varying form, through much of his writing of the next three decades. "We

can thank our stars," he wrote, "that the men who founded our system of government understood so well the corruption of power, and that in the common law we have a storehouse of inherited techniques for the protection of the individual man."[12] To preserve this way of life, Dos Passos, like many former pacifists of the 1920s and 1930s, entered wholeheartedly into the war against Germany and Japan. He made lengthy tours of America and the Far East and wrote extensively in support of the war effort.

By the mid-1950s, Dos Passos' miscellaneous writing in prose had fallen into the two complementary forms he was to pursue for the rest of his career. On the one hand he became a spokesman for basic right-wing positions—that labor unions were a threat to freedom, for example, or that liberals were weak on the dangers of international communism. On the other he defended, in the many interviews and addresses in which he discussed his life and work, his shift from the Left to the Right. In one of his most cogent summaries of this defense, he argued in 1959 that the shift was more apparent than real, that he had been devoted throughout his career to depicting "man's struggle for life against the strangling institutions he himself creates." What had changed in the course of his life was the nature of the principal threat to freedom—from "organized money" to the power of the modern state. He himself, however, in defense of individual freedom had remained "monotonously" consistent.[13]

Dos Passos' career as a whole, however, presents so awesome an instance of absolute change that it is difficult to accept a single explanation, including his own, for the variance. The writer who in the early 1930s had written for the *New Masses*, defended the rights of labor at Harlan, and voted for William Z. Foster, in the 1960s wrote for the *National Review*, attacked the power of labor unions, and voted for Barry Goldwater. And the writer who in his first major essay, "A Humble Protest," had attacked modern industrialism for its deleterious effect on the human spirit, in his last major essay, his 1971 "On the Way to the Moon Shot," applauded the products of applied science and industrial strength as evidence of "a fresh assertion of man's spirit."[14]

There are, as Townsend Ludington points out convincingly in his biography of Dos Passos, no easy solutions to the problem of accounting for this massive change in Dos Passos' social and political allegiances. Was it the result of an innate conservatism, derived in part from his father's beliefs, at last finding its role and voice after the "wild oats" of youthful rebelliousness—a state of mind that found its natural setting in the "ultra-conservative calm"[15] of Dos Passos' Virginia estate during the last two decades of his life? Was it principally the effect of a loss of hope (or illusion) through advancing age, the writer who had looked forward in May 1919 to a liberating world revolution stating in 1968 that "now we know that the first of May will never come"?[16] Or was it the product of the true believer whose apostasy forces him into the complete opposite of his earlier faith? There is probably an element of truth in each of these explanations, as well as in several others.

What remains constant in Dos Passos' career is the elemental integrity and the almost constant vitality of his self-examination. The informing presence of a man of conscious values and beliefs invigorates Dos Passos' prose from the beginning of his career to its close, from the reportage of "Four Nights in a Garden" to that of "The Battle of San Francisco," from the controlled irony of "300 N.Y. Agitators Reach Passaic" to that of "Doves in the Bullring." Always the professional, Dos

Passos seldom wrote a bad sentence. But his writing is more than professionally correct; it also reveals one of the major expressive consciences of the modern American experience.

Notes

1. Townsend Ludington, *John Dos Passos: A Twentieth Century Odyssey* (New York: Dutton, 1980).

2. For an example, see ibid., 67. Dos Passos' lists in his "Literary Diary" for 1914–15 (in the Dos Passos Collection of the University of Virginia Library) suggest he read roughly a book a day.

3. In Camera Eye (28) of *Nineteen-Nineteen*; see *U.S.A.* (*Nineteen-Nineteen*) (New York: Modern Library, 1939), 9, 11.

4. For a listing of Dos Passos' contributions to the *Harvard Monthly*—as well as for a full listing of all of Dos Passos' prose from throughout his career—see David Sanders, *John Dos Passos: A Comprehensive Bibliography* (New York: Garland, 1987).

5. "Young Spain," *Seven Arts*, 2 (August 1917); see pp. 40, 47 below.

6. "Statement of Belief," *Bookman*, 68 (September 1928); see p. 115 below.

7. A major turning point was Dos Passos' anger at the Communist disruption of a socialist rally at Madison Square Garden in February 1934.

8. "The Writer As Technician," in *American Writers' Congress*, ed. Henry Hart (New York: International Publishers, 1935); see p. 170 below.

9. See *The Fourteenth Chronicle: Letters and Diaries of John Dos Passos*, ed. Townsend Ludington (Boston: Gambit, 1973).

10. "Farewell to Europe," *Common Sense*, 6 (July 1937); see p. 185 below.

11. "Farewell to Europe"; see p. 185 below.

12. "To a Liberal in Office," *Nation*, 153 (6 September 1941); see p. 199 below.

13. "Looking Back on *U.S.A.*," *New York Times*, 25 October 1959; see p. 137 below.

14. "On the Way to the Moon Shot," *National Review*, 23 (9 February 1971); see p. 298 below.

15. The phrase is Richard Whalen's in his interview with Dos Passos; "Conversation with Dos Passos," *New Leader*, 42 (23 February 1959); see p. 231 below.

16. "What Makes a Novelist," *National Review*, 20 (16 January 1968); see p. 271 below.

I

Finding a Way
(1914-17)

Insurgent Mexico

[A review of *Insurgent Mexico*, by Jack Reed.]

Ever since the beginning of the Mexican Revolution,[1] we have been deluged with books about that unhappy country, each of which claims the final and ultimate solution of the problem of the land's pacification. Everyone who has spent ten days on Mexican soil, it seems, deems himself qualified to propound his pet idea as to the reasons for Mexico's unrest, or his favorite criticism of our government's policy in a long and tiresome book, or a lurid magazine article. In "Insurgent Mexico," a collection of sketches, consisting mainly of articles published in the *Metropolitan Magazine*, Mr. Reed, who is, by the way, a recent Harvard graduate,[2] neither dogmatizes nor puts forward any panacea for the ills of Mexico; he is content to describe what he saw during the months he spent there as a correspondent.

The book as a whole contains some of the finest impressionistic descriptions of the life and scenery of Mexico that have ever appeared. The author has shown in his pictures a truly remarkable boldness and vividness; now and then, perhaps a little sensational, a little lurid, he is constantly redeemed by his accuracy of perception, and by his human, half-humorous, view. His startling vividness of description gives the sketches wonderful color and tangibility. To read them is to feel that you have been in Mexico, that you have felt the hot blast of the Mexican deserts, lived the passionate, picturesque life of the country.

"Insurgent Mexico" also deserves praise for its sympathetic understanding of the Mexicans. Since he writes neither as a disappointed monopoly seeker, nor as a jaded professional writer of books about the more disturbed parts of the world, Jack Reed reaches a comprehension of Mexican psychology denied to many a profounder student of this puzzling nation. He has the breadth to see a little the Mexican view, and his sympathy becomes at times almost admiration.

But the chief delight in "Insurgent Mexico" comes from a certain refreshing quality of adventurous youth. You find in all the adventures and descriptions the old spirit of daring and naive enjoyment of danger and excitement, altogether too rare in recent literature. This makes the book enjoyable even more for itself than for the knowledge of Mexico that can be gleaned from it.

Harvard Monthly, 59 (Nov. 1914), 67–68.

Notes

1. The Mexican revolution began in 1911 with the overthrow of dictator Porfirio Diaz.

2. Reed was graduated from Harvard in 1910. He is the subject of a biography in Dos Passos' *Nineteen-Nineteen* (1932).

Small Souls

[A review of *Small Souls*, by Louis Couperus.]

"Small Souls" is a notable novel. The first work of the foremost Dutch novelist to be translated into English, it reminds us that Holland still has a literature,—and, to judge from this example, a very important literature. In the first place the book is a vivid picture of present-day Dutch life in the upper middle class. It undertakes to give the history of a period in the existence of a large family, which the author centers about two people returning to The Hague after many years' absence. The scandal-mongering, carpingly-critical women, and the egotistical, preoccupied men are admirably portrayed. They have all small souls, lead petty, trivial lives; there is nothing great about any of them. Without a trace of didacticism, the novel is a tremendous satire, cold and unemotional, on the life of a small European capital.

Too much credit cannot be given for Couperus's vivid portraiture of his characters. The main figures stand out vividly from a crowd of struggling "small souls" —all of which are alive, even though dismissed with a few words; they are carefully, almost painfully drawn with a wealth of psychological detail. It is doubtful whether Thackeray or Tolstoy could have created such figures as Dorine, the aunt whose mania it is to run errands, or Constance, or the vixenish sister, Adolphine. There would probably be great difference of opinion about the author's success in drawing Adriaan, Van der Welke's thirteen-year-old son; but there is no doubt that it is an admirable attempt to do the nearly impossible.

The book has little plot; but the interest in the development of the characters is in its favor. "Small Souls" is translated into smooth English without the loss of its original flavor.

Harvard Monthly, 59 (Feb. 1915), 169.

Conrad's *Lord Jim*

A strangely subtle character study is "Lord Jim." It is the story of a young man, physically clean, and healthy, and charming, almost a boy, in fact, who is by nature and breeding "one of us," a gentleman; but who, by some minute flaw, fails under strain and plays the coward. He is a mate of an hulk of a steamer, the *Patna*, that carries East Indian pilgrims to Mecca. The boat runs into a derelict; so that her forward compartment becomes filled with water, leaving only an old rusty bulkhead, too rotten to repair, between the native passengers and drowning. The white officers and engine-room crew, who turn out to be abject creatures, prepare to slip away from the steamer unnoticed. Through pure excess of imagination, of power to visualize the horrors of the wreck he is sure is imminent, Jim's ability to act is paralyzed. At last, just as the captain's boat is pushing off, without knowing why or how, he jumps into it, and takes his place beside the cowards who are leaving the ship and passengers to their fate. As soon as he realizes what he has done he is horrified; but there is no going back. From that moment he and all the world think him a coward.

It is with the inquiry into the desertion of the *Patna* by her officers that the novel really begins. (By a miracle, the ship did not sink, but was towed into port by a French man-of-war). The only one with the pluck to face it out is Jim; the others vanish. From there on the story is a minute study, from the point of view of Marlow, the strange character who relates it, of Jim's subsequent life. Not even Marlow, however, can really understand Jim. He is constantly perplexed. His age, his caustic analytic temperament—everything combines to prevent his being in full sympathy with the boy.

"But as to me," he says in one place, after one of his early conversations with Jim, "left alone with the solitary candle, I remained strangely unenlightened. I was no longer young enough to behold at every turn the magnificence that besets our magnificent footsteps in good or evil. I smiled to think that, after all, it was yet he, of us two, who had the light, and I felt sad. A clean slate, did he say? As if the initial word of each our destiny were not graven in imperishable characters on the face of a rock."

Not until the end of the novel, if there, does Marlow profess to understand the man he is telling about. With marvellous skill, Conrad leaves it to the reader to do

Harvard Monthly, 60 (July 1915), 151–54.

that. The story ends with Jim's heroic, romantic death, still misunderstood by his friends, by the woman he loves, and by himself.

About Conrad's remarkable narrative method, nothing adequate has been written. It is so startlingly unique and so daring that one is hardly likely to give it its full credit. Or is it that its very freshness blinds us to its faults? The novel, or most of it, is told from the point of view of Marlow's strange and complex personality. With great art the close is written from the rabidly hostile viewpoint of Brown, an almost grotesquely repulsive adventurer, pirate, and cutthroat.

Chronological order is nearly entirely abandoned. The opening pages place you exactly in the middle of the story. Then the plot goes far back for a swift incident, a hint of the great turning point in Jim's life, at last returning to the chronological start of the narrative. The scene skips next to where Marlow is telling the story of the inquiry—"After dinner, on a veranda draped in motionless foliage and crowned with flowers, in the deep dusk speckled by fiery cigar ends. The elongated bulk of each cane chair harbored a silent listener. Now and then a small red glow would move abruptly, and expanding, light up the fingers of a languid hand, part of a face in profound repose, or flash a crimson gleam into a pair of pensive eyes overshadowed by a fragment of an unruffled forehead; and with the very first word uttered, Marlow's body, extended at rest in the seat, would become very still, as though his spirit had winged its way back into the lapse of time and were speaking through his lips from the past." Framed in this scene, it goes on, interwoven, complex, taking sudden leaps forward and back, constantly changing the point of view. But out of what would seem to be utter confusion, incidents and characters emerge with vivid distinctness, but of a haze of conjecture, of personal opinions, of interplay of personality, the characters appear gradually, becoming sharper, more actual, with each change of focus. The result is amazing, almost incomprehensible. You are dazzled by the vividness of portrayal. Jim, Jewel, the pirates and the Malays, and even the whimsical and sardonic Marlow are immensely alive.

Behind them floats an atmosphere, a vast impression of romance made actual. Tropical jungles, sunbaked seaports, the glittering blue Indian Ocean, unite to give an impression of romantic strangeness, yet of truth. Even the hideous, gargoyle-like villains, Cornelius and Brown and the crew of the *Patna*, seem as real as the horrid leering faces you sometimes see at night in the streets under the sudden glare of an arc light. The setting and the strange minor figures form a marvellous background against which moves the story, seen through the prism of Marlow's personality.

Never could enough be written about Marlow, that remarkable figure behind which the author hides his own individuality. He is the teller of "Chance," of "Youth," and of many others in that series of novels that has carried delicate analysis and realism into the field of Herman Melville and Ballantyne. The mere fact that Marlow does not lose actuality and "roundness" in the process, that he does not become a bundle of phrases and qualities, is one of the highest proofs of Conrad's uncanny power of characterization.

Indeed, Conrad's books are staggering achievements. You start with prejudices, with dislikes, you complain of his style; by the time you have finished you are cowed, wonderstruck. There is such a wealth of humanity in them; the treatment is so subtle! It is as though you were looking at life through some wonderful instrument, a microscope that, instead of magnifying, merely refines the outlines. Out of the mists and misapprehensions which cloud the minds of the characters, the reader has constructed for him actuality;—but actuality refined upon, laid bare, as it were, made transparent.

The great joy of reading Conrad, apart from the romance of it, from the liveness of it, lies in the fact that his books act as a sort of mental grindstone. When you have finished such a novel as "Lord Jim" or "Chance," your mind feels clearer, more efficient and capable than when you took it up. Your intellectual cobwebs have been blown away. You feel as if a little of Conrad's magic elixir had penetrated your own brain. But perhaps that is a priggish, ultra-literary pleasure to take in anything so full of color and humanity. In its romance, without a doubt, lies the fascination and the greatest enjoyment of Conrad's work.

The Evangelist and the Volcano

We were crowded into one of those things they call a "tally-ho" in the West, but that anywhere else would have a more humble name. We were tourists, all of us, and our cameras stuck into our neighbors' backs.[1] Gorgeous solemn mountains filed by on either side, as the vehicle jolted uncertainly over the uneven roads.

But the tourists were not looking at the mountains; they were talking about the War!

"It's all them Kings and Queens," announced a lady in a blue veil next to me, "gettin' land for their princelings."

"It ought to be stopped," the brisk woman in a man's cap exclaimed angrily, "takin' those nice young men out and shootin' 'em down. I would . . ."

A Canadian on the front seat turned around. "It would be if the German barbarians . . ." His voice was lost in the din of the discussion.

"If King George was made to fight, and the rest of them Kings——" The scorn with which the words were uttered defies expression, "then . . ." The prophetic sayings of my friend of the blue veil, evidently a lady of strong democratic ideas, were drowned by an emphatic speech on the part of the Canadian. And all the while the mountains and the solemn rows of spruce trees looked on impassively.

We Americans are a great people. We have wealth, industry, splendid sanitation, and a will—provided the operation can be made to pay—to reform the earth. We are a sort of epitome of the Anglo-Saxon spirit. So it follows naturally that we have, as a people, the completest inability to see anyone else's point of view. That is probably why the Anglo-Saxons conquered the world; and why America and American business methods were well on the way to conquer it, when something happened that our friend in the blue veil could not understand. She attributed it to the evil designs of George V and the Kaiser. Though others of us may not agree with her, we are equally at a loss to understand it. The War is a fact. Yet I doubt very much if any of us have the slightest realization of what it means.

The Nineteenth Century has collapsed; the good old materialistic nineteenth century, with its self-confidence and its comfortable cosmopolitanism. Out of its ashes, amid the stench of asphyxiating gases and the lurid inferno of the new war, has sprung something strange and stirring and horrible. Yet the war might be taking place on one of the moons of Jupiter and have as much effect on our thought as a

Harvard Monthly, 61 (Nov. 1915), 59–61.

people. To most of us it is merely an opportunity for indulging in the old humanitarian cant, that pours forth mechanically when certain subjects are approached. The intelligence of the process is equal to that of a slot machine sliding out chewing gum when you drop in a penny.

All this is a far cry from a stage load of tourists chattering empty headedly about the war. But these tourists, chattering empty headedly about the war, for the moment symbolized America. We are all engaged in chattering empty headedly about the war. Our minds are so clogged by a long course of the sentimental prejudices and other quack medicines of the nineteenth century that we don't realize that we live in the twentieth. Like Rip Van Winkle we must soon open our eyes to be startled by a new age that has appeared while we slept, drugged by the nasal voice of our uninspired puritan materialism. Events have flown ahead and left us to stumble aimlessly about the barren brick kilns of dead ideas.

Impossible, indeed, is it to tell how much the course of our civilization has been changed. We in America are too shocked and irritated; in Europe men's eyes are blinded by the stinging smoke of howitzer bombs.

But all the same, we can try to understand, to sympathize, to realize how our civilization's ideals are tottering. We can lose the idea that it is by some especial God-given virtue of our own that we are not, as Mr. Bryan puts it, "wallowing in the slime of war."[2] Above all we must realize that we are not isolated onlookers, that our destinies as well as those of the warring nations are being fought out on French and Turkish battlefields. If we felt our own interests were at stake, we should soon lose our national attitude of supercilious disapproval. We might come to understand that such a huge catastrophe is above and apart from all praise and blame.

As a nation, at present, we are like an Evangelist preaching a sermon to a volcano—from a safe distance.

Notes

1. Dos Passos made a trip to the far West and California in the summer of 1915.

2. William Jennings Bryan, Woodrow Wilson's Secretary of State from early 1913 to June 1915, was a strong proponent of American neutrality in the European war.

The Catholic Anthology and Georgian Poetry, 1913–1915

[A review of *Georgian Poetry, 1913–1915*, edited by Edward H. Marsh, and
The Catholic Anthology, 1914–1915.]

This seems to be an age of anthologies. Probably they are among the signs of "the revival of poetry"; whether a favorable sign or not is still to be questioned. Indeed, the function of such volumes as Mr. Braithwaite's annual collections of current verse seems to be the embalming, Egyptian fashion, of a quantity of stuff which would otherwise very happily disappear in the course of nature.[1] Well-meaning attempts they certainly are to heighten the poetic interest of the multitude; but I much doubt if anyone, except the contributors, reads them. They may, too, have a future utility in supplying material from which some scholar of super-Teutonic thoroughness can construct a thesis, say on "The Trend of Minor Anglo-American Verse in the Early Twentieth Century." The other sort of Anthology has, I believe, more of a place in the leavening with poetry of life today. Such a volume as *Des Imagistes*, containing the work of people of approximately the same artistic creed, is really an attempt to add something, to impose a new trend of thought on current literature.[2] Whether, however, these Imagist collections are to degenerate into the expression of a mere clique of writers is still to be seen.

These anthologies, the *Catholic Anthology*, and *Georgian Verse, 1913–1915*, are somewhere between the two types. Each has a vaguely predominant tone without any of the polemic character of the Imagist volumes. They afford an interesting contrast; for although both were published in London, the *Catholic Anthology* is a representative, if not of America, of Washington Square, as is the other of the general trend of contemporary English Verse. Neither contains anything of surpassing merit; probably they are more interesting as samples of what is being done for that reason.

The first thing that strikes you in *Georgian Verse* is the lack of war poetry. Everything is from that period—so far away now—when the nineteenth century was still living on into the twentieth. This distance from the present mood gives things of that time a beauty and wistfulness, a strange futility. Somewhere in that absurd book *Le Juif Errant*,[3] there is a description of Behring Strait. Two people on either side seem borne together for a moment by a mirage, only to slip back into the mists again and find between them a lashing ice-strewn sea. However meteorologically incorrect it may be, the description expresses the feeling one has in reading poetry written in the mood of that calm period before the war split the centuries apart.

Harvard Monthly, 62 (May 1916), 92–94.

Hence a great deal of the verse is strangely meaningless, seems a mere stringing to-gether of words. The redeeming feature lies in the aliveness and closeness to the soil of much of the work. You feel the fine old English naturalistic spirit rising to domi-nance. The poets have turned their backs on the city and are out on the purple moorland. This feeling has always been in the background of English poetry. In the poems of A. E. Housman and in the novels of D. H. Lawrence it has become aggres-sively the dominant note. It is neither the moralized landscape of Wordsworth, nor the hot-house vegetation of the romantic poets, but the triumphant earthiness ex-pressed by Chaucer in the beginning of the Prologue.

> "Whan that Aprille with his shoures soote
> The droghte of Marche hath perced to the rote,
> And bathed every veyne in swich licour,
> Of which vertu engendred is the flour."

Imperfectly expressed, to be sure, in form at times degenerating into Mother Goose doggerel, there is a splendid sense of life about this poetry, of love of mere living, of man's blood and bone, and the golden cornfields that are his setting,—a robustness that makes the faddy verses of the *Catholic Anthology* seem sallow and anaemic.

To be sure at times the poets are led astray into strange fatuities; so childish are some of the poems that you wonder how they got into the volume. However, the contributions of D. H. Lawrence and W. W. Gibson, and Gordon Bottomley's play, *King Lear's Wife*, are in themselves enough to make the volume of real interest.

I wish one could say as much for the *Catholic Anthology*. The most important feature is the sense of satire, of half humorous character-drawing, well represented, in its more sinister side, by Edgar Lee Masters' work. Then there is a certain atmo-sphere of city life, a really poetic feeling for it, which may, under more propitious circumstances, produce mighty things. As it is, the verse, laboriously free, straggles over dull pages. Affectation reigns. Such desolating attempts to be new, to be bold, to be smart, to be naughty, have hardly been seen since some of the excesses of the Nineties. Here and there, though, a gleam of real light, of art to come, appears in the turbid obscurity. Probably the very absurdities are a good sign; Lyly came before Marlowe and Shakespeare.

Certainly the best thing in the volume is *Hortense Robbins*, reprinted from Mr. Masters' *Spoon River Anthology*, a splendidly terse satire, which expresses the life of a thousand women in half a page. The poems of Harold Munro, too, have considerable beauty. *Milk for the Cat*, also printed in *Georgian Poetry*, is worthy of being placed beside Gray's poem about the cat drowned in the bowl of goldfish. Then several of Ezra Pound's things are very delightful; one always feels about his work that he might do twice as well if he wanted to. Outside of these, however, and *A Portrait of a Lady* by T. S. Eliot, there is little worth reading—except as an object lesson!

Comforting it is to think, that notwithstanding the virulent cover, smelling of *Blast*,[4] the volume is not likely to be read by the great public the modern poets are trying so hard to innoculate with the germ of appreciation. If they did, I fear they would turn—perhaps wisely; who knows?—with relief to their velvet-covered illus-trated Longfellows, and there seek peace from this nightmare of distorted originality by gently murmuring:

"Life is real, life is earnest"; life is not an empty, and very unpleasant, dream.

Notes

1. William S. B. Braithwaite edited such volumes as *The Poetic Year for 1916* and *Anthology of Magazine Verse for 1916.*
2. Edited by Ezra Pound and published in 1914, *Des Imagistes* was a collection of imagist poetry.
3. In English, *The Wandering Jew*, a popular novel by Eugène Sue, published initially in 1845.
4. A radical journal founded by Wyndham Lewis in 1914 and noted for its flamboyant covers.

A Humble Protest

There is a tendency abroad to glorify, in sounding journalistic phrases, the age in which we live and the "wonders of science" which have brought it about. Man is pictured as enthroned on a girder-constructed pinnacle, calling the four winds to his service, enslaving the sea, annihilating time and space with the telegraph ticker. It all makes excellent material for the Sunday newspapers, and for the addresses of railroad presidents. A splendid thing it is, indeed, to contemplate the freeing of man from the elements, from the old base bondages of wind and tide. "He is ready," continue the clergymen and speechmakers, "mighty in blue overalls, to lay his hand to the task of constructing the new, the clean, the sanitary civilization." Meanwhile— so goes the peroration—our men of science sweep the universe with their telescopes, run into corners the most elusive of stars, taking their snapshots as it were, and feeling the pulse of their chemical composition by means of the spectroscope. Others, at the same time, grow cells as our ancestors grew cabbages, and, through the agency of their powerful microscopes, walk in strange molecular gardens. Disease, with a capital D, is prostrate at the feet of medicine; even Death is receding, dejectedly dragging his scythe, before the incantations of Professor Metchnikoff.[1]

There is a round of applause and the audience goes home to partake of its canned dinners—gathered from all the ends of the earth, economists tell us: raisins from Greece; bananas from Cuba; lamb from New Zealand; eggs from China, all reunited on one menu!—after which they read popular works of science, or, if they are enlightened, unpopular ones in German, before getting what sleep they may amid the roar of the traffic outside their windows. Such is the way we regard science, bowing down to it as abjectly as ever bigot bowed before the image of the Madonna, making it, in every sense but the literal, the object of our worship, the new god of our century.

Humanity has a strange fondness for following processions. Get four men following a banner down the street, and, if that banner is inscribed with rhymes of pleasant optimism, in an hour all the town will be afoot, ready to march to whatever tune the leaders care to play. Today the tune is science. Then, there is something very pathetic in the way the mob is now and again deprived of its idols and banners, and left to wander muddleheadedly through meaningless streets. You may be sure, however, that before the day is up a new temple will have opened its doors,

Harvard Monthly, 62 (June 1916), 115–20.

where all the world will throng to do honor to the new god. Before long the priests will have distributed the words of the hymn, and all the crowd will be lustily singing, comfortable in companionship, the paeon of the new shibboleth. To this trick of the mind is added the tendency to believe, somehow, that what is, is right and must endure forever. Even in oneself it is hard to eradicate the idea, to realize that no state of society is inevitable or ultimate, and that, so far as the limitations of our perceptions go, its flux is eternal.

Once, long ago, it was faith in religion people thought eternal; then it was the tendency to liberty; now it is the scientific age.

Isn't it time, once more, to question; to try to discover where this steel-girded goddess, with her halo of factory smoke and her buzzing chariot-wheels of industry, is leading the procession of human thought which follows so tamely in her trail? What, we should ask, is the result on the life of men of the spirit of science: the pursuit of facts for their own sake? What is the goal of this mechanical, splendidly inventive civilization of ours?

Before attempting to protest against the present attitude towards these questions, it is necessary to face the inevitable, unanswerable, question: what is the end of human life? So far no one has done much more than obscure the issue with glowing catch-words. All the Christs, all the philosophers, all the scientists have cloaked it under a sounding phrase and passed on. "Reason," "Conformity of Will," "Godliness," "Life, Liberty and the Pursuit of Happiness," "Virtue": any of them will do, since impotence before the ultimate ends does not preclude the assumption that some finite state or point of view is, so far as personal opinion goes, the highest. Of course, your mode of attack on the whole problem depends on the particular patch of tapestry you pick out with which to cover the hole in your thatched roof of dogma. It might be possible to divide life's aims, always under the limitations of opinion, into two half-opposed ideals; thought and art; Plato and Michael Angelo. To be sure, they overlap in great measure; but each has an outer fringe independent of the other. One is the desire to create; the other the desire to fathom. Intangibly mixed up with them is a sense of beauty, quick-silver-like, three times dangerous to argue about, to dogmatize on, by which, somehow, we veneer the crudeness of the world and make it bearable—far more than bearable.

It is here that the fundamental question comes. How do these two things fare under the rule of science and its attendant spirits, Industrialism, and Mechanical Civilization?

Perhaps it is only fair to inquire first what alternatives there are to these twin guide-posts for humanity, which I may call thought and art. Is there any other path to the fullness of life? Surely material comforts,—three meals a day, and machine-made shirts,—are merely a rung in the ladder, not the platform of attainment. Surely work is not an end in itself; labor, the mere wearing away of muscle, is not ennobling. Surely the investigation, the tabulation of all the component parts of the external world is not the summit of life.

And I do not mean the end of life for the few, for the initiate, for the specially prepared ones; far indeed from any ideal is the present human pyramid where the few at the top are in the sunlight while the rest sweat in the filthy darkness of meaningless labor. However much one may desire the supreme individual, the superman, he is not to be got by degrading the mass of men from whose loins he must spring.

With these two supreme desires in mind; to fathom and to create, this civilization of ours, prostrate before the popular gods of materialism, on the one hand, and
the inner shrine of science, of divine fact, on the other, takes on a different aspect. If
it accomplishes nothing else the present war will conduce to a less receptive attitude. The stodgy complacency of the nineteenth century can hardly stand such a
shattering of beliefs. Men, at least those whose lives and souls are not sucked into
the whirlpool, will be forced to bring their ideals before the bar of criticism, to sift
them, to try them, to attempt to discover where they really lead. Indeed it is not
very hard, at the present hour, to reach the sceptical frame of mind required for the
breaking down of the modes of thought inherited from the last epoch. The war, the
growing acuteness of labor problems, the state of contemporary art, the growing
outward ugliness of life,—any of them can be used as an acid to sear away the old
complacency.

It is then that you find the question before you: What are the results of our
worship of this two-fold divinity: Science and Industrialism?

In the first place, positive knowledge has increased to an infinite degree. The
method of knowledge too, the aggregation of facts into a systematic whole, has been
firmly established. Then, through the omnipresent results of scientific invention,
life has, in one sense, become far easier, more luxurious, more refined. The world
has become very small, very united—(so we thought, until the war shattered, irre-
deemably perhaps, the cosmopolitan point of view). In short, man's dependence on
natural phenomena has been enormously lessened. Whether that dependence, increased fourfold, has not been merely transferred to a force more subtle is another
question.

It seems to me incontestable that since the Renaissance the greatest minds—
with few exceptions—have been engaged in the building up of science. Their vigor
and sheer intellect have affirmed in infinitely more striking terms the vague hy-
potheses of the Greek philosophers. The influence on all future thought of the mechanical view of the universe built up by Newton and his predecessors is impossible
to estimate. Their activity in the period following the artistic Renaissance, the development of the atomic theory which succeeded, and the promulgation of the
theory of evolution in the nineteenth century, are all gigantic milestones of human
achievement. These, with their train of minor accomplishment, have stimulated all
departments of thought and life. Most recently of all, the theories of probabilities
and the laws of thermo-dynamics have entirely changed man's point of view towards the universe.

All this is an achievement not to be tarnished by the most fulsome praise from
those people who run after every idea sufficiently old—or new, as the case may be,
—with glad hallelujahs.

With minds strengthened, and channels of thought infinitely deepened, men
of intellect would, one should have thought, have turned towards the problems of
human life and social intercourse, or, what is of more importance, to the vivider
living of life which lies in art and in abstract thought, with new vigor and keenness.
Has this been the case?

The race, comparatively speaking, has lived a short time under a state of con-
centrated civilization. Even so, amid the surging triumph of certain phases of the
intellect, it would have been reasonable for a man say of Shakespeare's day, sufficiently keen-sighted to have guessed at the importance of such a scientist as Harvey,

to imagine that the next two centuries would see a nearer approach to the solution of the important problems of life. Can the most blatant optimist claim that this has been so?—outside, to be sure, of a number of purely superficial things like sanitation, which have genuinely changed for the better. Except for the single triumph of liberalism over superstition in all its forms, religious, political, moral, which was the French Revolution, can we honestly say that life is intenser, that art is greater, that thought is more profound in our age than in the reign of Elizabeth? Are we not still as aimlessly struggling as before, plunging merely from one bondage into another? You cannot honestly affirm that opportunity for producing great art,—and art is certainly one of the touchstones, if not *the* touchstone of a civilization,—or even the opportunity for a general interest in the forms of beauty, is greater than it was three centuries and a half ago. Most thoughtful people will say it is less; and some will go so far as to insist that civilization has outlived art, has grown beyond the necessity for it, as it has grown beyond certain forms of religion, and black magic. In that case, would it not be that civilization had outlived life? There must be causes for all this, causes which can be rooted out; for it cannot be that man has gained the whole world only to lose his own soul.

May not some of the fault—if we admit there is a fault—come from the unreasoning acceptance of this new superstition: science? May not something be traced to the tendency this new superstition has, I believe, fostered, to slight the part man plays in the universe as man sees it? It is possible that, from over-preoccupation with what is at the other end of our telescopes and microscopes, we have lost our true sense of proportion. In learning the habits of the cells of a man's epidermis, it is easy to forget his body as a unit. In the last analysis, the universe is but as we see it: all is relative to the sense perceptions of the body. In this consuming interest in science, in knowledge of the exterior, in the tabulation of fact, haven't we forgotten the *Know thyself* of the Greeks? Not that we lack self-consciousness. Heaven knows, we tabulate our emotions as eagerly as our observations of the spectrum of Uranus! It is not that which we need.

In succession, Roman stoicism, Pauline Christianity, and the Ages of Faith have kept prisoner under varying bonds that humanism, that realization of the fullness of man, which was the heritage of the Greeks, and in another form, of Jesus. The French Revolution, to my mind, was a manifestation of it, a re-birth more important than the limited Italian Renaissance. The most tragic part of modern history lies in the fact that the glorious movement of liberation has in turn been conquered by that bastard of science, the Industrial Revolution.

Thus it is that the minor, but the infinitely more numerous part of the energies of the scientific spirit have been turned to building about us a silly claptrap of unnecessary luxuries, a clutter of inessentials which has been the great force to smother the arts of life and the arts of creation.

Under industrialism the major part of human kind runs in a vicious circle. Three-fourths of the world are bound in economic slavery that the other fourth may in turn be enslaved by the tentacular inessentials of civilization, for the production of which the lower classes have ground out their lives. Half the occupations of men today are utterly demoralizing to body and soul, and to what end?

In Samuel Butler's satire on humanity in general and on the English in particular, *Erewhon,* describing a fictitious nation rather after the manner of Swift, is a chapter called "The Book of the Machines." It tells fantastically how all complicated machinery was abolished in this country of Erewhon because the inhabitants feared lest it should eventually find itself consciousness and enslave the race of men. There is a flash of profound thought in the idea.

Has not the world today somehow got itself enslaved by this immense machine, the Industrial system. Millions of men perform labor narrowing and stultifying even under the best conditions, bound in the traces of mechanical industry, without ever a chance of self-expression, except in the hectic pleasures of suffocating life in cities. They grind their lives away on the wheels, producing, producing, producing. And of all the results of this degrading, never-ending labor, how little is really necessary to anyone; how much is actually destructive of the capacity of men for living, for the fathoming of life, for the expression of life.

How long will the squirrel contentedly turn his wheel and imagine he is progressing? Are we so certain of the benefits of all this that the last hundred years has given us that there must be no discussion of the question? Most people are very certain; but most people are always certain. In the Middle Ages most people had no qualms as to the doctrine of intolerance or the institution of serfdom.

Still, there is discontent among us. In the light of the flames of burning Belgium towns civilized men look at each other with a strange new horror. Is this what men have been striving for through the ages? Is this ponderous suicidal machine civilization? The rabies of Germany has been a fearful disillusionment. The one modern nation which, as well as having developed the industrial system to its highest degree, has a really great living art has suddenly slipped back into barbarism. The same civilization has produced Wagner and Von Tirpitz, the Eroica Symphony and the ruins of Rheims.[2]

This is the time of all others for casting up the balance sheet of Industrialism, of our scientific civilization. Shall we not find that man's material power has far outgrown his ability to put it to constructive use? Are we not like men crouching on a runaway engine? And at the same time we insensately shovel in the fuel with no thought as to where we are being taken.

Even if you deny entirely that Science and Industrialism, two forces at present bound up together, not inseparably I hope, have tended for evil, have they tended for good? Is life any broader, more intense, truly freer from material hindrances because of them? Can it be that we have abandoned our old benevolent gods only to immolate ourselves before a new Moloch—in futile sacrifice?

Notes

1. Élie Metchnikoff, a Russian-born Nobel Prize winner who devoted the final years of his life to efforts to increase longevity.

2. Alfred von Tirpitz, German naval commander, advocated unrestricted submarine warfare against unarmed merchant shipping; the Germans shelled the cathedral city of Rheims early in the war.

A Conference on Foreign Relations

Announcements of a conference to be held at Western Reserve University in Cleveland, on the subject of our foreign relations, have recently been sent out. Primarily for college men, its aim is to help create "an enlightened public opinion on a sound foreign policy." All phases of our international relations are to be discussed, it seems, and an attempt is to be made to arrive at some sort of plan for world-reorganization after the war. The conference is to be held under the auspices of the Federation of International Polity Clubs, and will last from June 21 to July 1.

If carried out successfully, this will be a rather significant event, indeed, one of national importance. In any case, the very existence of such a conference proves that discontent is abroad, discontent with the spineless and cowardly temporizing which has become the tradition of our foreign policy. People begin to realize that if we are to justify our boasted idealism, if the United States is to throw in its weight against the powers of darkness, some more aggressive attitude must be assumed: not an aggressive attitude in the old sense, it is true, but a policy of "constructive pacifism."

The *laissez faire* political dogmas of the past must, it is evident, be abandoned. International relations in a civilized world must not again be allowed to slip down the long path of competitive armament to inevitable war. Yet order can only be brought into the desperate chaos of our European world—I am not speaking of any but the European family of nations—by the action of strong and organized public opinion in all the great nations. To mould opinion in America, and to stir it into active life is the aim of this conference. If it steers clear of the Scylla of "grape-juice" moralizing and the Charybdis of long-haired ultra-socialism, and achieves a middle course of forceful commonsense, the results of this conference will be of the highest importance. What is more, people will go away from it to spread through the torpid wastes of certain parts of the nation the understanding that nationality entails responsibility, that it is useless to mumble sleepily "isolation," and that our old provincial slumbers must give place to an intelligent and unselfish use of our power for good in world-politics.

Harvard Monthly, 62 (June 1916), 126–27.

Against American Literature

If any mood predominates in American writing it is that of gentle satire. This tendency to satire, usually vague and kindly, sometimes bitter with the unconvinced bitterness of a middle-aged lady who thinks herself worldly wise, is the one feature pervading all that can be called American among the mass of foreign-inspired writing in this country. Washington Irving is typical of its least significant manifestation; Edgar Lee Masters, Edith Wharton and Katherine Fullerton Gerould of its modern—and bitter—form. Search as you may, you will find little not permeated by this tone, which, chameleon-like, changes with the variations of European thought, but remains in its fundamentals always the same. And there is no doubt that up to now it has well approximated the temper of the nation, has pretty faithfully represented that genial, ineffectual, blindly energetic affair, the American soul. Strange combination of words; for until recently we have troubled very little about our *âme nationale*, leaving that sort of thing to introspective and decadent nations overseas. But even if we are unconscious of it, we have a national soul, and it is this, or at least the external of it, which is so aptly reflected by the pervading tone of our literature.

This wholesome rice-pudding fare is, unfortunately, a strangely unstimulating diet; so we are forced to give it body—like apple jack—by a stiff infusion of a stronger product. As a result of this constant need to draw on foreign sources our literature has become a hybrid which, like the mule, is barren and must be produced afresh each time by the crossing of other strains. What is the reason for this state of affairs? Much of our writing, particularly in the upper realm of the novel, the region of Edith Wharton and Robert Herrick, is sincere, careful, and full of shrewd observation of contemporary life; yet I defy anyone to confine himself for long to purely American books without feeling starved, without pining for the color and passion and profound thought of other literatures. Our books are like our cities; they are all the same. Any other nation's literature would take a lifetime to exhaust. What then is lacking in ours?

For one thing American literature is a rootless product, a cutting from England's sturdy well branched oak tree, nurtured in the arid soil of the New England colonies, and recently transplanted to the broad lands of the Middle West. In other countries literature is the result of long evolution, based on primitive folklore, on

New Republic, 8 (14 Oct. 1916), 269–71.

the first joy and terror of man in the presence of the trees and scented meadowlands and dimpled whirling rivers, interwoven with the moulding fabric of old dead civilizations, and with threads of fiery new gold from incoming races. The result is glamour, depth, real pertinence to the highest and lowest in man. It is to be found, in one form or another, beneath the temporary scum of every established literature. This artistic stimulus, fervid with primitive savageries, redolent with old cults of earth and harvest, smoked and mellowed by time, is the main inheritance of the civilizations, the woof upon which individual artists may work the warp of their own thoughts.

America lacks it almost completely. The earth-feeling, the jewelled accretions of the imagination of succeeding ages, so rich in old English writing, seem to have lost their validity in the transplanting. The undercurrent, rooted in the people, often voiceless for whole epochs, which springs from the chants of Druids, from fairy-tales and terror-tales recited in wattled huts about the smoky fires of the woad-daubed Britons, and which has time and again revivified the literature of England, saved it from artificiality and courtiership, has been cut off from us. We find ourselves floundering without rudder or compass, in the sea of modern life, vaguely lit by the phosphorescent gleam of our traditional optimism. A sense of landscape, or else an imported, flushed, *erdgeist* feeling, has taken the place of the unconscious intimacy with nature—the deeper the less reflective it is—which has always lain at the soul of great writings. No ghosts hover about our fields; there are no nymphs in our fountains; there is no tradition of countless generations tilling and tending to give us reverence for those rocks and rills and templed hills so glibly mentioned in the national anthem.

The only substitute for dependence on the past is dependence on the future. Here our only poet found his true greatness. Walt Whitman abandoned the vague genteelness that had characterized American writing, the stiff product of the leisure hours of a *petite noblesse de province*, and, founding his faith on himself, on the glowing life within him, shouted genially, fervidly his challenge to the future. But, although sensibly unconventional in manners and customs, the American public desires its ideas well disciplined according to the conventions of ten years back; Walt Whitman failed to reach the people he intended to, and aroused only a confused perturbation and the sort of moral flutter experienced by a primly dressed old bachelor when a ruddy smiling Italian, smelling of garlic and sweat, plumps down beside him in the street car. Still, the day of Whitman's power may be in a rosy future, when Americans, instead of smiling with closed eyes, will look keenly before them.

Then there is the cult of the abstract. Perhaps it too grows out of our lack of root, out of our lack of spiritual kinship to the corn and wheat our fields grow, out of our inane matter-of-factness. American life, as much as an unsuccessful inventor, is occupied with smiling abstractions. This is particularly true of our religion, which under multifarious forms of Protestant Christianity is actually a muddled abstract theism. We have none of those local saints—tamed pagan gods, most of them—that have tied the Church in Europe so tightly to the people, to the soil, to the eternal powers of corn and wine and resurgent earth. One by one we have pulled from our god the garments of concreteness, the human qualities. Even the abolition of hell and the devil may have done much to tear religion from people's souls, and to place it in the chilly soil of convention where it at present languishes. There was something tangible and human about hell-fire which cannot be found in the vague notion of future harp-twanging for all "nice" people, that symbolizes most current religious faiths.

What is true of religion is true of art and literature. Worse than its lack of depth and texture is its abstractness, its lack, on the whole, of dramatic actuality. Compare say "The House of Mirth," a fairly typical American novel, with Turgenev's "Spring Freshets." The Russian stirs eyes and ears and nose and sense of touch, portrays his story with vivid tangibility; the American leaves an abstract impression of intellectual bitterness. It is not so much a question of technique as of feeling. In the same way match the dramatic power of Couperus's "Small Souls" with Mary S. Watts's "The Legacy," a novel dealing with the corresponding class of people in this country. Why should not our writers be as vivid as the Russian, express their life as dramatically as the Dutchman?

It is significant that, quite unconsciously, I chose the works of two women to typify American novels. The tone of the higher sort of writing in this country is undoubtedly that of a well brought up and intelligent woman, tolerant, versed in the things of this world, quietly humorous, but bound tightly in the fetters of "niceness," of the middle-class outlook. And when the shackles are thrown off the result is vulgarity, and, what is worse, affectation.

In all this may lie the explanation of the sudden vogue of Russian literature in this country. It has so much that our own lacks. There is the primitive savagery, the color, the romance of an age of faith suddenly burst in upon by European science, the freshness, rank and lush as the vegetation of early May. No wonder it is a relief to us Americans to turn from our prim colonial living room of thought, where the shades are drawn for fear the sun will fade the carpet Puritan ancestors laid there, to the bizarre pains and passions, to the hot moist steppe-savour of a Russian novel.

And it becomes harder every day for any race to gain the lesson of the soil. An all-enveloping industrialism, a new mode of life preparing, has broken down the old bridges leading to the past, has cut off the possibility of retreat. Our only course is to press on. Shall we pick up the glove Walt Whitman threw at the feet of posterity? Or shall we stagnate forever, the Sicily of the modern world, rich in this world's goods, absorbing the thought, patronizing the art of other peoples, but producing nothing from amid our jumble of races but steel and oil and grain?

"Well, isn't that enough?" I hear someone say.

Young Spain

[Dos Passos studied and traveled in Spain from October 1916 till February 1917, when he returned to America following the death of his father.]

The *senores* were from Madrid? Indeed! The man's voice was full of an awe of great distances. He was the village baker of Almorox, where we had gone on a Sunday excursion from Madrid; and we were standing on the scrubbed tile floor of his house, ceremoniously receiving wine and figs from his wife. The father of the friend who accompanied me had once lived in the same village as the baker's father, and bought bread of him; hence the entertainment. This baker of Almorox was a tall man, with a soft moustache very black against his ash-pale face, who stood with his large head thrust far forward. He was smiling with pleasure at the presence of strangers in his house, while in a tone of shy deprecating courtesy he asked after my friend's family. Don Fernando and Doña Ana and the Señorita were well? And little Carlos? Carlos was no longer little, answered my friend, and Doña Ana was dead.

The baker's wife had stood in the shadow looking from one face to another with a sort of wondering pleasure as we talked, but at this she came forward suddenly into the pale greenish-gold light that streamed through the door, holding a dark wine-bottle before her. There were tears in her eyes. No; she had never known any of them, she explained hastily—she had never been away from Almorox—but she had heard so much of their kindness and was sorry. . . . It was terrible to lose a father or a mother. The tall baker shifted his feet uneasily, embarrassed by the sadness that seemed slipping over his guests, and suggested that we walk up the hill to the Hermitage; he would show the way.

"But your work?" we asked. Ah, it did not matter. Strangers did not come every day to Almorox. He strode out of the door, wrapping a woolen muffler about his bare strongly moulded throat, and we followed him up the devious street of whitewashed houses that gave us glimpses through wide doors of dark tiled rooms with great black rafters overhead and courtyards where chickens pecked at the manure lodged between smooth worn flagstones. Still between whitewashed walls we struck out of the village into the deep black mud of the high road, and at last burst suddenly into the open country, where patches of sprouting grass shone vivid green against the gray and russet of broad rolling lands. At the top of the first hill stood the Hermitage—a small whitewashed chapel with a square three-storied tower; over the door was a relief of the Virgin, crowned, in worn lichened stone. The interior was very plain with a single heavily gilt altar, over which was a painted statue, stiff

Seven Arts, 2 (Aug. 1917), 473–88. Reprinted in part in *Rosinante to the Road Again* (1922).

but full of a certain erect disdainful grace—again of the Virgin. The figure was dressed in a long lace gown, full of frills and ruffles, grey with dust and age.

"*La Virgen de la Cima*," said the baker, pointing reverently with his thumb, after he had bent his knee before the altar. And as I glanced at the image a sudden resemblance struck me: the gown gave the Virgin a curiously conical look that somehow made me think of that conical black stone, the Bona Dea, that the Romans brought from Asia Minor. Here again was a good goddess, a bountiful one, more mother than virgin, despite her prudish frills. . . . But the man was ushering us out.

"And there is no finer view than this in all Spain." With a broad sweep of his arm he took in the village below, with its waves of roofs that merged from green to maroon and deep crimson, broken suddenly by the open square in front of the church; and the gray towering church, scowling with strong lights and shadows on buttresses and pointed windows; and the brown fields faintly sheened with green, which gave place to the deep maroon of the turned earth of vineyards, and the shining silver where the wind ruffled the olive-orchards; and beyond, the rolling hills that grew gradually flatter until they sank into the yellowish plain of Castile. As he made the gesture his fingers were stretched wide as if to grasp all this land he was showing. His flaccid cheeks were flushed as he turned to us; but we should see it in May, he was saying, in May when the wheat was thick in the fields, and there were flowers on the hills. Then the lands were beautiful and rich, in May. And he went on to tell us of the local feast, and the great processions of the Virgin. This year there were to be four days of the *toros*. So many bullfights were unusual in such a small village, he assured us. But they were rich in Almorox; the wine was the best in Castile. Four days of *toros*, he said again; and all the people of the country around would come to the fiestas, and there would be a great pilgrimage to this Hermitage of the Virgin . . . As he talked in his slow deferential way, a little conscious of his volubility before strangers, there began to grow in my mind a picture of his view of the world.

First came his family, the wife whose body lay beside his at night, who bore him children, the old withered parents who sat in the sun at his door, his memories of them when they had had strong rounded limbs like his, and of their parents sitting old and withered in the sun. Then his work, the heat of his ovens, the smell of bread cooking, the faces of neighbors who came to buy; and, outside, in the dim penumbra of things half real, of travellers' tales, lay Madrid, where the king lived and where politicians wrote in the newspapers,—and *Francia* and all that was not Almorox . . . In him I seemed to see generations wax and wane, like the years, strung on the thread of labor, of unending sweat and strain of muscles against the earth. It was all so mellow, so strangely aloof from the modern world of feverish change, this life of the peasants of Almorox. Everywhere roots striking into the infinite past. For before the Revolution, before the Moors, before the Romans, before the dark furtive traders, the Phoenicians, they were much the same, these Iberian village communities. Far away things changed, cities were founded, hard roads built, armies marched and fought and passed away; but in Almorox the foundations of life remained unchanged up to the present. New names and new languages had come. The Virgin had taken over the festivals and rituals of the old earth goddesses, and the deep mystical fervor of devotion. But always remained the love for the place, the strong anarchistic reliance on the individual man, the walking consciously or not, of the way beaten by generations of men who had tilled and loved and lain in the cherishing sun with no feeling of a reality outside of themselves, outside of the bare encompassing hills of their commune, except the God which was the synthesis of their souls and of their lives.

Here lies the strength and the weakness of Spain. This intense individualism, born of a history whose fundamentals lie in isolated village communities—*pueblos*, as the Spaniards call them—over the changeless face of which, like grass over a field, events spring and mature and die, is the basic fact of Spanish life. No revolution has been strong enough to shake it. Invasion after invasion, of Goths, of Moors, of Christian ideas, of the fads and convictions of the Renaissance, have swept over the country, changing surface customs and modes of thought and speech, only to be metamorphosed into keeping with the changeless Iberian mind.

And predominant in the Iberian mind is the thought *La vida es sueño*: "Life is a dream." Only the individual, or that part of life which is in the firm grasp of the individual, is real. The supreme expression of this lies in the two great figures that typify Spain for all time; Don Quixote and Sancho Panza. Don Quixote, the individualist who believed in the power of man's soul over all things, whose desire included the whole world in himself. Sancho, the individualist to whom all the world was food for his belly. On the one hand we have the ecstatic figures for whom the power of the individual soul has no limits, in whose minds the universe is but one man standing before his reflection, God. These are the Loyolas, the Philip Seconds, the fervid ascetics like Juan de la Cruz, the originals of the glowing tortured faces in the portraits of El Greco. On the other hand are the jovial materialists like the Archpriest of Hita, culminating in the frantic, almost mystical sensuality of such an epic figure as Don Juan Tenorio.[1] Through all Spanish history and art the threads of these two complementary characters can be traced, changing, combining, branching out, but ever in substance the same. Of this warp and woof have all the strange patterns of Spanish life been woven.

II

In trying to hammer some sort of unified impression out of the scattered pictures of Spain in my mind, one of the first things I realize is that there are many Spains. Indeed every village hidden in the folds of the great barren hills, or shadowed by its massive church in the middle of one of the upland plains, every fertile *huerta* of the seacoast is a Spain. Iberia exists, and the strong Iberian characteristics; but Spain as a modern centralized nation is an illusion—perhaps a delusion; for the present atrophy, the desolating resultlessness of a century of revolution, may very well be due in large measure to the artificial imposition of centralized government on a land essentially centrifugal.

In the first place there is a matter of language. Roughly four distinct languages are at present spoken in Spain: Castilian, the language of Madrid and the central uplands, the official language, spoken in the south in its Andalusian form; Gallego-Portuguese, spoken on the west coast; Basque, which does not even share the Latin descent of the others; and Catalan, a form of Provençal which, with its dialect, Valencian, is spoken on the upper Mediterranean coast and in the Balearic Isles. Of course, under the influence of rail communication and a conscious effort to spread

Castilian, the other languages, with the exception of Portuguese and Catalan, have lost vitality and died out in the larger towns; but the problem remains far different from that of the Italian dialects, since the Spanish languages have all, except Basque, a strong literary tradition.

Added to the variety of language, there is an immense variety of topography in the different parts of Spain. The central plateaux, dominant in modern history (history being taken to mean the births and breedings of kings and queens and the doings of generals in armor), probably approximate the warmer Russian steppes in climate and vegetation. The west coast is in most respects a warmer and more fertile Wales. The southern *huertas* (arable river valleys) have rather the aspect of Egypt. The east coast from Valencia up is a continuation of the Mediterranean coast of France. It follows that, in this country where an hour's train ride will take you from Siberian snow into African desert, unity of population is hardly to be expected.

Here is probably the root of the tendency in Spanish art and thought to emphasize the differences between things. In painting, where the mind of a people is often more tangibly represented than anywhere else, we find one supreme example. El Greco, almost the caricature in his art of the Don Quixote type of mind, who, though a Greek by birth and a Venetian by training, became more Spanish than the Spaniards during his long life at Toledo, strove constantly to express the difference between the world of flesh and the world of spirit, between the body and the soul of man. More recently, the extreme characterization of Goya's sketches and portraits, the intensifying of national types found in Zuloaga[2] and the other painters who have been exploiting with such success the peculiarities—the picturesqueness—of Spanish faces and landscapes, seem to spring from this powerful sense of the separateness of things.

In another way you can express this constant attempt to differentiate one individual from another as caricature. Spanish art is constantly on the edge of caricature. Given the ebullient fertility of the Spanish mind and its intense individualism, a constant slipping over into the grotesque is inevitable. And so it comes to be that the conscious or unconscious aim of their art is rather self-expression than beauty. Their image of reality is sharp and clear, but distorted. Burlesque and satire are never far away in their most serious moments. Not even the calmest and best ordered of Spanish minds can resist a tendency to excess of all sorts, to overelaboration, to grotesquerie, to deadening mannerism. All that is greatest in their art, indeed, lies on the borderland of the extravagant, where sublime things skim the thin ice of absurdity. The great epic, Don Quixote; such plays as Calderon's *La Vida es Sueño*, such painting as El Greco's *Resurrection* and Velasquez's dwarfs, such buildings as the Escorial and the Alhambra—all among the universal masterpieces —are far indeed from the middle term of reasonable beauty. Hence their supreme strength. And for our generation, to which excess is a synonym for beauty, is added argumentative significance to the long tradition of Spanish art.

Another characteristic, springing from the same fervid abundance, that links the Spanish tradition to ours of the present day is the strangely impromptu character of much Spanish art production. The slightly ridiculous proverb that genius consists of an infinite capacity for taking pains is well controverted. The creative flow of Spanish artists has always been so strong, so full of vitality that there has been no time for taking pains. Lope de Vega, with his two thousand odd plays—or was it twelve thousand?—is by no means an isolated instance. Perhaps the strong sense of individual validity, which makes Spain the most democratic country in Europe, sanctions the constant improvization, and accounts for the confident planlessness as common in Spanish architecture as in Spanish political thought.

Here we meet the old stock characteristic, Spanish pride. This is a very real thing, and is merely the external shell of the fundamental trust in the individual and in nothing outside of him. Again El Greco is an example. As his painting progressed, grew more and more personal, he drew away from tangible reality, and, with all the dogmatic conviction of one whose faith in his own reality can sweep away the mountains of the visible world, expressed his own restless, almost sensual, spirituality in forms that flickered like white flames toward God. For the Spaniard, moreover, God is always, in essence, the proudest sublimation of man's soul. The same spirit runs through the preachers of the early church and the works of Santa Teresa, a disguise of the frantic desire to express the self, the self, changeless and eternal, at all costs. From this comes the hard cruelty that flares forth luridly at times. A recent book by Miguel de Unamuno, *Del Sentimiento Trágico de la Vida*, expresses this fierce clinging to separateness from the universe by the phrase *el hambre de inmortalidad*, the hunger of immortality. This is the core of the individualism that lurks in all Spanish ideas, the conviction that only the individual soul is real.

III

In the Spain of today these things are seen as through a glass, darkly. Since the famous and much gloated-over entrance of Ferdinand and Isabella into Granada, the history of Spain has been that of an attempt to fit a square peg in a round hole. In the great flare of the golden age, the age of ingots of Peru and of men of even greater worth, the disease worked beneath the surface. Since then the conflict has corroded into futility all the buoyant energies of the country. I mean the persistent attempt to centralize in thought, in art, in government, in religion, a nation whose every energy lies in the other direction. The result has been a deadlock, and the ensuing rust and numbing of all life and thought, so that a century of revolution seems to have brought Spain no nearer a solution of its problems. At the present day, when all is ripe for a new attempt to throw off the atrophy, a sort of despairing inaction causes the Spaniards to remain under a government of unbelievably corrupt and inefficient politicians. There seems no solution to the problem of a nation in which the centralized power and the separate communities work only to nullify each other.

The attitude of Spain to the war is an outgrowth of this. The country is pretty evenly divided into Germanophiles and Frankophiles, as they are called, not from any broad convictions on world politics, but from the hope that the victory of one or the other will throw weight on the side of one of the contesting parties. The reactionaries, the clergy, and the ignorant priest-ridden classes—the high aristocracy and the lowest peasantry—are strongly pro-German, or rather, pro-Austrian. Perhaps the faint hope of a new Metternich sustains them. The liberals of all colors, the intelligenzia, and the munitions manufacturers, who have been growing very wealthy in the North, are fervidly pro-Ally. Then there is a further regional division:

the Basque provinces, Portugal, Galicia and Catalonia, the portions of the peninsula that have most connection with the modern world, are pro-Ally; the central and southern parts pro-German.

But the most important influence of the war on Spain is this. The cost of living is constantly rising, and labor is wretchedly underpaid. Meanwhile the governing classes plunder, the intellectual classes talk and prophesy and despair, and a few towns in the North, like Corunna, grow suddenly rich on munitions. But under the surface the moment comes nearer and nearer when the tension will snap. Famine is the mother of revolutions. The trouble is that the revolutionary classes have so many different aims. In Catalonia they want a republic and virtual autonomy from the rest of Spain. In Andalusia they want, very simply, food and decent wages. In Galicia they want to be let alone and allowed to grow rich in peace. Fear of failure is everywhere, a fear that any move may make matters worse, may lift again into the saddle the incubus of the clergy and the reactionaries. So Spain, hot with discussion, holds aloof from the war.

On every side, however, in thought if not in fact, the ice of national stagnation is breaking. The war of '98, which to us was merely an occasion for a display of school historybook style of patriotism, combined with an amazing skill in sanitation, was to the Spanish people a great spiritual crisis. It was the first thorough unmasking of the hopeless atrophy of their political life. From '98 indeed has sprung the present generation, a generation of men strangely sensitive and self-conscious, some despairing, some pressing on very boldly up the logical paths of Spanish thought—toward anarchism, toward a searing criticism of the modern world in general and Spain in particular. Gradually, laboriously, with unexampled devotion, these men are piecing together the tattered shreds of national consciousness. Not national consciousness wholly in the present capitalistic-patriotic sense, however, but something more fruitful, more local.

The two most important novelists in the younger generation, Pió Baroja and Blasco Ibañez well illustrate this mood. The first, who very probably is one of the foremost writers of our time, has spent his life in delineating Spain against the background of the world today, exposing her weakness with frank pessimism. Baroja's attitude has a certain affinity to the attitude toward America of the early Henry James, though as artists there is no comparison between them. The Spaniard has a sense of life, a bouyancy, a power to tell a story that make sickly beside them the pale artifices of the Anglo-American novelist. Far different, too, from James's quiet dissent from ideas American is Baroja's burning criticism of his country's inaction. Through him Nietzsche has reached the present generation, and a worship of things Anglo-Saxon, of the efficient Roosevelt virtues, which sounds strangely in the ears of Americans used to reacting in the opposite direction from their red-blooded national ethics. Blasco Ibañez, a belated Zolaist of slightly lurid tendencies, attacks Spanish life from the opposite point of view, from that of his socialist's vision of the world. He is less of an artist, but probably his ideas will be ultimately more fruitful than the old-fashioned cosmopolitanism and Anglo-mania of Baroja.

In the Spanish poetry of the day there is much the same sense of purpose. Rubén Darío, the Nicaraguan who dominated the Spanish-speaking world for the past decade, was full of his call to the Spanish peoples to unite, to build a new ideal of life that would defeat what he called the *Yankí* ideal of dollars and steel. In his bold metrical inventions, in his continual breaking of the conventional chains of

Spanish thought, he was the prophet of an era of solidarity for the Spanish peoples of the world, with a humaner literature and a humaner religion. Antonio Machado, writing his passionate love for the grey iron hills and the yellow plains of Castile, and for the dark reliant peasants who till their soil, has made his greatest poetry in attempts to stir his countrymen to realization and action. Throughout his strong repressed poems runs the plaint of the ancient glory of Castile, "fecund mother of captains in the old time, today bringing forth puny drill-sergeants." Another poet, Juan Ramón Jiménez, has introduced a prosody developed from the French vers librists which approximates in some measure the verse of Amy Lowell and Richard Aldington. He has substituted a vague, rather Celtic mood for the traditional clarity of Spanish verse, and a delicate irregular cadence for the heavy lilt of its ballad rhythms. He is the poet of Andalusia the gay, the center of the ruined dream of Moorish Spain, while Antonio Machado represents somber visionary Castile. And, in the same manner, each poet of modern Spain can be assigned to his province, to his *pueblo*. In literature the triumph of the commune over Madrid is near at hand.

The regional character of Spanish music of the present generation is even more obvious. This is probably largely due to the varied character of the rich store of still unexploited folk-music, roughly of Celtic origin in the North and West, and of African in the South and Levant, which up to the present has found no genius strong enough to fuse it into a truly personal work of art. Spain is saturated with this native music. Even the light opera of the cheaper theatres in Madrid has, when the source is not muddied by imitation Viennese tinsel and syrup, moments of great charm and true musical value. Often in a trivial and ill put-together *zarzuela* appear almost unconscious traces of old thrilling motives handed down from the Moors or the Celt-Iberian mountaineers. Perhaps Spanish music is in the condition of German music before Beethoven. No one has yet appeared to collect the scattered strands into a great racial art. Among recent composers, neither Granados nor Albéniz have to my mind thoroughly mastered their material. They and probably Falla and the other composers of the moment, who are so busily engaged in collecting and interpreting what they can of the stream of musical richness that flows past them, will be the stepping-stones for the genius who must follow to make of Spanish music a great and original expression.

First, however, in Spanish music as in Spanish painting, one influence must be overcome: Paris. Paris has hitherto done one of two things to Spanish artists; it has subdued them entirely to the prevailing French mode, or it has turned them into mongers of the picturesque, of romantic Spain, for export purposes. There seem, in Spanish art as in American, few personalities strong enough to gain the technique of Paris without becoming as enslaved as Circe's swine.

The great vitality of Spanish painting in recent years is partly due to the fact that it has been an expression of local schools. Sorolla was a thoroughly Valencian painter before he went to Paris, and his best work is that which shows most the influence of the local tradition. In Zuloaga can be seen again and again the influence of his uncle Daniel, the Castilian ceramist. In the Basque painters represented by the brothers Zubiaurre, localism in style and technique becomes almost a mannerism. Indeed it is hard to realize how much good painting is being done in small isolated groups in Spain. Seville, Granada, Bilbao, Corunna, Barcelona, Valencia, have all their circles of extremely active painters; while Madrid is the palm of victory. There live all the thoroughly successful artists, and those the war has driven away from the lotus-trees of Paris. But even in the rather vulgar and cosmopolitan—in the worst sense—artistic circle of Madrid, the cult of the god Success and of the god Foreignness has nothing of the power and universality it enjoys in corresponding circles in America. Perhaps the reason is that a sincere inborn sense of art is part of the heritage of all classes of Spanish society.

IV

It was after a lecture at an exhibition of Basque painters in Madrid, where we had heard a wonderful old man, with eyes that burned out from under shaggy grizzled eyebrows, denounce in bitter stinging irony what he called the Europeanization of Spain. What they called progress, he had said, was merely an aping of the stupid commercialism of modern Europe. Better no education for the masses than education that would turn healthy peasants into crafty putty-skinned merchants; better a Spain swooning in her age-old apathy, than a Spain awakened to the brutal soulless trade-war of modern life . . . I was walking with a young student of philosophy I had met by chance across the noisy board of a Spanish *pension*, discussing the exhibition we had just seen as a strangely meek setting for the fiery reactionary speech. I had remarked on the very "primitive" look much of the work of these young Basque painters had, shown by some in the almost affectionate technique, in the dainty caressing brush-work, in others by that inadequacy of the means at the painter's disposal to express his idea, which made of so many of the pictures rather gloriously impressive failures. My friend was insisting, however, that the primitiveness, rather than the birth-pangs of a new view of the world, was nothing but the last affectation of an over-civilized tradition.

"Spain," he said, "is the most civilized country in Europe. The growth of our civilization has never been interrupted by outside influence. The Phoenicians, the Romans—Spain's influence on Rome was, I imagine, fully as great as Rome's on Spain; think of the five Spanish emperors;—the Goths, the Moors;—all incidents, absorbed by the changeless Iberian spirit . . . Even Spanish Christianity," he continued, smiling, "is far more Spanish than it is Christian. Our life is one vast ritual. Our religion is part of it, that is all. And so are the bull-fights that so shock the English and Americans,—are they any more brutal, though, than fox-hunting and prizefights? And how full of tradition are they, our *fiestas de toros*; their ceremony reaches back to the hecatombs of the Homeric heroes, to the bull-worship of the Cretans and of so many of the Mediterranean cults, to the Roman games. Can civilization go further than to ritualize death as we have done? But our culture is too perfect, too stable. Life is choked by it."

We stood still a moment in the shade of a yellowed limetree. My friend had stopped talking, and was looking with his usual bitter smile at a group of little boys with brown bare dusty legs who were intently playing bull-fight with sticks for swords and a piece of newspaper for the toreador's scarlet cape.

"It is you in America," he went on suddenly, "to whom the future belongs; you are so vigorous and vulgar and uncultured. Life has become once more the primal fight for bread. Of course the dollar is a complicated form of the food the cave man killed for and slunk after, and the means of combat are different, but it is as brutal. From the crude animal brutality comes all the vigor of life. We have none of it; we are too tired to have any thoughts; we have lived so much so long ago that now we are content with the very simple things,—the warmth of the sun and the colors of the hills and the flavor of bread and wine. All the rest is automatic, ritual."

"But what about the strike?" I asked, referring to the one day's general strike that had just been carried out with fair success throughout Spain, as a protest against the government's apathy regarding the dangerous rise in the prices of food and fuel.

He shrugged his shoulders.

"That, and more," he said, "is new Spain, a prophecy, rather than a fact. Old Spain is still all-powerful."

Later in the day I was walking through the main street of one of the clustered adobe villages that lie in the folds of the Castilian plain not far from Madrid. The lamps were just being lit in the little shops where the people lived and worked and sold their goods, and women with beautifully shaped pottery jars on their heads were coming home with water from the well. Suddenly I came out on an open *plaza* with trees from which the last leaves were falling through the greenish sunset light. The place was filled with the lilting music of a grind-organ and with a crunch of steps on the gravel as people danced. There were soldiers and servant-girls, and red-cheeked apprentice-boys with their sweethearts, and respectable shop-keepers, and their wives with mantillas over their gleaming black hair. All were dancing in and out among the slim tree-trunks, and the air was noisy with laughter and little cries of childlike unfeigned enjoyment. I thought of a cheap dancehall in America. How much healthier this seemed, in the open air, without restraint or hidden obscenities, this merrymaking of people who were so unaffectedly at ease in the world.

Here was the gospel of Sancho Panza, I thought, the easy acceptance of life, the unashamed joy in food and color and the softness of women's hair. But as I walked out of the village across the harsh plain of Castile, grey-green and violet under the deepening night, the memory came to me of the knight of the sorrowful countenance, Don Quixote, blunderingly trying to remould the world, pitifully sure of the power of his own ideal. And in these two Spain seemed to be manifest. Far indeed were they from the restless industrial world of joyless enforced labor and incessant goading war. And I wondered to what purpose it would be, should Don Quixote again saddle Rosinante.

Notes

1. Juan Ruiz, archpriest of Hita and author of the medieval poem *Libro de Buen Amor*, and Don Juan Tenorio of fourteenth-century Seville, one of the prototypes of the legendary lover Don Juan.

2. Ignacio Zuloaga y Zaboleta, a painter of Spanish folk life.

II

A Radical Perspective
(1920-37)

In Portugal

[Dos Passos lived in Spain during 1919–20 while writing *Three Soldiers*. In late September 1919 he spent a week in Portugal after learning that a revolution was imminent there. General Sidoñio Paes had led a military dictatorship in Portugal from December 1917 to December 1918, after which a republican form of government was restored. This government had withstood a monarchist revolt in January 1919, but was under increasing pressure from both the Left and Right during the period of Dos Passos' visit.]

Opposite me on the train to Lisbon sat a monarchist. He was very lean, had violet rings under his eyes, and a tightly stretched parchment face. He orated all night, bouncing up and down on his seat, and when he reached the climax of his eloquence, as he did frequently, his eyes flared in a most extraordinary way. As he kept handing me most tasty little patees which he took out of an inexhaustible paper bag, I felt excellently disposed towards him, and cheered in the pauses. He said that Portugal was a *pequenha Russia*, and that only a monarchy strongly supported from the outside, could keep the working people from taking control altogether. The place was not worked with soviets and with the infamous doctrines of Malatesta and Sorel.[1]

Later, in Lisbon I heard much the same story from the paternal white-haired old gentleman who edited the leading "Liberal" newspaper. His cure was "a strong conservative government" with the usual work and reconstruction and no-strike tag. Portugal, he said must fulfill her obligations to her great ally. As I left I sprang something on him. How about the rumor that the royalists in the January revolt had landed in Oporto from an English vessel? The Duke of Palmella had been sheltered in the American Legation, hadn't he?[2] The paternal old gentleman went to the door and shut it hastily. Then he cleared his throat and said impressively, "Portugal will always look to England for help and advice. What we need is work and a strong conservative government."

The republic, entirely in the hands of the bourgeoisie, receiving its orders as to foreign policy from Great Britain, having done nothing to free the country from domestic or foreign capital, has fulfilled none of its promises. Illiteracy remains over 75 percent. Labor is worse paid than in any except the Balkan countries. The mineral wealth of the country is untouched, or else exploited by Great Britain. Portugal is a British colony without the advantages of British administration.

But in Portugal, as everywhere in the world, the giant stirs in his sleep. The story of Russia has spread among peasants and workmen. The first result was the November, 1917, peasant revolt in the province of Alemtejo, where the land is held in large estates. They proclaimed a communist republic, seized and divided the land and for weeks held out against the troops of Sidoneo Paes. The railway men in the southern part of Portugal struck in sympathy, and for a time it looked as if the revolution were at hand. The organization was insufficient, however. The centers in Lisbon were cut off, and Sidoneo Paes was able to deal with the rebellion with such severity and secrecy that not an echo was heard in the outside world.

Since that time syndicalist organization, on the model of the French C.G.T.,[3] has gone on vigorously, until now Lisbon and the south are excellently organized, while propaganda is making progress even with the clerical northern peasantry, who own their own land and form the most profoundly conservative force in the country. *A Battalha*, the organ of the C.G.T., is the best printed paper in Lisbon, and has now the third largest circulation. Of the editors Joaquin Cardoso is a typographer and Alexandre Vieira a college man and journalist. Cardoso told me that he personally had four separate trials pending, but he added, laughing, justice is less expensive in Portugal than in America.

A Battalha has in the eight months that it has existed become the center of the syndicalist movement. I know of no paper that seems so rooted in people's affection. A constant stream of people would pour through the office, asking advice, telling their troubles; old women would ask help for sons who were in prison; boys would take off their shirts to show on their backs the welts raised by the sabres of civil guards, all with a trustful, burning enthusiasm that will go far some day. After talking a couple of hours with Lisbon workmen, the days of the politician and of the bourgeois seem numbered. And they might be over now if it weren't for British Dreadnoughts.

If organize and wait is the motto of the C.G.T. shout and sing is the motto of the new tendency embodied in the Maximalist Federation whose organ the Red Flag, leads a lively and precarious existence. Their aim is to form the nucleus of a red guard which, while leaving all direction in the hands of the C.G.T. shall be ready from the first to fight the counter-revolution.

When I was talking to the editor of another "Liberal" newspaper this one not fatherly but youngish, in a tight black silk vest, with a monocle in his eye, we heard singing in the street outside that sounded suspiciously like the Internationale. "It's nothing," he said. "They'll be arrested soon. We need a strong conservative government to control this rabble. What Portugal needs is work and order so that we may fulfill our respons. . . ."

But I knew what he was going to say. I left in a hurry. I found out that it was the Young Syndicalists protesting against the arrest of some members of the Maximalist Federation. The Young Syndicalists mostly boys between fifteen and twenty, were arrested too. In the prison they continued singing the Internationale. The Fire Department was sent for and the hose turned on them; they sang louder.

When I left Portugal about a week later, they were still in prison, and still singing. People could hear them from adjoining streets, which was demoralizing. But it's hard to see what else syndicalists can do in Portugal but sing until something happens to the Dreadnoughts.

Madrid, Dec. 14, 1919.

Notes

1. Errico Malatesta, an Italian revolutionary, and Georges Sorel, French philosophical anarchist.

2. The duke of Palmella, a prominent monarchist, had taken refuge in the American legation in Lisbon after the failure of the January revolt.

3. The Conféderation Génerale du Travail, a French union with strong syndicalist leanings.

America and the Pursuit of Happiness

O wad some power the giftie gie us, . . .[1]

As we came out of the shallow ford we met a lean blackish man with a very elongated face and yellow horseteeth. He was enthusiastic when he heard I was an American. "In America there's liberty," he cried and slapped me on the back so hard I nearly fell off the donkey. "En América no se divierte," in America people don't enjoy life, muttered the boy who owned the donkey, kicking his feet that were wet and cold from the river into the burning apricot-colored dust of the road. The three of us followed arguing, the sunlight beating wings of white flame about us. "In America there is freedom," said the blackish man. "There are no rural guards; road menders work eight hours and wear silk shirts and earn fabulous sums; there is free education for children and at forty everyone owns an automobile." "I don't care if the whole country is made of gold," cried the boy angrily. "People don't enjoy life there. An old sailor in Malaga told me, a man who fished for sponges, and he knew. It's not gold people need, but bread and wine and to enjoy themselves. We are poor here and have to work all day long, but we have dances and fine weather and pretty girls and this coast is so beautiful this gentleman"—pointing to me—"has come all the way from Madrid just to see it. No, I should not go to America except perhaps to get out of the army. There's nothing worse than the army. 'En América no se divierte.'" As he spoke there became suddenly vivid in my mind the phrase "pursuit of happiness." The donkey had stopped in front of a little wineshop under a trellis where broad dusty gourd leaves shut out the blue and gold dazzle of sun and sky. "He wants to say: Have a little drink, gentlemen," said the blackish man. In the green shadow of the wineshop there was a smell of anise and a sound of water dripping. When he had smacked his lips over a small cup of thick yellow wine he pointed at the donkey-boy. "He says people don't enjoy life in America." "But in America they are very rich," shouted the barkeeper, a beet-faced man whose huge girth was bound in a red cotton sash, and he made a gesture suggestive of coins, rubbing his thumb and forefinger together. Everybody roared derision at the donkey-boy.

Still, the consensus of opinion among the working people of Spain who had been to the United States seemed to be that people didn't enjoy life there, that money was easy, that there were many policemen, and that elevators and automatic lunchrooms and electric sky signs were marvels surpassing all things.

Nation, 111 (29 Dec. 1920), 777–78. Copyright The Nation Company, Inc., 1920. Reprinted in part in *Rosinante to the Road Again* (1922).

Among intellectuals, doctors, lawyers, scientific people, the image was different. America was to them a glittering *fata morgana* of imperishable beauty, where the great domes of progress were builded on the Fourteen Points, on sanitation, energy, clean living, and child labor laws. They hoped in its image to build a shiny well-policed, deloused, and deodorized Spain. They talked of what we had done for Cuba, of the stamping out of yellow fever, and of the anti-typhoid vaccine. They called themselves the generation of '98 and felt that contact with the great youthful power of the United States, even in war, had been a regenerative impulse for old inert Spain. Unlike the working people they had not been to America.

All this was in the winter of 1920.[2] I had the privilege of watching the golden domes of the Spaniards' imagined America totter as the Fourteen Points crumbled, and at last go crashing to the ground. When I was in Spain in 1917 they were naming squares and children after Woodrow Wilson. In the spring of 1920 the newspapers spoke of the United States and Hungary in the same breath. A symptom is the history of the Spanish commission to the labor congress in Washington. The members of that commission were chosen by the Government and were, except for one Socialist, conservative liberals, full of faith in the League of Nations, hopeful of governments. They landed in the middle of the anti-Bolshevik hue and cry, when the great docile sewer of canalized hate was being turned away from the Germans against anyone who hoped, however vaguely, that the exploiting system of capital would not be eternal. Coming from a country where, at least in private, liberty of speech is complete, they found themselves among a people who had deliberately cut one-half the world out of their consciousness, where the mildest form taken by the fanatical worship of things established was an ostrich-like hiding of the head. The president of the commission, an ex-minister with at least one ruthless suppression of a strike to his credit, was, by some strange confusion, attacked in our press as a Bolshevik. The Socialists found themselves exposed to constant and sometimes official rudeness. The result was that when the congress broke up with nothing accomplished the Spanish liberals returned home with their ideals of the American democracy shattered, and the labor men with a firm conviction that in the United States lay the heart of the great octopus they were fighting.

When Araquistain,[3] in a series of articles in *España*, the lively radical sheet that comes out weekly in Madrid, described the United States as a malignant colossus trampling out the hope of the western world, he expressed the bursting, in the minds of Spanish intellectuals, of the brightly colored bubble of American idealism. From the loved refuge from oppression in how few years have we become for all the world one of the most hated of militarist nations!

The face of an old woman in a bakery in Belfort intrudes itself out of my memory, a hollow-eyed face, wrinkled, the color of beeswax. It was before dawn one morning a couple of months after the armistice. I noticed in the flickering gaslight the usual portrait of Wilson on the wall, the lean face they burned candles before in Italy and that for a short time in Germany they substituted for their stiff whiskered Hohenzollern. The old woman's eyes shone when she saw I was looking at the picture. "He will save us all, with his Americans," she said. Then again when she handed me the long loaf of hot fragrant bread: "You don't like war, do you, you Americans? You will see to it that there is never a war again. They killed my three sons and I don't hate them for it. That's what only he understands. That's why he and his Americans will end wars." And she turned away from me to stare at the picture again. There was not a word I could say to her, for already the false dawn was fading. Europe had turned to America full of extravagant hopes, like a sick man that has stored all his faith in a quack doctor; when no remedy appeared the faith turned suddenly to hatred.

Perhaps the hatred is no more justified than was the extravagant hope. The muddled inert forces of American optimism and good-will had found real if accidental expression in the Fourteen Points. For a moment it seemed as if those sluggish streams of true democratic feeling that had been rambling further and further underground in the years of topheavy industrial organization since the Civil War might have reached the surface in a really living fountain. Yet the tragedy of their drying up to leave American thought the same muddy bog as before may have been due only to the lack of a pump, of an efficient machine to bring clear water to the surface; a tradition in other words, something similar to the great agin-the-government tradition that England inherited from the turbulent seafaring folk that crowded into the island out of northern seas. It is that tradition that in spite of centuries of various imperialisms has kept Great Britain the leader of the world's desire for liberty. In America, too, there must be left enough of the swaggering independence of our pioneers, enough of the hardheaded individuality of our old Yankee skippers to form a steely rebellious core in the flabby dumpling of our national docility. In the present disorganization of our public opinion it is our Hun-haters and lynchers and Bolshevik-baiters, our Palmers and Burlesons who—through the efforts of the jingo press—are considered the typical Americans.[4] Europeans ask themselves in bewilderment what they can have seen in all this welter to pin their faith to. No other voice can be heard above the howling of the dervishes of militant capitalism. The barbarities of our marines in Haiti are known all over the world,[5] but the protest against the miserable business will soon be forgotten in the files of liberal weeklies. Yet no one can say that more Americans were involved in the chain of events leading up to the massacres than protested when the facts became known with healthy indignation. We have heard a great deal in these last years of the duty of the individual to his government; it is time something were said of the duty of the individual to his own integrity, to his conscience, in the good round eighteenth century term. Not until a large and aggressive body of our citizens has formed the habit of loudly and immediately repudiating every abuse internal or external of the government's authority and every instance of bullying mob intolerance will we as a nation show that "decent respect for the opinions of mankind" necessary to reconquer the confidence of the only body of foreign opinion whose confidence is worth having. Somehow, in these dark days ahead, a compact Opposition must be built up which shall keep up contacts with the outside world in spite of the Chinese wall reactionary journalism is building up about us. And particularly, for the sake of our peace with our nearest neighbors the Latin Americans, Spanish-speaking peoples must be made to feel that there is more in the United States than ignorance and intolerance and aggression, that there is a body of opinion that puts humanity before national interests and class interests. We must outshout the priests of Baal.

Then, perhaps, after all this bitterness, we shall have replaced the land where the streets are paved with gold of the immigrant's dream by a land toward which the lacerated peoples of Europe can again aspire, where in a certain elemental freedom of thought and action the foundations will have been laid for a life that people—in the sense the donkey boy on that blazing road in Spain intended—can enjoy, the "liberty and pursuit of happiness" of that original too long forgotten declaration of our aims.

Notes

1. Robert Burns, "To a Louse."

2. Dos Passos means the winter of 1919–20, not that of 1920–21. Wilson's idealistic Fourteen Points had collapsed in the face of nationalistic self-interest at the Versailles Peace Conference and the opposition of the United States Congress.

3. Luis Araquistain, a prominent Spanish author and journalist of the day.

4. A. Mitchell Palmer, attorney-general (1919–21), and Albert S. Burleson, postmaster-general (1913–21). Palmer was largely responsible for the Palmer Raids, which sought to deport radical aliens; and Burleson sponsored the censorship of radical journals by the post office.

5. U.S. Marines landed in Haiti in 1915 and remained in the country as a "peace-keeping" force until the mid-1930s.

In a New Republic

[This report and the following one, "The Caucasus under the Soviets," derive from Dos Passos' visit to Batum and Tiflis in August 1921 while ostensibly working for the Near East Relief Agency. The Georgian region, which had sought to become an independent republic after the fall of the czarist government, had recently been absorbed into the USSR as the republics of Adjara and Georgia.]

Behind a cracked windowpane mended with tapes of paper, Things sit in forlorn conclave. In the centre is the swagbellied shine of a big samovar, dented a little, the whistle on top askew, dust in the mouldings of the handles. Under it, scattered over a bit of moth-chewed black velvet, are two silver Georgian sword-scabbards, some silver cups chased with a spinning sinewy pattern, a cracked carafe full of mould, some watches—two of them Swiss in tarnished hunting-cases; one an Ingersoll, quite new, with an illuminated dial—several thick antique repeaters, a pair of Dresden candlesticks, some lace, a pile of cubes of cheap soap, spools of thread, packets of pins. Back in the shop a yellow-faced old man droops over a counter on which are a few bolts of cheap printed calicos. Along the walls are an elaborate Turkish tabouret inlaid with mother-of-pearl, a mahogany dressing-table without its mirror and some iron washstands. The wrinkles have gathered into a deep cleft between the old man's brows; his eyes have a furtive snarl of a dog disturbed on a garbage-pile. He looks out through narrowed pupils at the sunny littered street, where lean-faced men sit with their heads in their hands along the irregular curb, and an occasional droshky goes by, pulled by boney racks of horses, where soldiers loaf idly in doorways.

The old man is the last guardian of Things. Here, in Batum, possessions, portable objects, personal effects, Things, that have been the goal and prize of life, the great centre of all effort, to be sweat for and striven for and cheated for by all generations, have somehow lost their import and crumbled away and been trampled underfoot. The people who limp hungrily along the rough-paved streets never glance into the windows of the speculators' shops, never stop to look enviously at the objects that perhaps they once owned. They seem to have forgotten Things.

Only an occasional foreigner, off a steamer in the harbour, enters the old man's shop, to haggle for this trinket or that, to buy jewels to re-sell in Europe, or goes into back rooms, behind locked doors, to paw over furs or rugs that can be smuggled out of the country only after endless chaffering and small bribery. The night before we got to Batum, the boat was full of talk of this and that which might be picked up for nothing, *pour un rien, per piccolo prezzo*. People scrubbed up their wits, overhauled their ways and means, like fishermen their tackle the night before the opening of the trout-season.

Freeman, 4 (5 Oct. 1921), 81–83. Reprinted in part in *Orient Express* (1927).

Strolling through the tree-shaded streets of Batum one sees, as one glances into the houses, mostly high, empty rooms, here and there a bed or a table, some cooking-utensils, a scrap of mosquito-netting or a lace curtain across an open window. All the intricate paraphernalia, all the small shiny and fuzzy and tasseled objects that once padded the walls of existence have melted away. Perhaps most of them vanished during the war, under the grinding wheels of so many invading and occupying armies, the Russians, the Germans, the British, the Turks, the Georgians, resisting the Bolsheviki, and lastiy the Red Army. Now, after these years of constant snatching and pillage, of frequent terrified trundling of cherished objects into hiding-places seems to have come apathy. People lie all day on the pebbly beach in front of the town, stripped of their rags, baking in the sun, now and then dipping into the long green swells that roll off the Black Sea, or sit chatting in groups under the palms of the curious higgledy-piggledy Elysium of the Boulevard along the water front. With half-starvation has come a quiet effortlessness probably sweeter than one might expect, something like the delicious sleep that comes, they say, over men who are freezing to death.

Meanwhile, the poor remnants of what people persist in calling civilization lie huddled, tarnished and dusty, in the windows of the second-hand dealers. Things useful and useless, well-made and clumsily made, and little by little they are wafted away West in return for dollars and lire and English pounds and Turkish pounds that lie in the hoards with which the dealers, the men with the eyes of dogs frightened on a garbage-pile, await the second coming of their lord.

II

There is a bright sliver of the moon in the sky. On the horizon of a sea, sheening green and lilac like the breast of a pigeon, a huge sun swells red to bursting. Palmfronds and broad leaves of planes flutter against a darkening zenith. In the space of dust, outside of their barracks, Georgian soldiers are gathering lazily into a circle. They wear ragged greyish uniforms, some with round fur caps, some with the pointed felt helmets of the Red army. Many of them are barefoot. From off them blows a sweaty smell, discouraged, underfed. One man, seated, starts thumping with his palms a double shuffle on a small kettledrum held between his legs. The rest beat time, by clapping, until one man breaks out into a frail lilting melody. He stops at the end of a couple of phrases, and a young fellow, blond, sprucely dressed, with a clean white fur cap on the back of his head, starts dancing. The rest keep time with their hands and sing Tra-la-la, Tra-la-la to the tune in a crooning undertone. The dance is elegant, mincing, with turkey-like struttings and swift hunting-gestures, something in it of the elaborate, slightly faded, romance of Eastern chivalry. One can imagine silver swords and spangled wallets and gaudy silk belts with encrusted buckles. Perhaps it is a memory that makes the men's eyes gleam so, as they beat time, a memory of fine horses and long inlaid guns and toasts drunk endlessly out of drinking horns, and of other more rousing songs sung in the mountains at night of the doughty doings of the Knight of the Pantherskin.

III

On the walls of the theatre are some crude squares of painting in black and white, a man with a pick, a man with a shovel, a man with a gun. The shadows are so much exaggerated that they look like gingerbread men. Certainly the man who painted them had not done many figures before in his life. The theatre is a long tin shed that used to be a cabaret show of some sort, the audience mostly workmen and soldiers in which tunics open at the neck, and women in white muslin dresses. Many of the men and all the children are barefoot, and only a few of the women wear stockings. When the curtain goes up all romping and chattering stop immediately; every one is afraid of missing a word of what is said on the stage. It is a foolish enough play, an early-Victorian "sob-story," about a blind girl and a good brother and a wicked brother, and a bad marquis and a frequently fainting marquise, but the young people who play it—none of them ever acted before the Red army entered Batum three months ago—put such conviction into it that one can not quite hold aloof from the very audible emotion of the audience during the ticklish moments of the dagger-fight between the frail good brother and the wicked and hearty elder brother who has carried off the little blind girl against her will. When, at last, all wrongs are righted, and the final curtain falls on felicity, one can not help but feel, that in the lives of these people who crowd out through the dilapidated ex-beergarden in front of the theatre, the bareness of the hungry living-rooms and barracks they go home to have somehow been compensated for. In the stamping and the abandon with which the two heroes fought was an atom of some untrammelled expression which might perhaps replace in people's hopes and lives the ruined dynasty of Things.

IV

The secretary of the commission for schools recently set up in Batum was a black-haired man, hawk-nosed, hollow-eyed, with a three-day growth of beard. Under-nourishment and overwork had made his eyes a little bloodshot and given them a curious intense stare. He had a sheaf of pink papers in front of him on which he scribbled an occasional hasty word as if pressed for time. He spoke French with difficulty, digging it up word by word from some long-forgotten layer of his mind. He talked about the school-system the Russians were introducing into the new Republic of Adjaria, of which Batum was the capital. He explained how children's summer-colonies had already been started in several villages, how every effort was being made to get equipment ready to open the primary and secondary schools at the end of September. All education is to be by work, nothing without actual touch; he spread wide his hands, angular tortured painful hands, and closed them with a gesture of laying hold on some slippery reality. The words he used, too, were concrete, of the soil. From the very first, work . . . In summer, in the fields, the children must cultivate gardens, raise rabbits, bees, chickens, learn how to take care of cattle. They must go into the forests and learn about trees. Everything they must learn by touch . . . Then, in the winter, they must study their native languages and Esperanto. There will be schools here for Armenians, Greeks, Moslems, Georgians, Russians. The rudiments of sociology, arithmetic, wood-working, cooking, will be taught; for in our new republic every man must be able to attend to his wants himself. That will be the primary education. You see, nothing by theory, everything by practice. Then the secondary education will be more specialized, preparation for trades and occupations. Those who finish at the high schools can go to the universities to do independent work in the directions they have chosen. You see, merit will be according to work, not by theories or examinations. All through the school-course there will be instruction in music and gymnastics and the theatre; the arts must be open to anyone who wants to work in them. But most important will be nature; the young children must be all the time in the fields and forests, among the orchards where there are bees. It is in the little children that all our hope lies . . .

V

The daily train from Batum to Tiflis crawls along the flanks of a sun-seared valley, with a river winding silvery in the bottom of it. There are ragged people sitting on top of the coaches, and hanging in clusters from each doorway, and jamming the passageways. From the windows of the bug-smelling, sweat-smelling sleeping-compartments peer out hot travel-grimed faces. On a siding, we pass the long train of the Second Tank Division of the Red Army, an engine, then box cars, on the steps of them blond young soldiers lolling. Few of them look more than eighteen, they are barefoot and scantily dressed in canvas trousers and tunics. They look comfortable and at their ease, sitting dangling their legs from the roofs and steps of the box cars and sleepers. It is impossible to distinguish the officers from their men. From out the big club-car, with posters in the windows, boys lean out to wave at friends in the passing train. Beyond the club-car, come flat cars with equipment, and a row of big green-splotched tanks. "A gift of the British," says some one beside me. "They were Denikin's."[1]

The Tiflis train, with its cars jammed with humanity and vermin, gathers speed and tilts round a bend. At the sight of the green tanks, a look of relief and pleasure comes over the sweating faces in the windows.

In my compartment, a banker from Batum starts explaining why there are no more political parties in Russia. "Now these words Bolshevik, Menshevik, Socialist, have no meaning," he says. "Whether we are conscious of it or not, we are only Russians."

Notes

1. Anton Denikin, Russian counterrevolutionary general and leader of the White Armies in the Ukraine. His troops were supplied by the Allies, including England.

The Caucasus under the Soviets

First, anyone who reads this article must be warned against believing it. Not that it is an intentional falsification of "facts," but on account of the enormous difficulty of getting any sense out of the teeming sprouting suffering muddle of a new sort of life. One is sure enough of facts when they are dead and stuffed and neatly set in rows in a textbook of history, but when they are scuttling about your feet like lizards it's a very different matter; each time you grab at one you are more likely to find its dead tail in your fingers than its live and wriggling body. If you add to this that I know neither Russian, nor Georgian, nor Tatar, nor Turkish, nor any of the minor dialects that swarm in the Caucasus, and that I spent only about three weeks in the countries altogether. . . . Well, what sort of impression of New York would a Chinaman have who could neither talk to people in their own language nor read the signs if he went through on Election Day?

The Italian captain had insisted the night before we reached Batum that the soldiers of the Red Army had helmets with little red horns on them, como il diablo. So as the steamer slewed into the harbor, vivid green in the dawn after the purplish blue of the Black Sea, there was a great deal of snatching back and forth of the glasses among the few passengers, each one wanting to be the first to spy a Bolshevik. They were mostly merchants with small batches of goods to peddle, and looked forward to landing with the same rather inquisitive apprehension with which people look forward to taking ether for an operation. Meanwhile the quarantine launch had come alongside unobserved, and some mild looking people in visored caps and white tunics were discovered having a drink in the smoking room. The captain, when asked to produce the horns, twirled his enormous white moustache in a very terrible manner, and whispered, "Wait till you see the Red Guard."

The wharf, to be sure, was dilapidated. There were holes where the planks had disappeared, and the piles tilted in every direction. Seaward of it was the wreck of an old tanker, from which men and boys were diving into the water. On the wharf lounged a quantity of ragged youths, many of them barefoot, with long, bayoneted rifles in their hands. A skinny, light-haired boy of about eighteen, remarkable by a pair of big black boots, was striding up and down in front of them shouting orders. When the gangplank was let down a whole crowd of youngsters in tunics with pistols bouncing in holsters at their hips came on board. Referring to them, a Swede,

Liberator, 5 (Aug. 1922), 5–8.

who had come down to sell soap, said in a disgusted voice in his purest Stockholm French: "There are only boys running this country. Ce n'est pas serios. Ce n'est pas serios."

Batum is the capital of the new republic of Adjara. The Russians discovered that the inhabitants of that region, who are a tribe known as the Adjars, Moslem Georgians allied to the Lazzes, those fine piratical-looking people in floppy black turbans one finds as sailors and fishermen all over the Black Sea, were hankering after the rule of their brothers in religion, the Turks, and decided to keep them busy by giving them a government all their own. At least so I was told, as Herodotus used to say. In actual fact all the men whom I met among the commissars of Batum were Russians. The town is very war-seedy, full of ragged people without work, come from no one knows where, but there are a couple of ships unloading in the harbor; the electric light plant is working; there are many theatres and cinemas open, and the huge pebbly bathing beach is always crowded, so that I imagine that life there is no more stagnant than in Trebizonde or Samsoun or any other of the Black Sea ports that have been drained of their trade by the war and by the results of the chaos-creating Allied policy in the Near East.

As everywhere in Soviet Russia, great effort is being put into education. There were night schools for adults already started—the Bolsheviki had been in control about three months—and the secretary of the committee for education told me that they hoped in another month to open, besides the Russian polytechnic, day schools for primary education where the children would be instructed in their own languages. This in a city where the population is about evenly divided among Georgians, Armenians, Jews and Russians, and where as far as I could discover there had been no school before at all accessible to the common people. Moreover, there were theatrical companies playing in Russian, Georgian, Armenian, Tatar and Yiddish. The night I left, Mordkin, who, I had been told in Constantinople, had been shot as a spy by the Georgians, was to dance with the corps de ballet he has created at the Opera in Tiflis.[1] In addition to this there was the *agi-theatre*, a sort of acted chronicle of current events, and a number of moving picture shows.

There is an express train daily from Batum to Tiflis. It consists of a sleeper for civil employees, one for army officers and one for the public, as well as a few box cars for local traffic. When the Russians first seized Georgia they set the fare from Tiflis to Batum at 250 rubles, worth about a quarter of a cent, with the result that the trains were so crowded with joy-riders that people traveling on business could never find room; so the fare has now been raised to 180,000 rubles. Even at that price there are many more passengers than places, and people going for short distances seem mostly to travel on the roof. As a last vestige of old Russian luxury, hot tea is brought round frequently during the night; people sip it in their overcrowded coupés and talk about Pushkin and the future of Russia much as they did before the Revolution.

Tiflis has still its funicular and its silver belts and sulphur baths, and there are still restaurants where people cry Alaverdi! and drink bottoms up, but the swagger of it has departed. On the Golovinski Prospect, where they say the Georgian nobles used to swank in their long coats, ribbed in front with rows of cartridge boxes, and their collars and round hats of astrakhan, and their curved swords of silver incrusted with jewels, one sees nothing but beardless youths in the inevitable white tunics of Soviet Russia, belted in at the waist. At the Grusinski Club, home of

never-ending Alaverdis under the old regime, were the same boys, soldiers and officers of the Red Army mostly, and a good many women poorly dressed, but rarely
lacking a certain brilliance of walk and gesture, commissars and stenographers, and
the wives and mistresses of army officers: a subdued, quietly jolly crowd, not too
well fed, that listens attentively to the orchestra and gives a curiously respectful silence to the actors in the little open air theatre where there are plays every night in
Russian or Georgian.

Wandering about Tiflis, one gradually begins to feel a curious lack in the population. There are no old people, no gray-bearded people, no fat, petulant-looking
rentiers. Everywhere youth, slimness, a look of hope and inexperience. You can
walk the length of the main street at the most crowded time without seeing a man or
woman over thirty-five, I was almost writing twenty-five. I used to wonder whether
the old people had all died or been shot by the Tcheka[2] or whether they had withered away before the raw hard violence of this new mode of life.

And their lot is pretty wretched, that of the old people. They are most of them
entirely unreconciled to the new regime, and drag out an existence, selling bit by bit
everything they possess, today a rug, tomorrow a silver cup, the next day some
china, sitting behind drawn curtains in their stripped drawing rooms, brooding on
the improbable day when their wrongs will be avenged and the topsy-turvy world
set right. Not even the failure of Denikine and Wrangel[3] and the rest of the Allies'
puppets can make them understand that not all the king's horses or all the king's
men can put Humpty Dumpty together again.

At the Near East Relief, while I was staying there, we were pestered continually by strings of people coming to sell things, watches, swords, jewelry, cameras,
state documents, old coins; everything upon which it was possibly conceivable that
an American would set a money value turned up in the course of a day. And it is
not only among the ex-rich that this daily selling out goes on; the poor sell what they
have, too; for the government rations are slim, and no one in the Caucasus, from
the president of the Revolutionary Committee to the man who works in the match
factory, is paid a living wage. The result is that with bread about 5,000 rubles a
pound, everyone, except the speculators and the peasants, spends half his life in the
elaboration of pitifully inadequate means of scraping together food.

The peasants, as far as I could gather, are well off. Gradually all the detritus of
the country's wealth gets into their hands. There is immediate sale for anything they
produce, no matter how small the quantity, at enormous profit. As the Batum train
neared Tiflis crowds of peasants, each with a small sack of wheat or potatoes or
corn, climbed on the roof or on the bumpers or hung in clusters from the doors.
Most of the people would sell their goods, and as nothing they needed could be
bought, would exchange their paper rubles for some object of gold or silver from a
speculator's shop, which they would take home and hide against better times. Miles
away from Tiflis in every direction there were convoys of oxcarts on the roads
loaded with produce for the market, and for each of these cartloads a bit more of the
stored-up riches of the city would go to the peasants. It is the revenge of the land on
the cities that, too hastily built up through the nineteenth century, had sucked it dry
of its energies.

In spite of the profits, scared by the danger of government requisitions, uprooted by the vague uneasiness of times of crisis, many of the peasants have given
up work and wander about the railroads and flock in and out of the cities, ragged,

starving, looking for they don't know what. All efforts to settle them have been in vain. It must have been something the same in Europe before the coming of the year one thousand when everybody thought the end of the world was tomorrow, and men and women left their farms and their flocks to wander about, full of terrified anticipation of the trumpet blast that should split the earth and sky. So in Russia, and in all the vast plains of Central Asia to which the Caucasus is the gate, a tremendous millennial unrest has seized hold of the people. They wander from place to place free and starving and vaguely expectant, trampling as they go the last vestiges of the complicated machine of the social order. The huge unconscious weight of this army of chaos dwarfs to absurdity all the tweedledum and tweedledee of pro-Bolshevik and anti-Bolshevik.

It is those boys in white tunics belted in at the waist with the air of wistful inexperience on their faces who are tackling the dragon. To call them the Bolsheviki has no sense, for though the government is still communist controlled, certainly not more than half of those who do the actual work of administration are communists even in the Red Army. In the government of Georgia I couldn't find any communists at all outside of the president, Nidwani.[4] And throughout Russia there has been such a lack of men of education or ability that anyone not actually intriguing against the regime who has had the slightest smattering of either has found himself in a position of responsibility high up in the governmental hierarchy. As a result, while the communists in Moscow are still struggling ahead on the thorny path to Utopia, their government has been tending more and more towards a confused and untheoretical attempt to conserve what's left of the old civilization. My impression is that communism in Russia is a dead shell in which new broader creeds are germinating; new births stirring are making themselves felt, as always, in people's minds by paroxysms of despair. Communism and the old hierarchy of the Little Father both belong to the last generation, not to the men who have come of age in the midst of the turmoil. It is they who will recreate Russia.

It was only by staying too long in the youth-renewing fire that the heroine of "She," that famous She-who-must-be-obeyed, came to her distressing end.[5] I suppose that Russia is in the same case. There is a limit to the number of years of famine and turmoil and destruction that any country can stand without losing all energy and vitality. The collapse of the Roman Empire did Europe in for a good many centuries. Without this year's famine on the Volga, it's fairly certain that the modified Soviet system would have been going smoothly enough by winter to allow people's energies to be turned towards reconstruction of a liveable sort of existence. As it is, no one can tell what may happen. Russia is at what you might call the Napoleonic moment. An immense country where in the muck of paralysis uncoordinated energies seethe and splutter like damp firecrackers. Out of it anything, good or evil, can come: a wave of conquest sweeping the whole East, in which Europe will only be an incident, or a hive of peaceful activity, the construction of a proletarian state. Theories or no theories, the Russians have too good an instrument in the Red Army to stay at home and starve. The course of events depends a great deal on the attitude of the Allies, that is of England and France, and a great deal more on that of America, the only great power which as the result of the war has not lost all prestige in Asia. The organizing of an honest relief service for the forty millions who are starving in the Volga basin, backed up by the help of individual technicians in the factories and railroads, would afford superb means of opening up

Russia to the world and turning her energies towards the building up of a new civilization. What sort of co-operation the relief would get from the government, if the leaders believed the enterprise to be above suspicion of political aims, is shown by the absolutely free hand they give the Near East Relief in the Caucasus.

Of course the famine can't be blamed for everything. There are aspects of the communist governmental methods that have done a great deal to bring about, along with the blockade and the foreign invasions, the present paralysis. First the Tcheka, the Extraordinary Commission. I doubt if the Russian courts were ever much to boast of, but the present judicial system which, intentionally or not, terrorizes the population by its secret methods, is extremely bad. Summary disposal of opponents is a feature of any civil war, but when the tribunals continue on a military basis in time of peace the lack of security becomes intolerable. The investigations in our own army have proved the immense unfairness of courts-martial. As far as I could find out, in the Caucasus, where it must be admitted the courts have been extremely moderate, the only penalty for any sort of crime was shooting, and the opportunities given the accused to prove his innocence were distinctly slim. The result is that men in administrative positions are very much afraid of taking any responsibility for fear some roving commission may disapprove and send them before the Tcheka. Inaction brings the same danger, but is less likely to be noticed, so passing the buck goes on to an unprecedented degree. The idea that the state can requisition anything it sees fit at any time brings the same insecurity to property and trade even in the Caucasus, where the community of goods has not been proclaimed. There is no visible machinery for redress, and the result is that everyone is afraid of doing anything, and that stagnation becomes a habit not easily broken.

Why, as money is entirely a question of the printing press, the government does not pay larger salaries—and everyone who gets a salary is in government employ, it is hard to guess. Perhaps from a fear of driving the unfortunate ruble further down towards the infinitesimal. Anyhow no one is paid enough to be able to make the few indispensable additions to the government rations without cutting and contriving on the side. The result is that speculation in all articles flourishes, and bribery, always common among Russian officials, is as frequent as before the Revolution, if it has not increased.

That is the reverse of the medal, perhaps a state of affairs inevitable in any social overturn, particularly at a time like the present, when the first ardor of revolutionary enthusiasm has cooled, and hope of a near millennium has pretty much evaporated, and people think mostly about saving their own skins. In spite of all that, the Communist Party has done great constructive work and has indescribably cleared the air of the old brutalizing tyranny of the Church and the Grand Dukes. And in spite of the new sort of tyranny I don't think that there is any doubt that the mass of the people have infinitely more opportunities for leading vigorous and unstagnant lives than before the revolution. The extraordinary development of theatres is one thing. I don't think it's an exaggeration to say that everyone in the territories under Russian influence has a chance to see some sort of a play and to hear a concert at least once a week. In the centers more often. Then the skeleton, if nothing else, of a gigantic system of education has been set up. Like most communist innovations, it has been in the army that the educational system has worked best. If the 11th or Caucasus Army is at all typical, they have done wonders in the reduction of illiteracy, which according to the statistics of the month of June, 1921, has been cut down from 85 to 90 per cent before the revolution to 5.7 per cent. Even allowing for considerable optimism in the figures, this is a notable achievement. It is in the army, too, that through the clubs and soldiers' councils and conventions that the real basis of a self-governing community is being laid.

At the top of the yellow hill that overhangs Tiflis, sitting in front of a glass of wine of Kakhetia. A huge wind out of the east lashes my legs with the stained table-cloth. Further down the slope four soldiers sit huddled together and look out over the city and talk. The city sprawls in huge raw squares at our feet. To the right is a ruined castle, and under it in the gorge of the Koura the old Persian and Georgian town, clustering about the black and white ornamented lanterns of the Georgian churches. To the left great reaches of muddy river, bridges and railway tracks, the onion domes of an orthodox church, and the enormous layout of a Russian city. Then in every direction the heave and slope of great stratiated hills of a greenish ochre color, and in front beyond series after series of patched ranges, the whitish blue peaks of the Caucasus bar the northern horizon. And all the time the huge wind blows out of the east, driving clouds of dust across the city. In a shack on the hill top a mechanical piano is jigging into the wind an insane jumble of trills. To-wards the east, where the wind blows from, there are no mountains, only endless blue distance.

Asia, I say aloud to myself. This is Asia. Asia of cruel wind-swept immensities. Asia, where unnumbered unconscious multitudes roam over the great frost-seared, sun-seared steppes, mindless, uneasy, feeling perhaps the first stirrings of that impulse that has again and again caused the dykes to burst, and sent floods of strange-faced people to swirl over the face of the cosy town-dwelling world. To the crazy jingle of the mechanical piano the phrase throbs in my mind: the future lies with Asia. Then a new gust of wind comes, upsetting chairs and ricketty tables and the waiter runs out with the ends of his tunic flapping. The soldiers have gone home and the sky seethes with copper-tinged clouds like suds in a washtub.

The future lies with Asia, and it is the Russians who have the moulding of Asia. Trace out the frontiers on a map of the world. The Europeans, British, French, Dutch still cling to the fringes, but Russia has penetrated to the heart of the continent that is the mother of races. It is those young men in tunics belted in at the waist who sit in ragged uniforms, swinging their bare legs from the doors of the in-terminable shabby troop trains of the Red Army, who struggle at desks with the in-ertia of underfeeding and corruption and despair, who listen in the evening at the different clubs to Beethoven and Borodine and to endless harangues on the prole-tarian state, it is those fair-haired boys of the new generation—Ce n'est pas serios, said the disgruntled Swede at Batum—who have the moulding, in the east at least, of the future centuries.

Tiflis, 1921.

Notes

1. Mikhail Mordkin, head of the Bolshoi Ballet company during this period.

2. An acronym for the All-Russian Extraordinary Commission for Combatting Counterrevolution, the secret police of the Communist party, known for its ruthlessness.

3. Anton Denikin and Peter Wrangel, generals commanding White Armies in South Russia during the civil war of 1919–21.

4. Dos Passos means B. Mdivani (not *Nidwani*).

5. In Sir Henry Rider Haggard's novel *She: A History of Adventure* (1887), "She-who-must-be-obeyed" is an African queen who has lived for two thousand years but who, in the climax of the novel, is killed rather than revitalized in a fire of supernatural origin.

Baroja Muzzled

[A review of *The Quest*, by Pió Baroja, translated by Isaac Goldberg.]

No European literature suffered more than the Spanish from the rigid optimist grin that overspread the novel in the nineteenth century. From the time when the Byronic outburst that had followed the failure of the first revolution had evaporated in tears and pistol shots to the late 'nineties, everything was good humour, taste, and gentility. A writer was a well-bred person in a stock who hurt no one's feelings and told comical stories enlivened with an occasional tear for the benefit of prosperous merchants and their clerks and wives. Facetiousness and *genre* were the keynotes. The genial fatuity of the novels of Valdes and Juan Valera is almost incredible. A tremendous epic sense of events hardly saved Galdós from the same doldrums. It took the entire police court docket of murder, rape, and lunacy to wipe the smile off the face of Echegaray. Funnily enough it was the sugar trust and "Remember the Maine" that first shattered the complacent dream of order and progress. The jolt of the disasters of the war brought a new generation into consciousness. This was the famous generation of '98, men who read German and English and forgot to go to mass, and who started about everything that is going on in thought and writing in Spain to-day. A half a dozen of Baroja's novels will probably remain their most solid and typical expression.

Baroja was of a hardheaded seagoing race, studied medicine, read Dickens, Dostoevsky, Stendhal, Nietzsche, scorned the pomp and rhetoric of the professional literary man, and admired scientific thought above everything. He felt intensely the restlessness and disruption of the world about him in which the middle classes, dazed and bloated by the tremendous power and riches a century's industrial growth had brought them, were already losing control. An era was speeding to a climax. The early twentieth century was to bring decisive and sublime events. In all this there was no time for urbanity or literary punctilio. Writing should be colloquial, sarcastic, acid. A novelist was an advance agent of revolution who measured out and described what was to be destroyed.

This novel, The Quest, is the first of a trilogy called La Lucha por la Vida (The Struggle for Existence) that follows the history of a servant-girl's son through stratum after stratum of work and poverty. The narrative rambles with the casualness of a rogue romance of the seventeenth century through the slums and back lanes and cheap eating houses of Madrid. Manuel, the central figure, first helps his

Dial, 74 (Feb. 1923), 199–200.

mother in the boarding-house where she works, is thrown out of there for flirting with the landlady's daughter, is put to work for a shoemaker, falls in with all sorts of hobos and ragamuffins, is apprenticed to a greengrocer, is a baker's assistant, tries a hand at burglary, joins the *claque* at a theatre, is befriended by an elderly rag-picker and his wife, and is finally driven out of the last refuge of their house by the teasing fury of his love for their daughter who won't look at him. At the end he is completely down and out.

These novels are written in a language wilfully casual and unliterary. They are full of slang and racy talk. Baroja, like Dostoevsky, must one time have read much Dickens, for there appear the strangest echoes, as in the description of the boarding-house clock in the beginning of The Quest. But Dickens could never have told such a plain unvarnished tale.

It is a shame that, at a time when American writing could gain a great deal from the impact of Baroja's tart simplicity, his work should be foisted on us in such a muddy disguise. When some thousand years from now Americanologists try to decipher the inconceivable mass of print they will find in the ruins of Mr. Carnegie's libraries they will be much puzzled by the curious language in which certain books purporting to be translations from other tongues are written. A lively translation, however incorrect, into English, Yiddish, American, or any other language spoken in these United States, would have been worth while. This one is disastrously clumsy and insensitive, written in no language ever heard on land or sea. We can only hope that Baroja's vitriol is crude and searing enough to eat its way through this pulpiest of mediums and line out its swift etchings in spite of the translator and his dictionary. What we need, in this flood of muffled foreign literature that's overwhelming us, is someone to translate the translations.

Foreword to *Roger Bloomer*

[Dos Passos became friends with John Howard Lawson (1894–1977) while both
were serving in the ambulance corps in France and Italy during 1917–18; they
remained close until the late 1930s. *Roger Bloomer*, an experimental
expressionistic satire, was produced on 1 March 1923 by the Actors' Theatre.]

In a year or ten years or a hundred years there is going to be a theater in America.
The continuously increasing pressure in the grinding engine of industrial life will
force other safety valves than baseball and the movies and the Ku Klux Klan.
Something approximating a national theater is the most direct organ of group consciousness and will come into being, inevitable with the welding of our cities into
living organisms out of the junk heaps of boxed and predatory individuals that they
are at present.

But will the cities come alive? They will either come alive or be filled with ro-
bots instead of men.

There are all sorts of elements in our stage of the moment that will probably
be discovered later to have been the foundations of a genuine native tradition. Already plays like *Blue Jeans* and *Uncle Tom's Cabin* and *Ben Hur*[1] had a quality that
distinguished them from their British equivalents. The series of Ten-Twenty-Thirty
melodramas[2] and sob plays with their accompanying pie-slinging farces were a very
genuine expression of the period of crude industrial expansion when people's energies were so drained by the physical effort of building up the country and their own
fortunes that they had no need of safety-valves. Now the country is all built up and
the fortunes of the tenth that had luck, and here we are, walled in. The forced draft
puffs as hard as ever and the pressure rises, rises.

The theater hasn't kept up with the race. At the same time as the desire and
need for it has grown the actual stage has become more and more disorganized.
There are heaven knows how many playhouses in New York, but the only one of
them that has a definite audience and a definite tradition, that really exists as a theater apart from the building it uses, has for its language not English but Yiddish.

Roger Bloomer is a raw, unlabelled attempt to use the emotional possibilities
of the theater to their fullest extent for the expression of the commonest American
theme—a boy running away from home to go to the big city. Explosions of fresh vitality in any art necessarily destroy the old forms.

What we have in American theaters today is a great uncoordinated swirl of individual energy and mechanical skill, that if it could only be got into motion towards an end would produce something inconceivable. There is in the extraordinary skill with which vaudeville performers put themselves over individually to the

John Howard Lawson, *Roger Bloomer* (New York: Thomas Seltzer, 1923), v–viii.

audience in the short time allotted to them, in the satire and construction you get occasionally in burlesque shows and musical comedies, in the brilliant acting and producing it takes to get across trick melodramas and mystery plays, raw material for anything anyone wants to make.

So far no one has had the nerve or the muscle to tackle the amazingly difficult problem of fusing all this personal effort and mechanical skill into something immediate and alive, expressive of an emotion and a will.

There have been weak attempts in all sorts of directions, national theaters built, experimental clubs, fine beginnings made, but so far no man has surmounted the complications of play production to the extent of putting on a great show really creating a lasting monument to any aspect of New York. Say, something that would bear the relation to America that *Le Sacre du Printemps* and *The Cherry Orchard* bear to Russia, that *Les Maries de la Tour Eiffel* bears to France, that *Peer Gynt* bears to Norway.

Not so fast. The scaffolding is barely begun, it's too early to talk of putting the apex on the pyramid. What I mean is that given the unprecedented fever and inhumanness and mechanical complexity of American life, the monument must be tough and solid and lustily built to make a place for itself at all on this continent, where it will be unprecedented, looked at with suspicion and dismay, perhaps unnoticed for generations.

Perhaps our time will only manage to pile up foundations for others to build on, perhaps it wont even manage that. The New York theater today has no more to do with the daily existence of the average New Yorker, with his hungers and terrors, than it has with the pigtail of the living God at Lhasa. The burlesque shows and even the movies are much closer. The plays of Eugene O'Neill, including *The Hairy Ape*, have only touched the problem. *Roger Bloomer* is only a beginning.

Like everything else about the American theater, a criterion of judgment exists if at all, only in vague conditional prophecy. Before we can have standards of comparison, we've got to have plays, and audience, a tradition.

Notes

1. Three extremely popular late-nineteenth-century American melodramas, the first by Joseph Arthur and the last two adapted from popular novels by Harriet Beecher Stowe and Lew Wallace.

2. Melodramas produced by a cheap repertory company; tickets to such performances were generally scaled at ten, twenty, and thirty cents.

Building Lots

[A review of *Weeds*, by Pío Baroja.]

It's curious rereading after seven years—this trilogy of Baroja's of which "Weeds" is the central novel. Then I was a newcomer in a Madrid that had been unchanged for two or three decades, the Madrid of Galdós and the Cafe Suizo; the war was in its less horrible slaughterhouse stage; the first thing you did every morning was still to look out of the window to see if the great revolution had burst with the dawn; now Madrid is an Americanized town with its subway and its skyscrapers at Cuatro Caminos; soccer is taking the place of bullfights, and at last Spain is being sucked into the current of industrial life. The Pyrenees are leveled.

"La Lucha por la Vida" is the epic of a period in Spanish life, a not at all despicable period, of which the close was symbolized by Primo Rivera's coup d'etat last summer.[1] Then, in 1916, the three novels still seemed actual, fresh off the presses as a bulldog edition; roaming through the clattering Madrid streets with "Weeds" in one pocket and M. Garnier's dictionary in the other, you seemed to have the keys to every alley and wine-shop, to the iron-bound doors that opened on the breakneck stairs, with their invariable smell of scorched olive oil, of all the tenement houses, to every courtyard and rag market. These books led you through all the back lots and bad lands and cabbage patches that filled the valleys round the city, through suburbs like Kafir kraals out along the old royal roads where great painted carts drawn by four mules tandem navigated creakily like galleons, over the bare hills of the Castilian desert with the Sierra always bright and gleaming in your face. They were the true Baedeker to that seething maze of rebellious, unkempt, louse-bitten, soaring life that was Madrid, the clotted center and heart of the peninsula. Under the thin veneer of a nineteenth-century city the old Adam was still rampant. Everything was leading to the great revolution that was to be the old Adam's victory and transfiguration. The angels and demons were spoiling for Armageddon.

Now we have seen Armageddon, the marvelous year has been laid away among the other years in the smoothing presses of history. The old Adam wears Arrow collars and Walkover shoes and the machine he was to make his own is in the hands of Henry Ford and Mussolini and other less personable marionettes. From being the actual tidings from a picket on guard "La Lucha por la Vida" has become a document and a work of art.

Nation, 118 (9 Jan. 1924), 36–37. Copyright The Nation Company, Inc., 1924.

In spite of an unimaginative and frequently incorrect translation, "Weeds" and "The Quest," the two novels already published in English, are worthy, I think, of being set a little apart from the flood of translations out of all languages annually dumped into the receptive but expressionless maw of the American public. They are a genuine and non-literary account of an almost extinguished flare of revolt against the great machine. These humble people, Manuel, Jesus, La Justa, the Baroness, fitfully and helplessly as they stray along their appointed paths, are none of them mob minded; the old Adam glows in them at times; they are unwillingly driven to the treadmill. Their children, the inhabitants of the new white stone Madrid that has sprouted in five years, go consentingly. Business and sport, industry and prosperity are undisputed gods. The lazy, knotty-minded inhabitants of this old Madrid, contentious and noisy and fond of laughing, have disappeared like the goats that used to browse in the back lots full of shacks and beggars and little drinking dens where now straight fences of barbed wire mark off the limits of the Garden City. As a record these books are immensely valuable, and perhaps there is more than that to them. There is a dignity and restraint in the writing, a quietly distilled poetic energy that is very hard to describe. Baroja is a great novelist, not only in his time, on railway bookstalls and in editorial offices, but in that vigorous emanation of life and events that for some reason people garner up and desiccate in libraries and call literature. That's all there is to it.

Notes

1. General Primo de Rivera disbanded the Spanish Cortes on 13 September 1923 and established a military dictatorship.

Is the "Realistic" Theatre Obsolete?
Many Theatrical Conventions Have Been
Shattered by Lawson's *Processional*

[Lawson's play was produced by the Theatre Guild on 12 January 1925. Dos Passos' own "jazz play," *The Moon Is a Gong*, was produced by the Harvard Dramatic Club in May 1925.]

We may as well admit that for our time there are no questions of aesthetics. Least of all in the theatre, where the problem is now one of sheer existence. It is doubtful, anyway, if the stage will long be able to compete with the movies and radio and subsequent mechanical means of broadcasting entertainment and propaganda. Perhaps it will follow the bison and the dodo and the wild swan. Certainly it is among the last survivors of what might be called the arts of direct contact.

If the theatre is to subsist, it must offer something that city-dwelling people need extremely, something matchless, that can't be found anywhere else. A century that has to snatch its hasty life furtively between time clock and alarm clock requires the stimulant of some human externalization, warm and glamorous and passionate, that it misses in the chilly fantasmagoria of the movies or in the slightly curdled strains of radio music. Baseball, football, and prizefights fill the bill in one direction; jazz dancing, in another. But as America is racked more and more by the growing-pains of conscious adolescence, we have got to have some more organized and purposeful expression of our loves, fears, and rages. That is the theatre's one chance to survive.

I don't think that the people who control the theatres of New York today quite see their peril. They do understand that a change is coming over their audiences and that there are breakers ahead. The danger is freely admitted of the competition set up by the movies and, more recently, by the radio, which makes it unnecessary for people to move out of their pigeonholes in the evening. If the theatre were on firmer ground, there wouldn't be any competition, any more than there is competition between shoe stores and soda fountains. If the people connected with the stage only have the energy and imagination, the theatres can get back their own audiences—and more. For the theatre more than anything else welds into a sentient whole the rigid honeycomb of our pigeonholed lives. Since religion has failed humanity, the theatre is the focus of mass emotion.

Of course, nobody can deny that a great many serious and well-intentioned people have been trying all over these United States to create a theatre and audience for the last fifteen years. Mightn't the unhappy slimness of the results be due partly to the fact that most of these people's interests have been literary rather than theat-

Vanity Fair, 24 (May 1925), 64, 114. Copyright © 1925 (renewed 1953, 1981) by Condé Nast Publications, Inc.

rical? The theatres that have run a successful course in various parts of the world since people went out and sat all day on the stonecut seats of an Athenian hill have had various aims and motives, but none of them have been *literary*. The fact that a lot of good and bad plays have been preserved as literature is beside the point. The plays had their real being where they were acted and applauded and hissed by the populace as spectacular and emotional entertainment and nowhere else.

Various aspiring organizations that are trying to coax the American public into taking the theatre seriously, have never quite gotten away from the point of view that plays must be regarded primarily as masterpieces of literary effort, fraught with the culture of a by-gone age. As a result, their audiences consist largely of wistful and literary-minded people who seek in culture a dope to make them dream that they live in a Never Never Land, European, decorous, and unattainable to the Man-on-the-Street, in which the Beautiful and True hold sophisticated discourse in a Louis Quinze drawing room. As long as the theatre depends on that audience, it will be more occupied with the idiotic schism between Highbrow and Lowbrow than with wringing people's minds and senses and hearts. And an audience of unsophisticated hot-blooded people can't be got by whistling for it.

The result is that the few worthwhile plays being produced round New York don't fit the frames they are presented in. At best they do no more than generate a lot of articles by the critics and a lot of superliterary conversation. They are short-circuited by the non-theatrical state of mind in which they are presented and attended.

That doesn't mean that a great deal of very noble and arduous sweeping of the boards hasn't gone on. The throb of the drum in *The Emperor Jones* cleared many a pair of ears that had been until that time tuned only to suburban comedy. The chesty roar of *The Hairy Ape* made several people forget to read how The Well Dressed Man would wear his cravat. Among many frustrated searchers after messages a few people, at least, sat up and felt terror and awe and a speeding up of the blood from the Dead People's Ball in *The Crime in the Whistler Room*.[1] On top of all these comes *Processional* (John Howard Lawson's jazz play, produced by the Theatre Guild) as the straw to break the camel's back of the literary drama.

First it must be admitted that the audience of the best people that gasped when the curtain went up on Gorelik's painted drop to the sound of the Yankee Doodle Blues was only restrained by its all-too-evident good breeding and its respect for *ART*, in whatever aspect that puzzling divinity might show itself—and perhaps a trifle by its natural inertia—from rising *en masse* and shouting this noisy gibberish off the stage. Many of those cultured and educated people, warmers of orchestra chairs six nights a week, had never seen theatre before. Naturally they were shocked. We have been brought up to believe that the first convention of the theatre is that the events take place in a room, one side of which is imagined to be transparent. The audience, by the power of illusion, believes that what it sees going on on the stage really exists in the world of actuality. The great triumph of the realistic theatre was when people put their umbrellas up coming out of *Rain*.[2] I don't mean to underrate the things that have been done under that convention; a great many of its effects are more natural than nature—like glass flowers.

But there is another sort of theatre. On a wooden platform in a hall actors perform acts. Trained seals would be the simplest illustration of this; a ballet like Stravinsky's *Noces*, one more subtle, complex, and intensely humanized. Instead of the illusion of "reality," its aim is to put on a show which creates in a hall full of people its own reality of glamor and significance.

Processional is the first American play in our generation in which the convention of the invisible fourth wall has been frankly and definitely abandoned. In other plays, the subterfuge of a dream has been used to placate the critics whenever the author felt he needed to be positively theatrical. In *The Hairy Ape* we were told that it was all subjective, inside the man's mind. Meanwhile burlesque, musical comedy, and vaudeville have preserved, but more or less flippantly, the real manners and modes of the theatre. In *Processional* these are employed with passionate seriousness. The actors are actors, you feel the boards of the stage in every line, events take place against painted scenery, behind footlights, in the theatre. There is no attempt to convince the audience that, by some extraordinary series of coincidences, they have strayed into a West Virginia mining town in the middle of an industrial war. They are in a theatre seeing a show.

But why, everybody asks, go back to the humdrum and hokum of the Ten-Twenty-Thirty[3] when we are just beginning to convince intelligent people, readers of *The World*, subscribers to *Vanity Fair*, book buyers, theatre lovers, art collectors, that what they want is Adult Entertainment, real life honestly set down? Even the most friendly critics label *Processional's* most genuinely theatrical moments as satire and think that the author is poking fun at them. Actually, crude and comic and grotesque as many of the scenes intentionally are, the play is a very unsophisticated attempt to invade the audience's feelings by the most direct and simple means that come to hand. The fact that it does move and excite us, and succeeds thereby in reinstating the stage, makes it extraordinarily important.

The movies have made the theatre of the transparent fourth wall unnecessary and obsolete, just as photography has made obsolete a certain sort of painting. The camera and screen can transport the audience into circumstances, in the ordinary sense, real. It can show you what people who have been there recognize as West Virginia. The theatre can only bungle at it clumsily. Therefore, if the theatre is going to survive, it has got to find for itself a new function. Of course it is perfectly natural that the first attempt to climb wholeheartedly out of the blind alley of realism should be received with horror and consternation. American audiences are pathetically afraid of being moved either in space or time or in their feelings. That invited crowd the first night at the Garrick had the face of a maiden aunt who has been unwillingly coaxed by a small boy to take a ride on a roller coaster. They felt sick and held on desperately and prayed that it would stop. But as a trip to Coney Island on a Sunday afternoon will show you, there are a great many people in New York who are crazy to ride on roller coasters.

Most of them have given up going to the theatre because they don't feel they get their money's worth. So far, "advanced," "serious," "highbrow" plays have been aimed at the intellectual audience that wants something to talk about at a dinner or a tea. *Processional* is aimed at the people who like roller coasters. Perhaps in its whole run only ten people who genuinely desire motion will go to see it. Those ten people will be the nucleus of the audience of a theatre that will have nothing to fear from the competition of the radio or of the movies.

Processional is the Uncle Tom's Cabin of the new American Theatre.

Notes

1. A fantasy by Edmund Wilson produced at the Provincetown Playhouse in 1924.

2. A popular dramatization in 1922, by John Colton and Clemence Randolph, of Somerset Maugham's short story.

3. See p. 72 n. 2.

300 N. Y. Agitators Reach Passaic

[The United Front Textile Committee, a Communist organization, had initiated a series of strikes in the New Jersey textile towns, including Passaic. When police began arresting strikers for unlawful assembly, various New York intellectuals and radicals joined the picket lines and meetings and permitted themselves to be arrested in protest against the violation of free speech. Dos Passos participated in such a protest at Passaic in mid-April 1926.]

The people who had come from New York roamed in a desultory group along the broad pavement. We were talking of outrages and the Bill of Rights. The people who had come from New York wore warm overcoats in the sweeping wind, bits of mufflers, and fluffiness of women's blouses fluttered silky in the cold April wind. The people who had come from New York filled up a row of taxicabs, shiny sedans of various makes, nicely upholstered; the shiny sedans started off in a procession towards the place where the meeting was going to be forbidden. Inside we talked in a desultory way of outrages and the Bill of Rights, we, descendants of the Pilgrim Fathers, the Bunker Hill Monument, Gettysburg, the Boston Teaparty . . . Know all men by these presents . . . On the corners groups of yellowish grey people standing still, square people standing still as chunks of stone, looking nowhere, saying nothing.

At the place where the meeting was going to be forbidden the people from New York got out of the shiny sedans of various makes. The sheriff was a fat man with a badge like a star off a Christmas tree, the little eyes of a suspicious landlady in a sallow face. The cops were waving their clubs about, limbering up their arms. The cops were redfaced, full of food, the cops felt fine. The special deputies had restless eyes, they were stocky young men crammed with pop and ideals, overgrown boy-scouts; they were on the right side and they knew it. Still the shiny new double-barrelled riot guns made them nervous. They didn't know which shoulder to keep their guns on. The people who had come from New York stood first on one foot then on the other.

Don't shoot till you see the whites of their eyes. . . .

All right move 'em along, said the sheriff. The cops advanced, the special deputies politely held open the doors of the shiny sedans. The people who had come from New York climbed back into the shiny sedans of various makes and drove away except for one man who got picked up. The procession of taxis started back the way it had come. The procession of taxis, shiny sedans of various makes, went back the way it had come, down empty streets protected by deputies with shiny new riot guns, past endless facades of deserted mills, past brick tenements with ill-painted stoops, past groups of squat square women with yellow grey faces, groups of men and boys standing still, saying nothing, looking nowhere, square hands hanging

New Masses, 1 (June 1926), 8. Reprinted in *In All Countries* (1934).

at their sides, people square and still, chunks of yellowgrey stone at the edge of a quarry, idle, waiting, on strike.

The New Masses I'd Like

[The *New Masses*, one of the principal journals of the American far Left during the 1920s and 1930s, appeared initially in May 1926. Mike Gold, a member of the Communist party, was an editor of the magazine; Dos Passos was a member of the editorial board for some years, along with Edmund Wilson, John Howard Lawson, Max Eastman, and Eugene O'Neill.]

Mike Gold is responsible for these notes, for their existence if not for their disorder and scatterbrainedness. The other night he made off into the underbrush after calling me a bourgeois intellectual before I had a chance to argue with him. The salutary truth has rankled and finally come out in a rash of generalizations concerning professional writers, the labor movement in America, the NEW MASSES and people in general. Admitting that generalizations are worthless, here they are.

First a restriction about proletarian literature. It seems to me that people are formed by their trades and occupations much more than by their opinions. The fact that a man is a shoesalesman or a butcher is in every respect more important than that he's a republican or a theosophist; so that when he stops earning an honest living and becomes a writer, agitator, poet, idealist, in his actions if not in his ideas he becomes a member of the great semi-parasitic class that includes all the trades that deal with words from advertising and the Christian ministry to song writing. Whether his aims are KKK or Communist he takes on the mind and functional deformities of his trade. The word-slinging organism is substantially the same whether it sucks its blood from Park Avenue or from Flatbush.

And at this moment it seems to me that the word-slinging classes, radical and fundamentalist, are further away from any reality than they've ever been. Writers are insulated like everyone else by the enforced pigeonholing of specialized industry. As mechanical power grows in America general ideals tend to restrict themselves more and more to Karl Marx, the first chapter of Genesis and the hazy scientific mysticism of the Sunday supplements. I don't think it's any time for any group of spellbinders to lay down the law on any subject whatsoever. Particularly I don't think there should be any more phrases, badges, opinions, banners, imported from Russia or anywhere else. Ever since Columbus, imported systems have been the curse of this continent. Why not develop our own brand?

What we need is a highly flexible receiving station that will find out what's in the air in the country anyhow.

Under the grey slag of a print-pocked crust there are veins of lava to be tapped that writers at least know nothing about, among the shuffling people at strike meetings there are tentative flickers of thought that the agitators and organizers know nothing about, under the vests of fat men in limousines there are inquietudes that

New Masses, 1 (June 1926), 20. Reprinted in *The Theme Is Freedom* (1956).

mean something. In these terribly crucial years when the pressure is rising and rising in the boiler of the great imperial steamroller of American finance that's going to try to grind down even further the United States and the world, being clear-sighted is a life and death matter. If we ever could find out what was really going on we might be able to formulate a theory of what to do about it.

Why shouldn't the NEW MASSES be setting out on a prospecting trip, drilling in unexpected places, following unsuspected veins, bringing home specimens as yet unclassified? I think that there's much more to be gained by rigorous exploration than by sitting on the side lines of the labor movement with a red rosette in your buttonhole and cheering for the home team.

The terrible danger to explorers is that they always find what they are looking for. The *American Mercury* explores very ably the American field only to find the face of Mr. Mencken mirrored in every prairie pool.[1] I want an expedition that will find what it's not looking for.

I hope that it is not for nothing that the NEW MASSES has taken that dangerous word NEW into its name. The tendency of the masses has always been to be more disciplined in thought than in action. I'd like to see that state of things reversed for once. I'd like to see a magazine full of introspection and doubt that would be like a piece of litmus paper to test things by. I don't mean to start with the original chaos and make a new map of the world starting from 8th Street. The receiver has got to be tuned to a fairly limited range. That range has been vaguely laid down to be the masses, the people who work themselves rather than the people who work others. Within that range, wouldn't a blank sheet for men and women who have never written before to write on as no one has ever written before be better than an instruction book, whether the instructions come from Moscow or Bethlehem, Pa.?

But Mike says that scepticism is merely the flower of decay, the green mould on the intellect of the rotten bourgeoisie. He may be right. Anyway I don't think it is scepticism to say that November, 1917,[2] is in the past. It shows an almost imbecile faith in the word NEW and the word MASSES.

The NEW MASSES must at all costs avoid the great future that lies behind it.

Notes

1. The *American Mercury*, edited by H. L. Mencken and George Jean Nathan, specialized in satirical depictions of provincial American society.

2. That is, the Russian Revolution.

Spain on a Monument

[A review of *Virgin Spain*, by Waldo Frank.]

The retablo behind the high altar in a Spanish church is a voluminous and gilded and pedimented edifice with a central group of figures and tiers of statues of saints in niches on either side. It seems to me that in this book Waldo Frank has painstakingly constructed a retablo of Spain against a background of history books. In the center in the Virgin's place is his portrait of Isabella la Catolica. Ranged in rows on either side are the saints and martyrs each in his appropriate niche, Don Juan and the Knight of the Doleful Countenance, the Celestina and the Picaro, Santa Teresa and San Juan de la Cruz, El Greco and Velasquez, Torquemada and Loyola, Unamuno and Ganivet, Belmonte and Picasso. The plan is architectural, the carving is competent and thorough, but for some reason that I can't make out, the figures are rather lifelike than alive.

Perhaps it's the drapery, all these voluted bookwords, these mystical philosophic terms that obscure the outlines. (Perhaps they are merely over my head.) But I can't help feel that this psychological phraseology, so popular with all the *serious* writers of our time, is mere ornamental verbiage, like the swirling drapery on baroque sculpture where all the lines ingrow to a short circuit. The result is that this highly wrought work is a mere library piece, a static elaborate monument. You open the door and look at it, you go over the details, you nod your head sagely, mutter, *Yes, that's quite true*, and go away with your brain splitting with murky, contorted, and highly charged phrases and wonder why so fine a show should leave you so unsatisfied.

In the first place there's no factual information in it that you couldn't find in the New York Public Library. That in itself is depressing to me, who finds a fact, say that the little dogs of Ronda have two curls in their tails, always more enlivening and worthwhile than the most elegantly balanced pyramid of abstract ideas. I suppose the aim of such a book is rather to give you the intellectual and emotional background that will make you understand a fact when you come across it. The real ground for objection, then, is that these particular abstract ideas are not useful. The framework of Waldo Frank's retablo is academic, rather than real. I mean that it belongs to a reality that may once have existed but that events have relegated to the storeroom.

New Masses, 1 (July 1926), 27.

There is a place in Madrid called the Ateneo, an antique and dusty and extremely convenient library where the people who hung round the university and the writing professions used to gather to hear lectures and chat and look up books of reference. It was the only library I've ever seen where you could order tea and coffee in the reading room. I used to work there because it was the warmest place I could find that winter. In spite of the excellent coffee, the Ateneo had a peculiarly depressing smell of decaying concepts and amiable dead liberalisms. It was a museum of extinct scholastic monsters. I wonder if Waldo Frank didn't write this book there.

But even the gloom of the Ateneo was cut by an occasional shaft of light from the street, so much so that the Directorate sent the police down to close it up.

Virgin Spain is Spain seen through the not very often washed windows of the Ateneo. Some of the details, within the limits of the library, are excellent. The description of Seville, for example, as a pagan goddess leaning on the Giralda:[1] "She stirs her head and her arms in a half somnolent, half ecstasied dance, seeking her own image in the water." The description of gypsies dancing, the account of the Jewish mystics, of Queen Isabella, of the building of the Escorial, of the life of Cervantes, of the matriarchal principal are pithy and reveal very first rate understanding. The explanation of bullfights is the best I've ever read.

But I can't understand how Frank came to leave out all the confused and confusing tragedy of the Spain of our day, the gradual collapse of the bullfights before football, the influence of the Rio Tinto British-owned mines, the bloody farce of the Moroccan war,[2] the Jesuit control of the railroads, the breakdown of Catalan syndicalism, of the agrarian movement in Andalusia. These things are as much Spain as Philip IV and the Old Cathedral at Salamanca and much more important to us at the present moment.

I don't mean that such a book, a book that aims to construct a well-proportioned ornate frame for the classification of facts, events, experiences, accidents, should give us the latest news; but it should at least not ignore the whole tangled welter of industrial and working class politics through which Spain, the immaculately conceived immaculately conceiving Lady of Elche,[3] is being tricked, seduced perhaps, into the howling pandemonium of the new world, where in a copper mine or in the assembling room of the Hispano-Suizo,[4] she may be brought to bed of a birth less immaculate, but as portentous for us poor devils on street corners in America, as any of the childbearings of her mystic past.

Notes

1. The Giralda tower of the cathedral of Seville, a vestige of the Moorish occupation and a symbol of the city.

2. The Rif Revolt in Spanish Morocco during the early 1920s resulted in heavy Spanish losses.

3. La Donna de Elche, a famous Greco-Iberian sculpture of unknown origin, was of a patrician woman with a refined smile.

4. The Hispano-Suiza (not Suizo) was a large Spanish-made touring car of the 1920s and 1930s.

The Pit and the Pendulum

[Written after Dos Passos' visit in June 1926 to the prisons where Sacco and Vanzetti were held. The two men were executed on 23 August 1927.]

About dawn on Monday, May 3rd, 1920, the body of Andrea Salsedo, an anarchist printer, was found smashed on the pavement of Park Row. He had been arrested for deportation eight weeks before in the tail end of the anti-Red raids of the Department of Justice then running amok under A. Mitchell Palmer. The man had jumped or been thrown from a window of the offices of the Department of Justice on the fourteenth floor of the Park Row building. What happened during those eight weeks of imprisonment and third degree will never be known. At that time Bartolomeo Vanzetti was peddling fish in the pleasant little Italian and Portuguese town of North Plymouth. He was planning to go into fishing himself in partnership with a man who owned some dories. Early mornings, pushing his cart up and down the long main street, ringing his bell, chatting with housewives in Piedmontese, Tuscan, pidgin English, he worried about the raids, the imprisonment of comrades, the lethargy of the working people. He was an anarchist, after the school of Galeani.[1] Between the houses he could see the gleaming stretch of Plymouth Bay, the sandy islands beyond, the white dories at anchor. About three hundred years before, men from the west of England had first sailed into the grey shimmering bay that smelt of woods and wild grape, looking for something; liberty. . . . freedom to worship God in their own manner. . . . space to breathe. Thinking of these things, worrying as he pushed the little cart loaded with eels, haddock, cod, halibut, swordfish, Vanzetti spent his mornings making change, weighing out fish, joking with the housewives. It was better than working at the great cordage works that own North Plymouth. Some years before he had tried to organize a strike there and been blacklisted. The officials and detectives at the Plymouth Cordage Works, the largest cordage works in the world, thought of him as a Red, a slacker and troublemaker.

At the same time Nicola Sacco was living in Stoughton, working an edging machine at the Three K's shoe factory, where star workmen sometimes make as high as eighty or ninety dollars a week. He had a pretty wife and a little son named Dante. There was another baby coming. He lived in a bungalow belonging to his employer, Michael Kelly. The house adjoined Kelly's own house and the men were friends. Often Kelly advised him to lay off this anarchist stuff. There was no money in it. It was dangerous the way people felt nowadays. Sacco was a clever young fel-

New Masses, 1 (Aug. 1926), 10–11, 30. Reprinted in *Facing the Chair* (1927) and *In All Countries* (1934).

low and could soon get to be a prosperous citizen, maybe own a factory of his own some day, live by other men's work. But Sacco working in his garden in the early morning before the whistles blew, tilling beans, picking off potatobugs, letting grains of corn slip by threes or fours through his fingers into the finely worked earth, worried about things. He was an anarchist. He loved the earth and people, he wanted them to walk straight over the free hills, not to stagger bowed under the ordained machinery of industry; he worried mornings working in his garden at the lethargy of the working people. It was not enough that he was happy and had fifteen hundred or more dollars in the bank for a trip home to Italy.

Three years before Sacco and Vanzetti had both of them had their convictions put to the test. In 1917, against the expressed votes of the majority, Woodrow Wilson had allowed the United States to become involved in the war with Germany. When the law was passed for compulsory military service a registration day for citizens and aliens was announced. Most young men submitted whatever their convictions were. A few of those who were morally opposed to any war or to capitalist war had the nerve to protest. Sacco and Vanzetti and some friends ran away to Mexico. There, some thirty of them lived in a set of adobe houses. Those who could get jobs worked. It was share and share alike. Everything was held in common. There were in the community men of all trades and conditions; bakers, butchers, tailors, shoemakers, cooks, carpenters, waiters. It was a momentary realization of the hope of anarchism. But living was difficult in Mexico and they began to get letters from the States telling that it was possible to avoid the draft, telling of high wages. Little by little they filtered back across the border. Sacco and Vanzetti went back to Massachusetts.

There was an Italian club that met Sunday evenings in a hall in Maverick Square, East Boston, under the name of the Italian Naturalization Society. Workmen from the surrounding industrial towns met to play bowls and discuss social problems. There were anarchists, syndicalists, socialists of various colors. The Russian Revolution had fired them with new hopes. The persecution of their comrades in various parts of America had made them feel the need for mutual help. While far away across the world new eras seemed to be flaring up into the sky, at home the great machine they slaved for seemed more adamant, more unshakable than ever. Everywhere aliens were being arrested, tortured, deported. To the war heroes who had remained at home any foreigner seemed a potential Bolshevik, a menace to the security of Old Glory and liberty bonds and the bonus. When Elia and Salsedo were arrested in New York there was great alarm among the Italian radicals around Boston.[2] Vanzetti went down to New York to try to hire a lawyer for the two men. There he heard many uneasy rumors. The possession of any literature that might be interpreted as subversive by ignorant and brutal agents of the departments of Justice and Labor was dangerous. It was not that deportation was so much to be feared, but the beating up and third degree that preceded it.

On May 3rd Salsedo was found dead on Park Row. The impression was that he had been murdered by the agents of the department of Justice. There was a rumor too that a new raid was going to be made in the suburbs of Boston. There was a scurry to hide pamphlets and newspapers. Nobody must forget that people had even been arrested for distributing the Declaration of Independence. At the same time they couldn't let this horrible affair go by without a meeting of protest. Handbills announcing a meeting in Brockton were printed. Vanzetti was to be one of the speakers.

On the evening of May 5th, Sacco and Vanzetti with the handbills on them went by trolley from Stoughton to West Bridgewater to meet a man named Boda who they thought could lend them a car. Very likely they thought they were being trailed and had put revolvers in their pockets out of some confused feeling of bravado. If the police pounced on them at least they would not let themselves be tortured to death like Salsedo. The idea was to hide the handbills somewhere until after the expected raid. But they were afraid to use Boda's car because it lacked a 1920 license plate and started back to Stoughton on the trolley, probably very uneasy. When they were arrested as the trolley entered Brockton they forgot all about their guns. They thought they were being arrested as Reds in connection with the projected meeting. When they were questioned at the police station their main care was not to implicate any of their friends. They kept remembering the dead body of Salsedo, smashed on the pavement of Park Row.

About this time a young fellow of Portuguese extraction named Madeiros was living in Providence.[3] From confidence games and the collecting of money under false pretenses he had slipped into the society of a famous gang of professional criminals known as the Morelli gang. They lived mostly by robbing freightcars but occasionally cleaned up more dangerous jobs. Gerald Chapman is supposed to have worked with them once or twice. In the early morning of April 15, Madeiros and four other members of the Morelli gang went over to Boston in a stolen touring car and at a speakeasy on Andrews Square were told about the movements of the payroll of the Slater-Merrill factory in South Braintree which was to be shipped out from Boston that day by express. They then went back to Providence and later in the morning back again towards South Braintree. In the outskirts of Randolph they changed to another car that had been hidden in the woods. Then they went to a speakeasy to wait for the time they had chosen. Madeiros' job was to sit in the back seat and hold back the crowd with a revolver while the other two got the payroll. Everything came out as planned, and in broad daylight in the most crowded part of South Braintree they shot down two men and carried off the satchel containing some $5,000. The next day when Madeiros went to a saloon on North Main Street, Providence, to get his share of the swag, he found no one. In his confession made at Dedham jail he says he never did get paid.

When Sacco and Vanzetti were first grilled by the chief of police of Brockton they were questioned as Reds and lied all they could to save their friends. Particularly they would not tell where they had got their pistols. Out of this Judge Thayer and the prosecution evolved the theory of "the consciousness of guilt" that weighed so heavily with the jury. After they had been held two days they were identified by the police, Sacco as the driver of the car in the South Braintree holdup and Vanzetti as the "foreign looking man" who had taken a potshot at a paytruck of the L. Q. White company at Bridgewater early on the morning of Christmas eve, 1919.

In spite of the fact that twenty people swore that they had seen Vanzetti in North Plymouth selling eels at that very time in the morning, he was promptly convicted and sentenced to fifteen years in the Charlestown penitentiary. The fact that so many people testified to having bought eels was considered very suspicious by the court that did not know that the eating of eels on the last day before Christmas is an Italian custom of long standing. Later Vanzetti was associated with Sacco in the murder charge. On July 14, 1923, both men were found guilty of murder in the first degree on two counts by the Norfolk County jury, consisting of two real estate men, two storekeepers, a mason, two machinists, a clothing salesman, a farmer, a millworker, a shoemaker and a lastmaker.

Dedham is the perfect New England town, white shingleroofed houses, polished brass knockers, elmshaded streets. Dedham has money, supports a polo team. Many of the wealthiest and oldest families in Massachusetts have houses there. As the seat of Norfolk County it is the center of politics for the region. Dedham has always stood for the traditions of the Bay State. Dedham was pro-British during the war; even before the Lusitania the people of Eastern Massachusetts were calling the Germans Huns. Dedham has always stood for Anglo-Saxon supremacy, and the white man's burden. Of all white men the whitest are those descendants of Puritan shipowners and brokers and ministers who own the white houses with graceful colonial doorways and the trim lawns and the lilac hedges and the elms and the beeches and the barberry bushes and the broad A and the cultivated gesturelessness of the New English. When the Congregational God made Dedham he looked upon it and saw that it was good.

But with the decline of shipping and farming a threefold population has grown up in the ring of factory towns round Boston, among which Dedham itself sits primly disdainful like an old maid sitting between two laborers in a trolley car. There is the diminished simonpure New England population, protestant in faith, Republican in politics and mostly "professional" in occupation. Alongside of that is the almost equally wealthy Irish Catholic element, Democratic, tending to make a business of politics and of the less severely respectable trades and industries. Under both of these is the population of wops, bohunks, polacks, hunkies, dagoes, some naturalized and speaking English with an accent, others unnaturalized and still speaking their native peasant dialects; they do the work. These three populations hate each other with a bitter hatred, but the upper two manage to patch up their rancor when it becomes a question of "furriners." In industrial disputes they find that they are all hundred per cent Americans. Meanwhile the latest-come immigrants are gradually gaining foothold. The Poles buy up rundown farms and get the tired and stony land back to the point of bearing crops. The Italians start truck gardens in back lots, and by skillful gardening and drudgery bring forth fiftyfold where the American-born couldn't get back the seed they sowed. The Portuguese work the cranberry bogs and are reviving the shore fisheries. The American-born are seeing their own state eaten up from under their feet. Naturally they hate the newcomers.

The war exalted hatred to a virtue. The anti-Red agitation, the Ku Klux Klan, the activities of the American Security League[4] and the American Legion have been a sort of backwash of hate dammed up by the signing of the peace. It was when that pent-up hatred and suspicion was tumultuously seeking an outlet that Sacco and Vanzetti, wops, aliens, men who spoke broken English, anarchists, believing neither in the Congregationalist or the Catholic God, slackers who had escaped the draft, were arrested, charged with a particularly brutal and impudent murder. Since that moment the right-thinking Puritan-born Americans of Massachusetts have had an object, a focus for the bitterness of their hatred of the new young vigorous unfamiliar forces that are relentlessly sweeping them onto the shelf. The people of Norfolk County, and of all Massachusetts, have decided that they want these men to die.

The faces of men who have been a long time in jail have a peculiar frozen look under the eyes. The face of a man who has been a long time in jail never loses the tightness under the eyes. Sacco has been six years in the county jail, always waiting,

waiting for trial, waiting for new evidence, waiting for motions to be argued, waiting for sentence, waiting, waiting, waiting. The Dedham jail is a handsome structure, set among lawns, screened by trees that wave new green leaves against the robbins-egg sky of June. In the warden's office you can see your face in the light brown varnish, you could eat eggs off the floor it is so clean. Inside the main reception hall is airy, full of sunlight. The bars are cheerfully painted green, a fresh peagreen. Through the bars you can see the waving trees and the June clouds roaming the sky like cattle in an unfenced pasture. It's a preposterous complicated canary cage. Why aren't the birds singing in this green aviary? The warden politely shows you to a seat and as you wait you notice a smell, not green and airy this smell, a jaded heavy greasy smell of slum, like the smell of army slum, but heavier, more hopeless.

Across the hall an old man is sitting in a chair, a heavy pear-shaped man, his hands hang limp at his sides, his eyes are closed, his sagged face is like a bundle of wet newspapers. The warden and two men in black stand over him, looking down at him helplessly.

At last Sacco has come out of his cell and sits beside me. Two men sitting side by side on a bench in a green bird cage. When he feels like it one of them will get up and walk out, walk out into the sunny June day. The other will go back to his cell to wait. He looks younger than I had expected. His face has a waxy transparency like the face of a man who's been sick in bed for a long time; when he laughs his cheeks flush a little. At length we manage both of us to laugh. It's such a preposterous position for a man to be in, like a man who doesn't know the game trying to play chess blindfolded. The real world has gone. We have no more grasp of our world of rain and streets and trolleycars and cucumbervines and girls and gardenplots. This is a world of phrases, *prosecution, defence, evidence, motion, irrelevant, incompetent and immaterial.* For six years this man has lived in the law, tied tighter and tighter in the sticky filaments of law-words like a fly in a spiderweb. And the wrong set of words means the Chair. All the moves in the game are made for him, all he can do is sit helpless and wait, fastening his hopes on one set of phrases after another. In all these lawbooks, in all this terminology of clerks of the court and counsel for the defence there is one move that will save him, out of a million that will mean death. If only they make the right move, use the right words. But by this time the nagging torment of hope has almost stopped, not even the thought of his wife and children out there in the world, unreachable, can torture him now. He is numb now, can laugh and look quizzically at the ponderous machine that has caught and mangled him. Now it hardly matters to him if they do manage to pull him out from between the cogs, and the wrong set of words means the chair.

Nicola Sacco came to this country when he was eighteen years old. He was born in Puglia in the mountains in the heel of Italy. Since then up to the time of his arrest he has had pretty good luck. He made good money, he was happily married, he had many friends, latterly he had a garden to hoe and rake mornings and evenings and Sundays. He was unusually powerfully built, able to do two men's work. In prison he was able to stand thirty-one days of hunger strike before he broke down and had to be taken to the hospital. In jail he has learned to speak and write English, has read many books, for the first time in his life has been thrown with nativeborn Americans. They worry him, these nativeborn Americans. They are so hard and brittle. They don't fit into the bright clear heartfelt philosophy of Latin anarchism. These are the people who cooly want him to die in the electric chair. He can't understand them. When his head was cool he's never wanted anyone to die. Judge Thayer and the prosecution he thinks of as instruments of a machine.

The warden comes up to take down my name. "I hope your wife's better," says Sacco. "Pretty poorly," says the warden. Sacco shakes his head. "Maybe she'll get better soon, nice weather." I have shaken his hand, my feet have carried me to the door, past the baggy pearshaped man who is still collapsed half deflated in the chair, closed crinkled eyelids twitching. The warden looks into my face with a curious smile, "Leaving us?" he asks. Outside in the neat streets the new green leaves are swaying in the sunlight, birds sing, klaxons grunt, a trolleycar screeches round a corner. Overhead the white June clouds wander in the unfenced sky.

Going to the Charlestown Penitentiary is more like going to Barnum and Baileys. There's a great scurry of guards, groups of people waiting outside; inside a brass band is playing "Home Sweet Home." When at length you get let into the Big Show, you find a great many things happening at once. There are rows of benches where pairs of people sit talking. Each pair is made up of a free man and a convict. In three directions there are grey bars and tiers of cells. The band inside plays bangingly "If Auld Acquaintance Be Forgot." A short broadshouldered man is sitting quiet through all the uproar, smiling a little under his big drooping mustache. He has a domed, pale forehead and black eyes surrounded by many little wrinkles. The serene modeling of his cheek-bones and hollow cheeks makes you forget the prison look under his eyes. This is Vanzetti.

Bartolomeo Vanzetti was born in Villafalletto, in a remote mountain valley in Piedmont. At the age of thirteen his father apprenticed him to a pastry-cook who worked him fifteen hours a day. After six years of grueling work in bakeries and restaurant kitchens he went back home to be nursed through pleurisy by his mother. Soon afterwards his mother died and in despair he set out for America. When after the usual kicking around by the Ellis Island officials he was dumped on the pavement of Battery Park, he had very little money, knew not a word of the language and found that he had arrived in a time of general unemployment. He washed dishes at Mouquins for five dollars a week and at last left for the country for fear he was getting consumption. At length he got work in a brick kiln near Springfield. After that he worked for two years in the stone pits at Meriden, Connecticut. Then he went back to New York and worked for a while as a pastrycook again, and at last settled in Plymouth where he worked in various factories and at odd jobs, ditchdigging, clamdigging, icecutting, snowshovelling and a few months before his arrest, for the sake of being his own boss, bought a pushcart and peddled fish.

All this time he read a great deal nights sitting under the gasjet when every one else was in bed, thought a great deal as he swung a pick or made caramels or stoked brick kilns, of the workmen he rubbed shoulders with, of their position in their world and his, of their hopes of happiness and of a less struggling animallike existence. As a boy he had been an ardent Catholic. In Turin he fell in with a bunch of socialists under the influence of De Amicis.[5] Once in America he read St. Augustine, Kropotkin, Gorki, Malatesta, Renan and began to go under the label of anarchist-communist. His anarchism, though, is less a matter of labels than of feeling, of gentle philosophic brooding. He shares the hope that has grown up in Latin countries of the Mediterranean basin that somehow men's predatory instincts, incarnate in the capitalist system, can be canalized into other channels, leaving free communities of artisans and farmers and fishermen and cattlebreeders who would work for their livelihood with pleasure, because the work was itself enjoyable in the serene white light of a reasonable world.

Vanzetti has served six years of the fifteen year term. How many more of them will he live to serve? And the wrong set of words means the chair!

William G. Thompson, the Boston lawyer who is conducting the defence, who is making the moves in the law game that mean life or the Chair to these two men, is a very puzzled man. As a man rather than as a lawyer he knows that they did not commit the crimes of which they are accused. The refusal of the Supreme Court of Massachusetts to entertain his motion for a new trial, the attitude of his friends, of the press, of Governor Fuller try him sorely. He wishes he were well out of it. He wants to go on believing in the honesty of Massachusetts justice, in the humanity and fair mindedness of the average educated Harvard-bred Bostonian. The facts he handles daily compel him to think otherwise. He wishes he were well out of it. And the wrong set of words means the chair!

And for the last six years, three hundred and sixtyfive days a year, yesterday, today, tomorrow, Sacco and Vanzetti wake up on their prison pallets, eat prison food, have an hour of exercise and conversation a day, sit in their cells puzzling about this technicality and that technicality, pinning their hopes to their alibis, to the expert testimony about the character of the barrel of Sacco's gun, to Madeiros' confession and Weeks' corroboration, to action before the Supreme Court of the United States, and day by day the props are dashed from under their feet and they feel themselves being inexorably pushed towards the Chair by the blind hatred of thousands of wellmeaning citizens, by the superhuman involved stealthy soulless mechanism of the law.

Notes

1. Luigi Galleani (not *Galeani*), an Italian-American anarchist and editor.

2. Roberto Elia and Andrea Salsedo, anarchist printers, were arrested in New York in February 1920.

3. Dos Passos deals at length with Madeiros because the defense appeal of the conviction of Sacco and Vanzetti relied heavily on Madeiros's confession, made while he was imprisoned on another charge, that he and the Morelli gang were responsible for the robberies and murders for which Sacco and Vanzetti had been convicted. Another member of the gang, James F. Weeks (see p. 91), corroborated Madeiros's confession.

4. Dos Passos appears to mean the American Protection League, a quasi-vigilante organization devoted to ensuring commitment to the war effort.

5. Edmondo de Amicis, a prolific Italian writer who became a socialist late in his career.

A Lost Generation

[A review of *The Sun Also Rises*, by Ernest Hemingway.]

It's a dangerous thing to quote the Bible in the beginning of a book. It raises the readers' hopes as to the meatiness of the matters to be served up by the author, and sets up a standard of skill in word and phrase, not unbeatable, but pretty much unbeaten. This book starts out with Gertrude Stein saying, presumably to the author and his contemporaries, "You are all a lost generation," and with a passage from Ecclesiastes: "the passing of generations, the rising and going down of the sun, the whirling of the wind, the flowing of rivers into the sea."

Instead of these things of deep importance you find yourself reading about the tangled love affairs and bellyaches of a gloomy young literatizing Jew, of an English lady of title who's a good sport, and of a young man working in the Paris office of an American newspaper, the "I" who tells the story.

Backgrounds; Montparnasse, American Paris, the Dome, Rotonde, Zelli's and the Select, then Pamplona during the fiesta of San Firmin.

It's an extraordinarily wellwritten book, so wellwritten that while I was reading it I kept telling myself I must be growing dough-headed as a critic for not getting it. Paris is a damned interesting place even at its most Bohemian; the fiesta at Pamplona is the finest in Spain and that means something! The people are so vividly put down you could recognize their faces on a passport photo. What the devil am I grumbling about anyway?

I suppose I want the generations, the sun also rising, the declamation of "Vanity of vanities, saith the preacher," the rivers running into the sea and the sea not yet full. I have a right to expect it too. Hemingway's short stories have that.

I don't think that there is anything in the division that critics are always making between a subject and the way it is treated; a subject can be treated any way. A novel is an indissoluble entity made up of as many layers as an onion. The style of an onion is its layers. By the time you've peeled off all the layers there's no onion left. Then why am I saying the book is well written? I mean that anywhere I open it and read a few sentences they seem very good; it's only after reading a page that the bottom begins to drop out. Maybe the trouble was sitting down to write a novel; maybe if it had been packed into a short unbroken story it would have given that feeling of meaning a lot to somebody, to everybody and to nobody that good work has got to have. As it is, instead of being the epic of the sun also rising on a lost gen-

New Masses, 2 (Dec. 1926), 26.

eration—there's an epic in that theme all right—a badly needed epic—this novel strikes me as being a cock and bull story about a lot of summer tourists getting drunk and making fools of themselves at a picturesque Iberian folk-festival—write now to Thomas Cook for special rate and full descriptive leaflet. It's heartbreaking. If the generation of young intellectuals is not going to lose itself for God's sake let it show more fight; if it is, let's find a good up-to-date lethal chamber that's never been used before.

There's a conversation between "I" and a certain Bill that gives you a feeling that maybe the author was worried about these things. Like most Americans when they are saying what they mean, he has inverted it all into wisecracks.

Bill says to "I":

> "Say something pitiful."
> "Robert Cohn."
> "Not so bad. That's better. Now, why is Cohn pitiful? Be ironic."
> He took a big gulp of coffee.
> "Aw hell," I said. "It's too early in the morning."
> "There you go. And you claim you want to be a writer too. You're only a newspaper man. You ought to be ironical the minute you get out of bed. You ought to wake up with your mouth full of pity."
> "Go on," I said. "Who did you get this stuff from?"
> "Everybody. Don't you read? Don't you ever see anybody? Don't you know what you are? You're an expatriate . . .
> "You're an expatriate. You've lost touch with the soil. You get precious. Fake European standards have ruined you. You drink yourself to death. You become obsessed by sex. You spend all your time talking, not working. You are an expatriate see? You hang around cafes."

There's a lot in it. This is a novel of Montparnassia for Montparnassians; if it weren't so darn well written I'd say by a Montparnassian. There's a lot of truth in the old saying that Paris is where good Americans go when they die. When a superbly written description of the fiesta of San Firmin in Pamplona, one of the grandest events in the civilized uncivilized world, reminds you of a travelbook by the Williamsons,[1] it's time to call an inquest.

What's the matter with American writing anyway? Is it all just the Williamsons in different yearly models? If it is, the few unsad young men of this lost generation will have to look for another way of finding themselves than the one indicated here.

Notes

1. Alice and Charles N. Williamson were the joint authors of widely used automobile touring guides.

Paint the Revolution

[Dos Passos was in Mexico City from mid-December 1926 to March 1927.]

Even Cortez clanking across the dykes on his warhorse is said to have been struck by the beauty of the markets of Tenochtitlan. Your first morning in the City of Mexico. The sunlight and the bright thin air, the Indian women sitting like stone idols behind their piles of fruit or their bunches of flowers, the sculpture on old red colonial buildings and the painting on the pulque shops, all tie you up into such a knot of vivid sights that you start sprouting eyes in the nape of your neck.

Going to see the paintings of Diego Rivera in the courts of the Secretaria of public education straightens you out a little bit. They give a dramatic sequence to all this brightness and white glitter, to the terribly silent welling up of life everywhere. In tense earth colors that have a dull burnish to them he has drawn the bending of bodies at work, the hunch of the shoulders under picks and shovels of men going down into a mine, the strain and heave of a black body bent under a block of marble, men working at looms, in dye-vats, spooning out molten metal. Then there are the plodding dust-colored soldiers of the revolution, red flags and black flags of the Zapatistas, crowds in marketplaces, women hanging out washing, politicians making speeches, Indians dancing. Everywhere the symbol of the hammer and sickle. Some of it's pretty hasty, some of it's garlanded tropical bombast, but by God, it's painting.

Go round to the art galleries in New York. Look at all the little pictures, little landscapes after Cezanne, Renoir, Courbet, Picasso, Corot, Titian, little fruity still lifes, little modern designs of a stovepipe and a bisected violin . . . stuff a man's afraid to be seen looking at . . . a horrible picking up of crumbs from rich men's tables. Occasionally a work of real talent, but what's the good of it? Who sees it? A lot of male and female old women chattering round an exhibition; and then, if the snobmarket has been properly manipulated, some damn fool buys it and puts it away in the attic, and it makes a brief reappearance when he dies at a sale at the Anderson Galleries.

"A lotta bunk this revolution stuff in Mexico," said the salesman of brewing machinery coming down on the train from Laredo. "Peons don't know nothin' . . . It's only a lot of politicians fighting for the swag, when they're not hired by the oil companies. Why people down here don't know what the word means." He got off at Saltillo before I could find out from him what the word did mean.

New Masses, 2 (March 1927), 15.

And there's not only the Secretaria of education. When you're through looking at the three stories of frescoed walls, probably a good half mile of them, setting down in passionate hieroglyphics every phase of the revolution, you can go to the superb baroque building of the Preparatoria where Clemente Orozco is working. Orozco was a cartoonist and started with a bitter set of lampoons on the bourgeoisie; but as he worked he became a painter. His panels express each one an idea with a fierce concentration and economy of planes and forms I've never seen anywhere except in the work of the old Italian, Cimabue. Again the revolution, soldiers and peasants and workingmen and the sibylline faces of old countrywomen. Over the doors the sickle and hammer. Imagine a sickle and hammer painted (in three dimensions, no Willy Pogany pastels of Progressive Evolution as in the Rand School), over the door of the Columbia University library.

And that's not all. Roberto Montenegro is filling the walls of another school with a sober and lilting decoration. There's a library dedicated to Ibero-American Unity decorated by him with a huge map of South America and Mexico where the U.S. is left in anomalous darkness. And everybody complains that the good old days are over, that nobody is painting any more.

As a matter of fact the Sindicato de Obreros Tecnicos, the painters' and sculptors' union, that was the center of this huge explosion of creative work, has broken up. Everything that happened, happened in two years. In 1923 Diego Rivera came back from Europe, full of Picasso and Derain and the plaint of artists pampered and scantily fed by the after-the-war bourgeoisie. (In New York at that time we were trying to be modern and see the beauty of the Woolworth Building and sighing for the first Independents and the days of the, oh, so lovely Sienese tablas of Spumone degli Spaghetti.) He found an enormously rich and uncorrupted popular art in textiles and pottery and toys and in the decoration of ginmills, a lot of young painters fresh from the heartbreaking campaigns of civil war and eager to justify the ways of Marx to man, and José Vasconcelos as head of the department of education.

After Felipe Carillo, the great leader of Yucatan, had made a speech to the liberated Mayas, outlining a Socialist commonwealth, someone went up to him and said the speech was worthy of Lenin. "Fine," he answered, "who's he?"

It wasn't a case of ideas, of a lot of propaganda-fed people deciding that a little revolutionary art would be a good thing, it was a case of organic necessity. The revolution, no more imported from Russia than the petate hats the soldiers wore, had to be explained to the people. The people couldn't read. So the only thing to do was to paint it up on the wall.

So some thirty painters started a union, affiliated themselves with the Third International, and set to work. Everyone was to get the same wage for painting, a cooperative studio was to be started; "its fundamental aesthetic aim was rooted in the socialization of art, tending towards the absolute disappearance of individualism, characteristic of bourgeois epochs, thus approaching the great collective art of antiquity." As a basis of study they took the remains of ancient Mexican painting and sculpture. Easel painting they rejected as intellectual, aristocratic and onanistic. But this isn't the first time that painters have issued a manifesto. The extraordinary thing about this group is that they set to work and delivered the goods.

Xavier Guerrero went down to Teotihuacan and studied the methods of the ancient Indian painters there. They made chemical analyses of the pigments and varnishes used and after much experimentation, began to paint. Diego Rivera's first big decorative work had been in encaustica, in which he had been experimenting in Paris. Vasconcelos, whose boast was that he would spend as much on education as the war department spent on the army, was ready to give any competent painter wall space, a small wage, and materials. And so in an incredibly short time an enormous amount of work, not only in the capital, but in Jalapa and Guadalajara as well, was under way.

All this time there had been growing opposition. The students of the Preparatoria, sons of haciendados and oilsplattered politicians, objected to this new style of painting, and set about destroying the frescoes. The hammers and sickles over the doors made them uneasy. Intellectuals and newspaper writers, whose idea of painting was a chic girl drawn a la *Vie Parisienne* with sensually dark smudges under the eyes, kept up a continual hammering under which the Government began to weaken. Vasconcelos left the ministry of education. The Union broke up in personal squabbles, largely owing to the fact that to continue working under the Laborista government it became necessary to give up the Third International. Now Rivera, Orozco and Montenegro are the only three painters subsidized by the Federal government. The rest of them pick up a living as best they can in the provinces. Several of them are carrying on lively communist propaganda, through *El Machete*, which started as the Union's mouthpiece.

But, even if nothing more is done, an enormous amount of real work has been accomplished. Even if the paintings were rotten it would have been worth while to prove that in our day a popular graphic art was possible. Maybe it's not possible anywhere but in Mexico. As it is, Rivera's paintings in the Secretaria, Orozco's paintings in the Preparatoria, Montenegro's decorations are a challenge shouted in the face of the rest of the world. You're a painter? All right, let's see what you can do with a wall a hundred by sixteen and a lot of homely doors and windows in it.

All we have in New York to answer with are a few private sensations and experiments framed and exhibited here and there, a few watercolors like Marin's, and a lot of warmed-over truck, leavings of European fads.

If it isn't a revolution in Mexico, I'd like to know what it is.

An Open Letter to President Lowell

[Governor Alvan T. Fuller of Massachusetts had appointed a committee
consisting of President A. Lawrence Lowell of Harvard, President Samuel W.
Stratton of MIT, and Judge Robert Grant to advise him on the clemency appeal of
Sacco and Vanzetti.]

To the Editor of The Nation:

Sir: I am asking the courtesy of your columns for the enclosed open letter to
President Lowell of Harvard that no publication in Boston seems willing to publish.

John Dos Passos

Boston, August 9

As a graduate of Harvard University I feel that I have the right to protest
against the participation of the president of that university in the report on the
Sacco-Vanzetti case presented to Governor Fuller by his advisory committee. I feel
that you have put your name and indirectly the name of the university you represent to an infamous document. This is no time for mincing words. You have made
yourself a party to a judicial murder that will call down on its perpetrators the exe-
cration of the civilized world. What it means is that you are allowing a Massachusetts politician to use the name of Harvard to cover his own bias and to whitewash
all the dirty business of the arrest of these men at the time of the anarchist raids and
their subsequent slow torture by the spiteful and soulless mechanism of the law.
They have probably told you that this was a mere local decision on a Boston murder case, but to any man with enough intelligence to read the daily papers it must be
clear that somehow it has ceased being a Boston murder case. Sacco and Vanzetti
starving in their cells in the death house and the authorities of the State of Massachusetts building the electric chair in which to burn them to death have become
huge symbols on the stage of the world. The part into which you have forced Harvard University will make many a man ashamed of being one of its graduates.

Many of us who have watched the case for years felt that your appointment as
a member of the committee assured at least a modicum of fair play and of historical
perspective in the conduct of the investigation. This hope was pretty well shattered
when it was announced that the investigation was to be carried on behind closed
doors. If there was nothing to hide, why the secrecy? Since when have star chamber
proceedings been part of the American judicial system?

The published report has confirmed our worst forebodings. With inconceivable levity you counsel the electrocution of two men because it "seems" to you that

Nation, 125 (24 Aug. 1927), 176. Copyright The Nation Company, Inc., 1927.

the enormous mass of evidence piled up by the defense in seven years' heartbreaking work should be dismissed, like the rent in the lining of the cap that you wrongly assert fitted Sacco, as so trifling a matter in the evidence of the case that it seems to the committee by no means a ground for a new trial. Did the committee feel that the prosecution's case was so weak that they had to bolster it by fresh deductions and surmises of their own?

The report in its entirety is an apology for the conduct of the trial rather than an impartial investigation. Reading it, the suspicion grows paragraph by paragraph that its aim was not to review but to make respectable the proceedings of Judge Thayer and the District Attorney's office. Not in a single phrase is there an inkling of a sense on your part or on that of your colleagues of the importance of the social and racial backgrounds of the trial. Your loose use of the words "socialistic" and "communistic" prove that you are ignorant or careless of the differences in mentality involved in partisanship in the various schools of revolutionary thought.

This is a matter of life and death, not only for Sacco and Vanzetti but for the civilization that Harvard University is supposed to represent. The Sacco-Vanzetti case has become part of the world struggle between the capitalist class and the working class, between those who have power and those who are struggling to get it. In a man in high office ignorance of the new sprouting forces that are remaking society, whether he is with them or against them, is little short of criminal. It is inconceivable that intelligent reading men can be ignorant in this day of the outlines of anarchist philosophy. Instead of crying ignorance it would be franker to admit that as anarchists and agitators you hate these men and disapprove of their ideas and methods. But are you going to sacrifice the integrity of the legal system to that feeling? Are you going to prove by a bloody reprisal that the radical contention that a man holding unpopular ideas cannot get a free trial in our courts is true?

I cannot feel that either you or your colleagues have understood the full purport of your decision. If you had you would certainly have made out a more careful case for yourselves, one less full of loopholes and contradictions. It is upon men of your class and position that will rest the inevitable decision as to whether the coming struggle for the reorganization of society shall be bloodless and fertile or inconceivably bloody and destructive. It is high time that you realized the full extent of the responsibility on your shoulders.

As a Harvard man I want to protest most solemnly against your smirching the university of which you are an officer with the foul crime against humanity and civilization to which you have made yourself accessory.

                                                            John Dos Passos, '16

Sacco and Vanzetti

[A review of *The Life and Death of Sacco and Vanzetti*, by Eugene Lyons.]

The names of Sacco and Vanzetti are fading fast into the cloudland of myth where they are in danger of becoming vague symbols like God, country and Americanism. One of the most extraordinary things about industrial society of the present day is its idiot lack of memory. Tabloids and movies take the place of mental processes, and revolts, crimes, despairs pass off in a dribble of vague words and rubber stamp phrases without leaving a scratch on the mind of the driven instalment-paying, subway-packing mass. It is up to the writers now to see to it that America does not forget Sacco and Vanzetti so soon as it would like to. Czar Will Hays of the moving picture industry has thrown the glove in our faces by ordering all news films dealing with the most dramatic episode in the industrial war of our time to be taken from the vaults and burned.[1]

Eugene Lyons fires the first gun with this rapid and fluent account of the case from its beginning on a Brockton street car to its end the night of August 22, 1927, when the death house in Charlestown jail suddenly swelled to become the whole world. In this excellent pamphlet Lyons has done exactly what he set out to do, which was to write an account of this seven years of agony of the working class that would be immediately available to men of all languages and conditions. I can't imagine how this particular job could have been done better.

But there remain a lot of other jobs to be done. Every detail must be told and retold. Sacco and Vanzetti must not have died in vain. We must have writing so fiery and accurate that it will sear through the pall of numb imbecility that we are again swaddled in after the few moments of sane awakening that followed the shock of the executions. America must not be allowed to forget. All the elements on the public stage who consider themselves alive and who are considered alive, college professors, writers, labor leaders, prominent liberals, protested that they were mighty shocked and that *if* the state of Massachusetts went ahead with the executions. . . . Workers all over the country felt their blood curdle at the thought. Well, it has come to pass. Well, we have protested. Our blood has curdled. What are we going to do now?

New Masses, 3 (Nov. 1927), 25.

Notes

1. Hays, head of the Motion Picture Producers and Distributors of America (the Hays Office), had the power to censor films for suspect material.

Toward a Revolutionary Theatre

[The New Playwrights Theatre, subsidized principally by the financier Otto Kahn, was organized in the spring of 1927, when it had its first productions. Full seasons were offered during 1927–28 and 1928–29. Dos Passos was one of five Directors of the company, along with Mike Gold, Em Jo Basshe, John Howard Lawson, and Francis Faragoh. The theatre disbanded in the spring of 1929.]

Definition: By theatre I don't mean a building or an idea, I mean a group of people, preferably a huge group of people; part of the group puts on plays and the rest forms the audience, an active working audience.

By American I don't mean that the group's interests must necessarily be limited to America, but that they should be as deeply rooted here as possible.

By revolutionary I mean that such a theatre must break with the present day theatrical tradition, not with the general traditions of the theatre, and that it must draw its life and ideas from the conscious sections of the industrial and white collar working classes which are out to get control of the great flabby mass of capitalist society and mould it to their own purpose. In an ideal state it might be possible for a group to be alive and have no subversive political tendency. At present it is not possible.

This is big talk. Still the theatre is a matter which it seems to me demands flamboyant treatment. If it is to compete with the vast milliondollar ineptitudes of the billiondollar movies, and with the crafty skill in flattering the public of the smart real estate men who run Broadway, the revolutionary experimental futurist "revolting" (or whatever you want to call it) theatre, has got to be planned on a large scale. The day of the frail artistic enterprise, keeping alive through its own exquisiteness, has passed. A play or a book or a picture has got to have bulk, toughness and violence to survive in the dense clanging traffic of twentieth century life.

Still big talk. Now let's talk small. What have we got as a basis of operations? (I am assuming that there are people, hundreds, thousands, maybe ten thousand people in this city who would be willing to take part in such a theatre as I've outlined. If that's a false assumption, we'll learn soon enough.) There's the Workers' Theatre, a small room on South Washington Square with the rent unpaid. Unfortunately there's little else to say about it. It's a germ that has vast possibilities of development and that's about all. Then there's talk of building an auditorium in one of the new cooperative apartment houses in the Bronx, and then there is the New Playwrights' Theatre, target of all the critics' bricks, operating obscurely on Commerce Street (that a bunch of London-minded aesthetes once tried to rename Cherry Lane). It is from the vantage point of the latter that I write.

New Masses, 3 (Dec. 1927), 20.

The tunnel-shaped auditorium, gloomy at best, sloping down to a low proscenium, containing two hundred and forty uncomfortable seats, and some of them
busted, is about as far as anything could be from the circus-shaped hall we would
like to have; the tiny stage cramped into a picture-frame proscenium, is far indeed
from the series of platforms jutting out into the audience that are needed for mass
plays. Beggars can't be choosers. The thing at present is to operate even if we come
down to putting on a flea circus. Big talk won't get us anywhere. American cities are
full of the wrecks of theatres, derelicts from big talk in the past. Look at the
Century.[1]

On one side of the auditorium is a yard stacked with the debris of last season's
sets, upstairs is a workbench where the props are made, some cans of paint, a glue-
pot and a series of cramped dressing rooms where the long-suffering actors have to
sit motionless and silent waiting for their cues, as every step on the floor sounds
from the auditorium like an elephant doing a cakewalk. In the basement there are
some offices where the whitecollar slaves work on promotion and publicity and
where desperate efforts are made to stop the steady trickling out of the dollars.

That's about all the N.P.T. has in the way of a plant.

In intangible assets we are richer. It's very surprising how easy it has been to
find skillful, reliable and enthusiastic people willing to work in the theatre in spite
of the starvation salaries we are forced to pay. There is one thing about which there
is no doubt in my mind: at this moment the human material exists in New York out
of which the acting and the backstage of a great American theatre can be built. If we
don't do it, somebody else will. If we don't do it, it will be due to lack of organizing
skill and not through any deficiency in the crowd, in many ways raw and untrained,
but genuinely rich in potentialities, that has in such a short time been collected in
that ramshackle house on Commerce Street.

As I see it the three problems of a threatre of this sort (and I'm still assuming
that there is a need for it and a working energetic audience for it) are hokum, internal organization and money.

We live in an air saturated with hokum. Particularly if you try to do anything
in any of the so-called arts you are stiffled by all the exhalations left in the profession by the rotting egos of the discouraged sons of doctors, lawyers and ministers,
who for a century have used the arts as a mushy refuge from themselves. In a world
building out of polished steel and glass all this padded brocade round the necks of
sniffling geniuses is hokum and death to any sincere work. The first aim of an enterprise so dependent on human cooperation as a theatre must be the elimination of
hokum, individually and collectively.

With hokum cleared out I don't think internal organization offers very serious
difficulties. It's just a question of being willing to try all possible combinations of
people until you find one that works. After all if all the individuals in a given body
of people are more anxious to get certain work done than to find a niche for their
own personal neuroses they are likely to find some satisfactory way of dividing it.

The trouble about money is its intimate association with hokum. We are so
accustomed to part with our money only when drugged with the requisite dose, that
it is going to be difficult, say the wiseacres, for a dehokumized organization, no matter how efficient it is, to get money. The cure is not more hokum, but less money. In
spite of the enormous cost of everything connected with the theatre, it is possible
for such a theatre, by continual and heartbreaking economy, to be self-supporting

(assuming again the possibility of building up an audience of say ten thousand people, an audience that is not passive like a Broadway audience, but actively part of the theatre). Economy is most difficult because there is something about the very word theatre that connotes lavishness.

The group that solves these three problems, in its plays as well as in its organization, will create a real focus in American life. In method of presentation it will be something between high mass in a Catholic church and Barnum and Bailey's circus, both of which are rituals stripped to their bare lines. Vigor and imagination must take the place of expensiveness and sublety. When it's possible to put on a great play in a big theatre for a couple of thousand bucks and sell your seats at fifty or seventy-five cents, you'll have something worth having. But where are the great plays you say? The woods are full of them. Give them a theatre for an outlet and the life pressure of a hundred million people will do the rest.

Notes

1. A large ornate theatre on the upper west side, constructed in 1909 and largely unused during the 1920s.

A Great American

[A review of *Henry Ward Beecher: An American Portrait*, by Paxton Hibben.]

Before you start reading you wonder why in the dickens anybody should waste so much time on a preacher dead and out of style. When you finish the book you wish that Paxton Hibben had added a volume or two. He makes you see that there is something about Henry Ward Beecher that has meaning today. Not that the fifty-year-old headlines of the Beecher Case are intrinsically of more interest than the recent tabloid over-flowings over the disappearance of the sainted Aimee Mac-Pherson.[1] Put it this way. History is continually being remade to suit the mood of the present and immediate past. Going down a river in a canoe, you see the trees on the bank go by so quickly that the hills on the horizon seem to stand still, until all at once you look up and find that their shape has changed entirely. When we were kids in school American history was the Presidential Range and very little else; now the Presidential Range is flattening out fast and all we have is a meaningless jumble where the contours have not yet been pointed out and emphasized. This book establishes Beecher on the map as an outstanding American windbag, and Hibben as a darn good writer. The only thing I can think of to compare it to is Bazalgette's *Thoreau.* It seems to be better than Brooks' *The Ordeal of Mark Twain*, because it has more juicy facts in it and because it is less meticulously tacked to the fine edge of a thesis. Or perhaps it's that Beecher interests me more as a man than the immaculate Mr. Clemens.

The question is, why it is of value to dig up these portraits of dead and forgotten worthies? Doesn't Elmer Gantry do the same thing more immediately? Why spend years boning up on facts in a library when "fiction" puts your idea over with more speed than "history"? I don't think so. It seems to me that history is always more alive and more interesting than fiction. I suppose that is because a story is the day dream of a single man, while history is a mass-invention, the day dream of a race. A book like *Henry Ward Beecher* permanently enriches the national consciousness, while all our novels, unrelated and helpless fragments, drain off into the annual stream of gush emitted by the publishing houses.

This brings me to the point I have been trying to get at. Why is it important to enrich the national consciousness, why wouldn't it be much better from the human point of view to let the national consciousness sicken and die? That we know and feel how our fathers and grandfathers acted and thought and shouted and died does

New Masses, 3 (Dec. 1927), 26.

not necessarily mean that we are going to mould our lives after theirs, but it does mean that we have some sort of standard to measure ourselves by. Any agglomeration of people trying to live without a scale of values becomes a mindless and panicky mob. The sudden gusher of American wealth in the last fifty years has boosted into power—into such power as would have sent shivers of envy down Alexander's spine—a class of illassorted mediocrities, who have not needed even much acquisitive skill to get where they are. Aping them is a servile generation of whitecollar slaves and small moneygrubbers and under that, making the wheels go around, endless formless and disunited strata of workers and farmers kept mostly in an opium dream of prosperity by cooing radios, the flamboyant movies and the instalment plan. In all that welter there is no trace of a scale of values. The last rags of the old puritan standards in which good was white and bad was black went under in the war. In the ten years that have followed the American mind has settled back into a marsh of cheap cosmopolitanism and wisecracking, into a slow odorless putrescence. The protest that expressed itself in such movements as the I.W.W. and the Non-Partisan League[2] has pretty well petered out. If this mass of a hundred million people can sink any lower without disintegrating entirely . . . well . . . but that's where Henry Ward Beecher comes in. Beecher was this utter vacuum that is the American consciousness of today, in human form. He is essentially the archetype of the leader that a money-mad society has loved to pet and encourage, a preacher who could be trusted never to preach against the wind, to know invariably which side his bread was buttered on; and he was very fond of butter.

From Lyman Beecher to Henry Ward you have the break in the American mind that came when a farmers' and traders' democracy began to founder in a flood of gilt-edged securities. Lyman Beecher, hard, bitter, tricky, full of jokes and brimstone, preaching hellfire and damnation to a mercantile generation of Yankees, whiskered, headstrong and ranting; Henry Ward, his son, a soft-faced man with floppy lips, floundering unhappily through the crazy years of the Civil War, trimming, trimming, until he flopped himself at last into velvet in Plymouth Church in Brooklyn, free to pour everlasting anodyne gush into the ears of a fattening congregation of bankers, bondholders and war profiteers. In those two men you have the whole disintegration of the American mind. The father was a fanatic, the son was a spellbinder. And Henry Ward Beecher got away with it, he got away with a mushy aestheticism, that his contemporary Wilde was not quite able to carry off in England, he got away with adultery, lots of it. Since that day getting away with it has been the first and only commandment on the statute books. Well the papers are telling us that the American standard of living, gushing up in geometrical progression of dollar-years, is the highest in history. Maybe the American mind, assiduously emptying itself into vacuum, will get away with it. Will it?

At any rate we need more books like this book of Hibben's, more accurate and imaginative studies of the American past to set our compasses by.

Notes

1. MacPherson, a flamboyant American evangelist, disappeared for a month in 1926, claiming that she had been kidnapped.

2. A radical farmers' organization active from about 1915 to 1925.

A City That Died by Heartfailure

[In the summer of 1925, during one of his frequent visits to the villa of Gerald and Sara Murphy at Antibes, Dos Passos accompanied Murphy and Vladimir Orloff, a Russian emigré set designer, on a yachting expedition. One of their stops was Savona, which Dos Passos had visited with John Howard Lawson in 1917. In this memoir of his 1925 visit, X is Murphy, Y is Dos Passos, and Z is Orloff.]

Cities are like men except that they live longer. Like men they suffer from diseases, they are carried off young by consumption; in old age they die slowly of cancer or hardening of the arteries. Sometimes heartfailure or murder does them in in a few days. That's what we debated walking under the empty grey colonades of Savona: was it murder or heartfailure?

X, Y and Z had found themselves as a result of a train of circumstances running in a rakish twenty foot sloop before a heavy wind that became a gale fit to read about in the papers. X like Jesus was asleep in the cabin. By the time they were all awake and had got over their sense of speed and the joy of skimming through the moonlight between sea and sky it was too late to take in the balloon jib and the clouds had buried the moon. Eventually they found themselves at anchor in an L in the breakwater of Savona in the full sweep of the wind, yelling in various languages for a tugboat. The trouble was that they were outside instead of inside the breakwater. The tugboat came and the sloop, drenched and shuddering, was towed into the harbor.

The harbor was full of gaunt steamers under the driving rain. Here and there an arclight hung over the rainpocked water. They had lost their anchor outside, so they had to tie up against a bulky bark. Then, feverish with fatigue, they crowded into the gutted cabin and rolled as best they could in damp blankets and each fell down his individual elevatorshaft into sleep.

In the morning dragging ourselves unshaven out of the overwarmth of damp beds we climbed over the slippery rail of the pale green bark we were tied up against, staggered across a plank and were standing in the full untiring rain on a long empty quay in front of big black houses with staring windows. We walked along sniffing the wind for breakfast, turned hopefully up a long imposing arcaded street. It was as empty as one of those painted perspectives you see on the off side of old Lombard buildings. Then it was that X up and spoke out his mind: The trouble with this town is it's dead.

From that time on it was an autopsy. Once warmed with coffee they asked the waiter why the street was so deserted. It wasn't deserted the waiter replied, pointing to a thin and knock-kneed black kitten that was padding across the car track. At the same moment at the end of the street a trolleycar appeared. All watched it breathless. It drew near and rattled past and turned a corner. It was empty.

Lantern, 1 (Feb. 1928), 11–12.

Y had been in Savona during the war and had made lengthy speeches coming up the coast on its gaiety and charm, the crowded streets, the painted facades. As they followed the interminable arcade towards the station and the Albergo Diurno, he was razzed about it. He played for time; it was too early, he said, and at any rate it was raining.

In the Albergo Diurno they fell on our necks. They ran hot baths, they unlocked the doors of waterclosets, they offered to clean our shoes. The cashier was thin as a rail, had a touch of jaundice and spoke a few words of the language of Brooklyn. No, he admitted, business wasn't good, too much politics. Then there was the boycott.

Not even Sunday brought much change. A few automobiles turned out, there were people outside the movie theatres. What movement there was rattled round in the big arcaded streets. X noticed that the storekeepers sat with their backs to the doors, discouraged fat women knitting or dosing. When you went in they got up with a start. Gradually it began to seep in to us that everybody started when you spoke to them, people walked as if they were being followed, talked as if they felt they were being overheard; it was a town with the heebyjeebies.

Sunday afternoon we took to architecture. We were staring at the doorway of an old house where probably some rich shipowner had lived before the town had knuckled down to Genoa, when a pale sparrowlike little man whom we all immediately knew to be a schoolteacher, spoke to us in French. Round the corner of the next street there were more doorways and entrancehalls and ceilings. He would show them to us. From that we fell talking and little by little he made us look at all there was of antique splendor, a few old towers, carved staircases, a couple of painted ceilings, by the sea a huge fortress rising out of the rusty litter of a partly deserted foundry. In the fort we waited a long while in an upper courtyard very daintily painted and decorated with colored lights for the regimental festa while officers in skyblue cloaks, after a great deal of talking and scraping and bowing on the part of our little professor, fetched us a permit from the colonel to see the dungeon where Mazzini had been imprisoned, and from which he escaped. Coming out of the fortress X popped the question: What's the matter with the town? The little professor winced and said that there was nothing the matter with the town. Of course there was not quite the movement there used to be, but . . . And that was all we could get out of him.

One night a travelling circus performed manfully before the thinnest sprinkling of people in a cavernous mouldy green hall that had probably once been a vaudeville theatre. The ring was in the orchestra. There were chairs on the stage and round the edges. All the performers doubled; they worked like demons. The ushers reappeared as clowns. The man who did the bicycle trick sold seats and was the Swiss bellringer, the hind legs of the elephant did a dog and pony act. The Spartans that died at Thermopylae never stood up more proudly in a chilly, cringing world than did that circus. X, Y and Z came out warm and tingling from the company of heroes and walked gaily through the long, discouraged streets towards the harbor.

They stopped in front of an unexpectedly shining cafe that was crowded with people, that had bay trees in front of it. A smell of brasspolish and prosperity and rum punch came out of it. They went in past a resplendent bar. The room was full of young men with long frizzy hair, intellectual-looking young men playing chess. From upstairs came a sound of billiards. Everybody had an air of assurance that this cafe was *the right place*. They had no sooner sat down than a stout, redfaced, pigeyed, young man came over to them, with a big hand outstretched, a big hand unexpectedly soft when you shook it.

"Shake the hand that this morning shook the hand of Il Duce . . . at Parma. Yes we know who you are. It was a fascista who saved your lives by telephoning for the tugboat. A nasty storm, a ticklish situation . . . No, thank you, couldn't drink anything . . . Well . . . Tonio, a creme de menthe . . . You see I'm very hoarse, worn out . . . Thirty five hours on the train . . . It was a magnificent manifestation. You see I had to go, I'm chief of a squadron of blackshirts . . . No I didn't speak, not this time. Ah what a man, Mussolini, what a handshake he has, he draws you towards him when he shakes your hand."

"Ask him," said X, "what's the matter with the town, why are all those freighters laid up in the harbor, why aren't there any automobiles."

"Automobiles, there are thousands of automobiles . . . Ah the port. There's been a little trouble there. It was boycotted by the syndicate of maritime workers. There were a great many communists. It's only recently that the purification of the city has been complete."

"I should say it was."

"Yes, it was a fascista saved your lives. Last summer at Alassio an American was saved from drowning by a fascista. He paid a thousand lire into the party treasury to show his gratitude."

There was a silence. The chief of the blackshirt squadron sipped his creme de menthe, and looked at us with lire in his eyes.

"You understand we have many expenses. We have to travel all the time to go to conventions and manifestations. That all costs money. We have to keep up the dignity of our position. The rich people here are stingy, they stay in their houses, they never come out. Why the owners of casini 'll give more in contributions than the bankers. We get something out of the shopkeepers though." He leaned back in his chair and laughed showing all his teeth. "They have to give . . . The workpeople here are rotten with foreign ideas; they'd rather emigrate to France. But things are improving." He tapped himself on the chest. "We have borne the brunt of the work of purification . . . Colonel come over here," he called to a one-legged man in a long tightwaisted raincoat who stood at the bar. "There are the Americans."

The colonel stumped over to our table leaning on a heavy cane. He had stringy, black hair cut straight below his ears, and a gaunt twisted face. "He's listed for complete disability from the war. Show them . . ." The colonel held up a crimson, clawlike hand. The wrist had a hole through it between the two bones. At the same time he jiggled his wooden leg. "He's very brave and a dead shot with a revolver. He's bagged more communists than anybody."

Walking back to the boat through the silent purified streets of Savona Z, who was from Odessa, said "That man is exactly the type of a local Bolshevik boss." That was a hard morsel to swallow for one member of the party. After gagging a little he said it was a damn lie.

"When honest men start shooting each other up, it's always the things come out on top," said X in a philosophical tone.

"Pretty raw though about the thousand lire."

"If we don't get out of here soon they'll try to purify us," said Y, and recalled the itching palm that had been pressed to Il Duce's.

The tiny white cabin of the boat was snug and separate from the gaunt empty town, pleasant to go to bed in. The great hulks of abandoned freighters stood up all round cutting into black oblongs and upsidedown triangles the diffuse glare of scattered arc lights. It was pleasant to snuggle under the blankets in the narrow bunk and think that tomorrow we'd haul up the anchor and show a dainty pair of black heels to that great mass of brokenhearted stone and iron, and to the blackshirts who had purified it until there were no more workers.

Mr. Dos Passos on *Him*

[E. E. Cummings's play—a Freudian drama relying heavily on circus and
burlesque house devices—opened at the Provincetown Playhouse on 18 April
1928 and ran for 28 performances.]

To the Dramatic Editor:

Parallel with modernism in painting and with the psychology of Freud in the
field of science there has grown up in the half-century since Rimbaud a style of writing that might be called oblique in the sense that it attempts to generate feelings and
ideas rather than put them immediately up to the understanding, and direct in that
it aims to express sensations rather than to tell about them. People trying to "understand" such writing according to the method of plain narrative are likely to get
seized with a sudden panic, to close their eyes tight and say it's all nonsense. Algebra is a means of human expression, but the person unacquainted with its method,
opening an algebra book and trying to read it as if it were the Bible, would soon
think he was in a madhouse.

The majority of educated people have been taught to believe that the only way
of expression in words is the narrative exposition style: "On May first, eighteen
forty-two, towards the end of a sunny afternoon, a lonely rider might have been de-
scried wending his solitary way across the rolling hills of Glenmore Heath." Now
there's a nineteenth century sentence that everybody can understand because
they've read it a hundred times.

But since we have begun to explore the half mythical dark continent of consciousness, that method of telling about an event does not give us the satisfaction
that it once did. We want to recreate the event more immediately. Any event in relation to consciousness becomes an onion off which layer after layer can be peeled.

A writer of our time, instead of stating that "a solitary rider was wending,
&c.," would try to create in the reader the shambling bumpety bump of an ambling
horse or the sweet smell of the heather or the feeling of loneliness or the thoughts in
the man's head or the drifts of the various streams and eddies of his consciousness.
Or else he might try to slice the onion and give you the event and its corollaries in
their various relations to each other. To do this he might have to use shorthand or
the Morse code. That is the method of "Him." And the result, particularly among
professional writers, critics and the like who feel they know it all and that any use of
words other than according to their own habits that they learned in high school is a
personal insult to them, start snorting and blustering around and saying, "Rubbish,

nonsense." And the talk about not being able to understand new methods in music, painting, writing, comes, it seems to me, from trying to judge them by standards other than their own—as if a man should go into a restaurant and order lobster and then complain to the waiter that it wasn't juicy like steak.

"Him" seems to me to be a very direct and vivid presentation of the tangle of one man's consciousness in relation to his love for his girl. Tangle is not quite the right word because the artichoke that is fed leaf by leaf to the audience is fitted round its central theme with admirable logic. All this talk about onions and artichokes is an attempt to express the fact that the play is not built, like a detective story, out of a succession of events hung on the plot like a string. Its method is much more that of a Freudian analysis of a dream. It is the method of a scientist rather than of a storyteller. The tricks by which the successive discoveries are imparted to the audience are the tricks of a review rather than of a continuously plotted entertainment. How well it is done, how great a play it is cannot be decided until it is measured with others of its kind. I think, in the Spring of this year 1928, that it's a pretty darn good play. At any rate, it won't do you any good to curse at it for not being like "Broadway."

And as for Cummings being a nonsense writer—if this is nonsense, make the most of it.

John Dos Passos
New York, April 18, 1928.

They Want Ritzy Art

The New Playwrights Theatre ended its second season under a tremendous shower of brickbats from all sides. The critics of the capitalist press went into a sort of hysterical anvil chorus; nothing pleased them, not the plays nor the productions nor the acting nor the seats. One of these beaux arbiters of New York's taste even stretched professional etiquette to the point of advising people to stay away. Uptown the consensus of opinion was that the whole thing ought to be stopped. Downtown in radical circles we did not fare much better. The Daily Worker discovered "deviations." The socialist press said we were communists in sheep's clothing. If the theatre had any friends they managed very effectively to keep their mouths shut.

In the face of this whirlwind of enthusiastic disapproval why in thunder try to go on? chants the chorus of wellwishers.

Well why not? Theatrical reputation is a fickle thing, the probabilities are that the longer you keep up the more chance there is of a lucky break. Also in a moment when criticism shows a singular dearth of direction every man has to be a law to himself in matters of theatre, writing, painting. While the American Mercury and the new Ford continue to spread a thin varnish of Ritz over the whole United States there is a certain virtue in being unfashionable.

Let's see how the theatre has earned these many dishes of raspberries.

The enterprise started with a bang last spring in the mouldy barn of the 52nd Street Theatre. The first play was Loud Speaker, a social-political farce by John Howard Lawson, acted with admitted spirit on a "constructivist" setting. The play was not a worldbeater, but it would probably have been entertaining to the general public if everybody had not been so ready to gag at modernism, futurism or whatever you want to call it. The New York theatregoer and his pastors the critics express their profound unconscious dissatisfaction with the arts and their life in general by a hysterical fear of change or novelty. Their first reaction is to get up and walk out of the theatre at the first unfamiliar sight or sound; except when recent trips abroad have planted a seed of doubt. Maybe it's art. So they drape it with an ism, say that they can't understand it and remain limp in their seats, profoundly bored. If the ism is translated from a foreign language they may even allow themselves to be moved. After all the outré forms of art are a foreign language to the average New York audience, not that it is a particularly dull audience, but because it's

New Masses, 4 (June 1928), 8.

been for years confused, bullied and high-hatted by art-tasters of all kinds, critics and foreign importers. Well I suppose the public has a right to gag at an ism. It did. Flop.

The second play was Earth, by Em Jo Basse, a play about a small Negro community somewhere in the foothills, about men and women fighting the earth for a living, fighting God and voodoo and the terror of night and forest fires. The production revolved round a superb performance by Inez Clough. The play was acted and sung by Negroes. It got a certain amount of critical recognition but failed to attract much of an audience. Flop.

For the second season, in an attempt to put on productions more economically, the theatre was moved down to the little Cherry Lane Playhouse on Commerce Street. The first production last fall was The Belt by Paul Sifton, a play about the Ford system. You saw Henry Ford dancing the old-fashioned dances with his employees, all one big happy family, the automaton workers on the belt-conveyor, a riot when the factories shut down for a prolonged layoff. Some critics praised the play and the production, but the majority said rubbish, chaos, amateurishness, radicalism. By that time the big fight on propaganda was on. The underlying idea was that any play in the writing of which the author had a more serious aim than making money was highbrow or communistic or worse. Authors mustn't have opinions, particularly political opinions. The Belt did not make money for the theatre but it came near splitting even. Almost a success.

Next came The Centuries by Em Jo Basse, a broadly painted historical picture of the New York Ghetto. A few writers stood up against the by this time monotonous chorus of complaint on the score of dullness, amateurishness, chaos and radicalism. Nobody made any million dollars out of The Centuries.

The third play last season was The International, by John Howard Lawson, a satirical pageant of world war and revolution, with a chorus that was a cross between the chorus in a Greek play and the chorus in an uptown review. That rang the bell of critical disapproval. The venerable gentlemen from the capitalist press almost had apoplexy, they foamed and lost their breath thinking up adjectives with which to vent their sour disapproval and disgust. The radical press was more friendly but hardly less disapproving. People still shudder at the mention of the play's name. Flop.

The last production was a fantasy on Harlem in the manner of old time nigger-minstrels, Hoboken Blues, by Michael Gold. All the remaining bricks in anybody's satchel came down on it. With that the season ended amid the jubilation of the critics. Flop. General comment on season: Series of flops.

Now everybody admits that the six plays so far presented have had faults, but I think that we can claim that they bear in them a germ of growth in the American theatre, and that each of the plays had an individual freshness and integrity that, several years from now, will make having produced it worth while. My personal opinion is that both The Centuries and The International will turn out to be important landmarks in theatre history.

Due to financial difficulties and the problem of working out new methods of setting production and direction, the actual presentation of the plays has been faulty in many ways. But I get the impression that people who like the theatre have gotten considerable stimulus from some of the experiments made in production. It will be impossible for an organization like the New Playwrights Theatre to turn out finished and perfect productions for many years to come, and by the time its productions are complete, it'll probably have no function to perform.

What we haven't had has been the Ritzy finish that Americans are getting accustomed to, veneering everything in this country. What even our friends don't seem to see is that this sort of finish is incompatible with growth and experiment, and that the finish that we have been, however ineptly, groping for, is a finish from the inside out, solidity.

Next season, and there's going to be a next season, in spite of the heartfelt prayers of our many wellwishers, we are opening with a production of Singing Jailbirds by Upton Sinclair, to be followed by Airways, Inc., by John Dos Passos. The third production will probably be Picnic, by Francis Faragoh, and the fourth will be chosen from a number of plays that are at present under consideration. Among these is The American Beauty, by Paul Sifton, and Women at Four O'Clock, by Dawn Powell.

The critics will certainly be stacked against us but we hope to interest an ever-widening circle of radicals, workers and plain miscellaneous theatregoers in the possibilities of such a theatre.

The main difficulty in getting such an organization under way, aiming at breadth of scope, low prices, and plays that deal with things that matter to a large and largely workers' audience, is that the whole drift of American cultural life is against it. That tendency is that experiments in thought and presentation are for a few highbrows and that the general public that attends prizefights and baseball games will take only the most smooth-worn routine in the theatre. It may be that the task is an impossible one. All worthwhile human institutions spring from impossible tasks.

Hopeless or not, the fight for radical thought and expression in theatres and magazines and newspapers must be kept up. One by one the rallying points of protest are drowned in the great wave of Cal Coolidge prosperity, Cal Coolidge mean-heartedness and meanmindedness. The American mind is smothered in wisecracks, in five and ten-cent store Ritziness and in the rising imaginary billions of oil-prosperity. Still people will gamble with their money. They can be induced to take a chance with their minds and feelings once in a while. Even if they can't it's no time to abandon a theatre that at least can be a center of resistance.

Statement of Belief

[One of a series of "Statements of Belief" solicited by the *Bookman* from prominent writers.]

The only excuse for a novelist, aside from the entertainment and vicarious living his books give the people who read them, is as a sort of second-class historian of the age he lives in. The "reality" he misses by writing about imaginary people, he gains by being able to build a reality more nearly out of his own factual experience than a plain historian or biographer can. I suppose the best kind of narrative would combine the two like Froissart or Commines, or Darwin in "The Voyage of the Beagle." I think that any novelist that is worth his salt is a sort of truffle dog digging up raw material which a scientist, an anthropologist or a historian can later use to permanent advantage. Of course there's Chaucer and Homer and the Edda, but that's all way over our heads.

Bookman, 68 (Sept. 1928), 26.

The Making of a Writer

[A review of *120 Million*, by Mike Gold.]

Most writers whose work turns out later to be any good have to spend ten or fifteen years floundering about before they hit upon a method of saying what they want to say. Of course there are people in whom poetry bursts out in the first fire of puberty, and who suddenly attain a style of expression in early manhood like Keats and Shelley and Pushkin, but it's rare that they do much afterwards. Probably it's better that most of them die young. *120 Million* is a collection of rough sketches by the way, by a man who is being gradually forced to find a method by the pent up need to say what he has to say. In one or two of them he succeeds in saying it. Certainly "Faster America, Faster" is one of the best pieces of writing that has been printed in ten years.

As a writer Mike Gold is very lucky to have been born when he was and where he was. The New York East Side before the war was one of the most remarkable phenomena in history, a germ of an ancient eastern-european culture transplanted pure into the body of America the way a scientist would transplant a colony of bacilli for an experiment. To have been able to live from its beginning the growth of the leaven of Jewish culture in American life may not seem so important now, but from a vantagepoint of twenty-five years I think it will seem tremendously important. The amazing thing is that this rich loam has not yet produced a single American writer; it has produced isolated books like *Haunch Paunch and Jowl*,[1] but no writing to compare in historic importance with the East Side's great world-sweeping invention, jazz.

120 Million is a clear graph of a writer's development. It starts with a straight first rate sketch called "Coal Breaker," the sort of thing the *New Masses* and the *Masses* have published again and again, the writing, that is in some way the writing I like best, that is called forth by the first impact of the real grim world on the sensitive fibres of someone who has just discovered the secret magnificent pleasure of release through the written word. It's not always the work of youngsters by any means, for even if a man writes his first work when he's sixty there's likely to be a certain adolescent freshness about it, a tender or joyful indignation that makes the sentences take fire.

It's the next step that is the worst. The young man sits on the edge of his bed one morning and decides that he's a writer, that he's going to be rich and famous, or

New Masses, 4 (March 1929), 23.

116

poor and famous; and then he sits down to write, not to get something off his chest, but to make eyes at, that critics will damn or praise (it's much the same) in long columns of print. It seems to me that "God is Love" and the "Password to Thought—to Culture" were written in that mood. I don't know what's the matter with the "Two Mexicos," but I don't like it. It's only with the piece "On a Section Gang" that Mike Gold again hits his stride.

"On a Section Gang," "Love on a Garbage Dump," and "Faster, America, Faster" are the work of a man who knows his trade, who knows what he wants to say and how to say it. I can't praise them too highly. I think they are great stuff.

I said Mike Gold was lucky to have been born on the East Side. I think he was also lucky to have worked on a real garbage dump, instead of on the garbage dumps of dead ideas the colleges are, to have started life as a worker instead of as an unclassed bourgeois. A writer is after all only a machine for absorbing and arranging certain sequences of words out of the lives of the people round him. Great literature can only be grown out of the loam of a rich and sprouting popular life. American society is a sausage machine forever turning lively proletarians into bleached and helpless suburban business men. Mike Gold has the luck to get the nourishment for his writing from the meat before it has been fed into the hopper. Most of the other writers of our day are busily trying to find life and form in the grey gobs of mincemeat, afterwards.

120 Million is a pretty tall name, but as a promise, it's justified. All that's needed is for Mike Gold to go ahead and fulfill it. He's got the material and he's got a method of writing; the fact that he's a revolutionist assures him of contact with the liveliest and most undigested elements of American life. The fact that he accepts the discipline of the Workers' Party[2] gives him that inner peace and stability that comes from accepting any genuine discipline.

We know too little yet about the structure of the featherless bipeds to be able to say except in the vaguest way what it is that makes one man a tailor, another a carpenter, another a skillful exploiter of his tribe with the power of a hundred millions behind him, another a writer, a poet. The old idea of genius being a sort of spontaneous generation, the way they used to think worms came from slime, can I think be safely discarded. What I like best about *120 Million* is that it gives you a chance to see a poet developing before your eyes. Only it's just an inkling. Here's thirty years of raw history, the East Side growing up, Jewish life bursting the shell of its old ossified culture, bringing forth flowers in the rank soil of American slums; gangsters, songwriters, scientists,—and the helterskelter lives of millions of Mexicans, Negroes, Bohunks, Wops, Hungarians, Albanians, Polacks building a continent out of their sweat . . . and a man with his roots in all that, moulding it with the passionate conviction of a revolutionist. How can he help giving us the hard tense poetry we need? As Mike Gold says in his preface, *Let us persist.*

Notes

1. Samuel Ornitz's novel *Haunch, Paunch and Jowl* (1923).
2. The name of the Communist party in the early 1920s.

Did the New Playwrights Theatre Fail?

"In the face of these results which may be important in the history of the theatre, even important politically, and which were achieved in the midst of tremendous difficulties both human and material, one may fairly say that the failure of our enterprise is relatively unimportant". Piscator in the article translated in the July issue of the *New Masses.*[1]

This is a good text on which to hang a summing up of what the New Playwrights Theatre did and did not accomplish.

In the first place I think we can cross out political results. The American mind of all classes and denominations is too accustomed to keeping art or ideas in separate watertight compartments. Their influence on action is infinitesmal and only to be measured in generations and major emotional movements.

Now as for results in the theatre! I don't feel that the various people who have worked with and for the New Playwrights Theatre at different times need to be ashamed of their work or to feel that they wasted their time.

Loud Speaker, in spite of many crudities, was a fairly successful attempt to put a political farce into three dimensions, to break down the pictureframe stage and to turn a stream of satire on the audience vigorously and unashamedly. It was fairly natural that the audience, being used to the conventions of the pictureframe and to the carefully pigeonholed distinctions of farce, musical comedy, drama, didn't like it. Hatred of novelty is one of the main characteristics of the human organism. But if you want a new theatre, there's nothing to do but to have one and to let the audience recover its equilibrium as it can. You can't make an omelet without breaking eggs.

Earth was not a very successful production, but it was important as the incubator for the method of treating a play like a musical composition that was later so successful in *Singing Jailbirds* and that I think Em Jo Basshe is likely to develop still further whenever he gets a chance. The play itself seems to me to be a masterpiece.

The Belt was a success all along the line. It was a play that had something to say very much in the spirit of American workers; it said it simply and recklessly and the audience understood.

New Masses, 5 (Aug. 1929), 13.

The Centuries was an experiment with multiple stages carried on with great difficulty on account of the small size of the theatre. There were moments when the production came off. Anyway it was probably the first attempt in America to put an ethnological document on the stage, to move the audience with a slice of the history of a race instead of with episodes in the lives of individual puppets.

The International, I feel, was the most interesting experiment we made. Many people disagree with me I know. The form of farce-melodrama it seems to me is one of the best for transmitting large-scale ideas to an audience. The enormous popularity of this form in Russia at present more or less proves that. In Lawson's play it was combined with a series of direct lyrical outbursts like those of the choruses of Greek tragedy. In the production all the conventions of the pictureframe stage were dropped and an attempt was made to introduce the audience to a set of conventions much nearer those of the ballet or operatic pageant. You couldn't show 'em a thing. People of all shades of political opinion united in damning it. I think in many cases it was the successful scenes annoyed people most. It was obvious that there were many weaknesses in the last act of the play and that much of the acting was poor and a large part of the production rather sketched in than accomplished. But I think that the reason why the abuse was so universal was that in *The International* a new type of theatre was taken for granted. And everybody was trying to see it in terms of a three act problem play by Pinero.

Hoboken Blues was more or less of a failure, due partly to what Mrs. Eddy[2] used to call the malicious animal magnetism that by that time surrounded the theatre, and partly to the fact that nobody would take for granted the rather childish but unpretentious blackface minstrelshow method of presentation.

Singing Jailbirds was the best example presented of the method of production where the director treats the play as if it were a musical score. I think it got over so easily to the audiences because it did not depart too far from the methods of expressionism with which they were already familiar.

About my own play[3] I can only say that in spite of much adverse criticism, from my own point of view the production was very successful: the best acting we ever had and a method of setting and direction that made the audience accept the elimination of the proscenium arch and curtain without batting an eyelash.

It may seem silly to many people, my continued harping on abolishing the pictureframe stage where the audience let itself be tricked into imagining that it is *really* seeing a slice of life. I think it is very important. That form and content in the theatre are indissolubly linked is a sort of axiom that needs no argument. The revolutionary theatre will aim to justify the ways of politics (mass action) to the individual-in-the-mass much the way the Greek theatre justified the ways of the priestinterpreted gods to the citizens of the cityrepublics. The whole scale and category of ideas is entirely different from that of the bourgeois theatres which aimed to make the private lives of wealthy or hopetobewealthy people interesting, exciting, tragic or funny to them for a couple of hours after dinner. The first step towards realizing a revolutionary theatre seems to me to be to work with new tools. This neither radicals nor reactionaries are willing to grant, or the fact that the first attempts with new tools are sure to be clumsy.

Eisenstein said last summer that Meyerhold had carried the theatre as far as it was possible to take it in every possible direction and that the theatre was dead for the modern world.[4] I don't agree with him, though I think it is fairly obvious that all that function of the theatre which came to be more economically and successfully taken by the Talkies is doomed. It seems to me that the theatre still has enough vitality even in America to carve out an empire for itself if it can show enough flexibility to use the tools that are being discarded by dying circuses and vaudeville shows. It's nip and tuck and the theatre director must have the means to use each living instrument at hand and discard everything that shows the slightest taint of death and decay.

I think the New Playwrights Theatre failed, in the first place because authors are largely too preoccupied with their own works to make good producers and secondly because the problems involved were not seen clearly enough in the beginning. But the fact that it existed makes the next attempt in the same direction that much easier. One thing is certain: the time for half way measures in ideas or methods has gone, if indeed, it ever was.

Notes

1. Erwin Piscator, the German director, had written in "The Social Theatre" (*New Masses*, 5 [July 1929], 14) of the failure of his revolutionary theatre in Berlin.

2. Mary Baker Eddy, founder of Christian Science.

3. *Airways, Inc.*, produced in February 1929.

4. Dos Passos had met the Russian film director Sergei Eisenstein in Moscow in the summer of 1928; V. E. Meyerhold was an experimental Russian state director.

A Farewell to Arms

[A review of *A Farewell to Arms*, by Ernest Hemingway.]

Hemingway's *A Farewell to Arms* is the best written book that has seen the light in America for many a long day. By well-written I don't mean the tasty college composition course sort of thing that our critics seem to consider good writing. I mean writing that is terse and economical, in which each sentence and each phrase bears its maximum load of meaning, sense impressions, emotion. The book is a firstrate piece of craftsmanship by a man who knows his job. It gives you the sort of pleasure line by line that you get from handling a piece of wellfinished carpenter's work. Read the first chapter, the talk at the officers' mess in Gorizia, the scene in the dressingstation when the narrator is wounded, the paragraph describing the ride to Milan in the hospital train, the talk with the British major about how everybody's cooked in the war, the whole description of the disaster at Caporetto to the end of the chapter where the battlepolice are shooting the officers as they cross the bridge, the caesarian operation in which the girl dies. The stuff will match up as narrative prose with anything that's been written since there was any English language.

It's a darn good document too. It describes with reserve and exactness the complex of events back of the Italian front in the winter of 1916 and the summer and fall of 1917 when people had more or less settled down to the thought of war as the natural form of human existence when every individual in the armies was struggling for survival with bitter hopelessness. In the absolute degradation of the average soldier's life in the Italian army there were two hopes, that the revolution would end the war or that Meester Weelson would end the war on the terms of the Seventeen Points.[1] In Italy the revolution lost its nerve at the moment of its victory and Meester Weelson's points paved the way for D'Annunzio's bloody farce at Fiume[2] and the tyranny of Mussolini and the banks. If a man wanted to learn the history of that period in that sector of the European War I don't know where he'd find a better account than in the first half of *A Farewell to Arms*.

This is a big time for the book business in America. The writing, publishing and marketing of books is getting to be a major industry along with beautyshoppes and advertising. Ten years ago it was generally thought that all writers were either drunks or fairies. Now they have a halo of possible money around them and are respected on a par with brokers or realtors. The American people seems to be genuinely hungry for books. Even good books sell.

New Masses, 5 (Dec. 1929), 16.

It's not surprising that *A Farewell to Arms*, that accidentally combines the selling points of having a lovestory and being about the war, should be going like hotcakes. It would be difficult to dope out just why there should be such a tremendous vogue for books about the war just now. Maybe it's that the boys and girls who were too young to know anything about the last war are just reaching a bookbuying age. Maybe it's the result of the intense military propaganda going on in schools and colleges. Anyhow if they read things like *A Farewell to Arms* and *All Quiet on the Western Front*, they are certainly getting the dope straight and it's hard to see how the militarist could profit much. Certainly a writer can't help but feel good about the success of such an honest and competent piece of work as *A Farewell to Arms*.

After all craftsmanship is a damn fine thing, one of the few human functions a man can unstintedly admire. The drift of the Fordized world seems all against it. Rationalization and subdivision of labor in industry tend more and more to wipe it out. It's getting to be almost unthinkable that you should take pleasure in your work, that a man should enjoy doing a piece of work for the sake of doing it as well as he damn well can. What we still have is the mechanic's or motorman's pleasure in a smoothrunning machine. As the operator gets more mechanized even that disappears; what you get is a division of life into drudgery and leisure instead of into work and play. As industrial society evolves and the workers get control of the machines a new type of craftsmanship may work out. For the present you only get opportunity for craftsmanship, which ought to be the privilege of any workman, in novelwriting and the painting of easelpictures and in a few of the machinebuilding trades that are hangovers from the period of individual manufacture that is just closing. Most of the attempts to salvage craftsmanship in industry have been faddy movements like East Aurora and Morris furniture and have come to nothing.[3] *A Farewell to Arms* is no worse a novel because it was written with a typewriter. But it's a magnificent novel because the writer felt every minute the satisfaction of working ably with his material and his tools and continually pushing the work to the limit of effort.

Notes

1. An error for *Fourteen Points*, Wilson's proposals for the solution of international conflict.

2. Gabriele D'Annunzio, the Italian poet and nationalist, led a group that seized the town of Fiume in September 1919 after Italian claims to the town were rejected on the basis of Wilson's Fourteen Points.

3. Elbert Hubbard founded an arts-and-crafts center at East Aurora, New York (near Buffalo), in the mid-1890s; William Morris led an English arts-and-crafts movement during the same period.

Edison and Steinmetz: Medicine Men

[A review of *Edison, His Life and Inventions*, by Frank L. Dyer et al.; *Loki: The Life of Charles Proteus Steinmetz*, by Jonathan N. Leonard; and *Forty Years with General Electric*, by John T. Broderick.]

The book on Edison is the old-fashioned perfunctory two-volume life, evidently first published about 1910 and now revamped. In spite of much meaningless bombast and chapters so badly written that they convey no idea whatsoever, it has a full account of Edison's inventions, and contains much information (a little too much on the Horatio Alger side, perhaps) about Edison's early life that should be interesting to anybody who wants to know about the personalities that created the world we live in today. "Loki" is the up-to-date version of the same sort of thing. It attempts to be pithy and epigrammatic and to have the fashionable air that now seems to be considered necessary in biographies. The book contains some extremely interesting photographs that make it almost worth owning, and are indefinitely more informative than the text. A good deal of time is spent in glossing over Steinmetz's eccentricities, of which Socialism seems to have been the most sinful and glaring.

"Forty Years with General Electric" is as uninstructive as a book could well be. Still, the report of several conversations with Steinmetz gives it a certain historical value.

If the foregoing paragraphs seem grouchy and impertinent, it is due to the bitterness of a great many futile hours spent grubbing in the literature of the last fifty years of American industrial development. You have to read these books to believe how muddle-headed, ill-written and flatly meaningless they can be. You'd think that any youngster in a high-school composition course could do better with the material in hand.

For one thing, the writing was usually left to hired hacks and publicity men. The people who were actually doing the work had no time and no inclination to put themselves down on paper. But even if they had, I doubt if the result would have been very different. The men who counted in our national development during the last half-century seem hardly to have used the analytic or coördinating centers of their brains at all. They carried practicality to a point verging on lunacy.

Thomas Edison, who played the lead the other day in that amazing charade at Dearborn, where in the presence of Henry Ford and Harvey Firestone and Mr. Hoover and Mr. Schwab and Mr. Otto Kahn, and the regimented microphones of the world, he reconstituted the incandescent lamp as he had first built it at Menlo Park fifty years ago,[1] is one of the two or three individuals most responsible for the

New Republic, 61 (18 Dec. 1929), 103–5.

sort of world we live in today. It would be more exact to say that thousands of men of the Ford and the Edison type are its builders. Politicians made more noise, financiers and industrial organizers and bankers got more personal power and ate bigger dinners, but it was the practical mechanics who were rebuilding the city the capitalists lived in while they blustered and gambled with the results of other men's labor. When you think that Edison was partially or exclusively connected with putting on the market the stock ticker, the phonograph, the moving picture camera, the loudspeaker and microphone that make radio possible, electric locomotives, vacuum electric lamps, storage batteries, multiple transmission over the telegraph, cement burners, it becomes obvious that there is no aspect of our life not influenced by his work and by the work of men like him. Reading his life, you feel that he never for a moment allowed himself to envisage the importance of the changes in the organization of human life that his inventions were to bring about. And he would have resented it if anyone had suggested to him that his work would destroy homes, wreck morals, and help end the individual toiler's world he was brought up in. Henry Ford, less the mechanic and more the organizer, seems equally unconcerned with the results of his work in human terms. The newspaper accounts of the goings-on at Dearborn at the jubilee of the incandescent lamp, the press statements and the kittenish skipping-about in the limelight of all involved, make that appallingly clear. These men are like the sorcerer's apprentice who loosed the goblins and the wonder-working broomsticks in his master's shop and then forgot what the formula was to control them by.

I don't mean to minimize their achievements, which are among the greatest in history.

Good writing is the reflection of an intense and organized viewpoint towards something, usually towards the value and processes of human life. The fact that the writing that emanates even from such a powerful institution as General Electric is so childish is a measure of proof that the men directing it are muddled and unclear about their human aims. They know in a vague sort of way that they want to make money and to make good; most of them want to play the game according to the rules of their time and not to be a worse son-of-a-bitch than the next man, but the problem of the readjustment of human values necessary to fit their world is the last thing they think about. I suppose they would say it was none of their business.

That is why the little crumpled figure of Steinmetz stands out with such extraordinary dignity against this background of practical organizers, rule-of-thumb inventors, patent-office quibblers. Steinmetz felt every moment what his work meant in the terms of the ordinary human being.

Steinmetz was a hunchback, the son of a hunchback, a railroad lithographer in Breslau. He was born in 1865, and grew up under the pressure of the Bismarck steamroller that was grinding down the jumble of cities, states, nationalities, idealistic creeds and caste prejudices that was Germany, into a smoothly integrated empire for his masters, the Hohenzollerns. Steinmetz was a bright boy; mathematics for him was a compensation for poverty, for being deformed, for being a member of the under-dog class in the university. It was a closed garden, free from corruption and death as the New Jerusalem of the early Christians, where he was absolute god and master. If he'd been a less warm-blooded man, that would have been enough, but he wanted real life, too. So it was inevitable that he should become a social revolutionist. Chased out of Breslau, he fled across the border to Zurich; there he studied at the Politechnik and shook up the institution considerably with his ideas about electricity. He met a young Dane named Asmussen and with him came to America, in the flood-tide of European immigration to the Promised Land, in the days when men used to fall on their knees and kiss the soil of liberty when they landed in Castle Garden. He had the good luck to get a job with Rudolf Eichemeyer, who was an old German forty-eighter, electrical theorist and practical inventor, who had a plant in Yonkers for building dynamos and hat-making machinery. From then on, Steinmetz had no life outside of the laboratory—when General Electric bought out Eichemeyer, Steinmetz went along with the rest of the apparatus, first to Lynn and then to Schenectady.

At Schenectady for many years he was the bad boy of G.E. The directors of that organization soon realized that apart from enormous value as a technician, Steinmetz was a publicity asset. So the Sunday papers were filled with his gila monsters and his cactus plants and his unconventional ideas on various subjects, and they let him teach and talk Socialism and even write offering his services to Lenin. He was the little parlor-magician who made toy thunderstorms for the reporters and took dignitaries out to his summer camp and dumped them out of his canoe with all their clothes on. It was largely his work with the mathematics of electricity that made the large-scale use of alternating current possible and the use of high-tension electricity safe and easy. The transformers you see hunched in their little gabled houses along the lines of high-tension wires are all monuments to Steinmetz's formulas. The officials of G.E. had the attitude of Edison, who when he was asked whether he'd ever studied mathematics, said "No . . . I can hire a mathematician any time, but the mathematicians can't hire me." G.E. had hired its mathematician, and it was a funny, rare little animal and had to be allowed to range a good deal to be kept happy and contented.

Finally, he wore out and died. If he'd been living, he'd probably have been at Dearborn with his toy thunderstorm, grinning in the limelight with the rest of the grand old men.

On the whole, it's fitting that he should not have been there. Edison, Ford, Firestone have cashed in gigantically on the machine. They have achieved a power and a success undreamed of by Tamerlane or Caesar. America has cashed in gigantically on the machine, has attained in these fifty years since the day when Edison—having tried everything, even a red hair out of a Scotchman's beard, finally settled on the paper carbon filament for the electric light bulb—a degree of wealth and prosperity absolutely new in history. Steinmetz was not of the temperament to cash in on anything.

Reading Hammond's life and Leonard's and the various notes and articles published about Steinmetz since his death, you feel more and more that the men around him were not of the caliber to understand and appreciate him. They thought of him as a pet oddity and let it go at that. He was a man of a different race, the race of those who do not cash in. The average European view is that America does not produce first-rate men—men who do not cash in. We had Franklin and Jefferson, but that's a long time ago. In the great industrial parades of our day, it is the cashers-in who are at the wheel. Are the Europeans right?

That brings me to the preachment I started in with. The woods are full of young men who have enough sense of human value, who have in their veins enough of the blood of those who don't cash in, to be pretty good writers; it seems a shame that instead of picking up the easy garbage of European bellelettristic small-talk, they don't try harder to worm their way in among the really compelling events and personalities that are molding lives.

It's about time that American writers showed up in the industrial field where something is really going on, instead of tackling the tattered strawmen of art and culture.

Notes

1. Edward Bernays, one of the founders of public relations, had organized a celebration to commemorate the fiftieth anniversary of Edison's discovery of the electric light bulb. It was held on 21 October 1929, at the early American village reconstructed by Henry Ford at Dearborn, Michigan.

Back to Red Hysteria

Since April 1 there have been about four thousand arrests in the United States of members of the Communist party, alleged Communists, or working people attempting to go to meetings on subjects considered "radical" or "dangerous" by the police. Many of the arrests were for distributing leaflets or speaking in connection with the March 6 or May 1 demonstrations. In New York, William Z. Foster and Robert Minor are both in jail on convictions resulting from the unemployment demonstrations.[1] There have been arrests in California, Connecticut, Illinois, Indiana, Massachusetts, Minnesota, New Jersey, Pennsylvania, Wisconsin, Tennessee and in widely separated districts all over the country. The most important cases now being fought by the International Labor Defense[2] (occasionally with the help of the American Civil Liberties Union) are the following:

The Newark Case

The Communist party's candidate for Senator for New Jersey, an ex-preacher named Dozier W. Graham, and Domenico Flaiani were convicted under the sedition laws for speaking at a Communist meeting for organizing the unemployed, but were given suspended sentences. The interesting feature of the trial was that a defense witness named Langer was not allowed to testify because the judge ruled that an atheist who did not believe in rewards or punishments after death was incapable of taking the oath. The form of affirmation was ruled to apply only to Quakers or others who had religious scruples against swearing.

The Chester Case

Two young Communists arrested in front of the Viscose Mill at Marcus Hook near Chester, Pennsylvania, for distributing leaflets protesting against unemployment conditions were held under the Flynn Sedition Laws. Ray Pelz, twenty-three, was sentenced to pay a $5,000 fine, and to one to twenty years in the county jail, and Thomas Holmes, who was only eighteen, was sentenced to not less than eigh-

New Republic, 63 (2 July 1930), 168–69.

teen months in the Huntington Reformatory. The court cast doubts on the mental
fitness of Holmes (and of all who believe in the overthrow of the capitalist system),
and there is danger that he may be sent to an insane asylum. They were convicted
on the evidence of an "expert" named Lenon, who has testified at other radical
trials and who somehow got into the evidence a quotation from Radek about over-
throwing the government by force.

The Imperial Valley Cases

These constitute the first revival in six years of the California Criminal Syndicalism Act of 1919. The Agricultural Workers' Industrial League, a Communist-
controlled organization, has been organizing the migratory workers who handle the
crops in the Imperial Valley. Fair success against the lettuce growers encouraged
them to organize a strike against the cantaloupe growers, who retaliated by hiring
three stool pigeons to join the organization. Their revelations were the basis of the
charges, one of which was conspiracy to overthrow the government and ruin the
cantaloupe crop. Every effort was made to stir up sentiment against the Reds
through the press, and by the usual parade of deputies armed to the teeth. Nine men
were found guilty. Judge Johnson gave five of them the maximum sentence of one
to fourteen years on each of three counts, to run consecutively, meaning that the
state of California can keep them in jail forty-two years, if they live that long.

The Atlanta Case

On the afternoon of March 9, the Communist party attempted to hold a meeting in a hall on Auburn Avenue, Atlanta, Georgia. The meeting had been widely
advertised through the distribution of leaflets, one of which showed a picture of a
Negro and a white worker shaking hands. A little before the meeting was scheduled
to begin, Police Captain Fain drove up to the door and began telling Negroes on the
street not to go into the hall. Then, when Robert M. Hart, the chairman, got up to
call the meeting to order, Captain Fain called him to the door and asked, "Who's
the boss here?" He was told that the meeting had been arranged by M. H. Powers,
Communist party organizer. Powers and a young man named Carr came up and
argued with the police captain, claiming that the meeting was legal, but were taken
off to the police station. Meanwhile, Hart told the audience they had a right to stay
there. At the police station, Powers and Carr were released by Chief of Police Bea-
vers, as no charge was brought against them. While they were on their way back to
the hall, a man, who the police later admitted was a detective, dropped a tear-gas
bomb in the aisle, and the men in the hall started running out. At that moment Carr
arrived, breathless, and shouted from the door that there'd been no charges and that
the meeting was legal. Whereupon he was grabbed by a cop, was called a "damned
Russian Red," and rearrested. When Powers reached the door, he also was arrested
again, and the hall was cleared. This time they were held for "disorderly conduct
and throwing a tear-gas bomb," but the charges were changed in a few days to "inciting to insurrection and distributing insurrectionary papers," on which charge the
Grand Jury indicted them under a statute passed in 1861 as a Confederate measure
against "Negroes, slaves and free persons of color" who might incite the slaves to

insurrection. "Distributing insurrectionary papers" probably referred to Lincoln's Emancipation Proclamation. Then, in 1866, under the carpet-bagger administration, the statute was amended to exclude the word "slaves" and include white men, aiming at attempts of insurrection against the federal government. The statute has never been used from that day to this, and even in the Reconstruction period, I believe that there was only one indictment under it. The statute carries the penalty of death for inciting to insurrection, and of five to twenty years in jail for circulation of insurrectionary papers. That the authorities are going to try for the maximum penalty is shown by a remarkable statement to the press by Assistant Solicitor-General John M. Hudson, who said among other things:

> As fast as these Communists come here and publicly preach their doctrine of violent opposition to the laws of this state, we shall indict them and I shall demand the death penalty in every case.
> Before any other Communists undertake to come into our state and preach their revolutionary gospel, they would be wise to investigate our laws. They have plenty of teeth in them. I know of no stronger similar laws in the whole country. We will not tolerate Communists in Georgia.

Carr and Powers have been held without bail since their arrest, and for some reason Carr, a boy of nineteen, has been kept incommunicado in the death cell. Four additional indictments have been returned under this law: Mary Dalton, twenty, organizer for the National Textile Union, and Ann Burluk, nineteen, of the International Labor Defense, and two young Negroes were arrested on May 22 at a meeting of the American Negro Labor Congress. Two white residents of Atlanta, arrested at the same time, were released, but the Northern girls and the two Negroes were held for trial under the same charges as Powers and Carr.

Anyone who knows the bitter sentiment in Georgia against the labor organizations, and particularly against the assumption of racial equality in labor organizations, will realize how easy it will be to get a conviction, in spite of the youth of the defendants and the extremely thin evidence upon which they are held. Local American Federation of Labor officials, there as everywhere anxious to get rid, at any cost, of the Communists who are undermining their authority, seem to be wholeheartedly in support of the prosecution.

Furthermore, Atlanta business men are in a bitter mood; unemployment is growing there, and, according to Atlanta Life, "business conditions are worse than at any time since Reconstruction days." Various attempts by local boosters to keep their spirits up—such as the Junior Chamber of Commerce's Progress and Prosperity Parade—have turned out to be flops of the bitterest sort and have only added to people's uneasiness. All this will make it much easier to stage a race panic and send these young Communists to the electric chair.

It looks as if, particularly with unemployment increasing (it seems to me a curious and sinister detail that newspaper headlines now almost invariably speak of unemployed workers as "the idle," as if there were something innately vicious about not having a job) and Hoover prosperity severely shaken, to say the least, the struggle against working-class radicalism of the American governors and owners were going back to the acute stage of 1919. Now the arch-enemy is Communism instead of the I.W.W. One important question in connection with this fight is the attitude of the middle-class liberals. In 1919 we were hog-tied by War psychology and many of us were actually in the army, and, therefore, helpless, or else too muddle-headed, as a result of a series of stunning blows against our political faith, to take any attitude at all. Now we have no such excuse. By middle-class liberals I mean everybody who isn't forced by his position in the economic structure of society to be pro-worker or anti-worker. They are the only class to which neutrality is possible in any phase of the struggle. I don't know if they can have much effect on the outcome, but their attitude certainly can affect the conditions under which the fighting is carried on. If they are genuinely neutral, they can at least demand that the war be fought under the most humane conditions possible. What is our attitude (I speak as a writer, and therefore as a middle-class liberal, whether I like it or not) about it going to be? Even neutrality, with the major organs of information in the hands of the government and the industrialists, is going to be difficult, and to many even the coolest neutrality is going to look like Red radicalism.

Notes

1. Foster and Minor, both important figures in the Communist party hierarchy, led a New York City march of the unemployed in March 1930 and were jailed for six months when a riot occurred during the demonstration.

2. A Communist-controlled organization; Dos Passos supported several of its activities during 1930 and 1931.

Whom Can We Appeal To?

The brave boys in blue of the New York police force have done their bit for prosperity in the last month by beating a young Negro to death (the police say he died of apoplexy and not from the beating) and then shooting a Mexican Communist dead at the young Negro's funeral for good measure. If they don't like this country let 'em go back where they came from.

Well, that's class war. But isn't there anyone in this great and etc. city who feels that there ought to be rules even in class war? We used to be taught as kids, in that distant day when even intellectuals believed or pretended to believe in something, that mercy was one of the pillars of the shining edifice of civilization, that it was bad sportsmanship to jump on a man when he was down, that civilization was a system designed to keep the weak from being too often beaten up by the strong. Isn't there anyone in the United States who feels it sufficiently to his advantage "that civilization shall not vanish from the earth" (as Wilson was so fond of crooning in a sad musical voice) to make some protest in the face of the daily increasing barbarity of the attacks of the police and owners' mercenaries on working men whose main crime is hope for a better day for themselves and for the world?

I've used the word *civilization* three times and each time I found myself wincing as I tapped it out on the typewriter. The poor old idealistic catchwords have grown pretty rancid in the last fifteen years, but under the muck there's a core of sound meaning in some of them yet, and anyhow there's no other convenient way of expressing what I mean: the body of inherited repressions and carefully built up social instincts on which our spontaneous hatred of cruelty is based. I admit that civilized man likes cruelty about as much as he hates it, but anybody who's been in wartime fighting knows that he hates it too.

The most shocking thing about the Ohio prison fire was the small amount of protest it called forth.[1] It's as if the carnage of the European War and the years following it and the rapid mechanization of life had entirely dulled the imaginative response (putting yourself in the other man's place) that's biologically at the bottom of feelings of mercy and compassion. Now we are in the midst of a wave of redbaiting and legal lynching again, and nobody so much as bats an eyelash.

The question is, whom can you appeal to?

From "A Discussion: Intellectuals in America," *New Masses*, 6 (Aug. 1930), 8.

Writing about it in the *New Masses*, mostly read by people who are convinced already, is like pouring coaloil on a fire that's already lit, it makes it flare up a little; but it's a waste of coaloil. And I don't think that the atrocity-psychology so easily generated in the last war against the Germans is a useful weapon for radicals. It's too damned dirty. It tends to produce counter-atrocities. Much better shut up about the brutality of the enemy.

The class you could appeal to would be the class that had the least stake in the game.

I think that such a class exists, though its members don't know it. In *Middletown*, that extraordinary useful survey of a middle-western town from the point of view of academic anthropology,[2] the authors divide the American life they're studying into three groups: the Middle Class or Business Class, the Owning Class, and the Working Class. Naturally, the great majority of the Middle Class are mercenaries and dependents of the owners and even less open to feelings of humanity than the people on top. But there is a layer: engineers, scientists, independent manual craftsmen, writers, artists, actors, technicians of one sort or another, who insofar as they are good at their jobs are a necessary part of any industrial society. (In Russia this class held over, not half as much affected as people think by the revolution, and in spite of the confusion of its politics is now growing in numbers and power.) If you could once convince them of the fact that their jobs don't depend on capitalism they'd find that they could afford to be humane. The time to reach these people is now, when the series of stock market crashes must have proved to the more intelligent that their much talked of participation in capital through stockholdings was just about the sort of participation a man playing roulette has in the funds of the gambling house whether he's winning or losing.

As a writer I belong to that class whether I like it or not, and I think most men who graduate from working with their hands into desk jobs eventually belong to it, no matter what their ideas are. You can call 'em intellectuals or liberals or petty bourgeoisie or any other dirty name but it won't change 'em any. What you've got to do is convince the technicians and white collar workers that they have nothing to lose and that they can at least afford to be neutral, and that every new atrocity like the Marion Massacre[3] or the railroading of the organizers in Imperial Valley will make the world worse for them personally.

The most difficult thing you have to buck is the fact that along with the technical education that makes them valuable to the community they have taken in a subconscious political education that makes them servants of the owners. And the more education they have the deeper that psychology is ingrained. They should be made to realize that they have power and that by intelligent organization they could make themselves respected, that industry can't do without them any more than it can do without workers. At present even radicals of that group have much less real political development than any bunch of scissorbill hodcarriers that never heard of a union.

Still this is the weekly-magazinereading class that people appeal to when they talk about public opinion. Education and our professional deformation has made most of us too cowardly and too preoccupied with making a living and living respectably and raising children to want to make events, but through our technical training and our fair average of leisure we are the handlers of ideas. Ideas can't make events but they can color them. We can't affect the class war much but we might possibly make it more humane.

And you can't wait to be humane after a war is over, the last war proved that: you're down to plain savagery long before the war's over. And then it's this very class that howls the loudest. If the Russian technically trained classes had had any political ideas or any idea of what they wanted, the work of the Russian revolution would have been infinitely easier. It's the job of people of all the professions in the radical fringe of the middle class to try to influence this middle class, that most of them would rather not belong to, so that at least some of its weight shall be thrown on the side of what I've been calling civilization. It's a tough job, but somebody's got to do it.

Notes

1. A fire at the overcrowded Ohio State Penitentiary at Columbus on 21 April 1930 resulted in the death of over three hundred prisoners.

2. *Middletown: A Study of Contemporary American Culture* (1929) by Robert S. and Helen M. Lynd.

3. In a battle between striking textile workers and sheriff's deputies at Marion, North Carolina, on 2 October 1929 three strikers were killed and twenty-four wounded.

Translator's Foreword to *Panama;*
or, The Adventures of My Seven Uncles

The poetry of Blaise Cendrars was part of the creative tidal wave that spread over the world from the Paris of before the last European war. Under various tags: futurism, cubism, vorticism, modernism, most of the best work in the arts in our time has been the direct product of this explosion, that had an influence in its sphere comparable with that of the October revolution in social organization and politics and the Einstein formula in physics. Cendrars and Apollinaire, poets, were on the first cubist barricades with the group that included Picasso, Modigliani, Marinetti, Chagall; that profoundly influenced Maiakovsky, Meyerhold, Eisenstein; whose ideas carom through Joyce, Gertrude Stein, T. S. Eliot (first published in Wyndham Lewis's "Blast"). The music of Stravinski and Prokofieff and Diageleff's Ballet hail from this same Paris already in the disintegration of victory, as do the windows of Saks Fifth Avenue, skyscraper furniture, the Lenin Memorial in Moscow, the paintings of Diego Rivera in Mexico City and the newritz styles of advertising in American magazines.

Meanwhile, in America at least, poetry (or verse, or little patches of prose cut into inevitable lengths on the page, or whatever you want to call it) has, after Masters, Sandburg and the Imagists, subsided again into parlor entertainment for highschool English classes. The stuffed shirts have come out of their libraries everywhere and rule literary taste. Literary philosophies vaguely favorable to fascism, pederasty and the snobmysticism of dying religion, absorb the attention of "poets." A young man just starting to read verse in the year 1930 would have a hard time finding out that this method of putting words together had only recently passed through a period of virility, intense experimentation and meaning in everyday life.

For the sake of this hypothetical young man and for the confusion of Humanists,[1] stuffed shirts in editorial chairs, anthology compilers and prize poets, sonnetwriters and readers of bookchats, I think it has been worth while to attempt to turn these alive informal personal everyday poems of Cendrars into English, in spite of the obvious fact that poetry by its very nature cant be lifted out of the language in which it was written. I only hope it will at least induce people to read the originals.

Blaise Cendrars, *Panama; or, The Adventures of My Seven Uncles* (New York: Harper & Brothers, 1931), vii–ix.

Notes

1. An allusion to the New Humanists, a conservative literary movement of the 1920s led by Irving Babbitt and Paul Elmer More.

Harlan: Working Under the Gun

[A bitter and violent coal strike in Harlan County prompted the communist-controlled National Committee for the Defense of Political Prisoners to request of a number of prominent writers (all of whom were already members of the NCDPP) that they travel to Harlan to investigate conditions there. The group, led by Theodore Dreiser and including Dos Passos, Lester Cohen, Samuel Ornitz, Bruce Crawford, Melvin P. Levy, and Charles and Adelaide Walker, visited Pineville, Kentucky on 5 November 1931; Harlan on 6 November; and Pineville, Straight Creek, and Wallins Creek on 7 November. They returned to New York on 9 November. The report of the group was published as *Harlan Miners Speak* in 1932.]

Everybody knows that the coal industry is sick and that the men working at our most dangerous occupation (every sixth man is injured in the course of a year) are badly off, but few Americans outside of the miners themselves understand how badly off, or how completely the "American standard of living" attained in some sections during boom years, with strong unions working under the Jacksonville agreement,[1] has collapsed. The coal operators, who have been unable to organize their industry commercially or financially along modern lines, have taken effective common action in only one direction: in an attack against the unions, the wage scales and the living conditions of the men who dig the coal out for them. Harlan County in eastern Kentucky, which has been brought out into the spotlight this summer by the violence with which the local Coal Operators' Association has carried on this attack, is, as far as I can find out, a pretty good medium exhibit of the entire industry: living conditions are better than in Alabama and perhaps a little worse than in the Pittsburgh district. The fact that the exploited class in Harlan County is of old American pre-Revolutionary stock, that the miners still speak the language of Patrick Henry and Daniel Boone and Andrew Jackson and conserve the pioneer traditions of the Revolutionary War and of the conquest of the West, will perhaps win them more sympathy from the average American than he would waste on the wops and bohunks he is accustomed to see get the dirty end of the stick in labor troubles.

I: War Zone

I am sad and weary, I've got the
   hongry ragged blues,
Not a penny in my pocket
   to buy one thing I need to use
I was up this mornin
   with the worst blues ever had in my life
Not a bit to cook for breakfast
   or for a coalminer's wife.[2]

New Republic, 69 (2 Dec. 1931), 62–67. Reprinted in part in *Harlan Miners Speak* (1932) and *In All Countries* (1934).

The mines in Harlan County are in the forks and creeks of the upper part of the Cumberland River. A comparatively new coal field, first developed on a large scale during the boom in production that went along with the European War, its output is said to be a very high grade of bituminous. The miners were organized 90 percent by the United Mine Workers of America around 1917. In the 1920 boom a union miner was sometimes able, hiring several "chalkeyes" (inexperienced helpers) at $8 a day, to clear two or three hundred dollars a month. Railways pushed into the leafy valleys of the Cumberland range, fairly prosperous towns grew up. The population of Harlan County increased three or fourfold. Local business men who had managed to get hold of coal lands prospered on leases and royalties. Mountaineers who had lived poor and free on their hillside farms came down into the valleys to work in the mines and live in "patches" of temporary houses, put up by the companies. The race for riches went to the heads of the operators. The fact of having a little cash every two weeks went to the heads of the miners. The union turned into a racket and lapsed. Financiers skimmed the cream off the coal companies and left them overcapitalized and bankrupt. In the fat years no one thought of taking any measures of civic organization to help tide them over the lean years that were to follow—a typical American situation. Headlong deflation left the coal operators broke and the miners starving.

Last winter was pretty bad. When spring came along, the miners around Evarts began to think something ought to be done to revive the old locals of the U.M.W. of A. Wages had been steadily slipping. Conditions of safety were getting worse. A few old Wobblies and radicals began to talk class war; some of the youngsters began to wonder about socialism. A meeting was held in Pineville to talk about union organization. Two hundred men lost their jobs and were blacklisted. The coal operators, scared by the flood of anti-Red propaganda fed them through detective agencies and professional labor-baiting organizations, began to hire extra guards. Their position depended on their underselling the coal regions where traces of unionism still remained. Trusting to the terrible unemployment to break any strike that might be pulled, they took the offensive. In April they started evicting active union men from their houses. In the eastern counties of Kentucky every man considers himself entitled to carry a gun and to protect himself with it against insult and aggression. It was not long before a skirmish took place between miners and guards sworn in as deputies. This was followed, on May 5, by an out-and-out battle on the road outside of Evarts.

The townspeople of Evarts explain it this way: The town was full of evicted miners who seem to have had the pretty complete sympathy of the townspeople (the small merchants and storekeepers are against the mine operators because they force the miners to trade at the company commissaries). Feeling was running high. The mine guards made a practice of riding slowly through the town with their cars in second, machine guns and sawed-off shotguns sticking out of the windows, "tantalizing us," as one man put it. The morning of the fight, a rumor went around that the sheriff was going to bring in some carloads of scabs. Miners congregated on the road across the bridge from Evarts. The Coal Operators' Association claims that the miners were lying in ambush, an assertion which the miners deny. A carload of deputies came in from Harlan town. Shooting began, and lasted for thirty minutes. In the course of it three deputies were killed and several wounded; one miner was also killed and others wounded. Deputies then took Evarts by storm and arrested everybody they could lay their hands on. For some time the town had been under the cross-fire of their machine guns. The next morning Judge D. C. Jones—his wife is a member of the Hall family, which has mining interests in the vicinity—called a grand jury which the miners assert was illegally picked, made them a fiery speech denouncing I.W.W.'s and Reds. This grand jury returned thirty triple-murder indictments and thirty indictments for banding and confederating. Among those indicted were the town clerk and chief of police of Evarts. From then on through the summer the elected town officers of Evarts were superseded by the high sheriff's men, whose salaries are paid by the coal operators. No indictments were returned against mine guards or deputy sheriffs who had taken part in the battle, or against a mine guard who later killed Chasteen, a restaurant owner in Evarts who was on the miners' side.

About that time, so far as I can make out, the communist-affiliated National Miners' Union, which was conducting a strike against the Pittsburgh Terminal Company, sent organizers into eastern Kentucky, and N.M.U. locals began to be formed out of the wreckage of the old U.M.W. of A. In Evarts itself the I.W.W. seems to have had more influence than the Communists. The thing is that the miners felt that they were fighting for their lives and were ready to join any organization that would give them back solidarity and support them in their struggle against intolerable conditions. I talked to men who had joined all three unions.

Meanwhile the Coal Operators' Association was out to crush radicalism in Harlan County. The automobile of the I.L.D.[3] relief worker was mysteriously dynamited. The soup kitchen in Evarts, which was feeding four hundred men, women and children a day, was blown up. In an attack on another soup kitchen at the swimming hole near Wallins Creek, two union men were killed and several wounded. Union organizers were beaten and run out of the county. Bruce Crawford of Crawford's Weekly, who greatly annoyed Sheriff Blair by publishing the miners' side of the story, was mysteriously shot from ambush. Boris Israel, Federated Press correspondent, was seized on the steps of the courthouse at Harlan, taken for a ride in perfect Chicago style, thrown out of the car on a lonely road and shot. Houses were raided, and many union sympathizers (among them Arnold Johnson, a theological student, who was an investigator for the American Civil Liberties Union) were arrested and jailed on the charge of criminal syndicalism. The Knoxville News Sentinel, a Scripps-Howard paper which printed stories about the frightful plight of the miners, was taken out of the newsstands in Harlan and its reporters were so intimidated the editor never dared send the same man up to Harlan twice.

All this time in the adjacent Bell County, where living conditions among the miners are worse if possible than in Harlan, the high sheriff has told the coal operators that if they make any trouble, he will cancel the deputy commissions of the mine guards, with the result that there has been no bloodshed, although there have been successful strikes in several small mines along Straight Creek.

II: Enter the Writers' Committee

When my husband works in the coalmines,
   he loads a car on every trip,
Then he goes to the office that evenin

an gits denied of scrip—
Jus because it took all he had made that day
   to pay his mine expenses—
Jus because it took all he had made that day
   to pay his mine expenses.
A man that'll jus work for coal light an carbide
   he ain't got a speck of sense.

Breakfast in the station at Cincinnati. After that the train crosses the Ohio River and starts winding through the shallow valleys of the rolling section of central Kentucky. At lunch time to get to the dining car we have to walk through a federal prison car on its way to Atlanta. Change at Corbin onto a local train for Pineville. The Louisville papers say Governor Sampson is sending a detachment of militia into Harlan County. As we get near Pineville the valleys deepen. Steep hills burnished with autumn cut out the sky on either side. There's the feeling of a train getting near the war zone in the old days.

At the station is a group of miners and their wives come to welcome the writers' committee: they stand around a little shyly, dressed in clean ragged clothes. A little coaldust left in men's eyebrows and lashes adds to the pallor of scrubbed faces, makes you think at once what a miserable job it must be keeping clean if you work in coal. At the Hotel Continental Mr. Dreiser is met by newspaper men, by the mayor and town clerk of Pineville, who offer their services "without taking sides." Everybody is very polite. A reporter says that Judge D. C. Jones is in the building. A tall man in his thirties, built like a halfback, strides into the lobby. There's something stiff and set about the eyes and the upper part of his face; a tough customer. When he comes up to you you realize he must stand six-feet-six in his stocking feet. He and Mr. Dreiser meet and talk rather guardedly. Judge Jones says he's willing to answer any questions put to him about the situation in Harlan County. Mr. Dreiser and Judge Jones are photographed together on the steps of the hotel. Mrs. Grace of Wallins Creek, the wife of Jim Grace, a union organizer who was beaten up and run out of the county, comes up and asks Judge Jones why the sheriff's deputies raided her house and ransacked her things and her boarders' rooms. The interview comes abruptly to an end.

When the members of the committee settle down at a long table in a room off the lobby to decide on a plan of procedure, stories start pouring in. Mr. Dreiser, after questioning Mrs. Grace about her husband's former employment—a former miner now working in a store, he was prominent in organizing the N.M.U.—asks her how he was arrested:

A. I was not with him, but he was arrested in Letcher County. Neon. Him and Tom Myerscough were together.
Q. What were they doing?
A. They were trying to get the union organized. They were organizing against starvation. They were establishing a union for better conditions.
Q. What happened to him?
A. After they came to the house looking for him, he went away and stayed at a friend's house and then he and Tom went to Neon, Letcher County. There he was arrested and took to jail in Neon. Then he was turned over to the Jenkins' bunch of gunmen.

Q. Well, what happened then?

A. Him and Myerscough were turned over to the Harlan County bunch and they takes them over to the Big Black Mountains of Virginia. They bust him in the face and broke his cheek bone. They kicked him in the back. He ran into the woods and they fired at him.

Q. How many shots did they fire?

A. About fifty I guess.

Q. Did they hit him?

A. Well he was grazed at the elbow.

Q. What did he do?

A. He went on to Middlesboro and stayed at a friend's house. But I didn't know. When I first got word that Mr. Grace and Tom was held in jail, I didn't know whether he was in Harlan, Jenkins, or Neon. I goes out and went to get somebody to find out. We thought they were killed. I started to get hold of the I.L.D. and I just happened in where Mr. Grace was and I asked the lady whether her husband was there and I found out that Jim was there. His face and eyes was swollen black and blue. He was crazy as a loon.

Then she testified to raids on her house and her boarders' rooms being searched for I.W.W. and Com-MU-nist literature. Then an organizer for the union testified about having his house broken into and his guns seized (the possession of firearms is legal in Kentucky), a vice president of the Kentucky State Federation of Labor turned over some documents to the effect that when the state militia came in after the Evarts battle last spring the operators had promised the U.M.W. of A. that they wouldn't take that opportunity of importing scabs, and in spite of that had imported scabs. A young man brought a mysterious message warning the writers' committee not to attend the meeting called by the National Miners' Union at Wallins Creek on Sunday, as there'd surely be trouble there. Bruce Crawford told the story of his quarrel with Sheriff John Henry Blair: how Blair had gone to see him in Norton and complained of the attitude of his paper, had taken a subscription and left, and how the next time Crawford went to Harlan several shots had been fired at him as he crossed the swinging footbridge over the river, one of them nicking him in the ankle. The most moving testimony was that of Jeff Baldwin, whose brother Julius had been killed by deputies at the swimming-hole soup kitchen. His story was that two or more deputies had driven up the dirt road that leads up the hill from the main road to the shack where the soup kitchen was located, had stopped the sedan so that the headlights shone full in the door dazzling the group of miners standing around it, that one deputy, Lee Fleener by name, had first yelled "Put up your hands" and then immediately opened fire. Baldwin's brother and another man had been killed and he himself wounded in the shoulder as he ducked for shelter inside the shack. In spite of the fact that the coroner's jury had named Lee Fleener and other persons unknown as the murderers, no action had been taken by the county prosecutor.

Next day the committee went up to Harlan, a fine ride up the magnificent valley of the Cumberland River. Harlan is a lively little town; stores and bank buildings attest to the slightly flimsy prosperity of the boom period; the handsome courthouse takes away a little from the gimcrack air of a Southern industrial town.

Meanwhile, in a crowded room in the Llewellyn Hotel, miners and their wives were telling their stories:

Q. For how many years have you been a miner?

A. From twenty to twenty-five years.

Q. Have you done most of your mining here in Harlan County?

A. Since 1917. . . .

Q. When you were in good standing with this union [the United Mine Workers] how much did you make a day?

A. When we had a union here I could make from four dollars to five dollars to six dollars a day.

Q. How much did you make a month?

A. Anywhere maybe along from eighty dollars to one hundred.

Q. How much did you work for after the union broke up?

A. They kept cutting wages down till you hardly couldn't make anything at all. . . .

Q. This thirty dollars that you would get, was it in scrip or in cash?

A. No, sir, you hardly ever drew any money on that. You traded your scrip in at the store, the company store, and part of the time they had you in debt.

Q. Did you buy clothing at the company store or food?

A. Food. I couldn't get enough to buy clothes.

Q. How did you get clothing?

A. I generally sent out to beg and did the best I could.

This miner testified that since he'd been fired he had lived "on the mercy of the people." Being asked what criminal syndicalism, the charge on which he had been arrested and bonded over to keep the peace, meant to him, he said: "The best I can give it is going against your country, but that is something I never did do. I never thought about such a thing. . . . My family always fought for the country and I've always been for it."

Then Mr. Dreiser questioned a woman who refused to give her name, saying she was afraid her husband would lose his job if the boss found out she'd testified. They were living in a company house, where they'd been living for three weeks. In that time the husband had received only scrip.

Q. How do you manage to live?

A. We have just managed to exist. I will tell you that I've had just one dollar in the last three days to live on, my husband and myself and two children.

Q. I wonder how you distribute that money around.

A. We live on beans and bread. We don't get no dinner. . . . There don't none of you know how hard a man works that works in the mines and I'll tell you what I had to put in his bucket this morning for him to eat and work hard all day. There was a little cooked punkin and what you folks call white meat, just fat white bacon, and that's what he took to the mines to eat and work on and he had water gravy for breakfast and black coffee.

Q. And what's water gravy?

A. Water and grease and a little flour in it.

Q. What do you give the children?

A. They had the same breakfast and they don't get no dinner. . . . They're not in a situation to go to school because they have no shoes on their feet and no underwear on them and the few clothes they have, they are through them.

In the afternoon Mr. Dreiser visited Sheriff Blair in his office and asked him some questions. The sheriff said that the National Mine Workers was a Communist organization and that the U.M.W. of A. had not been, that he considered The Daily Worker and all other Communist, I.W.W. or Red publications illegal, and explained that most of the deputies he had sworn in were mine guards paid by the coal operators. He didn't know how many deputies he had sworn in. The only money they got from his office were fees for arrests and summonses. He brought the interview to a lively close by serving Bruce Crawford with a $50,000 civil suit for slander.

Next morning County Prosecutor Will Brock was interviewed. He said he approved of unionism, if it was a legal unionism like that of the U.M.W. of A., but that he considered all this I.W.W.-Communist agitation illegal and seditious. As an example of a fellow that he'd thought at first was decent and that had then turned out to be a Communist, he mentioned Arnold Johnson, investigator for the American Civil Liberties Union. The interview was made fairly tense by the interruptions of an attorney named Jones, who shares his office with him, who said he was just waiting to tell the whole damned bunch what he thought of them; on being asked about a deputy named Heywood who was reputed to be a Chicago gunman, he said grimly through his teeth: "All right, if you want to see him so bad, you'll see him." We learned afterward that his brother had been killed in the Evarts fight, and that he himself had taken part in raids on miners' houses.

III: The Meeting in Straight Creek

All the women in this coalcamp
   are sittin with bowed down heads
All the women in this coalcamp
   are sittin with bowed down heads
Ragged an barefooted an their
   children acryin for bread
No food no clothes for our children
   I'm sure this ain't no lie
No food no clothes for our children
   I'm sure this ain't no lie
If we can't get no more for our labor
   we will starve to death and die.

Straight Creek is the section of Bell County that has been organized fairly solid under the National Miners' Union. Owing, the miners say, to the fair-minded attitude of the sheriff, who has not allowed the mine guards to molest them, there has been no bloodshed, and a three weeks' strike ended the week before we got there with several small independent operators signing agreements with the union at thirty-eight cents a ton and allowing a union checkweighman. They say thirty-eight cents is not a living wage but that it's something to begin on. The committee had been invited to attend a meeting of the N.M.U. local at the Glendon Baptist Church and walked around the miners' houses first. The militia officers who accompanied us were impressed with the utter lack of sanitation and the miserable condition of the houses, tumble-down shacks set up on stilts with the keen mountain wind blowing through the cracks in the floor.

The midwife at Straight Creek, Aunt Molly Jackson, who later spoke at the meeting and sang these blues of her own composing that I've been quoting at the heads of the sections, was questioned by Mr. Dreiser:

> Q. Can you tell us something about the conditions of the people in this hollow?
>
> A. The people in this country are destitute of anything that is really nourishing to the body. That is the truth. Even the babies have lost their lives and we have buried from four to seven a week during the warm weather . . . on account of cholera, flux, famine, stomach trouble brought on by undernourishment. Their food is very bad, such as beans and harsh foods fried in this lard that is so hard to digest. . . . Families have had to depend on the Red Cross. The Red Cross put out some beans and corn.
>
> Q. Do they give it to everyone that asks?
>
> A. No, they stop it when they know a man belongs to the union.
>
> Q. What did they say about it?
>
> A. The Red Cross is against a man who is trying to better conditions. They are for the operators and they want the mines to be going, so they won't give anything to a man unless he does what the operators want him to. . . . I talked to the Red Cross lady over in Pineville. I said there's a lot of little children in destitution. Their feet are on the ground. They have come so far. They are going to get pneumonia and flu this winter that will kill them children off.
>
> Q. Did she offer to give you any relief?
>
> A. No, because they was members of the National Miners' Union. They said, "We are not responsible for those men out on strike. They should go back to work and work for any price that they will take them on for."

The meeting in the Baptist Church was conducted by a young fellow who'd been a preacher. Men and women spoke. Two representatives of the I.L.D. made speeches. One of the miners said in his speech that the reason they called them Reds was because the miners were so thin an' poor that if you stood one of 'em up against the sun you'd see red through him. All through the meeting a stout angry woman, who we were told was the bookkeeper at the Carey mine and the Red Cross distributor, stood in the aisle with her arms akimbo glaring at the speakers as if she was going to start trouble of some kind. All she did was occasionally to taunt the chairman with the fact that he owed her ten dollars. The high point of the meeting was Aunt Molly Jackson's singing of her blues:

> Please don't go under those mountains
>   with the slate ahangin over your head,
> Please don't go under those mountains
>   with the slate ahangin over your head
> An work for jus coal light an carbide
>   an your children acryin for bread;
> I pray you take my council
>   please take a friend's advice:
> Don't load no more, don't put out no more
>   till you get a livin price.

IV: Last Vestige of Democracy

This minin town I live in
  is a sad an a lonely place,
This minin town I live in
  is a sad an a lonely place,
For pity and starvation
  is pictured on every face,
Everybody hongry and ragged,
  no slippers on their feet,
Everybody hongry and ragged,
  no slippers on their feet,
All goin round from place to place
  bummin for a little food to eat.
Listen my friends and comrades
  please take a friend's advice,
Don't put out no more of your labor
  till you get a livin price.

Evarts is probably one of the few towns in the United States that still has democratic government. In spite of the fact that it's hemmed in on every side by coal-company property, that the chief of police and town clerk were arrested and charged with murder after the battle in May and that the town policing was done all summer by company guards, at the November election they put in a pro-miner town council by something like 200 to 80 votes. Most of the men at present on trial for their lives come from Evarts, and as far as I could find out from talking around, they have the complete sympathy of the local population. It is in Evarts that the union movement started, and there the miners were first accused of being Reds when it was discovered by the Coal Operators' Association that one of the U.M.W. of A. locals had taken out an I.W.W. charter. The miners on trial for murder were being defended by the General Defense Committee, the old Wobbly defense, that is unwilling to cooperate with the Communist-affiliated I.L.D. defending the criminal syndicalism and banding and confederating cases that have grown out of attempts to suppress the National Miners' Union. So far as I could make out, the county authorities consider members of either organization equally without human rights. Possibly the I.W.W. occupies a slightly better position, owing to its connection with U.M.W. of A. officials who have contacts with state (Democratic) politics, and to its soft pedaling of class-war talk. But the real point is that the situation of the miners is so desperate that they'll join anything that promises them even temporary help. I asked one man if he'd go to work again under the present scale, supposing he could get past the blacklist. He said, "You starve if you work an' you starve if you don't work. A man 'ud rather starve out in the woods than starve workin' under the gun."

The meeting at Wallins Creek took place in the high-school building and passed off without disorder, though you got the impression that the people who attended it were pretty nervous. The local small merchants seemed strong for the N.M.U. and somebody had put up a banner across the main street that read, "Welcome I.L.D., National Miners' Union, Writers' Committee." The next morning the committee packed up its testimony and left for New York, to be followed by the "toothpick indictment" of Mr. Dreiser[4] and a general indictment of all concerned, including the speakers at the miners' meeting, for criminal syndicalism.

Notes

1. An agreement (signed at Jacksonville, Florida in February 1923) between coal operators and miners, which stabilized prices and wages in the coal industry. The agreement lasted approximately three years.

2. As Dos Passos later explains (p. 143), the song lyrics accompanying his Harlan essay are by Molly Jackson, a local midwife and folksinger. "Discovered" by the NCDPP group during their Harlan stay, Molly Jackson was later in the 1930s to achieve considerable national popularity as a radical folksinger.

3. International Labor Defence, a Communist-controlled organization.

4. Dreiser had travelled to Harlan with his secretary. When local officials observed her entering his hotel room late at night, toothpicks were placed against the door. These were found undisturbed the following morning and Dreiser was subsequently indicted for adultery. Dreiser's defense was that he was in fact impotent.

Introduction to *Three Soldiers*

[*Three Soldiers* was originally published by George H. Doran Company in 1921.]

It is thirteen years since I finished writing this book. Reading it over to correct misprints in the original edition has not been exactly a comfortable task. The memory of the novel I wanted to write has not faded enough yet to make it easy to read the novel I did write. The memory of the spring of 1919 has not faded enough. Any spring is a time of overturn, but then Lenin was alive, the Seattle general strike had seemed the beginning of the flood instead of the beginning of the ebb, Americans in Paris were groggy with theatre and painting and music; Picasso was to rebuild the eye, Stravinski was cramming the Russian steppes into our ears, currents of energy seemed breaking out everywhere as young guys climbed out of their uniforms, imperial America was all shiny with the new idea of Ritz, in every direction the countries of the world stretched out starving and angry, ready for anything turbulent and new, whenever you went to the movies you saw Charlie Chaplin. The memory of the spring of 1919 has not faded enough yet to make the spring of 1932 any easier. It wasn't that today was any finer then than it is now, it's perhaps that tomorrow seemed vaster; everybody knows that growing up is the process of pinching off the buds of tomorrow.

Most of us who were youngsters that spring have made our beds and lain in them; you wake up one morning and find that what was to have been a springboard into reality is a profession, the organization of your life that was to be an instrument to make you see more and clearer turns out to be blinders made according to a predestined pattern, the boy who thought he was going to be a tramp turns out a nearsighted middleclass intellectual, (or a tramp; it's as bad either way). Professional deformations set in; the freeswimming young oyster fastens to the rock and grows a shell. What it amounts to is this: our beds have made us and the acutest action we can take is sit up on the edge of them and look around and think. They are our beds till we die.

Well you're a novelist. What of it? What are you doing it for? What excuse have you got for not being ashamed of yourself?

Not that there's any reason, I suppose, for being ashamed of the trade of novelist. A novel is a commodity that fulfills a certain need; people need to buy daydreams like they need to buy icecream or aspirin or gin. They even need to buy a

Three Soldiers (New York: Modern Library, 1932), v–ix. Reprinted in part in *Occasions and Protests* (1964).

pinch of intellectual catnip now and then to liven up their thoughts, a few drops of poetry to stimulate their feelings. All you need to feel good about your work is to turn out the best commodity you can, play the luxury market and to hell with doubt.

The trouble is that mass production involves a change in the commodities produced that hasn't been worked out yet. In the middleages the mere setting down of the written word was a marvel, something of that marvel got into the words set down; in the renaissance the printing press suddenly opened up a continent more tremendous than America, sixteenth and seventeenth century writers are all on fire with it; now we have linotype, automatic typesetting machines, phototype processes that plaster the world from end to end with print. Certainly eighty percent of the inhabitants of the United States must read a column of print a day, if it's only in the tabloids and the Sears Roebuck catalogue. Somehow, just as machinemade shoes aren't as good as handmade shoes, the enormous quantity produced has resulted in diminished power in books. We're not men enough to run the machines we've made.

A machine's easy enough to run if you know what you want it to do; that's what it's made for. The perfection of the machinery of publication (I mean the presses; obviously smalltime boom finance has made a morass of the booktrade) ought to be a tremendous stimulant to good work. But first the writer must sit up on the edge of his bed and decide exactly what he's cramming all these words into print for; the girlishromantic gush about selfexpression that still fills the minds of newspaper critics and publishers' logrollers, emphatically won't do any more. Making a living by selling daydreams, sensations, packages of mental itchingpowders, is all right, but I think few men feel it's much of a life for a healthy adult. You can make money by it, sure, but even without the collapse of capitalism, profit tends to be a wornout motive, tending more and more to strangle on its own power and complexity. No producer, even the producer of the shoddiest five and ten cent store goods, can do much about money any more; the man who wants to play with the power of money has to go out after it straight, without any other interest. Writing for money is as silly as writing for selfexpression. The nineteenth century brought us up to believe in the dollar as an absolute like the law of gravitation. History has riddled money value with a relativity more scary than Einstein's. The pulpwriter of today writes for a meal ticket, not for money.

What do you write for then? To convince people of something? That's preaching, and is part of the business of everybody who deals with words; not to admit that is to play with a gun and then blubber that you didn't know it was loaded. But outside of preaching I think there is such a thing as straight writing. A cabinet maker enjoys cutting a dovetail because he's a cabinetmaker; every type of work has its own vigor inherent in it. The mind of a generation is its speech. A writer makes aspects of that speech enduring by putting them in print. He whittles at the words and phrases of today and makes of them forms to set the mind of tomorrow's generation. That's history. A writer who writes straight is the architect of history.

What I'm trying to get out is the difference in kind between the work of James Joyce, say, and that of any current dispenser of daydreams. It's not that Joyce produces for the highbrow and the other for the lowbrow trade, it's that Joyce is working with speech straight and so dominating the machine of production, while the daydream artist is merely feeding the machine, like a girl in a sausage factory shoving hunks of meat into the hopper. Whoever can run the machine runs it for all of us. Working with speech straight is vigorous absorbing devastating hopeless work, work that no man need be ashamed of.

You answer that Joyce is esoteric, only read by a few literary snobs, a luxury product like limited editions, without influence on the mass of ordinary newspaper readers. Well give him time. The power of writing is more likely to be exercised vertically through a century than horizontally over a year's sales. I don't mean either that Joyce is the only straight writer of our time, or that the influence of his powerful work hasn't already spread, diluted through other writers, into many a printed page of which the author never heard of *Ulysses*.

None of this would need saying if we didn't happen to belong to a country and an epoch of peculiar confusion, when the average man's susceptibility to print has been first enflamed by the misty sentimentality of school and college English teachers who substitute "good modern books" for the classics, and then atrophied by the bawling of publishers' barkers over every new piece of rubbish dished up between boards. We write today for the first American generation not brought up on the Bible, and nothing as yet has taken its place as a literary discipline.

These years of confusion, when everything has to be relabeled and catchwords lose their meaning from week to week, may be the reader's poison, but they are the writer's meat. Today, though the future may not seem so gaily colored or full of changing hopes as it was thirteen years ago when I quit work on this novel that should have been worked over so much more, we can at least meet events with our minds cleared of some of the romantic garbage that kept us from doing clear work then. Those of us who have lived through have seen these years strip the bunting off the great illusions of our time, we must deal with the raw structure of history now, we must deal with it quick, before it stamps us out.

Provincetown,
June, 1932.

Whither the American Writer?
(A Questionnaire)

1.—Do you believe that American capitalism is doomed to inevitable failure and collapse?

If not, what reasons do you entertain as to why it will not collapse in the next decade?

2.—What position should the American writer take in the social crisis that confronts him?

    a. Should he keep out of it? If so why?

    b. Should he participate in it? If so why?

    c. Should he dedicate his art to its interpretation? If not, why not?

3.—What should be the relationship between a writer's work and the (radical) political party.

    (1) Should he strive to conjoin Art and Conscious propaganda?

    (2) Should he write what he feels regardless of the party's philosophy?

4.—Do you believe that becoming a communist deepens an artist's work?

    a. If so how?

    b. If not, why not?

    c. Would not becoming a socialist have the same effect?

    d. If not, why not?

5.—Which path will American literature in the next decade tend to follow, that of:

    (1) John Dos Passos and Michael Gold

    (2) Robinson Jeffers and Eugene O'Neill

    (3) Thornton Wilder

    (4) Cabell and Hergesheimer?

6.—Do you believe in the near possibility of a proletarian literature in America?

    a. If not, why not?

    b. Of what, in your opinion should proletarian literature consist?

Modern Quarterly, 6 (Summer 1932), 11–12.

John Dos Passos

1.—Sure, but the question is when. We've got the failure, at least from my point of view. What I don't see is the collapse.

> b. It might change pretty radically, and is changing into a centralized plutocracy like that of ancient Rome. Ten years seems a pretty short time for that to ripen and drop off the tree in. Of course if enough guys shake the tree . . .

2.—a. How the hell can he?

> b. It will participate in him, right in the neck.

As a producer and worker, any writer who's not a paid propagandist for the exploiting group (and most of them will be) will naturally find his lot with the producers.

> c. The writer's business is to justify God's ways to man as Milton said. For God read society, or history.

3.—(1) Art is an adjective not a noun.

> (2) It's his own goddam business. Some people are natural party men and others are natural scavengers and campfollowers. Matter of temperament. I personally belong to the scavenger and campfollower section.

4.—a. I don't see how a novelist or historian could be a party member under present conditions. The communist party ought to produce some good pamphleteers or poets. By the way, where are they?

> c. I personally think the socialists, and all other radicals have their usefulness, but I should think that becoming a socialist right now would have just about the same effect on anybody as drinking a bottle of near-beer.

5.—Better go to see a good crystal gazer.

6.—Theodore Dreiser is, and has been for many years, a great American proletarian writer. He has the world picture, the limitations, and the soundness of the average American worker, and expresses them darn well. Sherwood Anderson does too. So did Jack London. We have had a proletarian literature for years, and are about the only country that has. It hasn't been a revolutionary literature, exactly, though it seems to me that Walt Whitman's a hell of a lot more revolutionary than any Russian poet I've ever heard of.

> a. It seems to me that Marxians who attempt to junk the American tradition, that I admit is full of dryrot as well as sap, like any tradition, are just cutting themselves off from the continent. Somebody's got to have the size to Marxianize the American tradition before you can sell the American worker on the social revolution. Or else Americanize Marx.

> b. Stalin's phrase, "national in form, proletarian in content," is damn good, I think. The trouble is that "proletarian" is a word that means a band playing the Internationale, everything or nothing. Good writing was good writing under Moses and the Pharaohs and will be good writing under a soviet republic or a money oligarchy, and until the human race stops making speech permanent in print.

Four Nights in a Garden:
A Campaign Yarn

[Madison Square Garden in New York was the traditional site of final presidential campaign rallies. Dos Passos himself voted for William Z. Foster in the 1932 election.]

Foreword

It's curious that there has been so little comment anywhere on the most striking thing about the 1932 campaign: the resurrection of the boo. The only heartfelt expression of the campaign, so far as I can make out, was in that great rumbling, mouthfilling boo that has resounded from coast to coast.

Booing from the galleries gave the only life to the Republican convention in Chicago last June; it was the booing of McAdoo by Al Smith supporters as he stood waiting to speak with the nomination of Roosevelt buttoned up in his back pocket that gave the emotional climax to the Democratic festival a week later.[1] Mr. Hoover's campaign was widely punctuated by the great boo, in Detroit, in Des Moines, in St. Paul, even a little in Washington itself. We take our medicine tamely enough when it comes over the radio or the newsreel, but when we're in the actual presence of the controllers of our destinies, we boo. Something new in American politics.

Monday Night

So many people want to see Mr. Hoover that even Ninth Avenue is jammed, so crowded, indeed, that the cops can't get at the Communist demonstrators come to jeer, and their boos are lost in the shuffle of the enormous crowd. Ducking through the ranks of brave boys in blue who seem bent on not letting anybody, with or without a ticket, get into the hall, you can catch a glimpse of the placards of the unemployed council, peaceably massed under the L. After worming through five lines of cops I find myself in a push of people up a stairway and am catapulted into an aisle that comes to an abrupt end in a bunch of men and women mashed against a rail. Beyond their heads is the hall, a pink mist of faces and American flags and spotlights.

They are singing something about Hoover to the tune of *John Brown's Body*. The flags wave, the pink faces roar: ovation. A small, dumpling-shaped mannikin has appeared on the mannikin-packed platform in the middle of the hall. Through the glasses I can see as distinctly as in the newsreels, among the jowly faces of Republican magnates, the familiar jowls of Herbert Hoover. He's waving a hand in a short gesture, squinting from side to side into the glare. That man's not the boss type; more the confidential foreman.

A drunk behind me yells, "Rah for Roosevelt!" There's a considerable scuffle as two sweating ushers and a cop try to clear the aisle. In the middle of it I see a printed sheet drifting down from the balcony. I reach for it, but a little fat man beside me who looks strangely like a dick has grabbed it. His companion, an identical little fat man who also looks strangely like a dick, snatches it out of his hand. Over their shoulders I can read the headline, MR. HOOVER YOU'RE A LIAR.

The second little fat man who looks strangely like a dick folds it and puts it in his pocket. "Vat," says the man who first grabbed it, "you vill be taking from me my vatch next?"

At the other end of the hall a heckler is being ejected. That boo never had a chance. Everybody is quieting down. The Hoover mannikin has been set out by itself in a pool of white light. From where we jam against the rail we look intently into its left ear. A dry phonograph voice comes from the loudspeakers that hang from the shadowy ceiling in the center of the hall. Through the glasses I can see the mouth barely moving—the expressionless face when he turns our way; it's like watching a ventriloquist.

We are listening to Herbert Hoover's great speech in Madison Square Garden in the last week of the losing campaign of 1932.

After it's over, everybody piles out to catch trains, go home to bed, meet friends in speakeasies, drink coffee in one-arm lunch rooms. Streets still jammed. On a car stalled in the crowd down Eighth Avenue a group of young Jewish boys is chanting in unison, "We want Roosevelt." From brownstone steps on a cross street an elderly man is doing a big business selling *Daily Workers*. Nobody notices a few isolated sticks of red fire in the hands of organization stalwarts.

Motorcycle cops charge by, opening a lane in the crowd. A black limousine follows. To me it looks empty, but the skinny man on the curb beside me says he saw Hoover sitting in it.

"Sure he was in it, all hunched up wid a black robe thrown over him. Other cars all went out de oder way."

I'm carried across the street by the push of the crowd. Faintly from far away comes the sound of a boo that is echoed by the bubbling noise an old drunken Irishman is making in his throat as he lurches out of the way of a policeman's horse.

Wednesday Night

For the Socialists I sat in a box. The hall was full, but there was room to move around. The speakers were ranked in chairs on a platform at the end of the hall. The speeches were very long. Judge Panken[2] spoke a long time about the achievements of the Socialist government of Vienna. A Negro from uptown spoke warmly and well: socialism was the only hope for the Negro people. Mr. Broun[3] (in person) made a brief appearance.

Everybody agreed with what everybody said. The only novelty was the youngsters from Columbia, Hunter, City College, New York University who paraded around with placards, COLUMBIA VOTES SOCIALIST, and similar mottos. Things dragged so that Norman Thomas did not begin to speak until around eleven.

Here was a good speech, a handsome dignified presence, a forceful way of talking, smoothed by a faint reminiscence of the Episcopal pulpit, as if he were always on the edge of dropping into, "Dearly beloved brethren."

Norman Thomas made the outstanding personal success of the campaign. Strange that so many people balked when it came to voting for him.

When he first came on there was great animation among the cameramen. Flashlight bulbs flickered like heat lightning. He was posed with his hand in the air, holding a large red flag in the attitude of the resurrection angel, leaning over the desk and looking into the crowd.

His speech was well put together (I thought I could detect a faint cloud cross Mr. Hillquit's face at the mention of a capital levy).[4] Everybody wanted to hear the speech, but the Long Island Railroad and the Staten Island ferry are mightier than salvation by Socialism, and the audience was melting away all through it.

When we got out we looked for the cheering crowds outside so feelingly described by the speakers. A lot of people but no real jam, as there had been to see Hoover. Not even a boo.

Saturday Night

At the Democratic rally the attitude of the cops was quite different. Instead of keeping people out of the Garden, they were inviting them in. Again it was pink with American flags. A crowd, but not the eager jam there had been to see Hoover. A theatrical manager would have said, "A lot of paper in this house."

Outside of the customary ovation for Al Smith (as customary as the clapping whenever Dixie is played in New York), and a certain courtesy uproar for our next president, the only real emotion I could feel in the crowd was in the deep throaty boos that shook the loudspeakers every time Hoover's name was mentioned. There's no hatred so strong as the hatred of the crowd for its fallen hero.

The Democrats had a better band than the Republicans, but worse speeches. For a long time a procession of candidates appeared on the rostrum, making remarks that smacked somehow of a high school commencement, each depositing a small identical bouquet at the feet of John F. Curry.[5]

When they saw the face of Surrogate O'Brien[6] even the two Greeks sitting in front of me, whose main anxiety before had been to get hold of some of the American flags that were being distributed free, winced.

Not a word of Jimmy Walker, not a word of Acting Mayor McKee.[7] Regularity on every face including the benign countenance that Colonel Lehman[8] wears below his genteel bald head.

People were pretty well choked with regularity by the time Frank, preceeded by the Roosevelt smile, and Al with "raddio" on the tip of his tongue, came in to do their Damon and Pythias act.

Their speeches gained a certain dignity from the fact that they made no mention of the candidacy of Surrogate O'Brien and dropped no incense before the noble Democratic leader, Curry; but where are campaign speeches now?

Going out, it was a happy bunch of wardheelers and district leaders that hurried to their beer. Seabury was stopped,[9] McKee was on the leash, the Tammany van was safely included in the big Democratic parade to Washington. But the ordinary voter was thinking of Hoover. Boo.

Sunday Night

Where was the Forgotten Man in all these meetings, the citizen of Hooverville, the down and out guy you find wherever you look for a second under the thinning veneer of comfort and the American standard? Or is Al Smith right in saying he doesn't exist? Depends on what you mean by exist. Maybe a few of him went to stand outside and crane and boo at Hoover, but the people you rubbed elbows with in the hall were of the stiffest small respectability.

The forgotten man didn't go to the Socialist meeting, and he'd have been out of place among the Deserving Democrats. Where is he? Maybe it's the rain or the fact that it costs 41 cents to get in, or maybe it's something else, but he isn't in evidence at the Communist rally and celebration of the Fifteenth Anniversary of the October Revolution, either.

The minute you step in the hall, though, you feel there's more life in the air. People look younger and livelier than at the other meetings. When they sing the *Internationale* they sing it as if they meant it. The speeches are short, boiled down to sets of slogans. The meeting starts at a high tide of enthusiasm.

Cheers for the Communist Party and the triumphant workers and peasants of the U.S.S.R., boos for Hoover and for Norman Thomas and Morris Hillquit.

After the crowds of dignitaries of the other meetings, the wide empty platform, with its short row of speakers on spindly chairs and the big upsidedown 5 that's going to be used later in the pageant, gives you a feeling of almost ominous emptiness. The audience is cheerful, orderly, neatly dressed, fills all the seats; the ushers are lively-looking youngsters with wide red bands across their chests; the organized cheering is brisker than at the Socialist meeting, but the voices of the speakers are small and dry and far away.

Foster is sick, broken down under the strain of bucking a hostile continent.[10] His speech is going to be broadcast from his bedroom. The feeling of far-awayness and emptiness is enormously intensified. Is it that we're ten thousand miles from Moscow? When his voice starts coming over, the accent and intonation of a native American workingman fills the hall with warmth. Hathaway[11] has to finish reading it for him; his voice is American, too. It's a good speech, well put, with a New England canniness in the phrases that Foster has never quite lost, but it leaves the meeting with a sense of loneliness and abandonment that nothing can cure, not even the announcement that the cheering thousands outside are being beaten up by the cops. I looked outside; about as big a crowd as the Socialists had.

The chairman tells us to be sure to stay for the pageant and begins to read the results of the German elections. The German Communists have won two million votes, eleven seats in the Reichstag. We feel for a moment the tremendous intoxication with history that is the great achievement of Communist solidarity.

Then Earl Browder begins to speak; a well thought-out, carefully enunciated statement of the party's aims in the election. But there is something dry and pithy in his voice that fails to hold the crowd. Suburban train-schedules, the perennial hopeless struggle of the New Yorker to get ahead of the crush in the subway, begin to wield their enormous power. People are drifting out.

A series of resolutions is voted automatically and the pageant comes on. It's better planned than executed, but still it's better than pageants usually are. It describes the triumph of the Five Year Plan in Four. Where's Hooverville? Where's the Forgotten Man? Where's the great boo of 1932?

We walk out between triple rows of chesty cops. The cops look happy. It's their last mass-meeting before the election.

Epilogue

Democratic landslide. We have half a million Socialists; the Communists and Coin Harvey are about tied.[12] The National Broadcasting Company at enormous expense suspends its regular programs so that the GREAT RADIO AUDIENCE may get the full benefit of the election returns; this it considers a form of public service.

Well, was it all worth while? Is it the ineptitude of democracies? Or is it that our political machinery was conceived in terms of the stagecoach? Or is it that we like Hooverville and overcrowded jails and the third degree and pellagra and babies dying for lack of milk? Or is it all a capitalist plot hatched at the Bankers' Club? Is the great boo of 1932 the death rattle of rugged individualism or is it the first syllable of a new word? Is the forgotten man trying to remember?

Notes

1. Roosevelt and Al Smith were contesting for the Democratic nomination; William G. McAdoo had risen at the convention to announce California's support of Roosevelt, support which gave him the nomination.

2. Jacob Panken, a socialist and judge of the municipal court of New York.

3. Heywood Broun, a well-known newspaper columnist of the time.

4. Morris Hillquit, national chairman of the Socialist party and candidate for mayor of New York in the 1932 election.

5. Curry was leader of Tammany Hall, the Democratic party organization of New York.

6. John P. O. O'Brien, a court surrogate of New York City, was the Democratic candidate for mayor.

7. James J. Walker, a Democrat, had resigned as mayor of New York on 1 September 1932, after charges of corruption were made against his administration; Joseph V. McKee, also a Democrat, was then appointed acting mayor.

8. Herbert H. Lehman was lieutenant governor of New York and Democratic candidate for governor.

9. It was the work of Samuel Seabury's investigating committee that had led to the resignation of Mayor Walker.

10. William Z. Foster, Communist party candidate for president; Foster suffered a heart attack after the election.

11. Clarence Hathaway, editor of the Communist newspaper the *Daily Worker*.

12. The Communists received a little over 100 thousand votes. Coin Harvey, that is, W. H. Harvey, was the author of *Coin's Financial School* (1894), a tract arguing for the free coinage of silver. The candidate of the Liberty party in the presidential election of 1932, Harvey in fact received some 50,000 votes or half that of Foster.

Thank You, Mr. Hitler!

[Hitler was named chancellor of Germany in January 1933; the Nazi-rigged
Reichstag fire occurred on 27 February, and on 23 March the Reichstag voted
Hitler dictatorial powers.]

A good whang on the back of the head from a policeman's night-stick will often give
a man a sense of reality that nothing else will. That is, if it doesn't knock him clean
out of his wits. The events now taking place in Germany should give a salutary
awakening jolt to all Americans whose lives do not directly depend on the exploiting of their fellowmen. Fantastic, incredible are the reports in the metropolitan
press; through the formlessness of the correspondents' despatches you can feel the
crumbling of their world under them. But what's happening in Germany is neither
fantastic nor incredible. It is the norm of the world of industrial war, strikes, repression of labor unions, Scottsboro, Harlan, Boston of the Sacco-Vanzetti case, Washington of the Centralia massacre, California of the Southern Pacific, the Los Angeles
of Inspector Hines.[1]

The owning and exploiting groups in Germany, in this case the industrialists
and the junker landowners, found that the exploited were getting a little too powerful for them, so, out of the maniac elements always ready to be stirred up in any society, and the grotesque sediment of feudalism that still underlies the German
mind, they rigged this pretty little Nazi picnic for them. Our owners and exploiters,
our bankers and power magnates will gladly do the same thing for us whenever they
feel we need the dose. Suppose American finance had taken the trouble to put
money behind the Ku Klux Klan, to put the necessary press and advertising facili-
ties at its disposal: imagine the results. They didn't feel their power sufficiently chal-
lenged at the time to try it. But what about the next time? You can imagine Southern business men and professional Nordics reading Hitler's speeches at this
moment with a certain interest. . . . And when it comes to a necktie party our best
people can make the square-heads look like pikers.

Do we want to keep the thin veneer of "civilization" that the ever increasing
brutality of the conflicts of the industrial era makes daily more precarious? Do we
believe that human life has some chance of retaining a few of the decencies built up
through the centuries? Do we believe that it is possible to chain the madman of can-
nibal exploitation that underlies every human community? Americans who don't
want to live in a society of slaves can no longer look to Europe for moral countenance. That continent, between the false mustache of the Jew-baiter Hitler and
Mussolini's castor oil squint, has sunk back to the cultural level of the Thirty Years
War.

Common Sense, 1 (27 Apr. 1933), 13.

We can only rely on ourselves and our past and our future. Repudiation of Europe is, after all, America's main excuse for being. We haven't got much civilization; but some of it is our own and we can't afford to lose any of it. If it's going to be saved it'll be saved from underneath, by the workers and producers, manual and intellectual. The men on top have minds geared only for profit, for their own power and easy money. When they're sitting pretty, they'll loosen up with an occasional college or scientific foundation, but if they get into a jam, they'll wreck the works to save themselves as light-heartedly as the German industrialists and landowners set the fire of Hitlerism to destroy the frail decencies of German life.

It's the choice, as the old signer of the Declaration of Independence put it, of hanging together or else assuredly all hanging separately. Young men of the left, farmers, mechanics, railroad men, miners, garment workers, engineers, chemists, teachers, writers, thinkers . . . the tar and feathers are just around the corner!

Notes

1. Referred to are the Scottsboro Boys case of 1931, in which a group of Alabama blacks were railroaded on a rape charge; the conflict between coal miners and operators in Harlan County, Kentucky, in 1931; the execution of Sacco and Vanzetti in 1927; the 1919 Armistice Day gun battle between IWW and American Legion groups at Centralia, Washington; the control of California political and economic life by the Southern Pacific Railroad throughout the late nineteenth and early twentieth centuries; and the activities of the "red squad," a Los Angeles police unit led by Captain William Hynes (not *Hines*) during the late 1920s and early 1930s that specialized in the harassment of left-wing groups.

Doves in the Bullring

[Dos Passos was in Spain during the summer of 1932 to work on a book about the Spanish republic. King Alfonso had abdicated in April 1931, and a republic was established. In the election of 1931 a republican-socialist coalition won by a large majority. The "Socialist Minister" who spoke at the rally, as Dos Passos recalled in his autobiography, *The Best Times* (1966), was Fernando de los Rios.]

It was a hot Sunday morning in July. Members of the Socialist Party had come from all over northern Spain for the big meeting in Santander. They had come with their red gold-lettered trade-union banners, with their wives and children and lunches in baskets and leather canteens of wine. They had come in special trains and in busses and in mule carts and on bicycles and on foot. The bullring held about ten thousand; every seat was taken, agreeable mildly intelligent looking people mostly, mechanics, small storekeepers and farmers, shoemakers, tailors, clerks, school teachers, bookkeepers, a few doctors and lawyers; for this part of the world a quiet characterless crowd, but a big crowd.

The proceedings began by the singing of the *Internationale* by a bunch of school children in white dresses with red bows. They sang it very nicely. It passed the time while we waited for the speakers to arrive. The more important dignitaries seemed to be late. Then when the speakers filed onto the stand set up in the broiling sun in the center of the bullring, everybody sang the *Internationale* again, standing, red bunting waved.

Somebody may have gotten the idea that it would be effective to send up two white pigeons with red ribbons round their necks, but (maybe it was the heat or that the ribbons were tied too tight or that the pigeons were sick) the pigeons couldn't seem to fly, they fluttered groggily over the heads of the crowd, and crashed against the wall of the bullring. One of them managed to rise over the roof of the stands and disappeared into the sizzling sunny sky, but the other fell back into the crowd. People tried to coax it to fly, to give it a starting toss into the air but it was too weak. It finally came to rest in the middle of the bullring, right in front of the speaker's stand. It stayed there all through the speaking, a very sick looking pigeon indeed. I kept expecting it to flop over dead, but it just stood there teetering, with its head drooping.

The first speakers were local leaders, working men or trade-union officials. They spoke simply and definitely. The fight at home, as all over the world, was between socialism and fascism, the kind of order the workers and producers wanted and the kind of order the exploiting class wanted. The Socialist Party had no choice but to go ahead and install socialism right away (cheers) . . . through a dictatorship if need be (more cheers). When the deputy to the Cortes spoke he was a little

New Masses, 10 (2 Jan. 1934), 13. Reprinted in *In All Countries* (1934).

vaguer, he talked more about world conditions and the course of history and economic trends, but in the end he could think of no other way of finishing his speech than by promising socialism (wild cheers). But when the Socialist Minister spoke (cheers, cries of *Vivan los hombres honrados*, Hurray for honest men) things became very vague indeed. It was very hot by this time, the Socialist Minister was a stout man with a neat academic beard. Neither the stunning heat nor his obvious sweating under the black broadcloth suit introduced a single tremor into his long carefully modulated sentences. He used the classical form of address, subjunctives and future subjunctives and future conditional subjunctives and conditional subjunctive futures. He brought in history and literature, philosophy and the fine arts as if he was speaking to his students at the university, and he ended with a throaty oratorical period that quite took the audience's breath away. The gist of it was that the Socialist Party was the party of discipline and order and that the best thing sincere Socialists could do was stay at home and pay their dues and leave talk about attaining a socialist state in the interest of the workers to their betters, their political leaders who had the interest of all humanity at heart and understood the need for law and order and were honest men besides. The interests of all humanity demanded confidence and discipline from the Socialist Party.

When the speaking stopped, the sick pigeon was still teetering in the center of the bullring. With as much discipline, but perhaps with less confidence than they'd had that morning, the members of the Socialist Party grouped themselves for the parade through the center of town. Everybody was telling everybody else that the watchword was order.

By that time it was afternoon and very hot indeed. The Socialist Party members with their banners and their children and their lunch baskets marched without music through the center of the town to the beach, mild, straggling, well-mannered and a little embarrassed. All the cafés were full. The people sitting at the café tables were telling examples of the type of Spaniard who's hated in Mexico. A gachupin, pear-shaped men with gimlet eyes and predatory lines on their faces, jerkwater importers and exporters, small brokers, loan sharks, commission merchants, pawnbrokers, men who know how to make two duros grow where one had grown before, men who'd discovered the great principle that it's not work that makes money. They'd never been much before, mostly they'd had to scrape up their livings in America, at home the hierarchy, the bishops, the duchesses, the grandees and the Bourbons had high-hatted them off the map, but now the feudal paraphernalia was gone, the gachupinos were on top of the world. They sat silent at their tables looking at the embarrassed socialists straggling by. There are a great many socialists; it took them a long time to pass with their banners and their children and their red ribbons and their lunch baskets. The silent hatred of the people at the café tables was embarrassing to them. They filed on by as innocent as a flock of sheep in the wolf country.

The Business of a Novelist

[A review of *The Shadow Before*, by William Rollins, Jr.]

The business of a novelist is, in my opinion, to create characters first and foremost, and then to set them in the snarl of the human currents of his time, so that there results an accurate permanent record of a phase of history. Everything in a novel that doesn't work towards these aims is superfluous or, at best, innocent day-dreaming. If the novelist really creates characters that are alive, the rest follows by implication. A record of his time is fairly easy to establish for any writer with the knack of honest observation and a certain amount of narrative skill. It's the invention of characters, which is work of an entirely different order from the jotting down of true-to-life silhouettes and sketches of people, that sets the novelist apart from the story-teller or commentator. We have published in this country in the last fifteen years a good deal of excellent narrative writing and a number of fairly truthful stories, but the whole direction of American life tends so towards emphasis on the function of a person or event rather than on the person or on the event, that, in spite of all the gabble from college professors, editors and politicians about individualism, we hardly ever create in our fiction living and rounded characters. We do the snapshot, the silhouette, the true-to-life spittin' image very well, but that is as different from the real invention of a personality out of the tangle of functions, sense reactions, memories, habits that are observable in the people we know, as a photograph is different from the person photographed.

I suppose Henry James was the American writer who most concerned himself with the creation of characters, but he suffered so from New England obsessions and from the fear of the flesh out of which people are made that his characters are dim (though accurate) diagrams of frustrations. In "The Shadow Before," William Rollins has taken these obsessed frustrations, clothed them with flesh, placed them in the battle of their time and described them with a horrified gusto for suffering, hysterical, enjoying, nightmare-ridden man that is in the great line of Dostoevsky and Dickens. "The Shadow Before" is not a book about a textile strike; it is the living invention of certain people undergoing a textile strike. The strike, the town, the social struggle, are real and profoundly moving because the people are real, not the other way round, as is usual in novels describing topical events.

Harry Baumann, crazy with money and racial hypersensitiveness, the gutted New England family of the Thayers, Ramon the pushing immigrant, Lawrence

New Republic, 78 (4 Apr. 1934), 220.

Marvin the so completely American labor leader, Doucet the Canuck millhand, Micky, Olsen the bobbin boy, are intimately, bitterly, tenderly, hysterically created. You know them as if you'd lived with them in the same boarding house, worked in the same office or shop with them, gone to school with them. Things about them haunt your memory as they do about people you've known intimately in your own life, like the smell of the boy who sat next to you in class, his expression when he picked his nose, the slight cast or the twinkle in a friend's eye, the feel of somebody's handshake or of some kid's biceps when you roughhoused with him at recess. I don't know any recent book that brings you into such chokingly close contact with the people in it. Reading it you feel towards them the changing teetering balance of love and hate, attraction and repulsion, you feel for real people you know and meet every day.

This vivid, alive material, so full of sentimental pulsation, is organized almost like a piece of music. The wording appeals continually to the ear, so that your head becomes full of the throb; *thump* of the looms that fills the huge low buildings of the textile mills, and the lives of the people who work in them from bobbin boy to engineer and foreman. When you've read it you've been through a strike.

It's no use describing it. "The Shadow Before" is a first-rate novel; the thing to do is to read it.

The World We Live In

[A review of *The Land of Plenty*, by Robert Cantwell.]

If a visitor from Mars or Moscow, puzzled by the spineless confusion of everything he ran into in the United States in these years, wanted to get an idea of the show as a whole, I can't imagine a better book to put into his hands than Robert Cantwell's second novel, "The Land of Plenty." The book is written with a deadly devastating accuracy that takes the heart out of you, but when you finish it you know more than you did when you began it. It's extraordinary how much the book covers. The method of covering the whole show is to take a very small part of the show in a factory for lumber products and builders' supplies in a town on the Pacific slope and to describe minutely two incidents and the people involved in them. The first incident is the accidental shutting off of light and power when the night shift is working on a rush order the night before the Fourth of July. The second incident is the equally accidental seizure of the plant by the picket line in the strike that results from the confusion of the shutdown. The word accidental is not quite right here, because both accidents are sudden overturns of the balance of forces of which the structure of the book is made up. But after all that's what accidents are.

"Laugh and Lie Down," which seemed to me an excellent novel, was marred by a curious dead veil that hung over it, like the pall of smoke from the forest fires over his town that Robert Cantwell is so fond of describing. It was original, accurate, direct, but somehow the full implications of the story did not quite come through. "The Land of Plenty," in spite of the moments when the story seems lost in the actual confusions and uncertainties of our lives, comes through with terrific force. The thing is that the invention of a new way of looking at the world about us, a new and unique imaginative classification of the hodgepodge of consciousness, which is what first-rate writing has got to be, is not attained in a couple of years. Original stuff is not easy to write and often at first it's not easy to read. Original writing is discovery, but the balance between discovery and understanding has got to be maintained. If the writer goes too far toward discovery, nobody can read him. If he goes too far toward understanding, all he does is ring up on the cash register of the magazines the current clichés and the slogans of the day. The writer has to be continually transforming his tools while he's using them. It's natural enough that, just as in prizefighting and in trapeze work in the circus, it is the immediate meretricious effects and not the exhibitions of science that get the big hand.

New Republic, 79 (16 May 1934), 25.

"The Land of Plenty" is full of genuine, unshowy science. To get the difference between imaginative creation and successful journalism, all you have to do is to compare it with a work of clever reporting like "I Went to Pit College."[1] "The Land of Plenty" really molds your perceptions and leaves them different from what they were when you began it; when you have read it you have undergone the town and the forest fires, the noise and sweat and grease of the big plant on the mud flats, the feel of the dirty overalls and the tremor of the panels going under the saws, the slimy rocks round the piling at low tide, the uselessness of the outworn equipment of Fourth of July, State College, Saturday Evening Post ideas with which the bosses, the foremen and the workingmen are trying to cope with the monstrously efficient machines they run and are run by. Reading "I Went to Pit College" leaves you as far away from the miners it describes as you are from a bum you've felt sorry for and slipped a nickel to; "The Land of Plenty" puts you right in the shoes of the men and women who work in and exploit the lumber business. Some of it is not too hellishly agreeable to go through, but then discovery is not an entirely agreeable pastime. The reader is helped by some fine moments of catastrophic wartime humor, like the conversation between MacMahon the manager and Carl the efficiency man, when they both fall through the conveyor in the dark, or the dinner with Mr. Digby the big boss at the MacMahon's house after the riot. If the material of the book were completely clarified, and if the people—Robert Cantwell has a very good ear for the way people talk—were completely created, this would be a very great novel; as it is, it is an instructive and important attempt to work out a method of dealing truly and from the inside with industrial life. This is going to take longer than a day or a year to work out.

It seems to me that this novel is written more from the inside than any Russian book about a factory I've read. After all, we've been accustomed to machines longer than the Russians have and ought to begin to know something about them. To tell truly, and not romantically or sentimentally, about the relation between men and machines, and to describe the machine worker, are among the most important tasks before novelists today. The job has only begun. I think Robert Cantwell is as likely to discover a method of coping with machinery, which is now the core of human life, as any man writing today.

Notes

1. *I Went to Pit College* (1934) by Lauren Gilfillan (pseudonym of Harriet Gilfillan), a first-person account of life in a Pennsylvania mining town.

The World's Iron, Our Blood, and Their Profits

[A review of *Merchants of Death*, by H. C. Engelbrecht and F. C. Hanighen;
Iron, Blood and Profits, by George Seldes; and "Arms and the Man,"
an article in pamphlet form from *Fortune* magazine.]

Since whoever reads these words, man or woman, young or old, stands an excellent chance of meeting his end in the next war, either by poison gas, shell fragment or machine gun bullet, any description of the preparation of the machinery of slaughter ought to be of pretty direct and personal interest to everybody. *Merchants of Death* and *Iron, Blood and Profits* cover about the same ground. Both books contain a mass of valuable material that so far as I know has not been published before in English. Neither book is the careful analytic study of the armaments business that we so much need but both are worth reading. The *Fortune* pamphlet is a fine summary of the main points of the European situation, but neglects entirely the American end. I wish I knew some way of putting one of these books in every college classroom and every voting booth in the country. If every American who could read and write could get a tenth of these facts into his head, the work of the warmakers would be made considerably more difficult. They are particularly to be recommended to the readers of Hearst papers.

The armament trade is not the whole story of the forces that are making for war but it is the spearhead of the profits system. In it the growing powers of nationalism and monopolistic business reach their climax in a logical absurdity. The picture of nations allowing their citizens to sell munitions to the enemy with which to blow their own armies to hell is a great cosmic joke. It is a joke that greatly prolonged the last war and in the next is likely to cost many millions of men their lives. The point of the joke is getting clearer every day. The point is that nationalism, even in its latest madhouse frenzies under Mussolini and Hitler, is still, like advertising, an arm of big business. Nations as we know them today, were the invention of business and it is natural that business should still consider itself slightly above patriotism and that the strongest international should still be the international of profits. Randolph Bourne pointed out that war was the health of the state, a study of the armament business indicates that in war the health of the state is somewhat neglected in favor of the health of the profit system.

This does not mean that the Schneiders and the Krupps and the DuPonts have ever met in a room to conspire to bring new wars on the human race, or have agreed on any explicit system for squeezing the maximum of profits out of an existing war. The point is that they don't need to. The great businesses, like the feudal lords of

Student Outlook, 3 (Oct. 1934), 17–18.

the middle ages, exist in a continual state of war among themselves, but being similar organisms they naturally behave in a similar way towards the societies on which they prey (or as a business man would put it, from which they exact profits in return for valuable services). The men running the armament business may very well be genial and patriotic gentlemen, very kind to their chauffeurs and butlers, who wouldn't hurt a fly themselves, but the organic logic of business makes it necessary for them to do everything possible to foment wars to liven up the trade; this makes them more dangerous to society than all the firebugs and homicidal maniacs in the world. It is largely due to their propaganda that the greatest patriot, today, is popularly conceived to be the man most willing to see his fellow citizens maimed and strangled in war. If it were not so prevalent, this attitude would seem crazy to the bloodthirstiest moron in a hospital for the criminal insane.

The story in outline is this: in Europe the most powerful coherent force in politics, finance and the press is the net of overlapping groups of steel and iron trusts in France and Germany. Four years of the bloodiest war in history were not enough to break up the unity of the ironmasters. It is thoroughly proved that businessmen of all the belligerent countries kept up a trade with the enemy in chemicals, nickel, copper and foodstuff up to very nearly the end of the last war. After the peace the Krupps had the effrontery to sue the Armstrong-Vickers company for their royalty on the German grenade cap the British firm had been using on its products all through the war. By common consent the mines and smelters in the Pas de Calais, on the French side, and the Bassin de la Briey on the German side of the lines were not shelled or bombarded, though neither belligerent had scruples about shelling and bombing civilian populations. After all what's a man worth? The pittance he can produce by his work. You can't buy and sell a cathedral. A mine or a smelter is worth real money. That's all ancient history. The danger to Western civilization at present is the subsidizing of reactionary and militarymad politicians and demagogues by the steel and armament interests. Thyssen and Hugenberg and some French interests subsidized Hitler in Germany, and the Comité des Forges (the public relations end of the French Steel combination) is spending a great deal of money to start a similar movement in France. In England the armament firms are not quite so completely in the saddle, but armament and shipbuilding interests form the very core of the governing class. The leaders of these firms, whose whole lives have been geared to nothing but the acquisition of money and power at any cost, can't help wanting war and working for it. If they were not the most ruthless and predatory members of their class they wouldn't have gotten themselves into the positions of power they now occupy. Any list of yearly dividends will give you the difference in their profits in war years and peace years. The armament makers hope for war just the way the farmers want spring rains. They'd just as soon have it in China as in their own back yard, but war they've got to have. The chances seem very good that they will have their wish.

The situation in America is harder to make out clearly, partly because we are nearer to it and partly because it is more difficult and dangerous to get the facts. Even the American businessman is willing to see the beam in the European business man's eye.

However, Mr. Shearer, the man who boasts he broke up the Geneva disarmament conference, was kind enough to shed a little light on the subject when he sued the shipbuilding interests that had sent him to Geneva at $25,000 a year for

$250,000 more that he felt he was entitled to as a result of his great success.[1] There is no question that the steel and shipbuilding interests are working tooth and nail against disarmament. War orders are the real gravy in the business of the great monopolies. Of all the current rackets patriotism pays the best. You can hardly turn on the radio without hearing some Navy League speaker denouncing pacifists. With the warmakers occupying all the avenues that direct people's minds and destinies it is surprising that we are still at peace at this moment. Possibly it's only the fear of the extreme effective deadliness of the methods industrial science, the overpowerful slave of capitalism, has perfected that keeps the gentlemen in the director's office from forcing the world once more into that supreme heaven of capitalist wellbeing, when profits are in the hundred percents and every protesting voice can be muzzled and labor kept in line by the firing squad, war.

As things are now it is not only the makers of machine guns and shells who are in the armament business. Any chemical or dye plant is a potential poison gas factory. The whole metallurgical industry, the cotton goods industry, the growers of cotton and foodstuffs stand to make more money in war than in peace time. Add to that the fact that industrial peace furnishes such a miserably unsatisfactory livelihood, if any livelihood at all, that many thousands of young men would be ready to go to war at the drop of a hat for the excitement and a dollar a day and the slum and the uniform. The logic of the profit system's need for war is so convincing that it seems a miracle that we have any peace at all.

Against this huge agglomeration of thrones, principalities and powers, what are the forces? You have the inertia of the naked and helpless individual who wants to make his living, satisfy his needs, raise his family, be well thought of by his neighbors, and the social instinct that has been slowly woven out of centuries of struggles and revolts and sacrifices, a frail web of compulsions and inhibitions that makes for common action in the face of common needs. That's what people mean when they speak of order and civilization. It's frail enough, but its organic existence is proved by the extraordinary hysterical and lunatic manifestations that follow the destruction of the feeling of human solidarity. Anybody who remembers the state of mind of noncombatants in the last war will admit that their mental condition was such that in peace time they would have been shut up in asylums as homicidal maniacs. Humanly speaking it's almost a relief to think that in the next war there won't be any non combatants.

Of course the nationalists will tell you that the feelings of solidarity and self-sacrifice induced in a nation at war are the finest flower of the social instinct. The trouble with their argument is that industrial war, like industrial peace, is a business of profit. Nationalism, under the profit system is the supreme imposition on human credulity. The doughboy in khaki and the machine operative in overalls are both grinding out their blood and their muscle for the power the glory and the dividends of the gentlemen in the director's office. I don't say that war would be impossible in a socialized state where everybody would get what profit there was, but it would be much less likely for the reason that war, while it is the apotheosis of money profits, is admittedly the destruction of real wealth. A socialized society would be interested in building up and conserving its wealth, instead of burning it up for the benefit of the gentlemen in the director's office. This for the moment is beside the point. The immediate question facing every man and woman in the organized world is how they shall save their lives and their children's lives from the exploitation, in war and peace, of the gentlemen in the director's office.

To fight an enemy you've got to know him. As the great monopolies that control oil, steel, aluminum, textiles, have to struggle harder and harder for their profits, they will have to impose scarcity and war and to destroy the last vestiges of the forms of commercial democracy. While there is any liberty of publication left the facts about the making of wars should be spread far and wide. These books are a valuable beginning. Somebody ought to follow them up by a serious analytic study of the whole business. But knowing the facts is only half the battle. You must know how to act on them. If a man finds himself locked up in a room with an angry gorilla it doesn't help him very much to know the animal's scientific name. Still he's better off than if he were under the illusion that the gorilla was a benevolent old gentleman in a Palm Beach suit.

Notes

1. William Shearer had lobbied against disarmament at the Geneva Conference on the Limitation of Naval Armaments in 1927 on behalf of American shipbuilding interests.

Two Views of the Student Strike

[A national student strike to protest against war occurred on 12 April 1935. Dos Passos' contribution to *Student Outlook* on the strike accompanied a contribution by Dr. T. W. Macquarrie, president of San Jose State Teachers College.]

April 6, 1917,[1] is certainly a date to be commemorated. It marks one of the great steps back from the hope and promise of American democracy.

In the last eighteen years, in spite of the enormous advance in industrial technique, civilization, measured as we have been accustomed to measure it, in the terms of man's humanity to man, has steadily retrograded, until now we find ourselves with the whole battle for freedom to fight again. Hardly a vestige remains of the elementary human rights that the history of the Western peoples has been one long struggle to establish.

The real aim of militarism in war and peace is, always has been, and always will be, oppression.

War is the last line of defense for the entrenched interests that arrogate to themselves the name of the nation they exploit.

The next war, more than any other, will be a war against the mass of the people in behalf of monopolies drunk with financial power. It will bring with it the complete obliteration of personal liberty.

Every inch of ground we lose, every infringement of human dignity we allow will make the fight to recover those hopes of progress and the peaceful organization of society that seemed so attainable, to Americans at least, a generation ago, harder and longer and more tragic.

Soon, the free man's right to speak out will have been gassed out of existence by the barrage of venal propaganda from the screen, the radio and the commercial press, or stamped out by martial law. Before it is too late we must make every effort to stir up the memory of the original aims and impulses of democratic government. For young men and women it is a battle for life as well as for everything that makes life worth while. If anything can bring the country to its senses their protest can.

Notes

1. The date America entered the First World War.

Student Outlook, 3 (Apr. 1935), 5.

The Writer As Technician

[The American Writers' Congress, a convention of radical writers, took place on 26–27 April 1935 in New York. Although Dos Passos did not attend the convention, he contributed "The Writer As Technician" to the volume devoted to addresses delivered at the convention.]

Anybody who can put the words down on paper is a writer in one sense, but being able to write no more makes a man a professional writer than the fact that he can scratch up the ground and plant seeds in it makes him a farmer, or that he can trail a handline overboard makes him a fisherman. That is fairly obvious. The difficulty begins when you try to work out what really distinguishes professional writing from the average man's letters to his family and friends.

In a time of confusion and rapid change like the present, when terms are continually turning inside out and the names of things hardly keep their meaning from day to day, it's not possible to write two honest paragraphs without stopping to take crossbearings on every one of the abstractions that were so well ranged in ornate marble niches in the minds of our fathers. The whole question of what writing is has become particularly tangled in these years during which the industry of the printed word has reached its high point in profusion and wealth, and, to a certain extent, in power.

Three words that still have meaning, that I think we can apply to all professional writing, are discovery, originality, invention. The professional writer discovers some aspect of the world and invents out of the speech of his time some particularly apt and original way of putting it down on paper. If the product is compelling, and important enough, it molds and influences ways of thinking to the point of changing and rebuilding the language, which is the mind of the group. The process is not very different from that of scientific discovery and invention. The importance of a writer, as of a scientist, depends upon his ability to influence subsequent thought. In his relation to society a professional writer is a technician just as much as an electrical engineer is.

As in industrialized science, we have in writing all the steps between the complete belt conveyor factory system of production and one man handicraft. Newspapers, advertising offices, moving picture studios, political propaganda agencies, produce the collective type of writing where individual work is indistinguishable in the industrial effort. Historical and scientific works are mostly turned out by the laboratory method by various coworkers under one man's supervision. Songs and ballads are often the result of the spontaneous feelings of a group working together. At present stories and poems are the commonest output of the isolated technician.

Henry Hart, ed., *American Writers' Congress* (New York: International Publishers, 1935), 78–82. Reprinted in part in *Occasions and Protests* (1964).

Any writer who has ever worked in any of these collective undertakings knows the difficulties of bucking the routine and the office-worker control that seems to be an inseparable part of large industrial enterprises, whether their aims are to make money or to improve human society. It is a commonplace that business aims, which are to buy cheap and sell dear, are often opposed to the aims of the technician, which are, insofar as he is a technician and not a timeserver, the development of his material and of the technical possibilities of his work. The main problem in the life of every technician is to secure enough freedom from interference from the managers of the society in which he lives to be able to do his work. As the era of free competition gives way to that of monopoly, with the corresponding growth of office-worker control, inner office intrigue and other stifling diseases of bureaucracy, it becomes increasingly hard for the technician to get that freedom. Even in a country that is organizing to build for socialism, instead of for the growth of the wealth and power of a few bosses, the need for functional hierarchies on an enormous scale and the difficulty of keeping the hierarchies alive through popular control, makes the position of the technician extremely difficult, because, by his very function, he has to give his time to his work instead of to "organizational problems." When you add the fact that the men behind the desks in the offices control the police power, indirectly in this country, but directly in many others, which can at the whim of some group of officials, put a man in jail or deprive him of his life and everything that makes life worth living, you can see that the technician, although the mechanical means in his power are growing every day, is in a position of increasing danger and uncertainty.

The only name you can give a situation in which a technician can do his best work, and be free to give rein to those doubts and unclassified impulses of curiosity that are at the root of invention and discovery and original thinking, is liberty. Liberty in the abstract is meaningless outside of philosophical chessgames. Then too the word has taken on various misleading political colorations. In America it means liberty for the exploiter to cut wages and throw his workers out on the street if they don't like it; in most of the newspapers of the world it means something connected with the privileges of the commercial classes. But, underneath, it still has a meaning that we all know, just as we know that a nickel is a nickel even if the Indian and the buffalo have been rubbed off. A writer, a technician, must never, I feel, no matter how much he is carried away by even the noblest political partisanship in the fight for social justice, allow himself to forget that his real political aim, for himself and his fellows, is liberty.

A man can't discover anything, originate anything, invent anything unless he's at least morally free, without fear or preoccupation insofar as his work goes. Maintaining that position in the face of the conflicting pulls of organized life demands a certain amount of nerve. You can see a miniature of the whole thing whenever a man performs even the smallest technical task, such as cleaning a carburetor, or taking a bead on a target with a rifle. His state of mind is entirely different from that of the owner of the car who wants to get somewhere, or of the man himself a second before he put his eye to the sight, all of a fluster to win the match or in a panic of fear lest his enemy shoot him first. This state of mind, in which a man is ready to do good work, is a state of selfless relaxation, with no worries or urges except those of the work at hand. There is a kind of happiness about it. It is much nearer the way an ordinary day-laborer feels than it is the way a preacher, propagandist or swivelchair organizer feels. Anybody who has seen war knows the astonishing difference between the attitude of the men at the front, who are killing and dying, and that of the atrocity-haunted citizenry in the rear.

At this particular moment in history, when machinery and institutions have so outgrown the ability of the mind to dominate them, we need bold and original thought more than ever. It is the business of writers to supply that thought, and not to make of themselves figureheads in political conflicts. I don't mean that a writer hasn't an obligation, like any other citizen, to take part if he can in the struggle against oppression, but that his function as a citizen and his function as a technician are different, although the eventual end aimed at may in both cases be the same.

To fight oppression, and to work as best we can for a sane organization of society, we do not have to abandon the state of mind of freedom. If we do that we are letting the same thuggery in by the back door that we are fighting off in front of the house. I don't see how it is possible to organize effectively for liberty and the humane values of life without protecting and demanding during every minute of the fight the liberties of investigation, speech and discussion that are the greatest part of the ends of the struggle. In any organization a man gives up his liberty of action. That is necessary discipline. But if men give up their freedom of thought what follows is boss rule thuggery and administrative stagnation. It is easy to be carried away by the temporary effectiveness of boss rule, but it has always ended, in small things and in great, in leaving its victims stranded bloodless and rotten, with all the problems of a living society of free men unsolved. The dilemma that faces honest technicians all over the world to-day is how to combat the imperial and bureaucratic tendencies of the groups whose aims they believe in, without giving aid and comfort to the enemy. By the nature of his function as a technician, the writer finds himself in the dangerous and uncomfortable front line of this struggle.

In such a position a man is exposed to crossfire and is as likely to be mowed down by his friends as his enemies. The writer has to face that. His only safety lies in the fact that the work of an able technician cannot be replaced. It is of use and pleasure to mankind. If it weren't for that fact, reluctantly recognized, but everywhere and always recognized, the whole tribe of doubters, inventors and discoverers would have been so often wiped out that the race would have ceased to produce types with those peculiar traits.

It's an old saying, but a very apt one, that a writer writes not to be saved but to be damned.

I feel that American writers who want to do the most valuable kind of work will find themselves trying to discover the deep currents of historical change under the surface of opinions, orthodoxies, heresies, gossip and the journalistic garbage of the day. They will find that they have to keep their attention fixed on the simple real needs of men and women. A writer can be a propagandist in the most limited sense of the word, or use his abilities for partisan invective or personal vituperation, but the living material out of which his work is built must be what used to be known as the humanities: the need for clean truth and sharply whittled exactitudes, men's instincts and compulsions and hungers and thirsts. Even if he's to be killed the next minute a man has to be cool and dispassionate while he's aiming his gun.

There is no escaping the fact that if you are a writer you are dealing with the humanities, with the language of all the men of your speech of your generation, with their traditions of the past and their feelings and perceptions. No matter from how narrow a set of convictions you start, you will find yourself in your effort to probe deeper and deeper into men and events as you find them, less and less able to work with the minute prescriptions of doctrine; and you will find more and more that you are on the side of the men, women and children alive right now against all the contraptions and organizations, however magnificent their aims may be, that bedevil them; and that you are on the side, not with phrases or opinions, but really and truly, of liberty, fraternity, and humanity. The words are old and dusty and hung with the dirty bunting of a thousand crooked orations, but underneath they are still sound. What men once meant by these words needs defenders to-day. And if those who have, in all kinds of direct and devious ways, stood up for them throughout history do not come out for them now to defend them against the thuggery of the bosses and the zeal of the administrators, the world will be an even worse place for men, women and children to live in than it is at present.

Grosz Comes to America

In the last twenty-five years a change has come over the visual habits of Americans, something like what must have happened to Winslow Homer when, after half a lifetime grinding out stifflydrawn imaginings of current events as a newspaper artist, he suddenly broke out in his watercolors into a new world of sunlight and clouds and ocean. From being a wordminded people we are becoming an eyeminded people.

As I remember how things were when I was a child, the people my parents knew had hardly any direct visual stimulants at all. There were engravings on the walls and illustrated magazines and reproductions of old masters even, but the interest in them was purely literary. The type of drawing current in the late nineteenth century had such meager conventions of representation that it tended to evoke a set of descriptive words instead of a direct visual image. I am sure that my parents enjoying a view from a hill say, were stimulated verbally, remembering a line of verse or a passage from Sir Walter Scott, before they got any real impulse from the optic nerve. Of course there were a few oil paintings in the upstairs bathroom, those mysterious little works done by forgotten members of the family that you used to find in the dark upper halls of family residences left over from the nineteenth century, little landscapes that people had been reluctant to throw away because they were "handpainted" oils, but that were kept out of sight in the less seen parts of the house. As I remember them in my mother's house in Washington they tended to include a millwheel and a patch of woolly blue water towards the center of the canvas. They meant a lot to children but no grown person ever thought about them: the graphic arts consisted of newspaper and magazine illustrations, illustrations of literature in a book or on the wall, portraits and old masters.

I must have been well along in college before I looked at a picture directly, and then it was because I'd been reading Whistler's *Gentle Art of Making Enemies* and went into the Boston Art Museum to see what his painting was like. It must have been at about the same time that I first heard the music of Debussy. My generation in college was full of literary snob-admiration for the nineties. I can still remember the fashionable mood of gentle and European snob-melancholy the Whistler pastels produced, with their little scraps of red and yellow and green coming out of the dovecolored smudge. At that I think the titles affected me more than the pictures.

Esquire, 6 (Sept. 1936), 105, 128, 131. Reprinted in *Interregnum. . .*, by George Grosz, ed. Caresse Crosby (New York: Black Sun Press, 1936) and *Occasions and Protests* (1964).

Still I must have been somewhat stirred visually because I seem to remember getting hold of a box of pastels and making dovecolored smudges of my own. The trouble was that it soon became obvious that almost any combination of pastel blurs was as agreeable to look at as any other, and my enthusiasm for that sort of thing began to flag.

The Armory Show was a real jolt,[1] though I can't remember any picture I saw there, and it is associated in my mind with a torn yellowbacked volume of Van Gogh's letters a friend lent me along with a very bad translation of *Crime and Punishment*. In spite of all the kidding about the *Nude Descending Stairs*, I didn't recognize it when I saw it again at the Modern Museum in New York. The most I got from cubism at that time was a tingling feeling that a lot of odd things I didn't know about were going on in the world. I imagine I still thought Andrea del Sarto, of whose works we had photographs in the library at home, real top notch in the painting line, that is if I thought about the matter at all. Through George Moore I'd learned the names of the French impressionists but thought of them as literary figments like the Goncourts. The first time I was in Madrid the Velasquez paintings gave me most pleasure. I remember being rather scared by the Goyas and Grecos in the Prado. One rainy day in Toledo, I did go in to see the Count of Orgaz,[2] though, and it probably began to bite in without my knowing it.

Right after that, in short glimpses of Paris during the war, I found myself walking up and down the rue de la Boètie and the little streets on the left bank looking at pictures in the windows of the few dealers that weren't bolted and barred behind iron shutters, and really seeing them. Then in Italy, on leave the next winter, the frescoes on the walls became suddenly more important than anything else.

What started me off was going into Giotto's chapel in Padua one fine wintry day after an airraid. A big domed church was burning on the other side of town sending up one long straight plume of smoke. The chapel was all banked up with sandbags and the fellow I was with and I were both eating some sort of round sausages of chocolate and filbertnuts, a Paduan specialty that seemed delicious to us at the time, and as we looked up at the walls, standing there with our caps in our hands, shivering in the cellar chill, we felt that feeling of great permanence. Perhaps it was enhanced by the knowledge that the chapel might be blown to hell the next moonlight night. It was a feeling of the permanence of the perfectly imagined forms colored and spaced with such sober magnificence. We felt good all day afterwards.

After that the appetite for painting grew fast. On leave I did hardly anything but look at frescoes and paintings, discovering Piero della Francesca and Uccello and the *Last Judgement* in the Orvieto Cathedral and the City Hall in Siena and the cemetery walls in Pisa and the paintings in the catacombs at Rome. Back in Paris after the armistice there were Cézannes to see and the bold inventions of Picasso and Juan Gris and the feeling that great days were beginning. Since then in spite of my early training being verbal I tend to take a painting visual end first.

I think something of the sort has happened to many Americans of my generation, and even in a greater degree to the generations younger than us, so that an appetite and a taste for painting is growing up in this country very fast. Display advertising and the movies, though they may dull the wits, certainly stimulate the eyes. In New York the visual attack of the showwindows of Fifth Avenue stores almost equals in skill and scope that of the windows of the picture dealers on the Rue de la Boètie in the heyday of the school of Paris. It's not entirely because we are considered the freest spenders that artists who find Europe more and more impossible to live in tend to settle in the U.S. There is growing up here—fifteen years ago how we wise guys would have sniggered at the suggestion—the sort of previous atmosphere of appetite and enthusiasm that might make great work possible if any painters should be found who were men enough to do it.

Thus far outside of purely domestic painting, whittling and ironwork, of which those little bathroom pictures I spoke about were the last representatives, American art (always excepting Winslow Homer) has been first English provincial, then French impressionist provincial, school of Paris provincial and now it leans towards becoming Mexican provincial. We haven't yet done anything important in that direction. Young Americans with a taste for that sort of thing have felt that they had to go abroad somewhere to do it and have come home devout faddists, useless to themselves and to the culture of their country. But now in the last few years Europe (due to the abundant sprouting of the dragons' teeth the old men so sanctimoniously sowed round the green baize at Versailles) instead of being the land of liberty and art young middlewestern highschool students used to dream about, has become so stifling to any useful and rational human effort that suddenly the tables are turned. In the arts as in science America has become the refuge of the traditions of western European culture.

One can't help wondering whether we'll muff our opportunity the way our bankers (provincials too) muffed their chance to take the financial primacy away from London after the armistice.

Anyway there's a Chinaman's chance that we may come to something. The fact that firstrate men who can't live in their own countries feel that they can breathe here makes you feel good about the country. The fact that George Grosz, the great visual satirist of our time, has come to live here, has taken out papers and considers himself an American makes you feel good about the country.

It was in Paris on the Boulevard St. Germain some time during the Peace Conference that I first saw a German booklet of drawings by Grosz. It must have been in a bookstore, I suppose, but I somehow connect it in my memory with a magnificent colored drawing of cirrhosis of the liver in the window of the Society for the Suppression of Alcoholism opposite the old abbey. I suppose it was because what Grosz was representing was cirrhosis of nineteenth century civilization.

It's hard to reimagine the feelings of savage joy and bitter hatred we felt during that spring. We were still in uniform. We still had to salute officers, to go into outoftheway bars to talk to our friends who happened to be wearing the bettergrade uniforms. But with the armistice each one of us had been handed his life back on a platter. We knew what dead men looked like and we weren't dead. We had all our arms and legs. Some of us had escaped G.O. 42.[3]

The horsechestnuts were in bloom. We knew that the world was a lousy pesthouse of idiocy and corruption but it was spring. We know that in all the ornate buildings, under the crystal chandeliers, under the brocaded hangings the politicians and diplomats were brewing poison, fuddled old men festering like tentcaterpillars in a huddle of red tape and gold braid. But we had hope. What they were doing was too obvious and too clear. It was spring. The first of May was coming. We'd burn out the tentcaterpillars.

We knew two things about the world (two things that most of us have since forgotten), we knew that unorganized industrial life was becoming a chamber of horrors, and we knew that plain men, the underdogs we rubbed shoulders with, didn't go out of their way to harm each other as often as you might expect, that they had a passive courage the topdogs had never heard about and certain ingrained impulses towards social cohesiveness, the common good. Loafing around in little old bars full of the teasing fragrances of history, dodging into alleys to keep out of sight of the M.P.'s, seeing the dawn from Montmartre, talking bad French with taxidrivers, riverbank loafers, workmen, *petites femmes*, keepers of *bistros*, *poilus* on leave, we eagerly collected intimations of the urge towards the common good. It seemed so simple to burn out the tentcaterpillars that were ruining the orchard. The first of May was coming.

We felt boisterous and illmannered. Too many sergeants had told us to wipe that smile off your face, too many buglers had gotten us out of our blankets before we'd slept our sleep out. The only restraint that had survived the war was this automatic social cohesiveness among men that seemed to come on whenever they slipped for a moment out from under the thumbs of the bosses. If the old edifice crashed the bosses who lived in all the upper stories would go with it. They had already shaken the foundations with their pretty war, their brilliant famines. Their diligent allies, typhus, cholera, influenza were working for them still. Now their peace would finish the job. A couple of heaves and down she'll go. When the dust clears we'll see whether men and women are the besotted brutes the gold braided bosses say they are.

Finding Grosz's drawing was finding a brilliant new weapon. He knew how the old men, the fat men looked. He drew them as they grewsomely were. Looking at his work was a release from hatred, like hearing wellimagined and properly balanced strings of cusswords.

May first came and went. And another. And another. Outside of Russia the edifice trembled but it still stood. In the great halls at Versailles, Locarno, Geneva generals and dignitaries clustered in front of the camera to pin medals on each other, seemingly unconscious of the rotten smell of corpses from the cellar.

At home we went in for normalcy and Teapot Dome.[4] We kept cool with Coolidge. The automotive boom began. America was filling the world with jazz and Ford cars and electric iceboxes. Americans poured over Europe to buy up artobjects cheap in the devaluated currencies. Americans still felt whole enough to make wisecracks about the bloody farce. We felt we had good comfortable seats for the last act of the European tragedy.

Those who didn't have any seats at all, who were actors in fact, felt differently. George Grosz's drawings will show the future how Europeans felt while their culture died of gas gangrene, just as Goya's drawings show us the agony of Europe a century before under the last convulsive stamping of the ironshod heels of the feudal church and the feudal army. Their impression is not verbal; (you don't look at the picture and have it suggest a title and then have the title give you the feeling) but through the eye direct, by the invention of ways of seeing.

The impact naturally was much sharper on Europeans who came of age during the war years than on Americans and sharpest of all on Germans. The generation of Germans who had begun their schooling in the nineties and were in their twenties when war broke out found themselves under a pressure almost unequalled in European history. They grew up in a respectable, easygoing, beerdrinking, sausageeating, natureloving world where everybody went to hear the band play in the *tiergarten*

Sundays and was delighted to shine the shoes of his superiors, and if he didn't like it he could go to America. They had hardly begun respectfully and agreeably to occupy the situations to which God and the Kaiser had called them when they were goosestepping to the railroad station and in another fortyeight hours were being slashed to pieces by the French seventyfives.

George Grosz was born in Berlin in '93 and spent most of his boyhood at Stolp in Pomerania. His parents were Prussian Lutherans. His life developed at the exact point of greatest strain in the European social structure, in the more impoverished section of the middle class. His drawings must have shown promise in school because he was sent to Dresden to learn academic pencilwork and charcoal from casts of the antique. He started making his living by drawing for comic papers. He studied in Berlin. The summer of 1913 he spent in Paris.

Grosz had too much Prussian and too much Lutheran in his bones to feel at home in Paris, but he must have been stirred by the fact that the full tide of European painting was running through the less prosperous studios of Montmartre and Montparnasse. *Bohème* was attaining real eminence under Guillaume Appolinaire, its last poet and king. Out of student traditions of the cult of oddity, the romantic libertarianism of *les bourgeois à la lanterne*, scraps of science and anthropology, and the pressures on sensitive young men of a social system tottering to collapse and its releases, the modern point of view towards painting was coming into being. In spite of the romantic bohemian tradition of spontaneous artistic flareup (the sideshow charlatan tradition) painting suddenly became a matter of experiments and theories followed up with almost scientific rigor. In the fads and isms of the painters and writers of that time there was a core of real effort to cope with reality. Grosz seems never to have espoused any of these causes but his work shows the influence of all of them, particularly of Italian futurism and of cubism. He used what elements he needed out of all the various methods of seeing that flourished and disappeared. His interests lay not in the studio or in the metaphysics of color and form, but in the everyday life as he saw it of men and women sleeping, dressing, eating, going to work, drinking, making love, and in their dreams and their wants. He was a satirist and a moralist.

Like Swift in another age and working in another medium, Grosz was full of the horror of life. A satirist is a man whose flesh creeps so at the ugly and the savage and the incongruous aspects of society that he has to express them as brutally and nakedly as possible to get relief. He seeks to put into expressive form his grisly obsessions the way a bacteriologist seeks to isolate a virus or a microorganism. Until he's done that no steps can be taken to cure the disease. Looking at Grosz's drawings you are more likely to feel a grin of pain than to burst out laughing. Instead of letting you be the superior bystander laughing in an Olympian way at somebody absurd, Grosz makes you identify yourself with the sordid and pitiful object.

Experiments in the visual arts (the invention of new ways of seeing things), are made because, due to the way the apparatus that makes up the mind is made, old processes and patterns have continually to be broken up in order to make it possible to perceive the new aspects and arrangements of evolving consciousness. The great enemy of intelligence is complacency. The satirist in words or in visual images is the doctor who comes with his sharp and sterile instruments to lance the focusses of dead matter that continually impede the growth of intelligence. Without intelligence it is impossible to cope with the intricacy of nature or with the madhouse every man carries within him. No one with any sensitiveness to words who has read Swift can ever be so complacent again about his position as a human being. Grosz's work combines visual freshness with a bitter satirical intensity that few complacencies can survive. When complacency goes young intelligence begins.

Notes

1. Dos Passos saw the famous Armory Show of experimental French art in Boston in the spring of 1913 while a student at Harvard. The show included Marcel Duchamp's cubist *Nude Descending a Staircase.*

2. *The Burial of Count Orgaz* by El Greco.

3. The army regulation prohibiting fraternization between officers and enlisted men.

4. The Teapot Dome scandal of Warren Harding's administration involved the fraudulent sale of government oil leases.

Introductory Note to *The 42nd Parallel*

[*The 42nd Parallel* was published originally by Harper & Brothers in 1930.]

The 42nd Parallel is the first volume of *U.S.A.*, a long narrative which deals with the more or less entangled lives of a number of Americans during the first three decades of the present century. The volumes that follow are called *1919* and *The Big Money*.

In an effort to take in as much as possible of the broad field of the lives of these times, three separate sequences have been threaded in and out among the stories. Of these *The Camera Eye* aims to indicate the position of the observer and *Newsreel* to give an inkling of the common mind of the epoch. Portraits of a number of real people are interlarded in the pauses in the narrative because their lives seem to embody so well the quality of the soil in which Americans of these generations grew.

This method was used with the idea of coping with the particular job in hand rather than from any generalized theory about novelwriting. In fact I don't think any such theory holds water. The shape of a piece of work should be imposed, and in a good piece of work always is imposed, by the matter. That's more or less of a commonplace of a considerable body of literary criticism.

The difficulty comes when you try to put into words how this occurs. If several people describe the same scene, say a man and a woman sitting at a table in a room and talking, the results are sure to be very different. Through a bunch of such descriptions a number of identical stereotypes will appear which will reveal the commonplace attitudes and the common grounds of the human group the narrators belong to. But there will also be found here and there in the accounts an occasional phrase or mental slant that tends to break the stereotype and to give some added insight or breadth to the event and to relate it in some new or fresh way to the experience of the group. That's the point where creative writing becomes of permanent value, as absolute discovery is of value in science. At the same time that's the point where many readers will feel annoyance and strain. Leaving the groove hurts. An effort of adjustment is demanded of the brain. People feel pain when the stereotype is broken, at least at first. Then gradually they become accustomed to the discovery and it in turn becomes a stereotype. There are long periods in history when no such breaking of stereotypes occurs and time-honored attitudes and phrases take on a liturgical insignificance and the standard of excellence becomes the exactness with which the stereotypes are repeated.

The 42nd Parallel (New York: Modern Library, 1937), vii–ix.

It may be that we are entering such a period now after a period of considerable fertility and tolerance of invention. Or it may be that we are merely in a lull to be followed by a new outburst of inventiveness and a new broadening of the field of language on the part of a young generation forced to make a fresh set of adjustments to a changed world. At any rate one thing is certain, the great advance made in American writing which can be roughly dated from Dreiser's final overthrow of the genteel tradition, has now become a commonplace of journalism, advertising and the applied arts of the trade, much as many of the discoveries of cubists and surrealists in painting have become the commonplace of the windowdresser and designer. There certainly has been no period in history when every slight imaginative advance has been so fast exploited and absorbed by the great mass of the population. For proof all you need is to compare the text of contemporary advertising in *Fortune* or *Life* with that of, say, the *Saturday Evening Post* of the years around 1910.

This does not mean that a limit has been reached, but it means that, like the pioneers who had to move west into the prairie as soon as the farm they'd just cleared could grow a good crop of corn, writers who want to do primary inventive work will have to keep moving forward into the wilderness. The pure scientist has to do the same thing.

No one will thank them for their work. Age and fatigue will overcome them with no roof over their heads; they'll come to bad ends. But so long as men are found among us who, confronted by welltilled fields yielding a rich harvest to the second generation of exploiters, can't help feeling an intolerable itch to push on beyond, to test continually slogans, creeds and commonplaces in the light of freshly felt experience, American writing will continue alive. When that race dies out or is forcibly extinguished by the pressure of civil war or robotmaking organization we shall settle down to the routine and sterility that seems in certain periods of low vitality so congenial to the race.

Provincetown, July, 1937.

III

The Return to Roots
(1937-71)

Farewell to Europe

[Dos Passos went to Europe—more particularly Spain—in the spring of 1937 in connection with a film that he and Ernest Hemingway were preparing in aid of the Loyalist cause. It was during his trip to Spain that Dos Passos' close friend José Robles was killed by the Communist secret police.]

The people of Western Europe are facing this summer a series of tragic dilemmas. Of the hopes that dazzled the last twenty years that some political movement might tend to the betterment of the human lot, little remains above ground but the tattered slogans of the past. These old slogans still have enough magic in them to make them useful to gang leaders with a knack for organizing and a will to power, but their appeal is now of a pie-in-the-sky order and tends to be enforced with the bayonet or, in the case of a friend, with the butt end of a rifle. Out of them is brewing a partisan fanaticism that equals in savagery that of the wars of religion. And the organizers of victory have at hand the greatest arsenal of destructive machinery that's ever been brought together on this planet.

If there are any of us left in America who really want liberty for ourselves and our fellows, it's time we started using our wits. The Atlantic is broad enough to protect us against air raids, but it can't protect us against the infectious formulas for slavery that are preparing in Europe on every side.

What Hope from Mother England?

Certainly Great Britain, the ancient mother of civil liberties, is going to be very little help to the democratic idea in the near future. The impression I got, from a few days in an England still bedraggled with coronation bunting, was that the ruling class, now in the form of the heavy industry–big banking clique typified by Stanley Baldwin,[1] has managed to reduce the middle and working classes to a point of physical and moral malnutrition where revolt is impossible. The tories are going to have their own way for a long time to come. The British Empire has reached that classical point in the development of empires where the interests of the ruling clique are definitely opposed to the interests of the aggregation as a going concern.

The only question is whether the victim will be devoured slowly, or whether death will be attended by violent convulsions. At the present it looks as if the ruling class anaesthetics had been so skillfully applied by Dr. Baldwin that dissolution would be a long twilight process. There is talk of reviving the Defence of the Realm Act[2] but it will probably not be necessary. All possible opposition is paralysed by

Common Sense, 6 (July 1937), 9–11.

two great dilemmas; first, a left-labor policy in foreign affairs means war with the fascist powers, and the British workman is stolidly and with good reason pacifist; and second, Stalinist Russia's monopoly of the socialist hopes of the world has much slowed up the labor movement at home; the British workman would rather be mildly oppressed by Mr. Chamberlain's bluecoated flatfeet than shot without trial,[3] or more gruesomely with a trial, by the Communist Party, and thank you very much, sir.

Unhappy Predicament of the French

In European affairs England (Mr. Baldwin's heavy industry–big banking England), is still dominant, and the Metternich policy of fighting popular rule, or any change that affects property, by any means that arise, continues triumphant. From behind the stained liberal curtains the singularly unplausible puppet of Mr. Anthony Eden[4] is from time to time stuck out to gibber nineteenth-century platitudes for the benefit of the office force at Geneva, the American press and the Anglican clergy. In France this Metternich policy has been ably seconded by the Quai d'-Orsay. Whether Mr. Blum[5] is himself a willing assistant at the Foreign Office guignol or is merely following the policy of the lesser evil will not be discovered until he writes his memoirs. Certainly the French people are not happy about their predicament. Nobody really feels that the Paris Exposition is going to solve the class war.

France gives you none of the feeling of a dead country that England does, though politically there is the same paralysis on the left. You feel that the stalemate there is due rather to a balance of vigorously opposite forces than to blood and bones ethnic breakdown. As in England the great dilemma that blocks social advance is that a socialist or a truly democratic policy can hardly avoid being a war policy, and that the only vigorous leadership on the left comes from the Communist Party which is in turn hogtied by the internal and international politics of the Kremlin. Ably seconded by the British, the heavy industry–banking block is able to keep a knife at Mr. Blum's throat by threatening civil war and a German and Italian invasion. Meanwhile the French helplessly watch themselves slipping from the position of a first class power, watch the Italians occupying the Balearic Islands and ready to cut communications with the African empire, and the Germans fortifying Morocco and the Basque border.

It's hard to see what the solution can be other than a civil war deadlier than the civil war in Spain. Certainly sympathy with loyalist Spain is the one bond that is holding the French left together during Mr. Blum's *pause*, and the active help to Spain of the French Communist Party is the one policy that holds the esteem of the French working class. This has forced the Right into a pro-German policy that is headed straight for high treason, and has afforded Mr. Blum the opportunity for the complete ascendancy he enjoys in parliament and among purely politician circles. His fatal weakness is that this ascendancy stops short of the banks and the industries where high treason is part of the day's work. Once his assault on the Bank of France failed, and once he was manoeuvered by Mr. Metternich-Baldwin into tolerating the Fascist aggression in Spain he became helplessly part of the windowdressing of the banking and heavy industry forces that are out to crush the working class of Europe at whatever cost.

Behind the Lines in Spain

In Spain the working class has defended itself with a magnificent heroism that will remain one of the bloodstirring episodes of European history. Meanwhile behind the lines a struggle as violent almost as the war has been going on between the Marxist concept of the totalitarian state, and the Anarchist concept of individual liberty. More and more as the day to day needs of the army become paramount over the turbulent effort of the working class in revolt against oppression, the Communist Party forges ahead as the organizer of victory. The anarchists and the socialists with their ideas of individual and local freedom and selfgovernment have given way step by step before this tremendously efficient and ruthless machine for power.

It is the Communists who have been able to attract the young men who want to see the war won. It's the Communists who have been able to obtain and canalize the help of the other Communist Parties of Europe and of the antifascists from all over the world who threw themselves into the breach to save Madrid. It's the Communists who have been supple enough to ally themselves with whatever Anti-Franco forces, small proprietors, shopkeepers, or political adventurers might temporarily be useful to win the war. On the debit side, it must be admitted that they have brought into Spain along with their enthusiasm and their munitions, the secret Jesuitical methods, the Trotzky witchhunt and all the intricate and bloody machinery of Kremlin policy.

The question which cannot be answered now is whether the Spanish people will have paid too high a price for the fine new army they have organized, and whether the Communist Party, once its social objectives are gone or translated into pie in the sky, won't turn out to be only one more magnificent instrument for power, which means a magnificent instrument for oppression. Anyway the die is already cast. It will be impossible to turn the clock back entirely in Spain, because an immense amount of spontaneous social reorganization has gone on; but the chances are that further changes will be in the direction of a centralized military state, possibly somewhat modified in the direction of personal liberty by the need to conciliate the instinct against centralisation of the masses and to cope with the economically cellular character of the peninsula. That is, unless the fascist combination wins. In spite of the seemingly overwhelming forces on the fascist side such a victory seems inconceivable to anyone who has felt the spirit of loyalist Spain. It would mean the final blotting out of hope for Europe.

Return from the Napoleonic Wars

The Atlantic is a good wide ocean. An American in 1937 comes back from Europe with a feeling of happiness, the relief of coming up out into the sunlight from a stifling cellar, that some of his grandfathers must have felt coming home from Metternich's Europe after the Napoleonic wars, the feeling all the immigrants have had when they first saw the long low coast and the broad bays of the new world. At least we still have alternatives.

Sure, we've got our class war, we've got our giant bureaucratic machines for antihuman power, but I can't help feeling that we are still moving on a slightly divergent track from the European world. Not all the fascist-hearted newspaper owners in the country, nor the Chambers of Commerce, nor the armies of hired gun-thugs of the great industries can change the fact that we have the Roundhead Revolution in our heritage and the Bill of Rights and the fact that the democracy in the past has been able, under Jefferson, Jackson, and Lincoln, and perhaps a fourth time (it's too soon to know yet) under Franklin Roosevelt, to curb powerful ruling groups. America has got to be in a better position to work out the problem: individual liberty vs. bureaucratic industrial organization than any other part of the world. If we don't it means the end of everything we have ever wanted since the first hard winters at Plymouth.

Notes

1. Baldwin, a Conservative, had been prime minister of Great Britain on two occasions during the 1920s and again from 1935 to late May 1937. He had been responsible for the successful suppression of the British General Strike of 1926.

2. A World War I measure that gave the government extraordinary powers to regulate industrial production and commerce.

3. Neville Chamberlain became prime minister in late May 1937.

4. Eden was British foreign secretary.

5. Blum, a socialist, was leader of France's Popular Front government from June 1936 to June 1937.

The Communist Party and the War Spirit: A Letter to a Friend Who Is Probably a Party Member

[The "friend" is John Howard Lawson. Dos Passos had known Lawson since 1917 and had been especially close to him during the mid-1920s when they shared an interest in experimental theatre. The two writers corresponded at length in the fall of 1937 about Dos Passos' essay "Farewell to Europe."]

To come back to your sense of being let down by things I have written since I came back from Spain! There's nothing I can do but state once more what I think our attitude should be in this very difficult moment of history. I'm speaking of the attitude of Americans who feel with the very simple hopes and needs of the plain man, who makes his living plodding among the snarling machineries of our world, rather than with the perhaps more dramatic enterprises of the holders of power and the fruits of power. After all there are still enough of us (it's a big country) who base our politics on that feeling to be able to lay claim to at least a part of the tradition we like to call American. I think most of us feel intense sympathy with the Loyalist cause in Spain. I know I do, especially as, outside of my own country, the Spaniards are the people in the world I have most liking for. But I don't think we should allow ourselves to be blinded by that sympathy to the great complexity of the political situation all over the world. I think that the effort to get at the true picture of what is going on will be more of a help to our friends and in the long run do more harm to our foes than indiscriminate cheering for the side we consider in the right.

As I take it, your argument is, in its simplest terms, that the world situation consists of war between Fascism, demagogic military dictatorship for the purposes of reaction on one side, and the principle of progressive popular rule on the other side, of which you feel the Communist Party is the spear head. I gather that you think that the capitalist democracies of France, Great Britain and the United States can eventually be counted on to fall into line on the side of progress and that, if the progressive countries can manage to destroy the reactionary dictators, pressure on the Soviet Union will be relaxed and the world movement of the producing classes to take over the instruments of production and power will go on. The basis of our difference is that I don't think that this is a true picture of the lineup of forces in the world today. In fact, I have come to think that this way of looking at politics is one of the chief dangers hanging over that so easily destroyed quality of organized life that we still have no better name for than liberty.

Common Sense, 6 (Dec. 1937), 11–14.

Democracy and War

After all, didn't most of us who are now around forty see enough of the effects of one war for democracy not to want to help start another? And during the last war the engineers of victory, in this country at least, had to cope with an anti-militarist habit of mind, the result of long years of peace, that will not hamper them in the next. The plans of the War Department are well known. The next war that this country is engaged in will mean that the military, and whatever capitalist and bureaucratic interests happen to be most powerful at the moment, will attempt to set up a totalitarian state. Goodbye Bill of Rights. The totalitarian state is the logical partner of totalitarian war. Now if we don't want the capitalist democracies in a war in which the first step will be that they will cease to be democracies even in the very limited sense in which they are now, we must stop generating the war spirit in the blind enthusiasm of our antifascism.

The basis of war spirit, the nature of which those of us who saw anything of the rear in nineteen seventeen and eighteen must remember, is the easy intoxication of partisan hatred. White is white and black is black. Whoever is not with us is against us. Don't forget that many people take active pleasure in the lynching spirit of wartime, with its complete suspension of inhibitions against violence, just as a few even take pleasure in the actual business of butchering their fellow man. War, whether in a good cause or bad, lets loose all the basic antisocial passions that it's the business of civilized society to keep chained up, and once it starts it follows its own laws, that have little to do with progress or democracy. If we had a democratic industrial system, it is barely conceivable that we might be able to fight a democratic war, but with the present set-up it is inconceivable, no matter what bunting phrases the war is dressed in.

For the last twenty years we have been able to watch the workings of war psychology as applied to the internal life of the Soviet Union. The declared aims of the Bolsheviks were, from the viewpoint of any democrat who values democracy more than property, admirable. The question is whether the dictatorship method didn't make these aims impossible to attain.

After twenty years of absolute rule we have seen the ruling Communist Party come to the point of reintroducing at least a facade of what Marxists used sneeringly to call bourgeois democracy. Americans find themselves asking the question, wouldn't it have been less costly to stick as near as possible to democratic processes all through? Has the price in human misery and repression been so high as to warp the whole great enterprise in the direction of personal and bureaucratic despotism? In the organization of victory have the Bolsheviks forgotten the aims for which the war was endured?

The American Heritage

However you answer these questions, I think you will admit that as far as this country is concerned, they are not instantly pressing. If we are on the road to a dictatorship it is certainly not to a communist dictatorship. We have our class war all right and our class war psychology, as anybody can find out by talking for a few minutes with any bankclerk or with anybody who lives off the interest of stocks and bonds, but civil war has not yet destroyed the fabric of the democratic state. After all, representative majority rule, however far from perfect, is the only political method yet discovered that allows for peaceful changes in the balance of power within a society. Occasionally the democratic state breaks down as it did in this country in sixty-one; this time, in spite of the tension and growing pains of the New Deal period, it has not broken down, at least not yet. In my opinion the one hope for the future of the type of western civilization which furnishes the frame of our lives is that the system of popular government based on individual liberty be not allowed to break down.

The forces against popular government are so immense and so inherent in the organization of society under bureaucratic monopoly capitalism that popular government needs every force it can muster to survive and to evolve. This is one of the moments when democracy has got to go ahead or quit. To go ahead it has got to permeate the industrial process.

You and the other partisans of the Communist Party in this country, and the many liberals with whom you are collaborating, are doing all you can to help the Spanish people in their desperate fight against fascist traitors at home and fascist invading armies, and I admire you for it; but I feel that the way you are doing it is a danger to the basic habits of mind that engender the democratic point of view. *After all*, we must remember where our enthusiasm for brave little Belgium led us. The great danger in letting our enthusiasm for fighting fascism in Europe get the better of us is that it shows every sign of being the first trickle of a flood of irrational emotion that may very well end in our fighting another war for the defense of the British Empire and the topdog capitalist bloc of nations. If liberals and progressives let themselves become infected with the war madness, what kind of a bulwark of sense will they be able to put up for the rest of the population once the radios begin to bark for war? We can give our unqualified respect to the men who have gone to risk their lives to help the Spaniards fight, without letting ourselves be organized into a cheering section by the left politicians back home. Everybody who has really seen war close to can recognize the difference between the matter-of-fact attitude of the actual worker in the machinery of fighting and the sadistic delirium of non-combatants screaming for the blood of an enemy they have never seen. Those of us who write and talk will be a great deal more useful in the long run if we try to make clear the actual truth of what is going on, and that is a full-time job.

Fascism versus Intelligence

If you are going to fight Fascism you have got to fight it at home. Fascism is a disease of sick capitalism, not a disease of democracy. The cure for Fascism is intelligent popular government. The roots of Fascism are not in certain wicked demagogues named Hitler and Mussolini, but in the jitters of monopolists in Paris, London, and New York, who fear a rising of the working class of the world more than they fear the loss of their own empires; in the desperation of a bewildered middle class; and also, we must add, in the lag behind events of the leadership of the working-class movement. World capital is in the position of the Romans during the decadence of the empire, arming and taming some of the barbarians to get them to fight the others. The emperors of money power can't fight their own battles any more than the Roman emperors could. Like the Romans they are willing to lose something in order not to lose everything. Like the Romans too, they'll end by being trampled under by the barbarian hordes. The question is whether there's any part of the world where their fall will not bring down the whole fabric of society with it.

I think that in America we have reason to hope that the republic has still enough life and youth and flexibility to survive the collapse. Our defense will lie in an informed, hardheaded population that has some means of getting a true picture of the world it's trying to live in. That's why freedom of speech, publication and assembly are of greater importance to us now than ever before. The answer to Catholic propaganda and Wall Street propaganda is not Communist propaganda or Loyalist government propaganda but the plain, unvarnished truth, or as near as we can get to it.

The more charged with emotion any given situation is, the more difficult it is to strike the common denominator of plain fact. That's why I feel that these quasi-wartime emotions being whipped up in the middle class are so dangerous, because they are attacking the section of the public that reads most and discusses most and can help most to clear away the verbal smoke screen under which politicians conduct events. Up to a couple of years ago if you wanted to get the real lowdown about current history you went to the nearest liberal radical or progressive. Now you are likely to get as vague and emotionally colored a picture from a radical intellectual as you would from the banker's daughter. The truth isn't the opposite of a lie; it's something different.

What is the Truth in Spain?

"That's all very well," you'll say, "but what are you going to do about the Spanish people who are fighting for their lives? Outside of the Communist sympathizers and the antifascist liberals who is collecting money to send them ambulances? How else can we do it than by whooping it up for our side?" I'm all for sending them ambulances. I'd be for sending them machine guns if there were a way to do it. But I'm also for trying to keep as clear as possible in our own minds the terrible predicament in which the Spanish people find themselves. And I'm for sending help in such a way that the sufferings of the Spanish people shall not be exploited by any group of politicians, no matter how much I agree with what they say, or be made the football of international diplomacy as were the sufferings of brave little Belgium in nineteen fourteen. We've got to try to understand what's happening, and that's not easy.

The tragedy of the republican movement in Spain that has been striving for more than a century to break through the bonds of a bankrupt feudal society is that, now as in the last century, it has not produced leaders capable of steering a way through the tangle of European powerpolitics and at the same time keeping the aims of "The Republic of Workers of Hand and Brain"[1] clearly before the masses of the people. July a year ago the republic was forced into war against the reactionaries under the leadership of the same group of muddleheaded politicians (they weren't muddled because they were liberals; they were muddled because their liberalism was muddled) who made the reactionary revolt possible in the first place by their policy of talk loud and do nothing. It's as if the North had had to fight the Civil War under Buchanan instead of under Lincoln. The people themselves without any government help held off the military revolt in the first days, and nipped it in the bud in all the great cities except Seville, but they developed no leaders with which to replace the garrulous and inefficient crew in office.

With a magnificent spontaneity antifascists of all creeds flocked to Spain to help defend Madrid at a period when most of the political leaders had bolted or were ready to bolt. Among them of course were many Communists of various factions.

Exactly how it came about that the Kremlin decided to help is not known. Whether the propelling force was the revolutionary idealism of the Soviet masses, or Kremlin policy that calls for the defence of democratic France as a military ally in spite of the fact that democratic France seems to love her enemies better than her friends, or both, the Russians began to send in arms, food supplies and technical help. It was natural that help from the Soviet Union should produce a great wave of enthusiasm for the Communist Party, which grew very rapidly. To a people who were fighting death from the machine-guns of Franco's Foreign Legion in the front and his firing squads in the rear, Communist help was life itself. The terrible thing for Spain's confused and vigorous movements for social renovation was that the Communists entered Spain at a moment when their party was infected by the internal feud of the Trotsky heresy hunt, at the moment in its history when it was least flexible, at the moment when, in the west at least, it had abandoned the social program of seizing the instruments of production for the working class that had called it into being in nineteen seventeen. The Communists took to Spain their organizing skill, their will to rule, and their blind intolerance.

The result has been that instead of being the rallying point for all the progressive elements in the peninsula the Communist Party has, as it gained in power, set itself to eliminating physically or otherwise all the men with possibilities of leadership who were not willing to put themselves under its orders. Whoever is not with us is against us. Instead of getting wider as its army becomes more powerful the popular base of the republic is, I fear, getting narrower. The workmen and country people have produced some fine military leaders, but the tragedy of their situation is that they have produced no political leader able to supersede the liberal journalists and intellectuals who had made a mess of the republic in the first place. These men are now as unable to control the communists upon whom the army's munitions depend, as they were unable to understand or direct the workers who were calling for the seizure of the instruments of production or the military leaders who were planning the Fascist revolt in the very offices of the republic.

There is still a chance that Dr. Negrin with the help of the French left may be able to steer Republican Spain into somewhat the same sort of small proprietor's compromise with powerful capital that Campañys, a really skillful politician of steadfast purpose, has for a long time envisaged in Catalonia.[2] What one wonders is if such a solution, which would have been possible even under the Fascist generals, will be worth the terrible sacrifices of the civil war.

The question is what we in America can do, or could have done, to help. You certainly must realize that a war's like an epidemic. The weapons against it are quarantine and medical aid. Spreading the disease doesn't help the original sufferers. The way we could have helped fight the Fascists in Spain was by exposing the Fascist sympathizers in our own State Department and by uncovering the forces in the Catholic hierarchy and the banking world which originally put the United States on the side of the enemies of the Spanish people. Our business is now to learn the lessons, so that we'll be able to meet a similar situation in America when it comes.

The only weapon we have is telling the truth, or as near as we can get to it. We live in a time when the true history of international events is enormously hard to come by. The truth is not in atrocity stories or partisan propaganda. Lashing ourselves up into a partisan fever will only make us the prey of whatever propaganda the warmongers want to put over on us. Last time they got us to hate the Huns and the first thing we knew we were persecuting the wobblies. This time we ought to be more careful. We have the enormous luck, shared by few of the inhabitants of Europe, of not having yet to take sides for life or death in any of these quarrels. The place to fight Fascism is in your own home town. Fascism thrives on the war spirit. Fanning the war spirit is preparing the ground for the destruction of our own rights and liberties. The war spirit means the end of the flexibility of mind necessary for progress and change and social readjustment. At least let's not have the war spirit until the shooting begins.

Notes

1. Spain, in its constitution of 1931, was declared to be a "Republic of Workers of All Categories."

2. Juan Negrin, a socialist, became prime minister of Spain in May 1937; Luis Campañys was president of Catalonia, which had been established in 1932 as an autonomous region within the Spanish republic.

The Death of José Robles

[Malcolm Cowley, in his review of Dos Passos' novel *Adventures of a Young Man* in the *New Republic*, 99 (14 June 1939), 163, had commented that Robles had been "arrested as a Fascist spy. People who ought to know tell me that the evidence against him was absolutely damning." Cowley's comment echoed the official Party line on the death of Robles.]

Sir: I did not intend to publish any account of the death of my old friend José Robles Pazos (the fact that he had once translated a book of mine, and well, was merely incidental; we had been friends since my first trip to Spain in 1916) until I had collected more information and possible documentary evidence from survivors of the Spanish civil war, but the reference to him in Mr. Malcolm Cowley's review of my last book [The New Republic, June 14] makes it necessary for me to request you to print the following as yet incomplete outline of the events that led up to his death. As I do not possess the grounds of certitude of your reviewer and his informants, I can only offer my facts tentatively and say that to the best of my belief they are accurate.

José Robles was a member of a family of monarchical and generally reactionary sympathies in politics; his brother was an army officer in the entourage of Alfonso of Bourbon when he was king; one of the reasons why he preferred to live in America (he taught Spanish Literature at Johns Hopkins University in Baltimore) was his disagreement on social and political questions with his family. He was in Spain on his vacation when Franco's revolt broke out, and stayed there, although he had ample opportunity to leave, because he felt it his duty to work for the Republican cause. As he knew some Russian he was given a job in the Ministry of War and soon found himself in close contact with the Russian advisers and experts who arrived at the same time as the first shipment of munitions. He became a figure of some importance, ranked as lieutenant-colonel, although he refused to wear a uniform, saying that he was a mere civilian. In the fall of 1936 friends warned him that he had made powerful enemies and had better leave the country. He decided to stay. He was arrested soon after in Valencia and held by the extra-legal police under conditions of great secrecy and executed in February or March, 1937.

It must have been about the time of his death that I arrived in Spain to do some work in connection with the film "The Spanish Earth," in which we were trying to tell the story of the civil war. His wife, whom I saw in Valencia, asked me to make inquiries to relieve her terrible uncertainty. Her idea was that as I was known to have gone to some trouble to get the cause of the Spanish Republic fairly presented in the United States, government officials would tell me frankly why

New Republic, 99 (July 1939), 308–9.

Robles was being held and what the charges were against him. It might have been the same day that Liston Oak, a one-time member of the American Communist Party who held a job with the propaganda department in Valencia, broke the news to José Robles' son, Francisco Robles Villegas, a seventeen-year-old boy working as a translator in the censorship office, that his father was dead. At the same time officials were telling me that the charges against José Robles were not serious and that he was in no danger. Mr. Del Vayo, then Foreign Minister, professed ignorance and chagrin when I talked to him about the case, and promised to find out the details. The general impression that the higherups in Valencia tried to give was that if Robles were dead he had been kidnaped and shot by anarchist "uncontrollables." They gave the same impression to members of the United States embassy staff who inquired about his fate.

It was not until I reached Madrid that I got definite information, from the then chief of the republican counterespionage service, that Robles had been executed by a "special section" (which I gathered was under control of the Communist Party). He added that in his opinion the execution had been a mistake and that it was too bad. Spaniards I talked to closer to the Communist Party took the attitude that Robles had been shot as an example to other officials because he had been overheard indiscreetly discussing military plans in a café. The "fascist-spy" theory seems to be the fabrication of romantic American Communist sympathizers. I certainly did not hear it from any Spaniard.

Anybody who knew Spaniards of any stripe before the civil war will remember that they tended to carry personal independence in talk and manners to the extreme. It is only too likely that Robles, like many others who were conscious of their own sincerity of purpose, laid himself open to a frame-up. For one thing, he had several interviews with his brother, who was held prisoner in Madrid, to try to induce him to join the Loyalist army. My impression is that the frame-up in his case was pushed to the point of execution because Russian secret agents felt that Robles knew too much about the relations between the Spanish war ministry and the Kremlin and was not, from their very special point of view, politically reliable. As always in such cases, personal enmities and social feuds probably contributed.

On my way back through Valencia, as his wife was penniless, I tried to get documentary evidence of his death from Republican officials so that she could collect his American life insurance. In spite of Mr. Del Vayo's repeated assurances that he would have a death certificate sent her, it never appeared. Nor was it possible to get hold of any record of the indictment or trial before the "special section."

As the insurance has not yet been paid I am sure that Mr. Cowley will understand that any evidence he may have in his possession as to how José Robles met his death will be of great use to his wife and daughter, and I hope he will be good enough to communicate it to me. His son was captured fighting in the Republican militia in the last months of the war and, as there has been no news of him for some time, we are very much afraid that he died or was killed in one of Franco's concentration camps.

Of course this is only one story among thousands in the vast butchery that was the Spanish civil war, but it gives us a glimpse into the bloody tangle of ruined lives that underlay the hurray-for-our-side aspects. Understanding the personal histories of a few of the men, women and children really involved would, I think, free our minds somewhat from the black-is-black and white-is-white obsessions of partisanship.

Provincetown, Mass.

The Situation in American Writing:
Seven Questions

We are publishing below the replies to a questionnaire submitted to a representative list of American writers. A second group of answers, received too late for publication in this issue, will be printed in the Fall number. Contributors will include Sherwood Anderson, Louise Bogan, Horace Gregory, R. P. Blackmur, William Troy, Lionel Trilling, Robert Penn Warren, James Agee, and Robert Fitzgerald. The questionnaire follows:

1. *Are you conscious, in your own writing, of the existence of a "usable past"? Is this mostly American? What figures would you designate as elements in it? Would you say, for example, that Henry James's work is more relevant to the present and future of American writing than Walt Whitman's?*
2. *Do you think of yourself as writing for a definite audience? If so, how would you describe this audience? Would you say that the audience for serious American writing has grown or contracted in the last ten years?*
3. *Do you place much value on the criticism your work has received? Would you agree that the corruption of the literary supplements by advertising—in the case of the newspapers—and political pressures—in the case of the liberal weeklies—has made serious literary criticism an isolated cult?*
4. *Have you found it possible to make a living by writing the sort of thing you want to, and without the aid of such crutches as teaching and editorial work? Do you think there is any place in our present economic system for literature as a profession?*
5. *Do you find, in retrospect, that your writing reveals any allegiance to any group, class, organization, region, religion, or system of thought, or do you conceive of it as mainly the expression of yourself as an individual?*
6. *How would you describe the political tendency of American writing as a whole since 1930? How do you feel about it yourself? Are you sympathetic to the current tendency towards what may be called "literary nationalism"—a renewed emphasis, largely uncritical, on the specifically "American" elements in our culture?*
7. *Have you considered the question of your attitude towards the possible entry of the United States into the next world war? What do you think the responsibilities of writers in general are when and if war comes?*

Partisan Review, 6 (Summer 1939), 26–27.

John Dos Passos:

1. In relation to style and methods of writing, I hardly think of the past in chronological order. Once on the library shelf Juvenal and Dreiser are equally "usable." The best immediate ancestor (in Auden's sense) for today's American writing is I think a dark star somewhere in the constellation containing Mark Twain, Melville, Thoreau and Whitman.

2. The audience is probably the people who read books other than best sellers. I doubt if it has expanded much in the last ten years, though in the preceding five years it certainly expanded. It may very well be shrinking now.

3. The critics for the daily press, and all newspaper writers live in a very special world. I think they are more influenced by the ebb and flow of headlined fashions, and by the varying standards in social prestige of that world than by any direct advertising pressure. Advertising probably determines the space given a book, and in the long run I think it will be found that the various publishers' lists get respectful attention in direct relation to the financial position of the concerns. After all, what do you want for three cents? Current newspaper criticisms are interesting to the social historian just as fashion notes are interesting. I doubt very much if they will take their place in the "usable past." There's not enough, but there is some first rate literary criticism around that, naturally, is very useful to a writer.

4. I've managed to do it so far, but it's nip and tuck.

5. Isn't an individual just a variant in a group? The equipment belongs to the society you were brought up by. The individuality lies in how you use it. My sympathies, for some reason, lie with the private in the front line against the brass hat; with the hodcarrier against the strawboss, or the walking delegate for that matter; with the laboratory worker against the stuffed shirt in a mortarboard; with the criminal against the cop. When I try to use my head it's somewhat different. People are you and me. As for allegiance; what I consider the good side of what's been going on among people on this continent since 1620 or thereabouts, has mine. And isn't there one of history's dusty attics called the Republic of Letters?

6. On the whole I'm all for the trend towards American self-consciousness in current writing. Of course any good thing gets run into the ground. I think there is enough real democracy in the very mixed American tradition to enable us, with courage and luck, to weather the social transformations that are now going on without losing all our liberties or the humane outlook that is the medium in which civilizations grow. The reaction to home-bred ways of thinking is a healthy defence against the total bankruptcy of Europe. As I have come to believe firmly that in politics the means tend to turn out to be more important than the ends, I think that the more our latent pragmatism and our cynicism in regard to ideas is stimulated the safer we will be.

7. My attitude towards a war would entirely depend on what I thought its internal results would be, though it's hard to conceive of a war that would have good results anywhere. But how would I know when it began? We live in a very odd period in human history when it's very difficult to make broad generalizations about events or to label them beforehand. Practically I'd probably try to get back my old job driving an ambulance.

To a Liberal in Office

[Dos Passos spent much time in Washington during 1940 and 1941 preparing *The Ground We Stand On* (1941), his study of the origins of the American republic. It is not known if the "Liberal" to whom the essay is addressed is a specific individual or Dos Passos' conception of a general type.]

Wiscasset, Maine, August 25

Dear ———: No matter how good the intentions of a man in public service are when he starts out, I think you'll agree that it's exceedingly difficult for him to avoid leading a double life. While with one side of his mind he's trying to fulfil his duty to his fellow-citizens, with the other he's busy with his career and with the demands of the organized group he belongs to. Only too often the members of the aggregations of men that make up a government lose all contact with the public needs they were got together to serve. Whether a public servant shall be written down as an honest man or a scoundrel depends on what part of his energy and brains goes into selfless work for his constituents in proportion to the part he has to use to make his way in the competitive scramble. Naturally if I didn't think you were an honest man I would not be taking up your time and mine with this letter. Furthermore, I know that through a long train of years you have done your best to throw your weight on the side of free institutions. If I'm not mistaken, it is largely because you proved yourself a conscientious liberal that you reached a position of power and responsibility under the present Administration. I am writing to ask you to stop to think for a moment how your power is being used, and what kind of responsibility you have undertaken in this difficult time toward your fellow-citizens and toward yourself.

It has been said so often that democracy is at stake that the mere repetition of the words has dulled their meaning for us. Nevertheless, it's frighteningly true. It's another commonplace that we are living through one of those periods in history when old institutions are crumbling away and new institutions are being built up. The thing nobody tells us is that what these new institutions will be like depends upon how every man jack of us acquits himself today. It's up to us to ask whether we are letting ourselves be used to build jails or homes for free men.

As Americans our minds were formed in childhood to react favorably to such phrases as liberty, equality of opportunity, freedom of speech, but unfortunately nothing in our schooling gave us any inkling how to apply them to the problems of real life. They were the measuring sticks with which we appraised the world we grew up in. In many cases they tallied so little with the facts we encountered in that world that we tried to rip them out of our minds as old, rotten, sentimental lumber, and to

Nation, 153 (6 Sept. 1941), 195–97. Copyright The Nation Company, Inc., 1941

put in their place one of the authoritarian creeds that are turning civilization into a slaughterhouse today. A few of us, and you were one, held on to the old traditions. They took root again in our minds and grew strong enough to become the underpinning of all our political hopes, and of our system of personal ethics.

Now after a period of reform and helterskelter reorganization that has been, in spite of many wrong roads taken, productive of real living good in the national life, the United States finds itself virtually at war. The fact of being at war tends to freeze normal social and political processes inside a country. This freezing puts a very grave responsibility on the men in office at the time. Great inflation of the power of the state is inevitable. For the duration public opinion will be able to make itself felt only feebly and negatively. The whole duty of protecting the self-governing system and the liberties that are supposed to be the watchwords of the battle will rest on men already in administrative and political positions. This is the responsibility I am asking you, as a liberal, to face.

The general run of men, organized into any group or gang or institution or government, must necessarily be time servers whose emotions and ideas will be colored by the stronger minds among them. They will tend to behave as their leaders behave. Democracy depends upon the active support of a minority just as much as dictatorship does. The difference is that democracy depends upon a minority able to set for the rest the example of that minimum of civic courage necessary to make self-governing institutions work instead of upon a minority of goons ready to club down opposition to the boss's orders.

We can thank our stars that the men who founded our system of government understood so well the corruption of power, and that in the common law we have a storehouse of inherited techniques for the protection of the individual man. But institutions are continually changing as a result of the uses men put them to. Each temporary distortion leaves its mark. In a time of emergency the temptation to a man in office to get results no matter how is almost overwhelming. It is the business of liberals in positions of power to remember that free institutions depend on the "how" much more than on the results. Democracy is a method of social organization, not an end. War has always meant the triumph of authority; that is why all through our history our statesmen in war time have occasionally neglected efficiency in the totalitarian sense in order to secure liberties at home that were more important to them than transitory victories abroad. If in the present war, out of a blind desire to catch up to the Nazis, we neglect to preserve the democratic process, we shall wake up one morning to find that we've given our blood and paid our taxes in order to fasten on our necks the dominion of a bunch of war lords who speak American instead of German. A doubtful victory!

Already, before we've even started shooting at the enemy, the Administration, which I honestly believe is more devoted to the aims of democracy than any we have had for many decades, has committed a number of acts that tend to put the bases of self-government in jeopardy. The prosecution of the Minnesota truck drivers is so far the outstanding example. On July 15 a federal grand jury handed down in St. Paul, Minnesota, an indictment against twenty-nine men, some leaders and members of Local 544, a union of transportation workers powerful in the Northwest, and the rest members of the tiny group of the followers of the murdered Trotsky that goes under the name of the Socialist Workers' Party. The indictment was handed down under a Civil War statute that has never been brought out before, and under the new Smith Act, which I believe was aimed at the subversive activities of the agents of foreign governments. The men are charged with conspiracy to overthrow the United States government by force and violence.

Let's assume that it's all perfectly legal, that the Department of Justice believes these men intended to rise in insurrection, and that it has a right to stretch a point or two to accomplish the useful purpose of restraining them. Is it wise to take this moment, when the Administration is trying to unify the country for a mighty effort, for this particular prosecution? Let us even assume that a few thousand Trotskyist Marxist sectarians scattered over the country can be a danger to the government of the United States at a time when the Department of Justice itself has more employees than the Trotskyists have adherents. What I want to ask you is: which is more dangerous to that survival of the democratic process in this country for which I am sure you would gladly lay down your life—the uprising of a few fanatics who control a single local of a trade union or a situation in which the government undermines at home those four freedoms for which it is asking the nation to make every sacrifice abroad?

You must remember the Palmer raids, the deportations delirium, the crushing of the I.W.W., the Sacco-Vanzetti case, all the terrible perversions of justice after the last war that made American democracy a mockery to a whole generation of young men. Is it all going to happen again? Is the same lack of whole-hearted principle that wrecked Woodrow Wilson's crusade to set the world straight going to destroy the present Administration too? A great deal of the history of the next few years depends on whether the Administration will recognize that it has made a mistake in this one case. If it is allowed to go ahead, the prestige of government will become involved in getting these men in jail and keeping them there. And a precedent will have been set that bodes ill for this country's liberties.

Well, you say, suppose you are right, what can one man do about it? We must keep our eyes on the great aims of the Administration and admit that in war time we have to do things that we don't quite like. That argument has been the refuge of officialdom from Pontius Pilate down. It just does not hold water. It is to make these decisions that a man is chosen for the public service. During the last war while some officials were busy tearing down the American system, a few others were doing their best to build it up. In the end the structure of self-government was tough enough to stand those strains and the great depression too. Where the present moment differs from 1917 is that now the traditions of our system are weaker than they were then. Although there has been more vocal expression of them recently than in any period since the great years of this country's founding, the average man still has a hard time connecting the principles of democracy with his daily life. In this immensely confusing time it is impossible to evoke from the mass of unthinking men the passionate automatic response to the old war cries that came in 1917. Furthermore, the national life is honeycombed with political groups such as the Communists and the Coughlinites,[1] highly confusing in their line of talk and vowed to the destruction of the democratic method. They will continue to be a danger until that method has had time to prove its practical worth.

Meanwhile we can't afford to lose any ground. The great successes of the despotic systems have been based on the fact that the democracies did not have the singlemindedness or the courage to advance to the attack. For a long time to come we are going to continue fighting against despotism with one hand tied behind our backs. The conviction of these union leaders in St. Paul in a case where even the language of the indictment has the peculiar twist of Stalin's famous frame-ups in Moscow will be a severe moral blow to the American cause. The heavens won't fall, you say. It won't be the first time that men have been framed in this country or that the majority of men have stood by and seen injustice done. But the effects will snowball. We musn't forget that in France the heavens did fall. The great reason for the success of the despotisms has been that they are as wholehearted in their work as a gangster in the middle of a holdup. They can be routed by a democracy that is wholeheartedly, even recklessly, for freedom. Can't we be as reckless on the right side as they are on the wrong?

Perhaps I'm the one who is wrong in thinking it is because of their honesty and frank speaking that the defendants in this case now find themselves in jeopardy rather than because of anything really subversive in their actions. Perhaps the Department of Justice is right in contending that so small a group can really be a nuisance to American institutions. In any case the Administration is risking more than can possibly be gained. I am writing you this letter to try to get you to step for a moment out of the peculiar exigencies of your official position. At a time when we are asking our young men to give up the best years of their lives, and possibly their lives entire, to national defense, it is hardly too much to ask a public official to remember that he is a citizen before he is an official and that he must decide for himself whether his actions are tending to the defense or the destruction of the Republic. If this were not a time of grave peril it would be insufferable effrontery for me to sit here in a quiet room in a shady retired village writing a letter asking you to go sit on a park bench and make this decision—you who are working fourteen hours a day in a Washington office, straining every nerve to do what you can in that precarious daily piling of average on slippery average which is the best victory a man can hope for who is trying to accomplish something through the directed work of groups of other men. But in every train of events there is a moment when one decision determines a long future. This, it seems to me, is one of the times when a man has to speak his mind.

Notes

1. Followers of the Rev. Charles Coughlin, a right-wing extremist of the period.

An Interview with Mr. John Dos Passos

John Dos Passos said that he had been particularly interested lately in what happens to American writers when they reach middle age, what it is that confuses them, what checks their careers. He shook a last drop of gin and bitters out of the ounce-and-a-half measure onto the ice in his drinking glass. "No, I don't know the answers. I just wonder about it." Did he think that a possible cause might be a tendency to form such close attachments, to become so closely entwined in the lives of others, that detachment was lost, that the imagination was too much caught up in complicated relationships? The more formalized relationships of the Europeans probably helped European writers to avoid this.

"Yes, there is a possibility that that is so. The cool detachment of a young writer—well, that's hard to keep into middle age. And then I wonder if that curious anarchism that is possible here once a man gets on top doesn't cut a man off from life, from his material.

"The Sunday supplement heroes—no, that's dated—the gossip column heroes —they seem to have a hard time avoiding a tendency to become a little like movie stars going in ermine to premiers, living up to press notices. And that cuts them off.

"Of course in Scott's case," he continued, referring to F. Scott Fitzgerald, "the notices weren't important. Neither was the alcohol. He could do without alcohol, and did. It was something else that held him up for so long. What? I don't know. More than any one else I know he lived to write. Nothing meant much to him except in how it might be translated into words. A taste, a meal, a view was nothing in itself, it became important only in what he might make of it in words. He had so much talent that even when he announced that he was writing a pot boiler, and tried to write a pot boiler, the talent came through unmistakably. Yet there was something blocking him that he couldn't get around."

He mentioned possible blocks that were in the way of other writers who now are well known. Stage center, he suggested, has been rather too much for several of them. What about his own case?

"Well, I'm working on a novel,[1] making fairly good progress. But all this talk about puberty being so hard on kids. Puberty isn't in it with middle-age, not by a

Robert van Gelder, *New York Times*, 23 Nov. 1941, Book Review section, p. 2. Copyright © 1941 by the New York Times Company. Reprinted by permission. Reprinted in Robert van Gelder, *Writers and Writing* (New York: Scribner, 1946).

damned sight. I took a long time out from fiction to dig into history for my last book. Now I've come back to fiction and it seems to be going along all right. Of course, just lately, the last few weeks, I've been traveling more than writing. I made a fast trip to London for the P.E.N. Congress and then there were a lot of details here."

With no taste for the spotlight he makes quick trips to localities that seem to promise material for fiction. His writings have proved that he has a singularly unerring instinct for the important men and developments of a time. Where did he find the best hunting these days?

"In Washington when you go out for an evening you have a better chance of running into a good story, a man who is doing something that is new and interesting and really important, than you have in New York just now."

Spending most of the year at Provincetown, he said that when well into a story he usually wrote five or six hours a day. This is at one sitting, from about nine in the morning until two or later in the afternoon. The amount of work accomplished varies with each day—"there is no average that I've ever estimated." In Summer he spends the afternoons sailing or gardening. He finds that he is fairly successful at putting the work out of his mind when he leaves his desk. His eyes have been in bad shape for years, but he finds that they give him less trouble if he reads without glasses, even though this necessitates holding print very close to his eyes. "I was pretty worried about them for a time, but now I guess that my eyes will last about as long as I last." He tries to limit the use of glasses to occasions when he is driving or walking.

His books have been given the greatest praise, but rarely have had large sales. How has he escaped the temptation of trying to write for money?

"I haven't escaped it. I once tried to write a murder mystery, but it was no go. I couldn't handle it at all. But I haven't tried to do much writing for money because the way I *do* write is the only way I *can* write.

"You see, though, of course, I am a professional writer, the realization that I'm a professional has come very slowly to me. In the beginning I meant to be an architect. I wrote my first novels in the belief that as soon as I found the time I'd go into architectural work. The illusion that I was about to become an architect stayed with me a long time. And even now—even now I'm sort of looking forward to becoming a farmer.[2] But, of course, I have this novel to finish, and then I suppose there'll be another."

He denied that his novels have contained any considerable amount of direct autobiography, "though, on the other hand, autobiography certainly is all mixed in. There is a part of me in every character, naturally. That's why novelists rarely write good autobiographies. You start one and it becomes another novel—bound to. No, I make very little use of other people, directly. It is like those museum skeletons that are built up from a knucklebone, something like that, reconstructed from a part. Walking around London, for example, during the blackout you hear a few words, a part of a conversation, and in them you may find a situation, or a character. But it is all building up, reconstruction.

"Naturally, when I wrote of a childhood, that is autobiography to a large extent. There's no getting away from it. You can be a part of many other adults, but you've only yourself to remember when you write of a child."

Notes

1. *Number One* (1943), the second novel in Dos Passos' *District of Columbia* trilogy.

2. Dos Passos' father had owned farming land in northern Virginia. Dos Passos' hope soon to occupy it depended on the outcome of a complicated law case. In fact, the case was not settled until 1944 and Dos Passos did not settle on the property until 1946.

The Duty of the Writer

[Dos Passos had been named an American delegate to the international PEN Club
conference to be held in London. The conference met 11–13 September 1941, and
Dos Passos remarks were published in the record of the conference, *Writers in
Freedom*. E. M. Forster, whom he refers to at the opening of his statement, was
also a speaker.]

Mr. Forster very beautifully put the case of the writer as poet, laurel-crowned child
of the Muses, or as a rat swimming away from the sinking ship, according to your
taste. Well, Mr. Poet-Writer, I am all for you, if you can get away with it, but the
type of writer I am interested in now is the writer who is also a good citizen. We are
in a period when we have to forgo a good many luxuries. I know the writer who
works with all his might to be a good citizen is a necessity.

I cannot see how even the most immortal writer is more than the best possible
type of moving picture machine contrived to focus the present moment on the
screen of the future. The present is people and the future is people. The good writer
is like a sponge that sops up the lives of the people he lives with. When things are
easy, in fat illusionary ages like the nineteenth century—(we haven't shaken the
drugged security of that time, when all the good little children of the well-to-do always got a gold piece for Christmas, off our thinking apparatus yet)—it does not
matter much whether people are good citizens or not. The old ship of state jogs
along on its own inertia. But in times of war and crashing institutions there is not
much room in society for anybody who is not a good citizen.

Naturally, by good citizen, I do not mean being the humble servant of whatever power holds the reins of the police. And I do not mean that the perfection of
citizenship is for every writer to go around spouting hastily improvized ideas in
public the way I'm doing here. Whether an orator can be a good citizen is quite another problem.

To be a good citizen to-day, the writer has got to put his mind on the world
around him. He has got to understand—I do not mean complain about, I mean understand—the industrial set-up that is so ruthlessly changing the basis of society
and he has got to tackle the problem of power. His business is to justify the ways of
machinery to man. If it is the chilly stone wreaths of posterity you are thinking of, it
is the writer who combines these two ways of looking at the world into a masterpiece that will get them. The terrible thing about machinery is that it is so easy to
run. The problem is to control the man who has got hold of the throttle.

That is where I think the writer in the English language is at this moment in
history particularly important. I feel rather ashamed to say this before an international gathering. We have let our free institutions get into a sad state of disrepair,

Hermon Ould, ed., *Writers in Freedom* (London: Hutchinson, 1942), 24–26.

and other peoples have always been shown the seamy side of them. But they do exist. Scattered over the world, among all the English-speaking tribe, fragments of the Common Law and of self-governing institutions do survive, and to a certain extent they work: they use the only machinery mankind has yet invented that has successfully curbed the individual men and groups of men who have at different times gotten hold of the levers of power and used them for what they thought was their own advantage and what certainly was the disadvantage of their fellows. That is one of the things people mean when they drag out that battered old battleflag: democracy.

It is not by bombers alone that we are going to defeat Hitler. We are going to defeat him only if we invent a superior political system. But no political system will last long if it is left in the hands of the politicians. It has got to be under the continual inspection of the citizens. Our political system—I am speaking now about America—is all tangled up in the problem of how to apply self-government to modern industrial society. I imagine the problem is very much the same here in England. If we do not solve that problem we shall find that when we have cut off Hitler's head a hundred other Hitlers will spring up where we least expect them. Some way must be found by which the mass of citizens can keep control of the man at the switchboard. In spite of all our crimes and hypocrisies the English-speaking peoples still have in them the habits and traditions needed to make the rusty old machine of self-government work. It will mean shaking off our lethargy and bringing about a period of political growth as keen and ardent as the period of the Commonwealth in England, or of the War of Independence in America. The alternative is destruction.

That is where the writer comes in. The average factory worker or clerk or college professor is only dimly aware of what kind of society he is living in. It is the business of the writer to tell him. There are endless ways of doing the job—from journalism to epic verse, but that is the job that has got to be done and it has got to be done quickly. When you say *quickly* literature and the *aere perennius* fly out the window. Great works of the imagination are not produced quickly nor do they take quick effect on the popular mind. Well, Milton put off *Paradise Lost* to slave for the Commonwealth. I don't know that in the long run we lost anything by it. I feel that this is a time when every English language writer must go to work for the commonwealth, and if we succeed in setting self-government up on its feet again in the new world of massproduction—there is only a slim chance at best that we may succeed —but if we do, we are likely to find we have written some epics without knowing it.

A Preface Twenty-Five Years Later

[*First Encounter* is the title Dos Passos gave to the 1945 republication of his novel *One Man's Initiation—1917*, a work published originally by George Allen of London in 1920. Dos Passos wrote this preface shortly after returning from a trip of over two months to the South Pacific war zone as a correspondent.]

It just happens that I'm looking over this little book with a view to its publication at a time when I'm in the middle of writing up the notes of another tour to another front in another way. This narrative was written more than a quarter of a century ago by a bookish young man of twenty-two who had emerged half-baked from Harvard College and was continuing his education driving an ambulance behind the front in France. The young man who wrote it was about the same age as so many of the young men I was seeing and talking to last winter in the Pacific. All the time I was trying to imagine how I'd be thinking and feeling if I were that young man again, really in the war up to my ears, instead of being a middle-aged literary man getting a couple of quick looks at it as a correspondent.

There would be a number of differences.

For one thing I think the brutalities of war and oppression came as less of a shock to people who grew up in the thirties than they did to Americans of my generation, raised as we were during the quiet afterglow of the nineteenth century, among comfortably situated people who were confident that industrial progress meant an improved civilization, more of the good things of life all around, more freedom, a more humane and peaceful society. To us, the European war of 1914–1918 seemed a horrible monstrosity, something outside of the normal order of things like an epidemic of yellow fever in some place where yellow fever had never been heard of before.

The boys who are fighting these present wars got their first ideas of the world during the depression years. From the time they first read the newspapers they drank in the brutalities of European politics with their breakfast coffee.

War and oppression in the early years of this century appeared to us like stinking slums in a city that was otherwise beautiful and good to live in, blemishes that skill and courage would remove. To the young men of today these things are inherent deformities of mankind. If you have your club foot you learn to live with your club foot. That doesn't mean they like the dust and the mud and the fatigue and the agony of war or the oppression of man by man any better than we did. But the ideas of these things are more familiar.

Looking back it is frightening to remember that naive ignorance of men and their behavior through history which enabled us to believe that a revolution which

First Encounter (New York: Philosophical Library, 1945), 7–10.

would throw the rascals out of the saddle would automatically, by some divine order of historical necessity, put in their places a band of benign philosophers. It was
only later that some of us came to understand that when you threw out King Log
you were like as not to get King Stork in his place.[1]

Nobody had given a thought to educating us in the traditional processes of
self-government or in the rule that individual liberty, wherever it has existed in the
world, has come as the result of a balance between the rights and duties of various
contending individuals or groups, every man standing up for himself within the
framework of a body of laws and customs. Having no knowledge of the society we
had grown up in, or of the traditional attitudes that had produced in us the very ethical bent which made war and tyranny abhorrent to us, we easily fell prey to the notion that by a series of revolutions like the Russian the working people of the world
could invent out of their own heads a reign of peace and justice. It was an illusion
like the quaint illusion the early Christians had that the world would come to an
end in the Year One Thousand.

In reporting a conversation we had with a congenial bunch of Frenchmen one
night in a little town where the division was *en repos*, I tried to get some of this
down on paper. As an American unaccustomed to the carefully articulated systems
of thought which in those days were still part of the heritage of the European mind,
I remember being amazed and delighted to meet men who could formulate their
moral attitudes, Catholic, Anarchist, Communist, so elegantly. Reading it over I
find the chapter scrappy and unsatisfactory, but I am letting it stand because it still
expresses, in the language of the time, some of the enthusiasms and some of the
hopes of young men already marked for slaughter in that year of enthusiasms and
hopes beyond other years, the year of the October Revolution.

It was this sanguine feeling that the future was a blank page to write on, focus-
ing first about the speeches of Woodrow Wilson and then about the figure of Lenin,
that made the end of the last war so different from the period we are now entering.
Perhaps the disillusionments of the last quarter of a century have taught us that
there are no short cuts to a decent ordering of human affairs, that the climb back up
out of the pit of savagery to a society of even approximate justice and freedom must
necessarily be hard and slow. We can only manage one small step at a time. The
quality of the means we use will always determine the ends we reach.

Last winter, talking to the young men out in the Pacific I found that most of
them just hoped that what they would return to after the war would not be worse
than what they had left. This is not an age of illusions. We can only hope that it will
become an age of clear thinking.

Provincetown, Massachusetts. April 26, 1945.

Notes

1. In Aesop's fable, frogs appeal to Jupiter for a king. When they become dissatisfied with the log
that Jupiter named as king, Jupiter replaces it with a stork, who promptly eats the frogs.

There Is Only One Freedom

It is time we asked ourselves a few questions. After two years of a peace more dreadful in terms of human misery than the war years, we must think straight again.

It is not generally admitted in the United States that we can remain at peace only in a tolerably peaceable world. Only a world where the majority of men enjoy some small measure of freedom and prosperity can be peaceable. The aim of our foreign policy has presumably been to produce that kind of world, but it seems apparent to the most casual reader of headlines that about everything we have done ourselves or have allowed the other members of the United Nations to do has worked directly against that end.

The sudden failure of the will to victory in the United States about the time when the defeat of Germany and Japan became certain is a phenomenon that will puzzle historians for centuries to come. Of course, each of the peoples of the United Nations think they won the war. The British think they won it by their fortitude under bombing and by the brilliant work of their airmen in the Battle of Britain. The Russians think they won it by the immense holocaust they suffered. We think we won it by our industrial production, by our air force, and by our long-range bombers and our amphibian landings. Still, any unprejudiced observer will admit that neither Britain nor Russia would have had a chance against Germany, to say nothing of Italy and Japan, without the enthusiastic backing of the United States.

We have produced the most efficient industrial organization the world has ever seen. We have created a social structure which, though it still lacks alarmingly that climate for the cultivation of excellence that marks the really great civilizations, at least spreads the material benefits of civilized life more widely among the population than they have ever been spread before. And, yet, we find ourselves, in the years of our greatest national power, drifting without course or direction. Every move we have made has tended to produce a world strangled by despotism in which American institutions cannot easily survive.

Somewhere along the road the American people have lost that unspoken agreement on a few basic axioms that is needed to hold any social organization together. We have forgotten the principles upon which our nation's greatness was built. We have put a tangle of meaningless words in their place. What few policies we have been able to think up in world affairs, have been pushed into the defensive.

'47: The Magazine of the Year, 1 (Apr. 1947), 74–80.

Before the proponents of the American way of life can recapture the offensive we, here in America, have got to decide on what kind of nation we want.

Our time is running short. We are alone, United Nations or no United Nations, in a hostile world. Unless we can recapture the offensive by a practical policy that will set us to building the kind of a nation we want in the kind of a world we want we are headed again for war and for probable defeat. The situation of our republic has enough analogies with the situation of France before the French collapse to rob any American patriot of his sleep.

A majority of Americans, I think, are convinced that our foreign policy in the immediate past has been wrong. The fact that the State Department is less accessible to popular pressure than any other department of the Government makes us feel helpless about changing it. A new foreign policy in this country will come only in response to an overwhelming popular demand. There can be no popular demand until the people know what they want. The easiest way of finding out what kind of a foreign policy we want is to recognize the type of policy we don't want. The question we want to ask is: "What is our foreign policy doing to increase the areas of individual security and liberty in the world today?"

Nothing in nature stands still. Institutions either grow or they die. If what we want for the future is the growth and development of free institutions in America, we can take it for granted that the only favorable climate for their development will be in a world where civil liberties are on the increase. Has our foreign policy in the past contributed to the growth of civil liberty in the world of which we are a part?

Woodrow Wilson's policies, full of flaws as we now see them, tended, I think we can admit, in a general way in that direction. But what about more recent times? What about Fascism? We allowed the New York bankers to help establish Mussolini. We allowed Anglo-American finance to help prepare Germany for the arrival of Hitler. We did nothing to save from drowning the democratic republics, established on our own principles, of Germany or Austria or Czechoslovakia. We helped ruin the liberal republic in Spain through the Embargo Act and through official benevolence towards the Nonintervention Committee.[1] At Teheran and Potsdam our representatives, for reasons impossible to comprehend on the facts as we now know them, abandoned the peoples of Eastern Europe to slavery and destruction. In China, however good our intentions may have been, the result of our operations has been civil war!

Before we can have a new foreign policy we must blow aside the oratorical vapors and see what kind of a foreign policy we really have. The Communists say that it is the historic mission of the capitalist democracies to prepare the way for them. If our foreign policy is to be dedicated to proving them wrong, we must stop digging our own graves as we have dug the graves of our friends the world over. The alternative is ruin and enslavement for everybody, reactionary and progressive, rich and poor, Jew, gentile, and Negro, man, woman, and child. Lincoln's saying, that this nation could not endure half slave and half free is now true of the world. The time has gone by for the sort of musical phrases that made up Franklin Roosevelt's Four Freedoms that politicians could frame in wind, while they saw the opposite done under their noses. There is only one Freedom, freedom from oppression. We must save that in the world if we are to save the United States.

We have learned some important things in the last few years, but the things we have forgotten are even more important. The most important thing we have forgotten is the principle on which our political system is based, the principle that no man can be trusted with power over other men.

The working of self-government within the structure of civil liberties depends upon popular knowledge of that one basic truth. The government of laws established by the people's vote and consent, which has been the underpinning of every political system that allowed any measure of liberty to the individual man, is very far from the norm in human organizations. Normally the political strong men exploit the weak.

Call the setup communism, Fascism, or dictatorship, the results are the same. All you have to do is to watch a group of boys playing for a few hours to understand that a gang led by a boss is still the instinctive pattern of human society. The whole development of Anglo-Saxon law and of American institutions has been a search for expedients to curb the basic master-slave make-up in mankind. In so far as our institutions have succeeded in curbing this old Adam, they have produced a free society, in which the independent man could flourish as well as the boss. Since the politically weak people are usually the productive people (the politically strong are too busy getting control of their fellows to do any useful work) free societies have almost invariably become creative and prosperous. The danger has always been that, like Americans today, the citizens of flourishing democracies will forget the principles to which they owe their well-being, and slip back into the cycle in which democracy leads to demagoguery and demagoguery to despotism.

Another war in the near future—before our institutions for self-government have had time to recover from the numbing effect of the last and to adapt themselves to the breathless speed with which technology changes the industrial hierarchy—will almost certainly produce a bureaucratic despotism in this country.

If we are to chart a course that will lead towards increased freedom and dignity for the individual man and for a rich and progressive civilization, instead of towards stagnation and death, there is little time left for us. If we can't resurrect some system of principles to which our people can rally and in which they will find standards for judging the behavior of our political leaders, we will certainly continue our drift towards disruption and war.

It was not Hitler's strength but the lack of political principle among the leadership of Europe's democracies that produced the vacuum into which the ideas and armies of Nazism so easily rushed. It is not the success of the Soviet system but the collapse of the social framework of Europe, combined with the shortsightedness and the lack of principle of our leaders who dealt with the Russians, that have made the Kremlin the most powerful political force in the world today. We have become weak in so far as we have forgotten the master plan on which our greatness was founded: self-government under a system of law that protects the liberty of every citizen, strong and weak. If we can't stimulate new growth in self-government at home, we have little hope of developing a humane and practical policy towards the other peoples of the world.

What we were never taught in school is that the way of civilization is the hard way. The easy way is the way of decadence and barbarism. The old Adam is always waiting to trip us the first time that we make a false step.

The weakness of American political thinking today, and particularly of the strain of liberal semisocialist idealism that has for so long been the fashionable trend, is that it has never shaken off the optimism of the last century. The latter half of the 19th century was on the whole a period of easy expansion for the peoples of Western Europe and America. Everywhere the world was getting safer, old despotisms were breaking up, laws were becoming more humane, restraints on individual initiative were melting away. Labor-saving devices were beginning to take the ancient drudgery off the shoulders of the laboring man. People had a right to think that mankind was getting more civilized, that the century to come would be a period of unparalleled happiness for the human race.

By now it must be obvious that, judged from any conceivable humane standard, civilization in our time is on the downgrade. We must never forget that before the First World War, outside of Turkey and Russia and a few other backward regions, the whole world was open to travel and trade and immigration. If a man found he wasn't able to make a go of it under one government, he was free to pack his bags and move to another continent. Now the parts of the world where there is any freedom of movement at all become progressively fewer. Security of life or property under the law has vanished. Men writhe helplessly in a web of secret police, through which subservient and unruly alike can be uprooted, or enslaved, or extinguished.

Before we can start talking about foreign policy or domestic policy in any terms that can possibly be useful, we must face and understand the reality of the world we live in. If the free and humane civilization, which has been more or less the goal of the Western Nations, is possibly to come to life again, it will be through the wise and passionate effort of a generation of free men who insist on remaining free—men who will give themselves to the cause of freedom as wholeheartedly as our forefathers who founded this nation did. Institutions have their own laws of development, but in the long run they are what men make them.

Here is where we meet the great stumbling block that has, throughout history, pitched many a self-governing community back into slavery. The men who rise to power under free institutions belong to the same general human type as the men who find it so easy to rise on the backs of their fellows under a despotism. We can't do without them. They are the instruments through which the people manifest their political power. In America so far we have managed to curb the politicians and the military and to keep them as servants instead of masters of the nation. Since the days of Athens and Sparta, republics have had particular difficulty in keeping the allegiance of their public servants when they came into contact with foreign despots abroad. Weak as our foreign policy is, the instruments of it tend to be still weaker.

The sort of man who spends his life wheedling a pittance of power out of the voters feels an overweening personal attraction for the untrammeled wielder of the naked sword. In the old days when power in the outside world was expressed in rarified form by decorations and crystal chandeliers and visiting cards with titles engraved on them, we used to complain that our diplomats lost their heads, and, what was more important, their American patriotism, at the first sight of a duchess. Now they are tempted by stronger essences. There's a reek of omnipotence about a tyrant who has just signed a deskful of death warrants. He is master of his people and represents an eminence that a public servant hemmed in by the checks and balances of a government of law can never attain. Whenever an American citizen sees a photograph of some grinning public servant of his playing chess with a victorious head man, or exchanging toasts with a dictator, he should remember the old saying that eternal vigilance is the price of liberty.

The cure for perverted politicians is an aroused public conscience. The cure for a weak foreign policy is a strong policy based on practical principles. If we are to save ourselves and the world from the new dark ages of slavery and stagnation we must fall in love with freedom again at home. Men who are free themselves like to encourage it in others. Men who are engaged in building free institutions at home will find a way to frame a policy that will encourage free institutions among other peoples. Americans have done it before; we can do it again. Moral generosity was once natural to us.

Notes

1. The American Embargo Act of 1937 prohibited the shipment of arms to Spain; the Nonintervention Committee consisted of Britain and France, who agreed not to intervene in the Spanish Civil War.

Mr. Chambers's Descent into Hell

[A review of *Witness* by Wittaker Chambers. Chambers was a principal figure in the celebrated Hiss Case of the late 1940s and early 1950s. In 1948, Chambers charged that Alger Hiss, a former official in the State Department, had been a secret Communist agent for many years. Chambers was widely attacked as an unreliable informer, but he was in part vindicated by Hiss's conviction for perjury in 1950.]

It's not St. Augustine or Rousseau or Cellini; it is not one of the very great auto-biographies because it lacks their passionate zest for life in all its diverse and varied forms. But among the testimonials of the suffering spirit of man I think the book will stand high, somewhere between Dostoievsky's "The Possessed" and the narratives of the adventures of the light within like "Pilgrim's Progress" and George Fox's "Journal" that abound in the literature of seventeenth-century England. Amid all the hysterics that have characterized American writing during the last few years this is the only book I have seen that really penetrates into those depths where every man, in the agony of solitude, has at last to make his decision. No wonder Chambers keeps quoting the last line of Dante's "Inferno." It is the story of a descent into hell.

That there is something uplifting in the prospect of the immensity of pain that the human soul can contain is one of the great paradoxes that make life supportable. The appalling part of the book to me was the landscape that formed itself in my mind as a background to the gnawing agonies of the narrative; a landscape with figures of a society dedicated to its own destruction. How can it be that in a few short years we have sunk so low? A society or a nation has some aspects of a living organism. We all know that a living organism that fails to react to danger is sick or dying. The questions raised in the mind by the moral lynching of Whittaker Chambers by the right-thinking people of this country are so grave and urgent that a man breaks out in a cold sweat to think of them. Can it be that the "liberals" who control communications in the press and the radio and the schools and the colleges in this country have already crawled under the yoke of the Communist Party? I mean in spirit. We know they are not dues-paying members. Or has an immensely clever propaganda machine been able to make them dupes of a sinister hoax? Anyone who has heard the rumors being circulated right now in journalistic circles to the discredit of Robert Vogeler, the American businessman arrested and framed by the Hungarian Communists, will be struck by their similarity to the rumors circulated about Whittaker Chambers.[1] It is likely that both smear campaigns have the same origin. There is nothing appalling in the fact that Communist party members should continually try to discredit people who have turned against them or who have escaped from

Saturday Review, 35 (24 May 1952), 11. © 1952 Saturday Review Magazine. Reprinted by permission. Reprinted in *Occasions and Protests* (1964).

their dungeons. If they can't be eliminated physically, slander is the most convenient weapon. But what shall we say of the right-thinking men and women, of the men and women of position and education who repeat these slanders without investigating their origins and who refuse, in the light of all the evidence, to recognize the existence of a conspiracy of assassins bent on the destruction of the right-thinking liberals, as much as on the destruction of the rest of us? The day that this mystery becomes clear, the day when this strange delusion is swept out of the public mind, as was the deportations delirium that arose in another "liberal" regime, that day we will be able to go to bed secure in the thought that if the United States is doomed by forces of history too great for us to overcome, at least we will go down fighting.

Notes

1. Vogeler had been arrested as an American spy in Hungary in early 1948 while on a business trip. He confessed at his trial, was sentenced to fifteen-years' imprisonment, and was released by the Hungarian government in April 1951.

The American Cause

Not long ago I received a letter from some German students asking me to explain to them in three hundred words why they should admire the United States. "Young people in Germany," they wrote "as in other places in the world are disillusioned, weary of pronouncements on the slogan level. They are not satisfied with negations, they have been told over and over again what to hate and what to fight. . . . They want to know what to be and what to do."

This is what I didn't tell them: I didn't tell them that they should admire the United States for victories of our armed forces or because we had first developed the atomic bomb or the hydrogen bomb, or because we had shinier automobiles or more washing machines and deep freeze or more televisions or ran up more passenger miles of airplane travel a year than any other people in the world. I didn't tell them to admire us for getting more productive work done with less backbreaking than any other people in the world or for our high wages, or our social security system. I didn't tell them to admire us because our popular leaders had the sweetest smiles before the television cameras or because we lived on a magnificent continent that offered an unbelievable variety of climates, mountains, plains, rivers, estuaries, seashores. Some of these are very good things but they are not things that would help them "to know what to be and what to do."

This is what I told them: I told them they should admire the United States not for what we were but for what we might become. Selfgoverning democracy was not an established creed, but a program for growth. I reminded them that industrial society was a new thing in the world and that although we Americans had gone further than any people in spreading out its material benefits we were just beginning, amid crimes, illusions, mistakes and false starts, to get to work on how to spread out what people needed much more: the sense of belonging, the faith in human dignity, the confidence of each man in the greatness of his own soul without which life is a meaningless servitude. I told them to admire our failures because they might contain the seeds of great victories to come, not of the victories that come through massacring men, women and children, but of the victories that come through overcoming the evil inherent in mankind through urgent and warmhearted use of our best brains. I told them to admire us for our foolish trust in other peoples, for our failure

Distributed by the Spadea Syndicate, 1955. Reprinted in *The Theme Is Freedom* (New York: Dodd, Mead, 1956); text from *The Theme Is Freedom*.

to create an empire when empire building was easy. I told them to admire us for our still unstratified society, where every man has the chance, if he has the will and the wit, to invent his own thoughts and to make his own way. I told them to admire us for the hope we still have that there is enough goodness in man to use the omnipotence science has given him to ennoble his life on earth instead of degrading it. Self-government, through dangers and distortions and failures, is the American cause. Faith in selfgovernment, when all is said and done, is faith in the eventual goodness of man.

Spence's Point, October, 1955

PS to Dean Briggs

Looking back on it forty years later I find myself remembering the time I spent at Harvard as a period of afterglow. At nineteen and twenty I was mighty impatient with that afterglow. No more ungrateful brat ever ran for a nine o'clock across the old duckboard in the Yard. It was my fate to come in on the end of an era. Victorian scholarship had fulfilled its cycle. William James was dead. The afterglow of the great Transcendentalists had not quite faded from the Cambridge sky. Graduate students were still retailing awed anecdotes of Santayana. There had been a young poet named Tom Eliot, an explosive journalist named Jack Reed. They had moved out into the great world of hellroaring and confusion. I felt I'd come too late. Some of my undergraduate friends were trying to replace the ardors of the past with Oscar Wilde and Beardsley's illustrations and "The Hound of Heaven"; the mauve afterglow. I wasn't satisfied with any of it. I guess I wanted Periclean Athens right that day in the Harvard Yard.

It took me twenty years to discover that I did learn something at Harvard after all. Cambridge wasn't such a backwater as I'd thought. There was Robinson's Chaucer course, Henderson's History of Science. . . But it wasn't a question of scholarship: only years later did I begin to understand the uses of scholarship; it was the acquisition of a sort of an inheritance,—from "an age that is gone" just like in the song. Like for so many others, it was Dean Briggs who became the personification of that inheritance. Not that I appreciated him at the time. It wasn't that I didn't feel respect and affection for him as a man and, in the best sense of the word, a New Englander. The man was unashamedly himself. No one could help being moved by his lovely candor, his tenderhearted irony, the salty smalltown way he had of putting things.

But I thought of him as a museum piece, quaint, the way in these latter years we have come to admire American primitives; provincial. I was among his irreverent students who spoke of him as Aunt Betsy. Though we revelled in shocking him, we preferred most of the time to pretend that we were shielding him from the facts of life. What horrid little prigs undergraduates were in my day; I suppose they still are. In our idiot sophistication we thought of the dear Dean and his English 5 as hopelessly old-fashioned.

Brooks Atkinson, ed., *College in a Yard* (Cambridge: Harvard University Press, 1957), 63–68. Copyright © 1957 by the President and Fellows of Harvard College; © 1985 by Oriana T. Atkinson. Reprinted in *Occasions and Protests* (1964).

Of course he was. It's taken me a second twenty years to discover that his great value to me as a student was his old-fashionedness. He had an old-fashioned schoolmaster's concern for the neatness of the language, a Yankee zest for the ship-shape phrase, an old-fashioned gentleman's concern for purity of morals, to use a properly old-fashioned expression, and a sharp nose for sham and pretense which was neither old nor newfashioned but eternally to the point. As a professor he was perfectly accessible. After I graduated I often regretted I didn't take more advantage of his openheartedness.

The last time I saw him was in Paris in 1919, if I remember right, during the sham and fustian of the Peace Conference. He had been induced to come overseas on one of the fast proliferating commissions that were being posed to distract the public from Woodrow Wilson's failure to make the world as safe for democracy as we'd hoped. The Dean and Mrs. Briggs were housed, somewhat incongruously as it seemed to me, at the hotel du Quai Voltaire on the Left Bank. Who could imagine anyone less bohemian than Dean Briggs? I went to see them. As I remember I was still in uniform. The last time I'd seen him I'd been fretting and fuming because I was trapped in a backwater cut off from the main currents of life.

Well, in the three years that had passed since I'd turned in my last theme in English 5 I'd seen some life and a good deal of death. War had turned out a great teacher. I'd lost all pretense of collegiate sophistication but I'd come out with a prime case of horrors. I had seen too many men die in agony. I had the horrors too about the kind of world the gentlemen at Versailles were arranging for us poor buck privates to live in. All through those years in College I'd been honing for "the real world." By the time I went to call on the Briggses at the Quai Voltaire I already had a belly full of it.

There's a special musty smell about old Paris hotels, a mildewed grandeur; after all Paris has so often been the capital of the world. At that moment it was again. I found Dean Briggs and Mrs. Briggs shivering under shawls as they hovered over an alcohol lamp that was heating water for tea. The highceilinged room with its spangled chandelier was wretchedly chilly from the raw breath of the Seine under the windows. I never saw two people who looked so out of place. Although they had both aged noticeably since I'd last seen them, they had a fresh rustic look that delighted me. The Dean's eyes were as bright as if he'd just stepped off a New Hampshire pasture. Mrs. Briggs' cheeks were *applered*.

I've forgotten what we talked about—probably I was still shielding them from the facts of life—but I remember my delight in their country cousin look. Provincial, old-fashioned had become words of tenderness in my vocabulary. They were indeed travellers from another world. In wartime bombarded Paris of a few months before they wouldn't have seemed so out of place, but in the Paris of the Peace Conference they had the innocence of new born lambs. A soldier gets pretty sick of Mademoiselle from Armentières and all that sort of thing. Here was home, something more like home than anything I had ever known. I stayed on with them as long as I could. Too long I imagine. When I left to go out into the alluring treacherous streets of the city of light, to go out into the future, my future not theirs, a future where hope and disaster seemed about evenly matched and both seemed full of grime and bloodshed, I can still feel the wrench it took. I remember thinking, as I went down the stairs, that if it were possible to change lives with another man the way people do in the old Welsh stories, Dean Briggs even at seventy was a man

I would change with. He seemed so much younger than I and, in a way, more enduring.

Acceptance by John Dos Passos

[Dos Passos' response, on 22 May 1957 at a dinner in New York, on being awarded the Gold Medal for Eminence in Fiction from the National Institute of Arts and Letters.]

I wonder if any of you have ever noticed that it is sometimes those who find most pleasure and amusement in their fellow man, and have most hope in his goodness, who get the reputation of being his most carping critics. Maybe it is that the satirist is so full of the possibilities of human kind in general, that he tends to draw a dark and garish picture when he tries to depict people as they are at any particular moment. The satirist is usually a pretty unpopular fellow. The only time he attains even fleeting popularity is when his works can be used by some political faction as a stick to beat out the brains of their opponents. Satirical writing is by definition unpopular writing. Its aim is to prod people into thinking. Thinking hurts. There was once a man named Giordano Bruno who liked to call himself "the awakener of sleeping souls." You'll remember that he came to a rather uncomfortable end. In some times and places people have broiled the authors of unpopular works on beds of coals; in other times and places they have tried to educate them into conformity by starving them to death beyond the Arctic Circle. On the whole just not buying the man's books is a more merciful way of expressing popular disapproval.

Taking all these things into consideration I think it is a very handsome gesture on the part of the National Institute of Arts and Letters to pin a medal on my lapel. I'm very much touched and thank you very much.

Proceedings of the American Academy of Arts and Letters and the National Institute of Arts and Letters, 2d ser., no. 8 (1958), 193. Copyright 1958.

What Union Members Have Been Writing Senator McClellan

"I'm sorry I can't sign my name as it may mean my life or my livelihood. We may as well admit we are living under a labor autocracy—graft, rackets, intimidation, goons, etc. For fear of being bumped off, ostracized or deprived of making a living, I'm afraid to sign my name."

These sentences are from a letter by an American workingman, addressed to the Select Committee on Improper Activities in the Labor and Management Fields, popularly known as the McClellan Committee.

Congressional committees are accustomed to an enormous mail, but the correspondence reaching the McClellan Committee ever since its hearings started bids fair to set a record. Last February it was estimated that 100,000 letters had been filed away in the Committee's offices. Hundreds more pour in every week.

They come from every state of the union, from men and women in every trade and occupation: hod carriers and seamstresses, operators of draglines and makers of delicate dental equipment; from steelworkers, ditchdiggers, salesmen, miners, musicians and machinists. Letter after letter is written in fear, fear of violence and loss of job. This reporter read thousands of them. It was an awakening experience. This is no organized campaign. These letters come from the heart of the American people —spontaneously. It took great courage—and bitter experience—to write them. How many hundreds of thousands more disillusioned people are represented by these letters?

The member who protests against the way his union is being run does so at his own risk. "I'd never have another job on the waterfront if they knew I'd written this," a stevedore warns. A number of men typed a petition asking the Committee to investigate strong-arm methods used by their local business agent. "Can't sign names," they scrawled at the bottom of the sheet. "We'd be blacklisted." Some of them put it jokingly, "I'd sign my name but I don't like my undertaker."

Not all the writers have let themselves be terrorized; many are ready to fight. "You are our last hope," writes a union member. "I don't like to live in fear for the rest of my life, but if I am asked to testify I shall." Here's a courageous house painter: "The goons got nine tenths of the rank and file scared. That's the reason they don't come to meetings. I'll face any of 'em for you, Senator. I've lived 63 years

Reader's Digest, 73 (Sept. 1958), 25–32. Copyright ©1958 by the Reader's Digest Association, Inc. Reprinted in *Occasions and Protests* (1964).

now, how much longer can I live? But for God's sake give these young men a chance to raise their families!"

Many write in anger. "Is this the United States of America or where are we?—when a man has to see his family in want because he didn't approve of what the union officials were doing and had nerve enough to say so." A veteran writes: "Is this what I fought for in World War II?"

These are not cranks addressing the Senate Committee. None of them is opposed to unions as such. Many have devoted their lives to the labor movement. But they want labor leaders to be subject to the law like everybody else. Again and again they draw the distinction between the leaders and the rank and file. They feel that proper legislation, before it's too late, can save the labor movement.

"All labor will profit by these investigations," one man writes. "Your investigation has been rough on unions but all unions will be the better for it." "Clean up this mess," another pleads. "Make it so a man has a right to work and not have to bow down to them damn Hitlers."

Why, if there is so much discontent within the unions, don't we hear more of rank-and-file action? Senator McClellan himself asked that question in a speech which drew comment from union members.

"You state, Senator, that members can do a lot to clean up their unions by standing up for their rights," wrote a railroad worker. "We did just that and there are 50 men in this little mountain city walking the streets for a job."

This reporter traveled to the little mountain city to meet that worker. For his protection, let's call him Jones—though having lost his job, he has little more to lose.

It is a rainy Sunday afternoon. Jones and his friends have called a meeting of most of the 50 men, in the assembly room of their social club. Locomotive engineers, conductors, brakemen, switchmen, railway clerks—all so eager to tell about the raw deal they got that they keep interrupting one another.

"Don't have no respect for the rank and file. . . . All they care about's your money. . . . They've been in there too long."

It comes as a shock to an outsider because the railroad unions are among the oldest in America. "If you don't like the leadership why can't you put them out and elect somebody else?" this reporter asks. The whole room breaks into a loud horse-laugh.

"Mister, you don't understand," Jones says. "The only way you can get your ballot counted is by voting the way the boys upstairs want you to. They had it their own way so long they think we're a bunch of suckers."

An elderly railroad employe tells this story: Many years ago a union management made some bad investments of union funds. In 1927, the union faced bankruptcy. The management appealed to the members to bail them out by buying "loyalty certificates," which resembled bonds. When these didn't sell fast enough, the members were given a choice between a $100 assessment and a $100 "loyalty certificate." Six million dollars was raised in this way.

These "loyalty certificates" were supposed to pay four-percent interest. But they had a lot of small print, to the effect that they would be payable "at the discretion of the trustees when funds became available." They never became "available."

When a new industrial union for all operating railroad crafts was formed, these 50 workers decided to go along with it. They liked its constitution, which called for direct election of officers, limitation of salaries, the referendum and recall, local self-government and public accounting of funds. But they had reckoned without the union-shop contracts approved by the Railway Labor Act. When they joined the new union they were cited by their old unions. The men put up a long fight with the National Railway Adjustment Board and in the courts, but in the end they were fired.

The fight has gone on year after year. The rank and file of their old locals petitioned to have these men reinstated, but the leadership said no. "We've been under pressure for five years," one of the ousted men wrote the McClellan Committee. "You never knew which knock on the door would mean violence, or which phone call would be a threat. Don't sound like we lived in America, does it?"

A hundred thousand letters. A hundred thousand stories, each lighting up some dark corner of American labor life. The over-all story that emerges is that the leaders have taken over the labor movement. No place for the independents. No place for the idealist who organizes for the benefit of his fellow workers. The letters are desperately urgent. "Send your investigators now—tomorrow will be too late."

The writers of these letters are terribly earnest men, as this reporter can testify from long talks with many of them. Here's the story of a man who has just lost a battle for honest unionism inside one of the best internationals in the country. Let's call him Murphy because he's an Irishman, a husky bull-necked young fellow who was a paratrooper in World War II.

Five years ago Murphy was working in a plant in an eastern city. Many foreign-born workers there spoke little English and were getting a raw deal. It was dirty, dangerous work. Safety regulations were often neglected. The foreman contemptuously spoke of the men as donkeys. The independent union in the plant seemed to be company-dominated. So young Murphy found himself trying to stiffen the men's spines. He set up a class in English for them after work. He got an organizer from a great CIO industrial union, and threw himself into organizing the plant. They lost one election, petitioned the NLRB for another and won it.

Murphy was elected shop steward and chairman of the safety committee. His local sent him as a delegate to union conventions. A career was opening up for him as a labor leader. Still he wasn't satisfied with the way safety regulations were enforced at the plant and felt that some men were being discriminated against in the wage scale. He began to quarrel with the president of his local, a man we'll call Joe Cermak, whom he had helped elect.

Cermak's brother was the industrial union's field representative. These two had become labor professionals. Cermak did no more work in the plant, though he was paid full time. He sat in his office smoking cigars and drinking whiskey. He was building himself a $30,000 home and playing the stock market. Murphy was still sticking up for the rank and file, but Cermak was backed by his powerful brother. They intimated to Murphy that if he went along with them he could have a fine career—president of the local maybe, money and soft living. Let the donkeys do the heavy work.

It was a hard decision to make. Murphy wanted a nice life for his two small daughters. Yet he chose to fight. His wife began getting anonymous phone calls hinting that he'd better keep his nose clean. But the men in the plant believed in Murphy. He had enough votes lined up to take the presidency of the local away from the professionals at the next election.

The Cermaks decided to get rid of Murphy. They got help from management, which didn't like his harping on improved working conditions. When Murphy got into a dispute over safety regulations with his foreman, he was fired on charges of using abusive language. Murphy took the case to the state labor arbitration board. The union and management put their heads together to pick the arbitrator. Murphy lost his case and that was the end of one man's fight for the rights of his fellow workers. Fortunately he was able to take up a new career in a different type of work.

How can such a thing happen in a union whose leadership is reputed to be honest and intelligent? "Bigness," answers Murphy. The international president cannot keep an eye on the smaller locals. He must trust his field representatives. If a field representative keeps up his per capita on dues collected he's asked no questions and can build a little satrapy of his own. The men who lead unions for the money hate a troublemaker as much as management does.

"They just don't have time to pay attention to little guys like me," says Murphy. "We've got to have proper legislation because the United States is made up of little guys like me."

Not all the battles are lost, of course. Sometimes a courageous union member wins a round. Some of the Committee's letters tell of men risking their lives right now for what they consider their rights as Americans.

Here's one who drives a taxi in a teeming industrial city. Let's call him Bronski. When he came home from several years in the armed services he went to work for a new small cab company we'll call the Blue Cabs. But a larger company, the Red Cabs, had established a monopoly in the city and worked hand-in-glove with a powerful union. Both were entrenched at City Hall. Their union moved in to organize the Blue Cab drivers.

Although he'd always been a union man, Bronski didn't like the deal. He suspected that the professional labor leader who ran their local, whom we'll call Mr. Marino, was being paid by the Red Cabs to drive Blue Cabs off the street. So Bronski and some friends invited an organizer from another big out-of-town union to form a local for the Blue Cab drivers. They are only 200 men. They don't need to be protected from the management; the aggressive young fellow who owns the company gives his drivers a square deal. But they've got to protect themselves from Marino.

The fight is on. Marino calls a strike of Blue Cab drivers. A few Blue Cab drivers go out, but most of the men decide to cross the picket lines. The usual pattern of violence develops. Drivers are slugged, cabs are burned, passengers are intimidated; gasoline supplies are siphoned off, tires slashed. At the same time the Red Cab company is harassing the Blue Cab's management through the state public utilities commission and the state labor board.

Needless to say, there's no police protection for the Blue Cab drivers. When an out-of-town wholesaler sends in two tank trucks of gas for them in the middle of the night, a policeman is seen copying down the license numbers and turning them over to the Red Cab pickets. Meanwhile Marino lets it be known that the man who runs the Blue Cabs had better look out for lead poisoning.

At the height of the battle the Blue Cab drivers hold an election. They manage to keep Marino and his musclemen—all equipped with red armbands so that they won't slug each other—at bay at one gate of the compound while their men sneak out one by one through a back door to the voting machines. The vote is ten to one in favor of the Blue Cabs' own local.

Nevertheless, acts of violence keep up after the election, until the Blue Cab drivers decide one night that they are tired of going about their business in fear of their lives. They would show that two can play the game of terror. A mysterious fire destroys a couple of taxis belonging to the Red Cab company. Suddenly everything is quiet. No more bricks are thrown, no more drivers are beaten up. Marino is even heard to announce that the Blue Cabs' manager needn't be afraid to walk out on the street.

This young man never did let them scare him: that's the moral of the tale. A stranger from another city, he bought into this company without knowing he was buying into a hornet's nest. Once in, he decided to stay. Now, saving the Blue Cab company has become a crusade with him and his drivers. He feels he's risking his life for American principles.

The doors leading to this man's office have stout locks. He never stirs without a gun. He knows he has a long fight ahead, but he knows what he's fighting for. His Blue Cabs are still on the street.

There are plenty of brave men in American business and honest men in the labor movement. But many of them are beginning to feel that the odds against them are too great. In view of the testimony of Senator McClellan's mail pile it's no wonder they are discouraged.

Here's an elderly man in a Midwestern city, a member of a union in the entertainment industry, who's been collecting evidence for 30 years against the racketeers who control his trade. His best friend was shot dead for trying to get some of the crooks into court on that same evidence. . . . Here's a team of machinery movers. Their business is going to pot because the union makes them hire stumblebums who can't do the work. . . . Here are two brothers who have paid dues to the carpenter's union for 30 years. They can't work at their trade because they had a squabble with a business agent five years ago. . . . Here's a skilled lathe operator who's working as a janitor because the union's got him blackballed. . . . Here are a hundred thousand stories of grief and frustration.

But there is hope among them, too. These men believe in unionism and they believe in America. They aren't writing to the McClellan Committee just to air their grievances. The great majority of them are offering constructive programs.

As you read their letters, you can't help feeling pride in your fellow citizens. The letters are level-headed, reasonable; the suggestions offered are practical and carefully thought out. The Committee's chief counsel, Robert F. Kennedy, who has had experience with the correspondence of other committees, estimates that at least 30 percent of the suggestions for legislation deserve consideration in the drafting of new labor laws. He rates this percentage unusually high. Ten percent of usable suggestions, he says, is about average.

What do the writers of these letters want?

They want unions, but not the check-off or the union shop. They want union membership to be voluntary instead of compulsory. Some ask for right-to-work laws with teeth in them.

They want unions to be financially responsible under the law like banks and insurance companies.

They want the right to present grievances, without danger of reprisals, before the courts or the NLRB or the Department of Labor or some new federal agency.

They want self-government in the unions, freedom of speech and the right for all union members to elect their officers by secret ballot.

They want action. They want legislation. They want protection. They want democracy.

"We pray to God that we will some day get some laws passed in this country that will help us working people rid ourselves of these dictators so that we can govern ourselves."

Foreword to *Up from Liberalism*

The first duty of a man trying to plot a course for clear thinking is to produce words that really apply to the situations he is trying to describe. I don't mean a fresh set of neologisms devised, like thieves' cant or double-talk, to hold the uninitiated at arm's length. We have seen enough of that in the jargon of the academic sociologists which seems to have been invented to prove that nobody but a Ph.D. can understand human behavior. Plain English will do quite well enough, but the good old words have to be brought back to life by being used in their original sense for a change.

Only through a fresh approach, maybe through a variety of fresh approaches, can the terms through which we try to understand the events that govern our lives be reminted to the point of ringing true again. It is immensely heartening to those of us who would rather establish a true picture of the world we live in than one which is socially acceptable, to know that rash innovators are heartily at work. Thirty years ago the innovators called themselves radicals. Now mostly they call themselves conservatives.

The radicals of the period of the first of the century's great wars were trying to conserve something too. We were pretty conscious of the fact that we were trying to conserve the independence of the average citizen which we felt the power of organized money was bent to destroy. This was the underlying theme of the Populist agitation, of the Progressive and Socialist and Farmer-Labor parties. Through the referendum and recall and primary elections and labor unions and cooperatives we thought that something like the old townmeeting type of self government could be revived. The aim of all the diverse radical movements of that politically fertile period was somehow to restore the dignity of the man who did the work. Staid Single-Taxers, direct action IWWs and bombthrowing anarchists had the same eventual goal. They believed that if every man could be assured of the full product of his labor, the Kingdom of Heaven would be installed on earth. Their quarrel was about ways and means.

The history of the twentieth century has been the history of a series of denials of these hopes. We can now see that the radical view was grossly oversimplified. It made no allowance, among other things, for the fact that man is an institution-building animal. In our enthusiasm for the "producer" we underestimated the im-

William Buckley, *Up from Liberalism* (New York: McDowell, Obolensky, 1959), ix–xiii.

portance of the planner and manager in industry. Marx had shrewdly pointed out the class solidarities which were so obvious in nineteenth century England, but he was too near-sighted to apply his theory of classes to human societies in general, instead of restricting it to the particular phase of the industrial revolution he had under his nose.

Though Marx's proletariat may be somewhat better fed than it was a century ago, its individual members have made little if any progress toward that personal liberty and independence on which the dignity of man is founded. Each new development of industrial society, whether under Communist dictatorship or under the mixed capitalist-socialist systems that have grown up in the western countries, has reduced the stature of the individual man. In the West he has been able to trade his liberties for some increase in material wellbeing. The American standard of living in particular has become the envy of the world; so much so that even in the Soviet Union the Communist masters have been forced grudgingly to try to match these capitalist allurements.

As the millennial dream of a perfect society recedes into a science fiction future, the slogans of its votaries become the liturgy of a new ruling class. Opinions of the sort that sent Eugene Debs to jail or ruined Thorstein Veblen's teaching career have become the accepted platitudes of the academic groves.

Forty years ago a young man in college spoke ill of businessmen at some hazard. Profits were a sacred word. Advocates of labor unions were jeeringly asked if they had ever met a payroll. The tenets of the free market economy were as much a divine institution as The Ten Commandments. With the devotion of young Mormons on their missionary year, college graduates took to the road to sell bonds.

How different is the climate in the schools today! An apologist of the profit system often finds it hard to hold his job.

When Business abdicated in 1929 it was not the working class who took over, it was the new bureaucracy. The radical theorists from the colleges crowded into Washington. They were in the driver's seat and they knew it. Whether their work was good or bad is beside the point. The functions they exercised established them as a managerial class. The First World War had enormously increased the power of the Federal government. Under Roosevelt the labor union bureaucracies took their place beside the bureaucracies of the great corporations as economically dominant forces. Then the Second World War left government towering over both. Class realignments went along with the increasingly hierarchical organization of society. When the old regime businessmen fell from their thrones, the leaders of a new class took their places.

The "liberal" mentality which Mr. Buckley puts over a barrel in this book is, I am beginning to suspect, the ideological camouflage of the will to power of this new ruling class. I can't find any other explanation of these fits of hysteria, these fixations which time will prove to have been irrational, some of which are so amusingly documented in this book. The Communists are excellent propagandists who have developed an uncanny skill in putting their words in other people's mouths, but they are not that good. Only some such phenomenon as the solidarity and esprit de corps of a class recently risen to power can account for the lynching spirit aroused against those who have sought to dislodge any fraternity member, whether bureaucrat or college professor, columnist or commentator, from an entrenched position of power. This disparity between the provocation and the reaction is, as the emotions of the moment cool, what stands out more and more as the characteristic trait of the "liberal." Here is perhaps a key to the subconscious springs of liberal behavior.

As the nineteenth century Englishman defended his home as his castle, the modern American bureaucrat will defend the security of his job to the death. For security he will give up fame and fortune. This is certainly true of federal office holders, but why should it apply to white collar workers so generally? Could it be that they too feel a solidarity with the ruling class as against the common run of anonymous citizens they seek to manipulate?

This is not Mr. Buckley's theory. It is mine. Maybe new developments will prove it to be worthless. In any case, the sort of high-spirited analysis offered in this book should prove useful to anyone who is working towards an independent appraisal of this midcentury phenomenon of "militant liberalism."

Conversation with Dos Passos

[Dos Passos' interlocutor, Richard Whalen, was an editor of a Richmond newspaper.]

Spence's Point, Va.

The narrow blacktop winds placidly over the flat Tidewater farmland, through drowsy hamlets with names like Acorn and Farmer's Fork. At the Westmoreland County post office, a fly-specked general store with a dozen Negroes lounging on the sagging porch, the blacktop becomes a deep-rutted dirt road. A mile farther, half-hidden in the trees, a white sign reads: "Dos Passos Farms."

Another mile of deep cedar woods and the dirt track curves sharply into a broad pasture, where some fifty head of jet-black Aberdeen Angus are grazing. Set primly against a cluster of scrub pines is a two-story, red brick farmhouse with green shutters. A hundred yards beyond lies the gray Potomac.

This is Spence's Point, a remote corner of Virginia's history-laden Northern Neck (birthplace of George Washington and Robert E. Lee), where one-time radical John Dos Passos lives and writes in ultra-conservative calm. His father, a successful New York attorney, bought 1,800 acres here before the turn of the century. Dos Passos returned to his boyhood summer home in 1948, restored the 150-year-old tenants' house and has lived here intermittently with his second wife, teenage stepson and young daughter.

Tall, balding Dos Passos looks like a bookish country squire, casually dressed, modestly wealthy and comfortably insulated against the outside world. Yet his "disengagement" is more apparent than real. At 63, he has put ideology behind him. He rests his faith on the private virtues of the individual, and fears the coercive mediocrity that bigness breeds.

Walking with a scholar's stoop, he leads the way to his bright, white-walled back parlor, where coffee is waiting. Seated himself, he crosses his legs and lights a slender cheroot. A shy smile creases his oval, olive-skinned face, as though he were perpetually amused by some unspoken irony. He seems more inclined to listen than to speak, but, after a moment's hesitation, he responds quickly to a question, loosing a tumble of words, breathless and earnest. Then, as suddenly as a summer shower, the torrent halts and the smile returns.

Richard Whalen, *New Leader*, 42 (23 Feb. 1959), 20–21. Copyright © the American Labor Conference on International Affairs, Inc.

231

The suggestion that the youthful radical has become an elderly tory draws an amused snort from Dos Passos.

"I'm not a conservative," he says, smiling. "The conservatives must first discover what they have to conserve. I've been trying to escape labels all my life, but if I must have one, put me down for a 'Jeffersonian liberal'."

How did he come to Jefferson from a Marxist beginning?

"Slowly. I first became interested in Jefferson in the late 1930s. I felt a great personal need to seek an explanation of the New Deal, which was falling into bureaucratic lethargy and not turning out at all the way we had expected. Socialism, we believed, would revive democracy, with trade unions as the foundation. After World War I and the Soviet Revolution, we pacifists were convinced that the upheaval would be worthwhile if the people came out on top and gained control of the means of production. That was the theory; in practice, the people remained at the bottom. We were bursting with ideas, but the great weakness of socialism proved to be its lack of *politics*, the art of getting people to operate together without bopping each other on the head or eating each other."

And Jefferson?

"Jefferson and his contemporaries were immensely practical men, who understood *politics* from everyday experience as merchants and farmers. Running a large farm—making everyone do his share, making certain everyone was fed and clothed—was a political experience in itself. It taught the men of Jefferson's day the way power works. They saw government as utilitarian, responsive, working up from the local level, instead of down from the top. They wanted to protect the citizen on the fringes against domination by vested interests at the center.

"On the other hand, the theorists who put over the Wagner Act[1] didn't understand the way power works. They had an idea, but no sense of *politics*. I can't believe they wanted to deliver the workingman, bound hand and foot, to the labor bosses and racketeers. But they did."

Dos Passos rises and stuffs his hands into the back pockets of his baggy slacks. His glasses slide down on his nose as he paces to and fro. His artificial right eye, the result of the 1947 automobile accident that killed his first wife, gleams fixedly, in contrast to the soft, blinking left eye.

"Big labor and big business make big government inevitable; we can't go back to agrarian democracy. But we can read and learn from Jefferson, who would probably have considerable difficulty in keeping out of jail if he were alive today. Time doesn't kill ideas. If Jefferson were spreading his ideas on self-government today, they would cause almost as much alarm among the bureaucrats in Washington as among the bureaucrats in Moscow. If he were alive today, I wonder if his first move wouldn't be to stir up his political friends to call a constitutional convention to see if they couldn't readjust our method of government to meet our present needs."

Aren't we meeting our needs?

"I don't think so. We've experienced a dead period in the past few years because of prosperity. Now, the shoe seems to be pinching a bit. I think a more active period, for good or ill, lies ahead."

Was it merely "prosperity" that caused the "dead period"? How about McCarthyism?

"It seems to me that McCarthy was a clumsy man who tripped over a good cause. There *were* Communists in government. But the hysteria of McCarthyism was generated chiefly by those who opposed him. After you've seen a real witch-hunt, like Mitchell Palmer's [U.S. Attorney General in 1919–21], you can't take the 'McCarthy Terror' too seriously. Some people were inconvenienced, yes, but their shouts were out of all proportion to their injuries. All in all, the McCarthy episode was one of the strangest in this nation's history."

Has the novel survived the "dead period"?

"Of course. It always survives. The novel is alive today, though it's somewhat feeble. Too many people are stewing in their own juices; they're caught in their own time. Take Jack Kerouac and his *On the Road*. The tale's been told before, and better. There's little attention to style and no discipline. And this talk of a 'Beat Generation.' The whole subject of 'generations' seems to me to be a crashing bore. Some huckster picks up some idiotic and misleading classification, like 'the Lost' or 'the Beat,' and drums it into everybody's ears until you'd think they'd vomit. The odd thing is that they don't. All these pigeonholes relieve people of the effort to use their own minds. I say to hell with them.

"Now, the Pasternak book and the Djilas book were superb.[2] They show human standards still exist in the Communist world. Though they're written inside the Marxian framework, they're truthful and exciting . . . because the writers have tapped something deeper than their immediate surroundings. Djilas especially is exciting, but he offers no alternative. If he'd read Jefferson, Madison and John Adams, he would definitely have something different to offer. That's the great problem—there's no modern alternative to worship of the machine."

Dos Passos, who wrote and wept for Sacco and Vanzetti and a generation of lesser known radicals, isn't impressed with the Angry Young Men either.

"There are Causes today, great Causes for young writers to get stirred up about. But a curious dualism toward our economic system softens their anger and silences their protest. Instinctively, they desire freedom, yet they also feel government owes them something. They want opportunity, yet they crave security. Eventually, the mentality of the bureaucrat sets in. When I went to college, our professors were stuffy—but they had something to be stuffy about. They offered very definite ideals. They gave you something to rebel against. Nowadays, most professors offer the uninspiring notion that one idea is probably as good as the next. No wonder the young are silent.

"If the shoe begins to pinch, writers are likely to follow the banners again. Cultural and political progress interact. Today's tired liberal idealism reflects the apathy and self-interest of the bureaucrat. The revolutionists of yesterday have become the vested interests of today. And the bureaucratic mind is barren. When new rebels come along, something exciting may be produced. Unfortunately, literature usually happens after the fact."

Perched on the edge of his chair, lighting another cheroot, Dos Passos shakes his head and declines to give advice to young writers, except to "avoid people who offer advice."

"There are too many 'creative writing' courses and seminars, in which young writers are constantly being taught to rewrite the previous generation. They should be experimenting on their own. Every writer faces different problems which he must solve for himself."

All of his prose devices—running words together, the "Camera Eye" autobiography, the "Newsreel," the memorably incisive biographies of Henry Ford, J. P.

Morgan and Eugene Debs in *U.S.A.*—all these devices, according to Dos Passos, were "the result of thrashing around to try and get the stuff out as directly as possible." The "thrashing" continued in his last novel, *The Great Days*, which he wrote in the first-person "although it wasn't particularly autobiographical." Some reviewers hinted acidly that Dos Passos' own "great days" were behind him, but he confesses that he didn't read a single review. "I've been writing for a long, long time. If I'd paid any attention to my critics, I'd be in a sanitarium."

What lies ahead?

"Before senility?" he replies, arching his eyebrows.

First, there will be some journalism ("it helps to keep one's fingers and brain oiled"), then another novel, about two years off.[3] It will trace the labor movement from its cradle days with the Wobblies to the swank efficiency of the merged AFL-CIO. (Dos Passos began work on the book after reading the McClellan Committee transcripts and interviewing scores of union members.) Finally, as might be expected, the lights of Dos Passos' second-floor study will burn late as he writes another tribute to the good sense of the Master of Monticello.

Notes

1. The National Labor Relations Act of 1935, sponsored by Robert F. Wagner of New York, regulated labor relations and established the right of labor to organize.

2. *Doctor Zhivago* (1958) by Boris Pasternak and *The New Class* (1957) by Milovan Djilas.

3. *Midcentury* (1961).

Looking Back on *U.S.A.*

[Dos Passos' collaboration with Paul Shyre on a dramatic version of *U.S.A.*
opened at the Martinique Theatre in New York on 28 October 1959 and ran for
seven months.]

It's not entirely an accident that the first attempt at staging one of my books should
be concerned with "U.S.A." Though I don't remember being too conscious of it at
the time, as I look back with the advantage of thirty years of hindsight at the writing
of these three novels, it seems fairly obvious that my excitement over the "expressionist" theatre of the Nineteen-twenties had a good deal to do with shaping their
style.

"The 42d Parallel," part of the trilogy, must have gotten under way some time
during 1927. I remember that I carried some chapters with me to work on when I
went to the Soviet Union in the early summer of 1928. The years 1926–29 were the
only period of my life when I was involved in any way with the theatre.

At Harvard College, to be sure, I was interested enough to be punctual in attending whatever theatrical productions came to Boston. What I mostly remember
of those years were Urban's settings at the Boston Opera House and the Diaghilev
ballet. It was always the theatre-as-spectacle that attracted me. I loved the circus.
"Boris Godunov" still seems to me the greatest theatrical work of our time.

"Moon Is a Gong"

What contact I had with the other kind of theatre, the comedy of manners sort
of theatre, was through my friendship with Ed Massey, who was taking one of
George Pierce Baker's courses.[1] That was how in an (unpublished) early novel I
came to make one of the characters write a play.[2] This play was produced years later
by Ed Massey as "The Moon Is a Gong," and published in 1926 under the title I
preferred: "The Garbage Man," with the subtitle: "A Parade with Shouting." It was
the New York production of this "expressionist" work that resulted in my getting
entangled with an early attempt to establish a "labor" stage in this country: The
New Playwrights Theatre, which Otto Kahn put up the money for.

To tell the truth, at that time I was more interested in scene designing than in
the drama per se. I had followed with enormous enthusiasm the productions of Diaghilev's Ballet Russe in Paris during the years when it was dominated by Stravin-

New York Times, 25 Oct. 1959, sec. 2. Copyright © 1959 by the New York Times Company. Reprinted by permission.

sky's music. Some friends and I had been delighted to be allowed to help Gontcha-
rova paint some of the scenery for "Noces" in a loft over near the Place des
Combats.

Ed Massey had used settings of my designing for his "Moon Is a Gong" production. The work that appealed to me most when I was a director of the New Playwrights was planning and painting the scenery. I was a frustrated architect: in those
days I hadn't quite decided whether to put most of my time in on painting or writing.

The two things that caused me to lose interest in the theatre (as a career say)
were, first, the fact that I was by nature and training a morning worker, while in the
theatre everything constructive gets done after midnight; and second, a feeling of
the hopelessness of the struggle with the organized Communists—with whom I still
sympathized in some things—who were busily boring from within.

It was largely to get away from the personal problems of the New Playwrights,
as well as for a close look at the Russian theatre—which, embodied by Meyerhold
and Tairov,[3] seemed to me to lead the world at that time as Eisenstein did in motion pictures—that I went to the Soviet Union in the summer of 1928. Although
Stalin's terrible ice age had not yet clamped down on Russian inventiveness in the
arts, I found all the trends I was interested in pretty thoroughly embattled. By the
time I got back to New York—though somewhere in that period, I did write one
more play, a thing called "Fortune Heights" which oddly enough was produced in
the Soviet Union—I was already engrossed in the writing of "The 42d Parallel."

From that day to this, writing has kept me too busy to allow me time off for
more than an occasional watercolor. People don't choose their careers: they are en-
gulfed by them.

In helping prepare a text for this proposed dramatic reading, I have had to
skim over a good deal of the "U.S.A." trilogy. If there is a special Hell for writers it
would be in the forced contemplation of their own works, with all the misconcep-
tions, the omissions, the failures that any finished work of art implies. It's the relationship between the David Michaelangelo managed to hew out of the marble and
the David he wanted to make.

Naturally you do find passages that seem to come through. Invention isn't all
failure: I suppose in Hell the successful passages would fade away just as you were
starting to read them.

Political Change

People keep asking me whether my political ideas have changed. Of course.
Haven't yours? If they haven't where have you been all these years?

It's a boring question because none of the political slogans of the Twenties applies to the Fifties. All the concepts have been stood on their heads. "Liberalism,"
for example, used to be equated with enthusiasm for individual rights; now it tends
to mean identification with central governing power.

This much I can say: though youthful prejudice occasionally led me into what
I now see as distortions, on the whole the attitude of mind exhibited by the
"U.S.A." books doesn't seem to me too different from my attitudes today. What has
occurred is a complete transformation of the social background. What was white in

the Twenties is black in the Fifties and vice versa. The Communists who have a keen nose for heresy "smelled a Lollard" as early as "The Big Money." I can't see any particular virtue in consistency, but the basic tragedy my work tries to express seems to remain monotonously the same: man's struggle for life against the strangling institutions he himself creates.

Notes

1. Edward Massey was in 1925 to direct Dos Passos' *The Moon Is a Gong* in its Harvard Dramatic Club production. Baker's "47 Workshop" courses in playwriting and stage production attracted students from throughout the country.

2. In Dos Passos' unpublished novel *Seven Times Round the Walls of Jericho*, written largely in France and Italy during 1917–18, the character James Clough is a radical playwright who writes a play resembling *The Moon Is a Gong*.

3. V. E. Meyerhold and Alexander Tairov, Russian Formalist directors of the 1920s.

Contemporary Chronicles

[Dos Passos' introduction to a reading from his own works that he gave at Carleton College on 30 November 1960.]

For something like forty years I've been getting various sorts of narratives off my chest without being able to hit upon a classification for them. There's something dreary to me about the publisher's arbitrary division of every word written for publication into fiction and nonfiction. My writing has a most irritating way of being difficult to classify in either category. At times I would find it hard to tell you whether the stuff is prose or verse. Gradually I've come up with the tag; contemporary chronicle.

The sort of novel I started to try to write in the antediluvian days of the first World War was intended to be very much a chronicle of the present. It was a chronicle of protest. Dreiser and Norris had accustomed us to a dark picture of American society. Greedy capitalists were getting in the way of attainment of the Jeffersonian dream every American had hidden away somewhere in his head.

Three Soldiers my first long novel was an attempt to chronicle the feelings and frustrations of the natural-born civilian who found himself in the army. We were all natural-born civilians in the early years of this century. Now we are very much more regimented. It is hard to explain to young people born into today's regimented world how automatically their fathers and grandfathers resented the sort of forcible organization that has become the basis of today's social structure.

Manhattan Transfer which followed *Three Soldiers* was an attempt to chronicle the life of a city. It was about a lot of different kinds of people. In a great city there is more going on than you can cram into one man's career.

I wanted to find some way of making the narrative carry a very large load.

The period immediately before and after World War I had been a period of experimentation both in Europe and America. The Europeans have a sense of order and hierarchy that makes them love labels as much as the typical American tends to distrust them. Maybe trying to escape classification is one of our national vices. It certainly is mine. They called the sort of thing I wanted to do futurism or expressionism. I wasn't much interested in the labels on these various literary packages but I was excited by what I found inside.

In a war you spend a lot of time waiting around. While I was in the ambulance service in France and Italy I had managed to find time to read a certain amount of French and Spanish and Italian, poetry mostly.

Carleton Miscellany, 2 (Spring 1961), 25–29. Copyright by Carleton College, 1961.

The Italian futurists, the Frenchmen of the school of Rimbaud, the poets who went along with cubism in painting were trying to produce something that stood up off the page. Simultaneity, some of them called it. That excited me.

Why not write a simultaneous chronicle? A novel full of snapshots of life like a documentary film. I had been very much affected by the sort of novel that Stendhal originated in French with his *Chartreuse De Parme* and Thackeray in English with *Vanity Fair*. I remember reading *Vanity Fair* for the tenth time rather early in my life; after that I lost count. You might call these chronicle novels. *War and Peace* is another example.

In this sort of novel the story is really the skeleton on which some slice of history the novelist has seen enacted before his own eyes is brought back to life. Personal adventures illustrate the development of a society. Historical forces take the place of the Olympians of ancient Greek drama.

I had read James Joyce's *Ulysses* on my way home from Europe laid up with a bad case of flu in a tiny inside cabin down in the third class of a Cunarder.[1] It's a marvelous way to read a book. *Ulysses* got linked in my mind with Sterne's *Tristram Shandy*. They are both subjective novels. My interests were the opposite: I wanted to write objectively. I had been pretty well steeped in the eighteenth century from early youth. Sterne too had tried to make his narrative carry a very large load. In college I had been taken with the crystal literalness of Defoe's narratives and by Fielding's and Smollett's rollicking satire. Fielding and Smollett came easy to me because I'd been prepared for them by Captain Marryat's sea stories of life in the Royal Navy which gave me infinite pleasure when I was a small boy. I read enough Spanish to be interested in Pio Baroja's modern revival of the Spanish picaresque style.

I dreamed of using whatever I'd learned from all these methods to produce a satirical chronicle of the world I knew. I felt that everything should go in: popular songs, political aspirations and prejudices, ideals, hopes, delusions, crackpot notions, clippings out of the daily newspapers.

The basic raw material is everything you've seen and heard and felt, it's your childhood and your education and serving in the army, and travelling in odd places, and finding yourself in odd situations. It is those rare moments of suffering and delight when a man's private sensations are amplified and illuminated by a flash of insight that gives him the certainty that what he is seeing and feeling is what millions of his fellowmen see and feel in the same situation only heightened. Seen a little sharper perhaps.

This sort of universal experience made concrete by the individual's shaping of it, is the raw material of all the imaginative arts. These flashes of insight when strong emotions key all the perceptions up to their highest point are the nuggets of pure gold.

They are rare even in the lives of the greatest poets.

The journeymen of the arts have to eke them out with lower quality ore. A novelist has to use all the stories people tell him about themselves, all the little dramas in other people's lives he gets glimpses of without knowing just what went before or just what will come after, the fragments of talk he overhears in the subway or on a streetcar, the letter he picks up on the street addressed by one unknown character to another, the words on a scrap of paper found in a trashbasket, the occasional vistas of reality he can pick out of the mechanical diction of a newspaper report.

It was this sort of impulse that came to a head in the three U.S.A. novels. Somewhere along the line I had been impressed by Eisenstein's documentary films like the Cruiser Potemkin. Eisenstein used to say that his master in montage was Griffith of the *Birth of a Nation* fame. Montage was the word used in those days to describe the juxtaposition of contrasting scenes in motion pictures. I took to montage to try to make the narrative stand up off the page.

The chief difficulty you have to meet when you try to write about the world today is that the shape of society is changing so fast that the descriptive and analytical part of the human mind has not been able to keep up with it. The old standards of good and evil have broken down and no new standards have come into being to take their place. A couple of generations have been brought up on the theory that standards of behavior don't mean anything. The basic old rocky preconceptions—call them prejudices if you want—on which a writer, whether he was for them or against them, used to find a firm footing, have been so silted over with the double talk of various propagandas that he can't get a foothold on them any more. You are left wallowing in the quicksand of the theory that nothing really matters. Morals? ethics? How shall we behave? Let's just pull it out of the air. An old time Christian named John Bunyan called that quicksand the Slough of Dispond.

The generation I got my education from, the generation that cut its eyeteeth on the deceptions and massacres of the first World War had a fervent sense of right and wrong. We thought civilization was going to hell in a hack, and in some ways we were right. But we did believe too that if people used their brains the modern world could produce a marvelous society. There was a germ of truth in both conceptions. We suggested some radical remedies. The trouble was that when the remedies were tried in most cases the cure proved worse than the disease.

It was in the cards that the writing of a would-be chronicler like myself should become more and more satirical as the years went by.

I'm going to read you a few samples from pieces I've used in various novels for purposes of contrast or to explain some facet of the underlying tale, samples of what maybe you might call the "documentary" style.

Notes

1. Probably the spring of 1922, when Dos Passos returned to America on the *Aquitania* after traveling extensively in the Near East.

John Dos Passos

[Sanders' interview with Dos Passos occurred at Spence's Point, Virginia, on 2 July 1962 (not 1966, as cited in the *Paris Review* headnote to the interview). Portions of the interview appeared initially in the *Claremont Quarterly*, 11 (Spring 1963) and in the *Paris Review*, 46 (Spring 1969).]

INTERVIEWER: Is this the same farm where you spent your summers as a boy?

DOS PASSOS: This is a different part of the same farm. When my father was alive, we had a house down at the other end, a section that has been sold, which is now part of a little development called Sandy Point, that string of cottages you saw along the shore. We've been here for more than ten years now, but I don't get to spend as much time here as I would like to because I still have a good deal of unfinished traveling.

INTERVIEWER: Has this polarity between Spence's Point and your traveling had any particular effect on your writing?

DOS PASSOS: I don't know. Of course anything that happens to you has some bearing upon what you write.

INTERVIEWER: Perhaps it once led you to write that the novelist was a truffle dog going ahead of the social historian.

DOS PASSOS: I don't know how true that is. It's the hardest thing in the world to talk about your own work. You stumble along, and often the truffle dog doesn't get to eat the truffle . . . he just picks it up.

INTERVIEWER: Have you become the social historian at the expense of the artist?

DOS PASSOS: There's just no way that I can tell. I have to do what I'm interested in at the time, and I don't think there's anything necessarily inartistic about being the historian. I have great admiration for good history. All of my work has some certain historical connotation. Take *Three Soldiers*. I was trying to record something that was going on. I always felt that it might not be any good as a novel, but that it would at least be useful to add to the record. I had that idea when I began writing—with *One Man's Initiation*—and I've had it right along.

INTERVIEWER: Always, then, you have been observing for the record?

DOS PASSOS: Very much, I think.

INTERVIEWER: It must have been difficult to remain simply an objective observer.

David Sanders, in *Writers at Work: The "Paris Review" Interviews*, ed. George Plimpton, 4th ser. (New York: Viking, 1976), 68–89. Copyright © 1974, 1976 by the Paris Review. Reprinted by permission of Viking Penguin, Inc.

DOS PASSOS: Possibly, but I think I've tended to come back to center. I'm often carried away by emotions and enthusiasms for various ideas at one time or another, but I think the desire to observe, to put down what you see as accurately as possible, is still paramount. I think the critics never understand that because they always go on the basis that if a man writes about Mormonism he must be a Mormon, that if he writes about Communism he must be a Communist, which is not necessarily true. I've usually been on the fence in partisan matters. I've often been partisan for particular people, usually people who seem to be getting a raw deal, but that's a facet I share with many others.

INTERVIEWER: You've said that when you began observing you were a "half-baked young man" out of Harvard. Have you had any recent thoughts about that education?

DOS PASSOS: I got quite a little out of being at Harvard, although I was kicking all of the time I was there, complaining about the "ethercone" atmosphere I described in camera eye. I probably wouldn't have stayed if it hadn't been for my father, who was anxious for me to go through. At that time, the last of the old New Englanders were still at Harvard. They were really liberal-minded people, pretty thoroughly independent in their ideas, and they all had a sort of basic Protestant ethic behind them. They really knew what was what. I didn't agree with them then, but looking back on them now, I think more highly of them than I once did. But that essentially valid cast of mind was very much damaged by the strange pro-Allied and anti-German delusion that swept through them. You couldn't talk to people about it. When the war started in the summer of my sophomore year, I was curious to see it, even though theoretically I disapproved of war as a human activity. I was anxious to see what it was like. Like Charley Anderson in *42nd Parallel*, I wanted to go over before everything "went bellyup." When I got out of college in the summer of 1916, I was anxious to get started in architecture, but at the same time I was so restless that I had already managed to sign myself up in the volunteer ambulance service. My father was determined to put that off so we kind of compromised on a Spanish expedition, and I went to Madrid to study architecture. Then my father died in January of 1917, and I went ahead into the ambulance service. I suppose that World War I then became my university.

INTERVIEWER: Especially because you were in the ambulance service?

DOS PASSOS: . . . You *saw* the war. I don't know if it was on the more or less seamier side of combat, but in the ambulance service you did have a more objective point of view toward war. After all, the infantryman must be carried away by the spirit of combat, which is quite different from sitting around and dragging off the wreckage.

INTERVIEWER: What remains with you now about the First War—thinking back on it?

DOS PASSOS: Much of it I don't remember, really because I wrote about it; when you write about something you often never think of it again. I do remember little snatches of experience. The smells. They seem to linger on in the memory— the gas smells, the almond smell of high explosive, latrine and body odors. A terrible time, there has never been such a series of massacres, but all of us were glad to have seen it and survived it. In the ambulance corps, my capacities were largely concerned with driving a car without dumping people into ditches. As for the troops, they had an ambivalent feeling about the corps. Where they saw us in greatest volume was where an attack had been planned and was going to be mounted and a lot of people were going to be killed. They must have thought us a collection of scavenger crows.

INTERVIEWER: Did you go through this time thinking of yourself as a writer?

DOS PASSOS: I never felt I wanted to be a writer . . . I didn't much like the literary world as I knew it. I studied architecture. I've always been a frustrated architect. But there are certain periods of life when you take in an awful lot of impressions. I kept a good diary—very usual sort of thing—and I was consistent about putting down my impressions. But I had no intention, really, of being a writer then. It may have been Barbusse that got me going. Or more likely something to keep the dry rot from settling in the brain. Robert Hillyer and I began what we called the Great Novel, or more simply the GN. Our schedule then at the front was twenty-four hours on, twenty-four hours off, and I remember we worked on the novel in a cement tank that protected us from the shelling. We wrote alternate chapters. I sent the manuscript up to the University of Virginia the other day.[1] I didn't dare look at it.

INTERVIEWER: You mention the novels of Barbusse. Was it *Le Feu*, in particular, which made an impression?

DOS PASSOS: It impressed us a good deal at the time. It was the first of the novels that gave a picture of the massacres of World War I. He had a very good ear for the conversations of those involved. His other things weren't really very much. They were cultish works, like Rolland's *Jean-Christophe*, which impressed so many of us in our college days. One had to make a reassessment. I met Barbusse a number of times in Russia afterward. It was rather horrible: he was a combination of evangelist and Communist, and by that time he had become a mere mouthpiece for the Party.

INTERVIEWER: Then, after the war, you were at the Versailles peace conference?

DOS PASSOS: Not really. Sometime in the winter after the armistice they established a thing very much like the G.I. Bill. If you were a college student or a recent graduate, you could go to any university you picked over there, and I picked the Sorbonne. So I was around in Paris, I guess, from February to June of 1919. Of course, that was the peace conference period, and I talked to a lot of people connected with it in various ways. Most of them were observers. No, I wasn't taking notes on it.

INTERVIEWER: The question of combining politics and fiction has engaged a good many critics, often drawing from them the notion that it's very difficult to mix the two.

DOS PASSOS: Well, I don't know. Recently, I've been calling my novels contemporary chronicles, which seems to fit them rather better. They have a strong political bent because after all—although it isn't the only thing—politics in our time has pushed people around more than anything else. I don't see why dealing with politics should harm a writer at all. Despite what he said about politics in the novel being "the pistol shot at the opera," Stendhal also wrote contemporary chronicles. Or look at Thucydides. I don't think his history was at all damaged by the fact that he was a political writer. A lot of very good writing has been more or less involved in politics, although it's always a dangerous territory. It's better for some people to keep out unless they're willing to learn how to observe. It is the occupation of a special kind of writer. His investigation—using blocks of raw experience—must be balanced. Sartre in his straight, plain reporting was wonderful. I can't read him now. A writer in this field should be both engaged and disengaged. He must have passion and concern and anger—but he must keep his emotions at arm's length in his work. If he doesn't, he's simply a propagandist, and what he offers is a "preachment."

INTERVIEWER: Let's recall how you observed things when you were among the first American writers to see the results of the Soviet revolution. Did you speak the language?

DOS PASSOS: I learned French at an early age, and Spanish, and Portuguese. I tried Russian, but I didn't do very well with it. I used to get a special kind of headache over their verbs.

INTERVIEWER: Just how impressed were you on those first visits?

DOS PASSOS: My first glimpse of the Red Army was in 1921–22 when I was with the Near East Relief in the Caucasus. At that time it still seemed very hopeful that they would develop something that would be leaning forward instead of backward. You may remember having read in *Orient Express* how hopeful I felt upon observing that the pawnshop in Baku seemed to be going out of business. And, then, probably the period when I was in Leningrad and Moscow in 1928 was the time when I was very much on the fence because I tried to avoid politics entirely on that visit. I'd been working with the New Playwrights—Gold, Lawson—in New York, and I was very much interested in the theater. The Russian theater was still quite good, and so there was a great deal to see. I didn't know at that time that its development was just about coming to its end. Often things you think are just beginning are coming to an end. I spent about six months there in 1928. Even then it was a much more open period than any they had since except possibly the early part of the Khrushchev regime. People were still being introduced as Trotskyites, although Trotsky was in exile. Stalin hadn't really attained power the way he did after the purges. Most of the Russians I knew then were connected with the theater, and a few of them would shake their fists when they passed his picture. This was in '28. They already hated him. They knew more about him than I did. All those people disappeared in the purges.

INTERVIEWER: Would it be fair to say that at first you thought the Soviet experiment held some sort of promise for the individual?

DOS PASSOS: Yes, I thought it might. I always felt at that time that the Soviets might develop into something like the New England town meeting, but of course they became entirely different, something more like the boss-controlled conventions at home.

INTERVIEWER: What were your literary influences at this time—during the twenties?

DOS PASSOS: The futurists, Ungaretti in Italy in particular. I wasn't taken at all by D'Annunzio. He was a little too rhetorical for my taste. Then I admired Pío Baroja, the Spanish novelist, and Rimbaud, of course, and Stephen Crane, particularly *Maggie, Girl of the Streets*, in which Crane has a terribly good ear for conversation and the way people put things.

INTERVIEWER: Did Hemingway read Barbusse?

DOS PASSOS: Not as far as I know. Ernest and I used to read the Bible to each other. He began it. We read separate little scenes. From Kings, Chronicles. We didn't make anything out of it—the reading—but Ernest at that time talked a lot about style. He was crazy about Stephen Crane's "The Blue Hotel." It affected him very much. I was very much taken with him. He took me around to Gertrude Stein's. I wasn't quite at home there. A Buddha sitting up there, surveying us. Ernest was much less noisy then than he was in later life. He felt such people were instructive.

INTERVIEWER: Was Hemingway as occupied with the four-letter word problem as he was later?

DOS PASSOS: He was *always* concerned with four-letter words. It never bothered me particularly. Sex can be indicated with asterisks. I've always felt that was as good a way as any.

INTERVIEWER: Do you think Hemingway's descriptions of those times were accurate in *A Moveable Feast*?

DOS PASSOS: Well, it's a little sour, that book. His treatment of people like Scott Fitzgerald—the great man talking down about his contemporaries. He was always competitive and critical, overly so, but in the early days you could kid him out of it. He had a bad heredity. His father was very overbearing apparently. His mother was a very odd woman. I remember once when we were in Key West Ernest received a large unwieldy package from her. It had a big, rather crushed cake in it. She had put in a number of things with it, including the pistol with which his father had killed himself. Ernest was terribly upset.

INTERVIEWER: Have you ever had an equivalent sense of competition with your fellow writers?

DOS PASSOS: No, not at all. I've always thought you should concentrate on paddling your own canoe. Ernest's jealousy of Scott was really embarrassing—because much of it was at a time when Scott was going through a horrible experience in his own life. He was writing stories like "A Diamond As Big As The Ritz"—out of a state of mind which had so little to do with his literary energies.

INTERVIEWER: If we may return to your novels, is characterization particularly difficult in such a novel as *42nd Parallel* where J. Ward Moorehouse, who seems to personify the whole system being indicted, might be taken—I believe he has been taken—as based on Ivy Lee, the man who actually started the field of public relations?

DOS PASSOS: Well, Ivy Lee did have something to do with Moorehouse because I met Ivy Lee in Moscow—I've forgotten what he was doing there—when I was writing the book. We were at the same hotel. I was trying to learn Russian, a very painful process, and so it was quite a relief to find someone to talk English to. I had several rather interesting conversations with him. I think it was in the fall of '28, but I'm not sure what hotel it was. The Metropole? Anyway, I had done the first few chapters of *42nd Parallel* before I went, and then J. Ward Moorehouse was just emerging. I think those conversations with Ivy Lee probably had something to do with his completed portrait. Then, also, I knew quite a few advertising men in New York.

INTERVIEWER: I suppose a much more direct characterization of an actual figure occurs in *The Great Days*, doesn't it, with Roger Thurloe modeled as he is on Forrestal?

DOS PASSOS: That's closer to being an effort to produce a characterization of a living person, I think, than most of the others. I had met Forrestal a couple of times, but even so the characterization is pretty far off. I think if I had actually intended to do Forrestal, I would have done him as one of those portraits in *Midcentury*.

INTERVIEWER: Do you find it difficult to read anything written about your work?

DOS PASSOS: I never do, if I can help it. I know it has a bad effect on fellow writers. People sometimes send me articles about myself, and I bundle them off after a while to the University of Virginia for the professors to mull over. Occasionally I look at things, but I've generally managed to avoid stuff written about my work because there just isn't time to fuss with it. I don't think I've lost very much sleep by what you would call the critical reception of my work. I've been very fortunate in a way. If a thing is knocked in one place, somebody else may like it somewhere else. *The Great Days* was very much ignored in this country, but it went quite well in England and in Germany. I wouldn't have been able to make a living without the international market.

INTERVIEWER: What do you think of the considerable disparity between criticisms here and in Europe of your work over the past twenty years, or at least since *U.S.A.* was so well received in both places?

DOS PASSOS: I haven't followed it very much. I think there are a lot of American critics who try to pretend that I don't exist at all. They haven't read much of the stuff, and so they really don't know. When you do historical things, say, like *The Men Who Made the Nation*, a totally different set of people review it from those who review so-called fiction. There's this strange schizophrenia in American publishing between fiction and nonfiction, and so people who review nonfiction have never read any of the fiction. It works both ways.

INTERVIEWER: How much of the hostile American reception dated from *Adventures of a Young Man* in 1939, with the cues from left-wing reviewers?

DOS PASSOS: A certain amount, but still *Three Soldiers* was greeted with hostility all the way back in 1921. Of course I think they were wrong on *Adventures of a Young Man* because I don't think my position was so much changed. Politically it was, but from a human point of view I don't think it was so different.

INTERVIEWER: How have these differed in your orientation? The political and the human point of view? In going from *U.S.A.* to *District of Columbia* to *Midcentury*, have you, in effect, gone from big money to big government to big labor?

DOS PASSOS: To a certain extent, I think, yes. At different periods one seems more drastic than the other.

INTERVIEWER: It's a procession which points, perhaps, to this human consistency in your work.

DOS PASSOS: I think it probably does because I think that's what motivates it. It's a fact that I have tried to look at it from the point of view of the ordinary man, the ordinary woman, struggling to retain some dignity and to make a decent life in these vast organizations.

INTERVIEWER: In almost all of your work, then, there has been some opposition between individuals and systems?

DOS PASSOS: Always, yes. We've gone through a period when the industrial society has been very rapidly solidified. The Communist way is just one way of solidifying. What it seems to me they have done is to take the capitalist system and kind of freeze it, including a great many of its less agreeable characteristics, freeze it and turn it over completely to bureaucratic control.

INTERVIEWER: I've always wanted to know how *Manhattan Transfer* was written—more than *Three Soldiers* or the other two early novels which more directly follow your experiences. When you wrote *Manhattan Transfer*, were you trying to create an entirely new kind of novel? Or were you building from definite precedents?

DOS PASSOS: *Three Soldiers* had just raised quite a stir and had quite a considerable sale. I seem to remember writing some of *Manhattan Transfer* in Brooklyn, in a room on Columbia Heights that looked out on the harbor. I don't know how this question can be answered. I was trying to get a great many things in to give a picture of the city of New York because I had spent quite a while there. I was trying also to get a certain feeling in. Precedents? I don't think so. I never went in much for theories of that sort. At the time I did *Manhattan Transfer*, I'm not sure whether I had seen Eisenstein's films. The idea of montage had an influence on the development of this sort of writing. I may have seen *Potemkin*. Then, of course, I must have seen *The Birth of a Nation*, which was the first attempt at montage. Eisenstein considered it the origin of his method. I don't know if there were any particular origins for *Manhattan Transfer* in my reading. *Vanity Fair* isn't at all like it, but I'd read *Vanity Fair* a great deal, and I'd read eighteenth-century English stuff. Perhaps *Tristram Shandy* has certain connections. It's all subjective, while, in my stuff, I was trying to be all objective. Sterne made up his narrative out of a great many different things. It doesn't seem to have much cohesion, but if you read the whole book, it adds up to a very cohesive picture.

INTERVIEWER: What about the reception of *Manhattan Transfer*?

DOS PASSOS: One critic called it "an explosion in a sewer." Probably the person who helped the book most was Sinclair Lewis, who wrote a very favorable review.[2]

INTERVIEWER: What sort of plan did you have for *U.S.A.* when you began writing it?

DOS PASSOS: I was trying to develop what I had started, possibly somewhat unconsciously, in *Manhattan Transfer*. By that time I was really taken with the idea of montage. I had tried it out in *Manhattan Transfer*—using pieces of popular songs. By the time it evolved into such compartments as the camera eye of the *U.S.A.* trilogy it served a useful function—which in that case was to distill my subjective feelings about the incidents and people described. My hope was to achieve the objective approach of a Fielding, or a Flaubert, particularly as one sees it in Flaubert's letters, which are remarkable. In the biographies, in the newsreels, and even the narrative, I aimed at total objectivity by giving conflicting views—using the camera eye as a safety valve for my own subjective feelings. It made objectivity in the rest of the book much easier.

INTERVIEWER: You eventually closed down the camera eye—though *Midcentury* is the same as *U.S.A.* in its other formal aspects.

DOS PASSOS: After a while, you feel more in control of your subjective feelings. I didn't think that I needed it by then.

INTERVIEWER: Was *U.S.A.* a trilogy to begin with?

DOS PASSOS: No, it started to be one book, but then there was so much that I wanted to get in that it got to be three books very soon . . . before *42nd Parallel* was finished.

INTERVIEWER: Did you begin with the idea of just taking the years up to the war?

DOS PASSOS: No, I had the basic idea for the whole thing. It started with what I didn't then call a contemporary chronicle; I do call it that now because it seems a useful label. I think, if I can remember back, I started *42nd Parallel* with the idea of publishing a series of reportages of the times. I don't think I thought of the book as any sort of a novel. I thought of it as a series of reportages in which characters appeared and reappeared. It was to cover quite a long period.

INTERVIEWER: I've often wondered why some of them, like Richard Ellsworth Savage or Vag, didn't reappear in *District of Columbia* or *Midcentury*.

DOS PASSOS: I decided to try to close that group down. You have to make a fresh start every now and then.

INTERVIEWER: How did you come to add the portraits to *U.S.A.*? Did you get much editorial advice on this book?

DOS PASSOS: Eugene Saxton, first at Doran and then at Harpers, was a very friendly editor, but I don't think anybody gave me any advice. If they did, I doubt if I took it—I guess because I've been very hard to convince. I've always been very grateful for what they've been able to point out about misspellings and bad construction, but as far as the *gist* of things is concerned I've not been much moved. It's awfully hard to say how I came to add the portraits. It was trying to get different facets of my subject and trying to get something a little more accurate than fiction, at the same time to work these pieces into the fictional picture. The aim was always to produce fiction. That's why I was completely unable to understand the fiction, non-fiction dichotomy. I was sort of on the edge between them, moving from one field to the other very rapidly.

INTERVIEWER: Critics might drop labels altogether when they take up *U.S.A.*?

DOS PASSOS: It would be a good idea to look at it a little more objectively without preconceived ideas. That wouldn't mean that they would necessarily have to like it, but I think they would have a better basis for criticism.

INTERVIEWER: In connection with research, is a social life with literary people useful?

DOS PASSOS: Almost never. I hear a good deal more nonliterary conversation. Certainly useful to me in my line of work. I read very little. Yet the language does change—mostly through television and teenage jargon—and it's very hard to keep up with it. Knowing a younger generation helps. An academic community is pretty dreary, but the students, of course, are an interesting quantity. They come down from the University of Virginia and deliver themselves of the current doctrine. As do my daughter and step-son. It's very valuable. Word of mouth provides the great texture, not research.

INTERVIEWER: Incidentally, what is your opinion of the students of the New Left?

DOS PASSOS: Many of them seem to be going through something rather like a tantrum. An odd paranoia sweeping the country, I don't know exactly why . . . a mass hysteria . . . a combination of the St. Vitus' dance of medieval times and the Children's Crusade . . .

INTERVIEWER: What about other forms of activity? In the twenties you maintained a great interest in the theater.

DOS PASSOS: The theater didn't suit me really. I can't sit up all night. Everything in the theater is done after midnight. I lived in Brooklyn at the time, and we always finished so late that I had to walk back home across the Brooklyn Bridge. I never got home before three A.M. and being someone who's never been able to sleep later than seven in the morning, I just couldn't keep up the schedule.

INTERVIEWER: Did you ever run across Hart Crane on those walks?

DOS PASSOS: He was very much a night animal. I used to try to get him to go home to his bed for a change. I'd get him there all right, but then he'd hide in the entry and dart out again.

INTERVIEWER: He used to prod his creative impulse by writing to the noise of a phonograph turned up full volume.

DOS PASSOS: Yes, I've heard that. For me it would be too distracting . . . pleasure and pain equally divided. I find that simpler things get me going—diaries, for instance, especially if they turn up in old trunks . . .

INTERVIEWER: What is your ideal set of working conditions?

DOS PASSOS: All you need is a room without any particular interruptions. Some things I've done entirely in longhand, but now I tend to start chapters in longhand and then finish them on the typewriter, and that becomes such a mess that nobody can transcribe it except my wife. I find it easier to get up early in the morning, and I like to get through by one or two o'clock. I don't do very much in the afternoon. I like to get out of doors then if I can.

INTERVIEWER: You get all of your work done before you go swimming?

DOS PASSOS: Yes. Down here that's my regular routine.

INTERVIEWER: How much revising do you go through?

DOS PASSOS: I do a lot of revising. Certain chapters six or seven times. Occasionally you can hit it right the first time. More often, you don't. George Moore rewrote entire novels. In my own case I usually write to a point where the work is getting worse rather than better. That's the point to stop and the time to publish.

INTERVIEWER: How did *District of Columbia* become a trilogy?

DOS PASSOS: *Adventures of a Young Man* came by itself, and the Spottswood[3] family seemed to need more development. I began with the younger brother, went on to the older brother, and finished with the father. It worked out backwards.

INTERVIEWER: Was Glenn Spottswood's predicament in *Adventures of a Young Man* anything like your own in the later thirties? By his predicament I mean Glenn's feeling that he had been deceived while he worked on the Harlan County Defense Committee, the Scottsboro Boys Defense Committee, all of his encounters with the Communists.

DOS PASSOS: I wouldn't have known about conditions in Harlan County or what was behind either Defense Committee if I hadn't been through those experiences. I wouldn't have known how to describe them. Of course, I think you always have to have a little seed of personal experience, although it's often a very small seed, to produce the real verisimilitude, which is what you are looking for.

INTERVIEWER: In *Number One*, the novel about Glenn's older brother Tyler, there is an account of the third-term convention. Had you admired Roosevelt before that occasion?

DOS PASSOS: Yes, I certainly did. I thought he did very well all of his first term. I voted for him a second term, and then I regret to say that I voted for him for his third term. Now I think it would probably have been better for the country if Willkie had been elected, if anybody else had been elected, because it would have broken up the continuity of Roosevelt's extraordinary machine in Washington. I think Roosevelt would have come down as a really great president if he had only served two terms. I think he had done all the good he had in him, and there was only harm left. In that third term, the consolidation of the federal government really was the rebirth of bureaucracy, which had shown its head under Wilson and then faded away. That's what *The Grand Design* is about.

INTERVIEWER: It seemed to me that Roosevelt dominated that book, if not all of *District of Columbia*, in much the same way that Wilson did *1919*.

DOS PASSOS: I think so, although I fairly intentionally kept him behind the scenes. At that time I had done quite a bit of reporting around Washington. Reporting has always been an important part of my career. Between books, I've always done a few reporting jobs.

INTERVIEWER: One political question seems inescapable. In many of your books since the war, you write of the "abominable snowman" of international Communism, of having been among the first to see him, and having kept on seeing him through all of the crises, alliances, and thaws. Do you see him as clearly today?

DOS PASSOS: It's very hard to tell. It's almost impossible to have any view of present-day international politics without having a double standard of judgment. Our development and that of the Soviet Union have many things in common except that the Soviet Union is motivated by this tremendous desire for world conquest, more active sometimes and at other times less active. It may be that the people of Russia are not very much motivated by this passion for expansion any more. I'm not sure whether they ever were. I would like to know. I mean I don't think the mass of people is motivated at all because it's so hard for them to reach any conclusion. They are doped with ideology.

INTERVIEWER: Have you ever thought of going back there to check on it?

DOS PASSOS: It would be hard to. There might come a time when it would be interesting to go to Russia, but I don't think that time has come yet. I think there are certain phases of the development of Russian society which are on our side. Some Russians might be among our best allies because some of them really want much the same things that we do. But those particular people are helpless in the bureaucratic setup. Pasternak was a good example, I think, with his curious book, *Doctor Zhivago*. It seemed so much a voice from the past, like something of Turgenev's coming back to life. It was very attractive to me because it showed a side of the Russian people which I've had great sympathy with. It showed that that side of the Russian mind, that nineteenth-century humanism, still existed. Of course, Pasternak was quite an old man. Still, as long as they teach people to read and write and allow them to read nineteenth-century Russian literature, there are going to be more Pasternaks.

INTERVIEWER: Do you read many contemporary American writers?

DOS PASSOS: I don't get time for very much because I do so much reading of a research type in connection with things I am doing—documents. It's very hard for me to get time. I read Salinger with a great deal of pleasure, and I mention him simply because he has given me pleasure. *The Catcher in the Rye* and *Frannie and Zooey* were very entertaining books. I read a certain amount of Faulkner, and I'm very, very fond of some of his writing. "The Bear" and *As I Lay Dying*. "The Bear" is a marvelous hunting story. I liked *Intruder in the Dust*. He reminds me very much of the old storytellers I used to listen to down here when I visited summers as a boy, when I would hide in the shadows so that I wouldn't be sent off to bed. I'd listen till my ears would burst. I suppose what I like best in Faulkner is the detail. He is a remarkably accurate observer and builds his narratives—which sometimes strike me as turgid—out of the marvelous raw material of what he has seen.

INTERVIEWER: And Cummings' poetry?

DOS PASSOS: Oh, I've always enjoyed Cummings' poetry. I was very fond of Cummings personally. He was in college at the same time I was, I think a class ahead of me, and I saw quite a little bit of him there. We always met on much the same terms, although sometimes a year would go by when I didn't see him. He was the last of the great New Englanders.

INTERVIEWER: How does the work of some of the more committed left-wing writers of the thirties seem to you now? Michael Gold and Howard Fast, for example.

DOS PASSOS: Somebody credited me with a wisecrack about that time. Writers of the world unite, you have nothing to lose but your brains. Mike Gold wrote quite well. His first book, *Jews Without Money*, was a warm, human thing, very much influenced by Gorky, whom Gold admired greatly. Fast never interested me. His book on Tom Paine irritated me very much because I thought he completely falsified the picture. Generally, though, the writers who became CP members either stopped writing or became so boring nobody could read them.

INTERVIEWER: Have you known any of the Communist politicians, rather than the writers?

DOS PASSOS: I had a long conversation with Earl Browder, to whom I took a great dislike. He was a horrible fellow. I've met Foster and didn't like him.

INTERVIEWER: Did you discover a great disparity between Browder and Foster, on the one hand, and John Reed on the other?

DOS PASSOS: I had a great deal of sympathy with John Reed. I thought he wrote very well, and I think I liked his writings better than I did him. The only time I ever met him he was giving a talk, maybe about Mexico. It was at Harvard when I was an undergraduate. There was something indefinably Harvard Brahmin in his manner that threw me off at the time. I was a very intolerant young man in a bashful and retiring sort of way in those days. I hated college boys. From what Louise Bryant said privately, I suspect that John Reed was pretty discouraged before he died.[4]

INTERVIEWER: Have *you* been more optimistic about the world situation in the last five years or less so?

DOS PASSOS: It would be hard to say. I think I have probably become more so as I get older and a little less passionately involved, but then when they pull something like the operation in the Bay of Pigs, I become extremely pessimistic, particularly when nobody seems to understand its significance.

INTERVIEWER: What do you think of the academic treatment of modern literature?

DOS PASSOS: It seems to be rather confused, although I haven't followed it very much. The academic community is more likely to suffer from mass delusions than the general public. I don't know exactly why, but I suppose it's always been the case.

INTERVIEWER: Do you feel that your own most recent writing is generally misunderstood in this country?

DOS PASSOS: I wouldn't say that. Some people misunderstand it, naturally. They always will. It would be absurd to expect them to understand things. Also, if you deal with matters that touch people, you must expect to cause pain; particularly, if you hit at some target that is close to the truth. It always causes pain, agony. Naturally, they resent it.

INTERVIEWER: Have you ever thought that you have what has been called a Wayne Morse complex, an unwillingness to go along with a major party or major tendency?[5]

DOS PASSOS: There is a type of mind that does tend to say, as Ibsen did, that the minority is always right. Perhaps I agree with Ibsen in that.

INTERVIEWER: Have you tried other artistic forms? Poetry, for instance.

DOS PASSOS: I did quite a lot of that . . . but it took a different form . . . it got into certain rhythmic passages in *U.S.A.* I do a little painting, a watercolor or so. The prose can get too highcolored; a watercolor gets that drained off.

INTERVIEWER: Do you enjoy writing?

DOS PASSOS: That depends. Sometimes I do, and sometimes I don't.

INTERVIEWER: What is its particular pleasure?

DOS PASSOS: Well, you get a great deal off your chest—emotions, impressions, opinions. Curiosity urges you on—the driving force. What is collected must be got rid of. That's one thing to be said about writing. There is a great sense of relief in a fat volume.

Notes

1. *Seven Times Round the Walls of Jericho*, which remains unpublished. Hillyer in fact contributed only to the opening portion of the work.

2. "Manhattan at Last!" *Saturday Review of Literature*, 2 (5 Dec. 1925), 361.

3. The correct spelling is *Spotswood*.

4. Bryant, a journalist and companion of Reed, was with him when he died in Moscow in 1920.

5. Morse, a U.S. senator from Oregon, was noted for his independent views.

Faulkner

[A tribute occasioned by Faulkner's death on 6 July 1962.]

Faulkner's storytelling appeals to me so much, I suppose, because it is the kind of storytelling I remember as a child down in the northern neck of Virginia. Sitting in a row of men on some rickety porch after the dishes had been cleared off the supper table some hot August night when the dryflies shrilled, rocking and smoking or chewing tobacco—a man would start talking. Usually he didn't explain who the people were he was telling about. You were supposed to know that. It would be he or she or sometimes "what's his name?" did this or that. Gradually out of a web of seemingly disconnected incidents a story would evolve. Characters in situations scary or mirthful would take shape. A scene would light up as if you were there watching. Listeners would draw in their breath or laugh and slap their knees. I'd be sitting on the porch steps, keeping out of sight for fear somebody would notice me and send me off to bed, never minding the mosquito bites, listening till my ears burst.

Reading Faulkner brings that lost world back to me. It's so often an eleven-year-old boy who is the listener through whose ears the outlandish scrambled tales pour into the reader's blood. Faulkner's writing has a way of pouring direct into the bloodstream like a transfusion. It was his old-time rural storyteller's gift that enabled him somehow to keep his steaming turgid inventions—blood and thunder mixed with often false psychological subtleties out of the psychiatrist's clinic—within the margins of the tall story tellingly told. You are carried away whether you believe it or not.

At his best Faulkner's gothic caricatures of men and women, for all the clap-trap of the plots, come to life as Dickens' did. Always the emotions ring true.

Storytelling is the creation of myths. A good acting myth doesn't have to be plausible but it has to impose its own reality on mankind. I defy anybody who has been reading Faulkner to look at a map of the state of Mississippi without expecting to find Yoknapatawpha County there.

Faulkner's characters impose their nightmare reality upon you because they are built out of truths. The truth of the stirrings of the flesh and blood and passion of real men observed tenderly and amusedly and frightenedly, just as Homer made his goddesses and heroes real because he built them out of traits he knew in men and women. In Faulkner what I like best is the detail, the marvelously accurate ob-

National Review, 14 (15 Jan. 1963), 11. © by National Review, Inc. Reprinted by permission.

servations he built his narrative out of, the raw material of his inventions. Has there ever been a bear more real than Old Ben in The Big Woods? His unendingly cordial study of the struggle between the bloods of various races under one man's hide is truthtelling of the highest order. So are his descriptions of the happy symbiosis that builds up under certain conditions between men and discordant races and disparate backgrounds. The Chickasaw Indians who bought the steamboat, the hound dogs, the hunting dogs, the little fyce dogs, the horses, the mules, the trees, the streams and the swamps; and the kitchen clock, I think it was in *Soldiers' Pay*, that ticked out: Life, death; life, death.

And now the great storyteller is dead. I don't imagine death came too hard to him. He had met death before many times in his storytelling. His stories are full of the knowledge of death. He did not meet death as a stranger.

The Battle of San Francisco

[The leading contenders for the presidential nomination at the 1964 Republican national convention were Senator Barry Goldwater of Arizona and governors William W. Scranton of Pennsylvania, Nelson A. Rockefeller of New York, and George Romney of Michigan.]

San Francisco

Political conventions are as traditional as the circus. One of San Francisco's charms is that it is the most traditional of American cities. The perfect place for a convention. In the alternation of sun and mist, in the wild wind off the western ocean, the skyscrapers of universal megalopolis shine in a special light. The upthrust of the stubborn hills has forced groupings and intervals. The other building shows odd little decorative details you don't see anywhere else. Among the crowds on the streets there are faces you wouldn't see in New York or Chicago, oldtimer faces, prospectors' faces, cowpunchers' faces with eyes narrowed to count cattle on distant plains. People have a pleased look. Their frank enjoyment of the show is contagious.

All the young people are trotting about, old dowagers have crept out from under the pavings of Nob Hill. "I can't wait to see who it is," mutters an old lady in a porkpie hat as she stands breathless on tiptoe in the throng outside the St. Francis Hotel watching some much televised profile pass through the whir of cameras and the flicker of flashbulbs out of an automobile and up the steps into the slogan-infected lobby.

Trends and portents emerge from the cheerful confusion of the streets. On Sunday civil rights marchers filled nine blocks of Market Street. The scattered citizens along the sidewalks watched them in a strange silence. At first it was a straggle of well-intentioned, middleclass people shuffling along after a sound truck playing *The Battle Hymn of the Republic*. Then came the longhairs, the beards, the characters. The placards said a great deal more about stopping Barry Goldwater than they did about equal rights.

Next came the blue banners of Harry Bridges' Longshoremen,[1] and then rank on rank of young activists, clapping, shouting slogans, flourishing impromptu placards, singing in key, walking in step with long elastic strides. The parade becomes electric. There is force here. Disciplined and directed force. After forty years Lenin's revolution still has the militance and power to command so many of the gripes and frustrations of the world.

But the eager Commies aren't the only activists on the streets. The Young Americans for Freedom are something new on the political scene. Wherever there is a chance their candidate might appear, whenever some personality they approve of arrives, the YAF turns out in swarms. They wear Goldwater hats, Goldwater shirts and sweatshirts, badges the size of dinner plates. They have bands, bunting, guitar players, little crackers that go pop and send off a shower of colored streamers. They are cheerful, they are tireless, their "We Want Barry" placards bounce up and down, they never heard of frustration.

(Fascists, Hitler Youth, the Liberal journalists whisper behind their hands.)

In the hotels the journalists, counting radio, TV and the skillful busy bands of technical people who set up the machinery, outnumber the delegates. There are four thousand or more representatives of mass communications describing the behavior of a couple of thousand delegates and alternates. The stage managers outnumber the actors two to one.

The main arenas are the Mark Hopkins and the Fairmont up on the hill and the St. Francis and the Hilton downtown. On upper floors in suites behind closed doors the struggle goes on between the old and the new in the Republican Party. The stage managers of press and radio want things to go on the way they have been, routinely, for twenty years. But the direction of the play seems to be slipping out of their hands. The actors are making up their own speeches.

Starting with the Young Americans for Freedom, many of whom are too young to vote, moving through the state delegations, made up often of small businessmen new to politics, a different cast is taking over. Somehow the old machine, operated from the Eastern Seaboard, the machine that so deftly destroyed Robert A. Taft, has lost its power. Caught in a sort of nightmare horror, the Liberal journalists see the comfortable certainties they helped construct crumbling all around them.

There are times when the struggle surfaces so that even an outsider can see. The actors appear. There was Governor Scranton's press conference. Governor Scranton is a pleasant appearing gentleman, with an attractive wife who is quite skillful at answering questions tartly for the television viewers. He has been chosen for his agreeable qualities to lead the forlorn Grand Old Party.

After Rockefeller failed, after Romney didn't quite catch fire, all the hopes of the Liberal battalions focused on the Governor of Pennsylvania. His interlocutors are friendly. Their questions are all loaded to go off in the right direction. The Governor smilingly makes the perfect answers that would have sounded so right on the East Coast, but somehow here in San Francisco in 1964, they fall flat. The neat clichés no longer apply. Baal has always been so kind, but now when his priests call to him he answers not a word.

With General Eisenhower it is different. He steps up into the focused lights and cameras and microphones and says simply "I am Dwight Eisenhower, fire away."

For half an hour, with an air of gallantry and good health and good humor, he answers trick questions. He evades every trap set for him by the most skillful stage managers in the nation who are trying to beguile him into saying something damaging to Senator Goldwater. Eisenhower cheerfully refuses to have words put in his mouth on any subject whatsoever. He walks away from the crestfallen crew a gentleman very much to be respected.

The place to see Goldwater at his best was at the Masonic Temple addressing an audience of YAFs. He is a Mason and he dearly loves young people. He is entirely at home. His two sons introduce him. He explains why his stake is in the young people. He and his wife have raised a family. They've seen their children grow up. To a certain extent they have grown up with them. He speaks reminiscently of the old days when they all went fishing and hunting together, camping out, looking up out of their sleeping bags through the pinebranches at the stars and talking in whispers about God and man.

For the new generations he must help undo the mistakes of the old. The young understand what he means when he says that constitutional government was designed to protect the freedoms given us by God. Strength, Liberty, God. These are the words that bring cheers bursting from their throats till the white Masonic hall seems to swell with the roar. After all, he points out, the United States is still a very young nation.

Under the vast concrete shell of the Cow Palace, way out among the tawny hills of Daly City the stage managers are arranging the scenery and props for the final struggle. The place is so full of TV sets it is hard to tell where real life ends and where the flickering screen begins. Instead of listening to the real speaker you step into the corridor to see his simulacrum on the screen. The need to present the show before a world audience controls the timetable. A pyramid of TV apparatus dominates the hall. Great cables twine everywhere like lianas in a tropical forest. In the upper galleries you can see dim transparencies behind which groups of commentators sift and rearrange events as they occur. There the struggle, for a while at least, will be resolved. On the one side are the politicians and opinion makers who have had their say ever since the military victories of the Second World War were turned into a defeat of so many things America stands for. Behind them at a certain distance are the marching mobs of the frustrated who have never been told that the means through which abuses are remedied are as important as the remedies themselves. Behind Goldwater are the new groupings, people who look to American tradition as the source of victories for individual opportunity. It is the mightiest conflict in a generation.

Notes

1. The International Longshoremen and Warehousemen's Union, a left-wing union led by Harry Bridges, a Communist.

What Hope for Maintaining
a Conservative Opposition?

We do have a tendency in this country to think of Presidential elections the way we think of big games. The association is obvious. The general election comes in the fall, sandwiched in between the World Series and the really important football games. Great masses of Americans can't help thinking of it as just another athletic contest. The tendency is to yell like hell for our team while the game is going on, and then, win or lose, to go home and forget it.

It is very much to be hoped that, no matter who wins the big game on November 3, the men and women who are devoting so much to the Goldwater campaign will not go home and forget it. Even with Goldwater elected the Democrats will remain the majority party. If he loses the election he will already have won a major political victory. His capture of the machinery of the Republican Party means that for the first time in many years, the basis exists in American politics for a really effective opposition.

The mouthpieces of the established order shout to high heaven that the Goldwater campaign is a flash in the pan. The Liberal columnists make a great show of bewailing the demise of the Republican Party. What they are hoping of course is that once this campaign's over no one will dare raise a dissident voice again. There's an excellent chance that these hopes will be dashed. In spite of hell and high water the Presidential campaign of 1964 may well prove to be the beginning of a consistent application of the force of minority opinion to the power structure in Washington.

If it does nothing else Barry Goldwater's capture of the Republican nomination has proved that dissent exists on a large enough scale to be politically effective. The enormity of his crime in the eyes of the diverse vested interests of the powers that be is that he has had the courage to dramatize that dissent.

Win or lose in November, the most important part of the contest has only begun for the conservatives. Ideas have a way of surviving defeat. If ideas are vigorous and cogent enough they can even survive victory. In the remoulding of the structure of government which is the underlying aim of every political movement it is not always the plan of the victor that dominates in the end. In English and American politics particularly the majority party which won at the polls has time and again found itself borrowing measures and methods from the rejected minority.

National Review, 16 (20 Oct. 1964), 907–9. Copyright by National Review, Inc. Reprinted by permission.

During the great days of British political life in the nineteenth century the loyal opposition became a recognized part of the machinery of parliamentary government. The institution has developed to the point where the party out of power is expected to designate a shadow cabinet and an aspirant prime minister ready to take over as soon as the party in power loses its majority. During the years of Bull Moose and of old Bob La Follette's Progressives we developed an organized dissent in Congress very nearly as formidable as a British opposition party. Since representatives of the Establishment of those days had very little in their heads beyond an awed subservience to big business, the ideas of the dissenters dominated the legislative process.

Ever since Franklin D. Roosevelt inaugurated our peculiarly American form of Caesarism with the policy of "Tax, tax, spend, spend, elect, elect," there has been no really consistent political opposition in this country. Voices have been raised in remonstrance against this or that policy. Robert Taft spoke up in the Senate again and again on the side of civilized decency and rational common sense. He had his personal following but it was never well enough organized to wrest the machinery of the Republican Party away from the timeservers. Young Bob La Follette tried to continue his father's tradition of disinterested public service, but somehow in the process he lost touch with his constituents and, much to his country's loss, with life itself. Everybody knows what happened to his successor in the Senate from Wisconsin when he tried to make political capital out of the Communist infiltration in Washington.[1]

These were voices crying in the wilderness. They lacked the sort of support Senator Goldwater has been able to evoke: the young people carrying the word from house to house, organizing rallies, distributing literature, seeing that voters get to the polls, who are creating a new type of political pressure group.

It is a startling fact that during all the years since President Roosevelt's death, the most dedicated and continuing political movement in this country has been the hands of the Communists. In spite of their small numbers, and the drawback of the visible failure, obvious to anybody who reads the newspapers, of the various Communist governments around the world to produce a livable regime for their victims, their propaganda has remained the dominant influence during the past twenty years. It will take a very courageous and dispassionate historian properly to evaluate the influence of Communist propaganda and intrigue on Washington policies between 1944 and 1964. It will take all the energy the young conservatives of America can muster to effectively counteract it.

Let me say right here that I'm not suggesting that American conservatives should copy Communist methods. While these methods are certainly worthy of careful study, the fact that their basic aim is the destruction of self-governing institutions makes them useless to those whose hope is to preserve the American system. Further Communist tactics have become so formalized by forty years of successful use that they would not be too difficult to detect and checkmate, if you could once get people to admit their existence. These tactics can be defeated by new and original political methods in the hands of knowledgeable and dedicated people. They cannot be defeated without intelligent and lasting organization.

A Voice in Congress

It is highly probable that enough conservatives will have seats in the next Congress to form, if they roughly coordinate their plan of action, a minority strong enough to be listened to. Courage and brains will tell in the end. Remember the immense influence the Irish MPs had in the British parliament during the years of agitation for Irish independence.

So long as there is a Democrat in the White House, conservative congressmen will have to reconcile themselves to being cut off from federal patronage. They will have to make a point of explaining to their constituents in each case exactly why this patronage is being denied. This tactic alone will bring the methods by which the President controls Congress out in the open and will help restore a little of their lost independence to the Senate and House.

The votes of the conservatives in Congress would be given much more weight if continuous campaigns were going on in the states and cities for the capture by conservatives of local administrations, for the repeal of undesirable measures and for the passage of laws encouraging individual liberty and local self government.

Such campaigns will be met by virulent counterattacks from entrenched officeholders. Conservatives will need the encouragement and protection of a national organization roughly analogous to the organization for the Presidential campaign. No matter what happens on November 3 it is to be hoped that the conservative campaign will continue without a break. From the longterm view the congressional elections in '66 may prove every bit as important as the Presidential election in '64. The time will have come for such a campaign to present practical and affirmative projects. Conservatives will find themselves laying more emphasis on what they are for than on what they are against.

What we really need is a new edition of the Federalist Papers.

It was these public discussions between Hamilton and Madison and Jay that laid the theoretical groundwork for the Constitution of 1787. To rescue the aims of that Constitution from the inroads of the Supreme Court and of the executive bureaucracy a great deal of fresh thinking will be needed. That thinking will have to be based on a candid examination of American Government as it really works, and not as it is described in the euphoric statements of politicians.

The first consideration must be of ways and means to restore purpose and common sense to the foreign policy of the United States. What can be salvaged from the wreckage must be salvaged quickly. The present situation threatens not only the life and wellbeing of every American citizen but the survival of any kind of humane civilization in the world.

The bankruptcy of the policies of the State Department has been made painfully evident by the tragedy of Vietnam, the Congolese fiasco[2] and the paralysis of the United Nations. The American people and particularly Washington officials must be made to understand that these disasters are no accident. They are the result of a long train of mistakes dating back to Franklin Roosevelt's deluded notion that it was good policy to help the Communists strip the European powers of their colonies.

In these twenty years our foreign policy can boast, on the credit side, of the restoration of Germany and Japan, and of the temporary return to sanity under Truman's Administration which resulted in the Marshall Plan and the rescue of

Greece and Turkey. The rest of the story has been (with a few exceptions under Eisenhower and Dulles) of practical collaboration, under a smokescreen of anti-Communist palaver, with the Communists to destroy civilization in a large part of the world.

Bipartisanship in foreign policy has served as a cloak for innumerable follies and crimes. Had there been the sort of conservative opposition that now seems possible the protests of the conscientious and well informed men of both parties who have spoken out in remonstrance might have resulted in the curbing of some of the worst excesses of the Liberals in office.

Realpolitik & the Opposition

On the domestic scene the decisions which would have to be made by a conservative opposition are less urgent, but the problems are more complicated. For the purposes of a Presidential campaign, where everything has to be either black or white, it may be all right to talk about restoring free enterprise, but for practical purposes it will be necessary to spell out just exactly what that means.

As things stand today it is the mixed economies that are the going concerns. In the United States and in Western Europe and in Japan centralized direction of the economy through government control of credit and currency has on the whole worked pretty well. The semi-socialized, semi-capitalist nations—using the mass production techniques invented by free enterprise in America—are furnishing their populations with a material standard of living unheard of in human history. It is the completely socialized economies that have proved a failure. Most of them are only kept from starvation and collapse by food and subsidies furnished by the "imperialists" whom they denounce as their mortal enemies. Pure free enterprise, untrammelled by government controls or unassisted by government handouts, just does not exist in the world.

The business of a conservative opposition, to my way of thinking, would be to see that the inevitable greed for power of the men at the governmental controls didn't run away with the economy. The socialist side, "the public sector," as Washington officeholders like to call it, can readily be puffed up to the point of strangling the energies of the nation. Power breeds corruption as inevitably as a corpse breeds maggots. It will take all the political skill an opposition party can equip itself with to keep bureaucratic control within bounds. An economy isn't only statistics fed into a computer, it's men and women trying to make a living. An opposition party will have to work night and day to strengthen those elements in the mixed economy which offer the maximum scope for individual initiative and the maximum opportunity for youth and brains to come to the fore.

The vital drive, the biological urge for survival, which animates the conservative movement, springs from the feeling many young people have that the heavily socialized society they see being fostered by bureaucratic empire-building all around them will deprive them of the opportunity which their fathers had to develop their lives in freedom.

This problem of bureaucratic giantism is a poser. It's a problem that is recognized as urgent in Moscow even more than it is in Washington. It's a question of discovering a technique for the really efficient functioning of administrative offices.

Under any regime modern society will demand a great deal of administrative and regulatory machinery. The problem is how to keep it efficient. There is a law of diminishing returns in bureaucratic bigness. Nobody has found a way of repealing the other law that applies, Parkinson's. Bureaucracies grow by their very nature; the more they grow the less efficiency they bring to the public service.

A very instructive investigation might be conducted by some future congressional committee to discover what proportion of the criminal ineptitude in Vietnam resulted from bureaucratic stagnation in the Pentagon and the CIA and the State Department, and what proportion resulted from mistaken policies of the top command.

What little we have been allowed to learn of Billie Sol Estes' activities in Washington[3] reveals a weird lack of communication between various agencies of the Department of Agriculture. It is possible that we are approaching in Washington the state of affairs in Brazil, under Goulart and his gang of balmy Liberals and Communist wreckers,[4] where, whether a man's business was legal or illegal, the only way he could get anything done was by bribing officials.

It took bureaucracy about three hundred years to bring *rigor mortis* to the Roman Empire. How long will it take to destroy the American republic?

The tasks laid out for a conservative opposition in this country are staggering to contemplate. With the campaign of 1964 rolling into history the time has come to plan for 1966.

Notes

1. An allusion to the Senate career of Joseph McCarthy of Wisconsin.
2. During the civil war in the Congo, which followed the withdrawal of Belgium in 1960, the United States supported the unsuccessful United Nations effort to resolve the conflict.
3. Estes, a Texas financier convicted of fraud in 1962, had been involved in large-scale suspect business dealings with various Department of Agriculture officials.
4. João Goulart, liberal president of Brazil; he was overthrown by a coup in April 1964.

The New Left: A Spook Out of the Past

Ten years ago it was Panmunjom.[1] Now it is the New Left. How is it possible for the stale dogmas of discredited Marxism still to appeal to young people in the colleges?

The record is there for any man to read.

Forty-nine years have gone by since Lenin and Trotsky seized power in what was then St. Petersburg and built the Communist Party out of the Bolshevik wing of the revolutionary Social Democrats. Whole libraries have filled up with the record of the heroisms, the frustrations, the failures, the massacres and famines which have resulted from the efforts of the Communist Party to impose the Marxist theory on the human race. Any student who wants to finger his way through the card catalogues can find clear and accurate accounts of the Russian civil war: of American relief of the consequent Russian famine in the early Twenties; of the power struggle between Stalin and Trotsky after Lenin's death, and Stalin's purges and the elimination of the more efficient peasants and of the small nationalities; and of Stalin's deal with Hitler which brought on the Second World War; and the endless daily killing and the destruction of every conceivable civilized value which followed the Communist conquest of China and North Vietnam.

Marxist Failures

The record is simple. In the past half century every form of Marxist revolution has been tried. In every case it has failed to produce a workable society. Each Communist dictatorship has provoked deeper misery and degradation than the last. The Marxist verbiage has degenerated into a cloak for the crudest forms of personal despotism. One thing only have the revolutions proved: under a sufficiently organized terrorist dictatorship revolt is impossible. The good men are shot down. The survivors go on living: man ends by accepting anything.

By one of history's mighty ironies it is in the Communist countries today that you find the oppression of working people that so horrified Marx when he studied early nineteenth-century industrialism in England: farm workers bound like serfs to the collectives, factory workers who dare not strike for better working conditions,

National Review, 18 (18 Oct. 1966), 1037–39. © by National Review, Inc. Reprinted by permission.

every man's life shackled tight in a net of bureaucratic tyranny, every human value turned topsy turvy in a deceitful smog of propaganda that neither Marx nor Engels ever dreamed of.

Meanwhile the more fortunate populations of Western Europe and North America have managed to produce fairly workable societies. In spite of the short-sighted demagogy of many of the politicians in charge, their governments have not been able, so far, greatly to hamper the fantastic productivity of modern mass pro-duction. Even if they have done very little to solve the basic problem which the en-thusiasts of fifty years ago believed socialism would have solved—the adaptation of modern industry to the spiritual and organic needs of the men and women who handle its machinery—at least they have left roads open to experiment and change.

The sudden recrudescence among American college professors and their stu-dents of the leftist delusions of the nineteen-twenties is particularly hard to under-stand at a moment when it is becoming obvious that a very considerable ferment is going on among their contemporaries in Russia and Eastern Europe. Even if the only foreign news you get is through TV, how can you help noticing that something is changing the minds of the victims of Marxist dogma? Very considerable groups of thoughtful people are desperately searching for a way out.

Their efforts to see clearly are obstructed on the one hand by the police power. Milovan Djilas is still in prison for having dared publish *The New Class*. Andrei Sinyavsky is serving seven years at hard labor in Siberia for the crime of having cir-culated (under the name of Abram Tertz) a novel which not only showed talent but a sense of humor.[2] Pasternak, probably the greatest Russian poet of his generation, was denied the Nobel Prize and hounded to his death. His offense was writing a narrative of the revolution in the candid humane tradition of the Russian classics. The police still rule the presses. The second difficulty the Communist educated writers have to cope with in their effort to find the truth and tell it is that they are not only prisoners of the barbed wire and the mine fields along their borders, but they are prisoners of an ideology which makes it impossible for them to draw ra-tional comparisons between man's condition under socialism and under what they still call capitalism.

No Pickets for Sinyavsky

In *The New Leader* for August 30, 1965 there was translated an article by Mi-hajlo Mihajlov called "Why We Are Silent" which admirably illustrates this diffi-culty. Mihajlov is the Yugoslav college professor who got into serious trouble for his appraisal of the state of the literary craft in the Soviet Union, called "A Moscow Summer." Mihajlov is obviously an honest man, an intelligent man, and a coura-geous man, but when he tries to compare conditions under "capitalism" with condi-tions under "socialism" he is helpless because he has no inkling of the complica-tions, the advantages or the shortcomings of the mixed economies under which we live in what we like to call the Free World. His notions about the United States date back to the anti-capitalist cartoons in the old *Masses* in the year 1910.

This sort of thinking—for all its limitations—is a far cry from the monolithic dogmatism of the old days. Mihajlov and the new Russian writers are people a man would like to talk to. You would think that our sociologists and historians who boast of their Marxist creed would interest themselves in the state of mind of their opposite numbers behind the barbed wire. Instead they avidly regurgitate the routine propaganda that comes from the desks of the foreign subversion departments of the police states.

With picketing as much the rage as crowding into phone booths or swallowing live goldfish was a few years ago, you would think that a few American students might have been found to picket for Sinyavsky and Daniel during their trial in Moscow. In Europe even party members raised their voices. In America the protest was so feeble as to be almost inaudible. Ever since the McCarthy hysteria it seems to be against the rules for American intellectuals to interest themselves in the realities of life in the Communist countries.

Just the other day I found myself in an assembly of men of letters discussing the pros and cons of government subsidies to the arts as part of the Great Society program. When I endeavored to suggest that some study of the workings of government subsidy in the Soviet Union might be to the point, nobody showed the slightest interest. Maybe I didn't speak loud enough.

We are reaching the heart of the matter. In the schools and colleges, as amid the whole caste of news gatherers and opinion moulders, for one man or woman who tries to look at the realities behind the catch phrases of international politics, ten accept them at their face value. Somewhere in the network of communications an inhibition has been set up against a rational examination of the forces that are fighting for supremacy in the world. This inhibition is to a certain extent the creation of organized propaganda, but it can also be thought of as part of a subconscious effort to cushion the pain of the failures of American statesmanship during the postwar period. This inhibition still exists. Its existence is the most effective weapon in the armory of the aggressors. As some spiders anesthetize their victims before devouring them, the Communists endeavor to anesthetize the thinking strata of the nations that stand in the way of world conquest. Those who are most influenced stoutly deny that they are under any influence at all.

If you told the professors and students, all in a flutter of self-righteousness under their black gowns and their mortar boards, who walked out on a speech by the Secretary of Defense at a recent college commencement,[3] that what they did was equivalent to throwing a hand grenade into a squad of American soldiers, they would say you were mad. Yet the statement is literally true.

It has been repeated *ad nauseum* that propaganda has added a new dimension to war but very few Americans yet understand what that means. If the President of the United States and his speech writers don't understand it, if the Administration leaders and most of the members of Congress don't understand it, how can you expect college students with the milk hardly dry behind their ears, who have been brought up in a solid ignorance of political or ethical principles, to understand it?

Does no one remember the importance Hitler gave to the pledges announced by British university students in the Thirties that under no circumstances would they fight for king and country? These pledges helped convince Hitler that the English would not oppose his conquest of Europe. Hitler was wrong. Many of these same young men squandered their lives recklessly in the defense of their homes: but a little forethought might have averted all that ruin.

The forces of destruction we face today are far more dangerous than they were in Hitler's day. It is folly to encourage this sort of emptyheaded exhibitionism, as the Administration spokesmen are doing, on the theory that dissent is per se a good thing.

Jail the dissenters, no. Try to talk a little sense into their heads, yes.

Take the case of Vietnam. How is it possible for any man not completely blinded by prejudice to read Marguerite Higgins' *Our Vietnam Nightmare* or the cool appraisal of Ho Chi Minh's methods in Hoang Van Chi's book translated under the title of *From Colonialism to Communism* without understanding that the tragic situation in Vietnam is the result of a carefully planned and patiently executed attempt at conquest from the North?

The question of the effectiveness of the methods used to remedy this situation by the Kennedy and Johnson Administrations is another matter. Plenty of room for dissent there. But every well-intentioned dissenter must couch his protest in such terms as to make it useless to the machines tirelessly turning out anti-American propaganda in Paris and Peking and Moscow.

There is plenty to protest about. A good deal, not all, of our foreign policy has been disastrously mishandled since the first strategic errors, which threw the peace of the world into jeopardy for a hundred years, were committed at Yalta and Potsdam. Pacifism, if we define it as an earnest and sophisticated effort to avoid war, still has a role to play. There have been times when even marching and picketing and lying down in the street by convinced pacifists would have been useful. Demonstrations would have been in order when we helped establish Castro in Cuba, or at the time of the Bay of Pigs, or of the neutralization of Laos, or of the untimely abandonment of the blockade during the missile crisis in Cuba. Intelligent pacifists should protest when they see that mistakes in foreign policy are about to be committed which will make fresh wars inevitable.

In the world we live in it is too late to demand the immediate withdrawal of American troops from Vietnam without giving aid and comfort to the enemy. When will the American politicians get it into their heads that when they are fighting one Communist Party they are fighting them all? There is a distinct connection between the murder of Newcomb Mott[4] and the President's determination to make a stand in Vietnam.

Certainly there are fissures and conflicts within the massive apparatus of international Communism; but the ideology, though somewhat tattered at home, continues to dominate foreign policy. Its destructive force is still immense. Read the history of the Khalifate. Bloody struggles for power in the seats of government hardly hindered the conquering march of the Muslim armies.

The tragedy, for the inhabitants of the Communist nations and for the world, is that, years after the Marxist theories have proved unworkable, when all the early brotherhood-of-man idealism has ebbed away from the centers of power, Communist organization for destruction and conquest still carries on as efficiently as ever.

It is no accident that when part of a graduating class walks out on a speech at some American college the event coincides with the disturbances of certain self-styled Buddhists in Saigon.

With a little sophistication it would be possible for the students and professors to protest to their hearts' content against war atrocities in Vietnam. All that is needed to make their manifestations unpalatable to the Communist propaganda mills is to include some mention of the torture and assassination of village leaders, the bombing of schools and hospitals and the Vietcong's long-term terrorizing of the civilian population. Gus Hall,[5] whose exultant countenance appears in so many press photographs, would soon be laughing out of the other side of his mouth.

In some ways the delusions of the New Left can be considered the last sour exhalations of the decaying Liberal creed. Many of its manifestations can be written off as adolescent exhibitionism. But I can't help feeling that there are forces for good among those young people. They can still be saved from the routine treadmill of Communist subversion. Already the more perceptive among them must understand that they are being made monkeys of.

The new generation has so many problems to face that it seems a tragic waste to have any of its energy, or its ability for self-abnegation, or its goodwill, lost among the spooks and specters of the Communist underground. Once these young people got it into their heads that destruction of the social order was no cure for any of the social ills, they would find the challenge of their lives in the dilemmas presented by the daily need to reorganize our society.

Take a few random examples of problems for which Marxism offers no solution:

As the United States becomes one vast suburb our cities tend to die at the center.

At the moment when the mass production system reaches the peak of its productivity and is on the verge of assuring a fairly abundant life for all, we discover that some ten per cent of the population has dropped out of reach of the current prosperity. The scheme of certain politicians to pauperize the so-called poor as a reservoir of captive votes is no answer at all.

With increasing affluence crime increases to epidemic proportions.

Air pollution confronts us with the question of whether we have to find a substitute for the internal combustion engine.

River pollution demands a new code of social ethics on the part of industrial management and municipal government.

Obsolete obsessions about greedy capitalists and exploited workers throw no light on these problems. Solutions, if they are found at all, will come from the application of inventive brains according to our American tradition of somehow managing to balance off the claims of personal liberty against the imperatives of efficient mass organization. For this task we need all the original thinking the new generation has to offer. A Left that was really new might be worth having.

Notes

1. The site of the peace negotiations during 1951–53 at the end of the Korean War.

2. *The Trial Begins* (1960).

3. The incident, involving Secretary of Defense Robert S. McNamara, occurred at New York University in June 1966.

4. An American businessman, Mott had wandered from Finland across the Russian border in September 1965. He was sentenced to eighteen months imprisonment and then, according to Russian accounts, had committed suicide in mid-January 1966 on the train taking him to prison.

5. General secretary of the Communist Party of America from 1959.

What Makes a Novelist

[Dos Passos' address on the occasion of his being awarded the Feltinelli Prize by the National Academy of Lynxes in Rome on 14 November 1967.]

It is a humbling experience for an inhabitant of the new world beyond the western ocean to stand up today, in this Corsini Palace amid all the incrustations of history and to confront the shades of the mighty dead. Galileo Galilei, what would he think? How about Benedetto Croce? That fastidious spirit might not approve at all. All I can say is that I am profoundly grateful, and particularly that I am grateful to the "Academy of the Sharp Eyes" for picking out the technique of narrative for special mention. Since I have spent my life wrestling with the problem of how to tell a story it is gratifying to receive this commendation as I near the end of it.

Though the series of novels which I now call Contemporary Chronicles began to take final form in the Thirties, the experiences that sparked them off date back to the years of the European war of 1914–1918. Even the most topical chronicler is always years behind the times. Like many others of my generation I got most of my education from the first war.

Some of the seeds sown in the course of this education have taken a lifetime to germinate. Those were years of colossal hopes and colossal disappointments. Civilization was torn and battered by every nightmare scourge out of the vision of John on Patmos, but at the same time the creative instincts showed a gift for survival. Invention and discovery in science, and to some extent in the arts; and to much greater in technology, continued unabated. Some minds met the challenge of disaster by an outburst of invention and experiment.

Driving an ambulance in the rear of combat is a job that tends to impress you more with the wreckage than with the glory of warfare. Being an American I was a naturalborn civilian. My first really finished novel, *Three Soldiers*, was an attempt to express the resentments and frustrations of the naturalborn civilian drafted into an army. Even then I was beginning to depart a little from the novel depending on a single hero which I had been brought up with. In my youth I had been an avid reader of Fielding and Smollett in English and Flaubert and Zola in French. I was already trying to do something different. In *Three Soldiers* I tried to build my story out of the contrasts between the attitudes and development of three very different men.

National Review, 20 (16 Jan. 1968), 29–32. © by National Review, Inc. Reprinted by permission.

The Novel: How Moribund?

Those war years in Europe were an instructive period for me as they were for many other Americans of my generation. War leaves you with a surprising amount of spare time. Days and days go by when your outfit is stalled some place waiting for orders. The volunteer ambulance service was after all a pretty comfortable way of getting a look at the massacres without really taking part in them. Even when we were in the front lines we usually had 24 hours on duty and 24 hours off.

I spent most of my spare time reading. I had known French from childhood and had steeped myself in Flaubert in college—particularly in his letters and in *Education Sentimentale*. I was pretty well versed in Stendhal. I carried volumes of Verhaeron and Rimbaud in my musette bag. I had recently learned enough Spanish to read Cervantes and Jorge Manrique and Pió Baroja, whose up-to-date version of the seventeenth-century picaresque delighted me.

Out of French and Spanish I managed to fudge a certain superficial acquaintance with Italian and even Provençal. I was very much enlivened by the works of the Italian writers then known as futurists, which I bought in a bookshop in the Galleria in Milan on my way to the Piave and the Brenta. All that was mixed up with Villon and Rabelais who were my private literary idols.

In college certain professors had assured me that the novel as a literary form was on its last legs. I refused to believe that the novel was dying. When I wasn't reading I was filling small notebooks with various trials and experiments in my own American form of the English tongue.

A combination of copious reading with vigorous action spiced with a little danger is enlivening to anybody young or old. For a young man in his early twenties it amounted to a complete refurbishing of the mental faculties. Added to that was the linguistic stimulation of being immersed in the ways of speaking of common soldiers from all sorts of different countries. This was before radio and television had reduced everybody's talk to a common denominator.

Part of my service was at the Italian front. We arrived soon after Caporetto. Aside from the excitement of the architecture—glimpses of Palladian buildings driving a Fiat ambulance through Vicenza—a breathtaking sight of Venice across a lagoon sheathed with a thin scrim of ice one winter day—there was the painting. I mention it because I am sure that the great narrative painting of the thirteen and fourteen hundreds profoundly influenced my ideas of how to tell a story in words.

Padua between airraids: when we looked, peeping through the sandbags, at Giotto's frescoes in the Arena Chapel the intensity of their homely narrative was immensely heightened by the feeling that perhaps we were the last men who would ever look on these masterpieces; and the feeling too that perhaps, perhaps, Giotto's gospel tales might be the last thing we would experience on this earth.

We Weren't Dead

There was, among many of the young people of my generation, a readiness to attempt great things. Giotto and Dante and Orcagna and Piero della Francesca—to mention only a few of the influences we were sopping up like sponges between bouts of driving the poor wounded back from the trenches on Monte Grappa—these men had made eternal their view of the world they lived in. It was up to us to try to describe in colors that would not fade, our America that we loved and hated.

The road had been opened for us. In the United States Crane and Dreiser had already transferred Zola's naturalism to the American scene. James Joyce was knocking established ideas on the novel into a cocked hat with his *Ulysses*. The influence of *Ulysses*, out of snippets printed in the little magazines, was already rampant long before the publication of the book. Artistic styles, like epidemics and popular songs, are borne in the air. They cross the wildest oceans, the most tightly barred frontiers.

From Europe, mostly through the painters of the School of Paris, the artistic ferment of the period between the Paris Exposition of 1900 and the outbreak of war in 1914 was spreading across the world.

After the armistice, during the winter of 1918–19 while still in the Army—the U.S. Army had taken over the old volunteer services the year before—I managed to get myself into what was known as the Sorbonne Detachment. Service men who had either started or finished college were allowed to attend European universities while waiting for their turn to be shipped home. I had become obsessed with the need to write a novel about soldiers. While I went through the motions of attending lectures at the Sorbonne I wrote and wrote in a little room on the Ile St. Louis.

Paris in those years really was the capital of Europe. So-called modern painting—how stale that word modern has become!—really was fresh from the palette in those days: les Fauves, the Cubists, Modigliani, Juan Gris, Picasso. This too, was the Paris of new schools of music. Satie presided over Les Six. There were Poulenc, and Milhaud. Stravinsky was beginning to be heard. The Diaghilev ballet was promoting a synthesis of all the arts.

Paris in 1919. It's hard to reimagine the feelings of savage joy and bitter hatred we felt during that spring. Most of my friends were still in uniform. I was an enlisted man. Never got confirmed even in the rank of sergeant. A doughboy with the rest of them. We still had to salute officers, to sneak into out-of-the-way bistros to talk to our friends who happened to be wearing gold or silver bars. But with the armistice each one of us had been handed his life back on a platter. We knew what dead men looked like and we weren't dead.

The horsechestnuts were in bloom. We knew the world was a lousy pest-house of idiocy and corruption, but it was spring. The Peace Conference was going on. We knew that in all the ornate buildings, under the crystal chandeliers, under the brocade hangings, the politicians and diplomats were brewing poison, huddled old men festering like tentcaterpillars in a tangle of red tape and gold braid. What they were doing was too obvious and too clear. The people of the world would wake up. It was spring. The first of May was coming. We'd burn out the tentcaterpillars.

We believed we knew two things about the world. We subscribed to two dogmas which most of us have since had to modify or scrap. We were convinced that life in the militarized industrialized nations had become a chamber of horrors and we believed that plain men, the underdogs we rubbed shoulders with, were not such a bad lot as they might be. They wouldn't go out of their way to harm each other as often as you might expect. They had a passive courage and certain ingrained impulses towards social cohesiveness, towards the common good. Loafing about in little old bars full of teasing fragrances of history, dodging into alleys to keep out of sight of the military police, seeing the dawn from Montmartre, talking bad French with taxi-drivers, riverbank loafers, workingmen, poilus on leave, petite femmes, we young hopefuls eagerly collected intimations of the urge towards the common good.

Nor Was the Novel

It seemed so simple to burn out the caterpillars who were running the orchard. The first of May was coming.

We felt boisterous and illmannered. Too many sergeants had told us to wipe that smile off your face. Too many buglers had gotten us up out of our blankets before we had slept our sleep out. It seemed to us that the only thing of value that survived the war was this automatic social cohesiveness among men that came on whenever they slipped for a moment out from under the spell of the demagogues.

The storied skyscrapers of civilization were tottering. If the old edifice crashed the bosses who lived in the upper stories would go down with it. They had already pretty well shaken the foundations with their pretty war, their brilliant famines. Their diligent allies, typhus, cholera, influenza were working for them still. Now their peace would finish the job.

"All together boys. A couple of heaves and down she'll go. When the dust clears we'll see whether men and women are the besotted brutes the bosses say they are."

This was all fifty years ago.

Now we know that the first of May will never come. Where the workers conquered they allowed themselves to be overwhelmed by regimes even more oppressive than the old regimes they had overthrown. But in these resentful hopes, in these crushing disappointments, these callow enthusiasms lay the roots of satire. By the time I had finished *Three Soldiers*, the book I was working on in Paris, I was beginning to dream of novels that would throw into sharp satiric focus the grandeurs and miseries, the crime and the heroism of the world I knew. I knew damn well the novel was not dead.

I'm speaking as if I'd been one of those exiles who spent their lives brooding over café tables. Actually the longest time I ever spent in that Paris was three months. But it happened to be in one of history's climaxes from which every bystander emerges changed and invigorated. I came away feeling that in the arts at least anything was possible.

After obtaining my discharge from the Army I found work in Spain as a foreign correspondent. Painting and architecture and walking through the countryside had already become as enthralling to me as politics. At that time most of my reading was back in the Middle Ages. The Poem of the Cid and the Archpriest of Hita;[1] perhaps I was trying to escape from that foreknowledge of the consequences of the Peace of Versailles we had all suffered from in Paris and from the dimming of our hopes in the revolutionary movement of the working class which for a while—to us impatient young men—had seemed destined to create a new world.

After finishing *Three Soldiers* I managed a certain amount of travel in the Caucasus and Persia and what was then known as the Mespot. I came away obsessed by the hideous miseries the common people suffer from the great readjustments of history. More than ever I felt a sense of kinship with individual men and women who although ground under the wheels manage to retain a certain alertness, a certain aloofness, a certain dignity. Even more than before I hated the demagogues and the politicians.

My head stuffed with everything I could absorb in Europe and the Near East I came back to America. New York was the first thing that struck me. It was marvelous. It was hideous. It had to be described. The lives of the men I had known so intimately in the Army, of their women friends and mine, had to be related to the bloody panorama of history. The style of writing had to be made up as I went along. It was all an experiment. As I worked I used occasionally to reassure myself with the thought that at least some of the characters and scenes and feelings I was putting down might prove useful for the record.

Some of the poets who went along with the cubism of the painters of the School of Paris had talked about simultaneity. There was something about Rimbaud's poetry that tended to stand up off the page. Direct snapshots of life. Rapportage was a great slogan. The artist must record the fleeting world the way the motion picture film recorded it. By contrast, juxtaposition, montage, he could build drama into his narrative. Somewhere along the way I had been impressed by Eisenstein's motion pictures, by his version of old D. W. Griffith's technique. Montage was his key word.

U.S.A. *Ad Infinitum*

I had already been affected, I must add in retrospect, by the sort of novel that Thackeray originated in English with *Vanity Fair* and Stendhal in French with *La Chartreuse de Parme*. You might call these chronicle novels. *War and Peace* is another example.

In this sort of novel the story is the skeleton on which some slice of history is brought back to life. Personal adventures illustrate the development of a society. Historical forces take the place of the Olympians of ancient Greek theater.

I started a rapportage on New York. Some of the characters out of abandoned youthful narratives got into the book, but there was more to the life of a great city than you could cram into any one hero's career. The narrative must stand up off the page. Fragmentation. Contrast. Montage. The result was *Manhattan Transfer*.

By this time I was thoroughly embarked on an effort to keep up a contemporary commentary on history's changes, always as seen by some individual's eyes, heard by some individual's ears, felt through some individual's nerves and tissues. These were the *U.S.A.* books. The narrative must carry a very large load. Everything must go in. Songs and slogans, political aspirations and prejudices, ideals, hopes, delusions, frauds, crack-pot notions out of the daily newspapers.

The *U.S.A.* narratives were never supposed to end. They were followed by other chronicles from other points of view. Intermittently, and always trying to look out from the vantage point of today, to let the matter mould the style, I've kept these narratives rolling in various forms, through the years.

Growing old is partly a process of outgrowing illusions. A man discovers that he can't explain to himself just how he acquired some of his cherished and passionately held convictions. Some of them seem to have appeared, quite fortuitously, by imprint. Everybody knows the story of the greylag goose that followed Konrad Lorenz around, because the bearded naturalist was the first thing it saw when it hatched out of the egg. Naturalists now call that process imprint. Young men, particularly, pick up dogmas as irrationally and mistakenly as that gosling picked its mother image. Neither are the old exempt from the process. Impacted illusions crumble only very gradually in the light of reason.

For the novelist or the historian who is trying to describe, in terms which might have some permanence—the permanence of Dante's *Inferno*, or of the ceiling of the Sistine Chapel, for examples—the problem of imprint is very crucial. Being human he can't be exempt from the dogmas and political passions of his time. Passions good and evil furnish the fuel that keeps the artistic process going. The writer's personal resentments and frustrations and enthusiasms furnish the head of steam that drives the engine. But to obtain the objectivity that is essential to good work he must keep his own mental processes, as well as those of the people he is describing, within the focus of his satiric lens.

The Writer as Hunter

During the last fifty years we have heard endless arguments on this topic. The artist must be *engagé*. The artist must be *degagé*. He must free himself from the propaganda and the demagoguery of his age. This discussion is fruitless. Artistic works to be of lasting value must be both engaged and disengaged. They must have a certain lift, a certain aloofness that separates them from the obsessions of the hour. At the same time they must encompass—in no matter how modest or fragmentary a way—the whole range of the human spirit.

The aim of narrative writing, or poetry or painting or abstract design has been the same since the time of Aristotle and long before. It has been to give the pleasure that all men feel in the expression of skill and through that pleasure in skill, to furnish the catharsis that comes from a heightened understanding, a simplification, a formalization of the unbearable turmoil of life clattering about men's ears. No matter what his method may be it is the narrator's objectivity, sometimes hidden, sometimes apparent, that gives humane value to his narrative. Keats was right when he exclaimed that beauty was truth and truth beauty.

For the novelist, his work is an endless struggle between his passions and prejudices and his need to turn them to good purpose in the objective description of the life around him.

Observing objectivity demands a sort of virginity of the perceptions. Each time he sits down at his desk a man has to clear all preconceived notions out of his head.

The sensitivity of a man's perceptions is in no way increased by the painful squinting of the eyes and the anxious straining of the ears. The state of mind of the dispassionate observer is somewhat analogous to the hunter's. An expert hunter in a duck blind, or walking behind his dogs round the edges of a cornfield or waiting by a deerpath in the woods, thinks of nothing. He forgets himself. He lets all his senses come awake to respond to the frailest intimations that come to his ears or his eyes of the movement of game. Really good shots, the fellows who really bring down the quail, are people who are able to forget who they are and become for the moment just an eye and an ear and a gun.

To report objectively some scene, some person, the gestures two people make when meeting on the street, the movement of some animal, the shape of some organism under the microscope, the writer has to fall just an instant into the hunter's state of unpreoccupied alertness.

The hunter has to know what to look for. For years he must have been building up a bank of experience. An expert ornithologist can give one glance into a thicket. Where I see only some English sparrows he can pick up a wren sitting on her nest and three different kinds of warblers. As a result of a lifetime of observation a good hunter can tell, from the slight disturbance of twigs and pinetags on a path through the woods whether it was a deer or a raccoon that just passed that way. The trained novelist has to develop this sort of capacity.

He has to conquer his own professional deformations. By the nature of his occupations the man of letters tends to become a man of words and not of deeds. His attention is likely to be on the name of the thing rather than on the thing itself. The literate man tends to believe that when he has named, labeled and pigeonholed some event, some sight, some manifestation of the manifold oddities of life, he has disposed of it. He is likely to apply the label before he has really observed the object. To observe objectively a man has to retain something of childhood's naive and ignorant state of mind. In my experience children and illiterate people often see things more exactly than educated men. The first-rate novelist like the first-rate scientist must be obsessed by his own ignorance. This conviction of ignorance is the first step towards understanding. Astonishment strangely quickens the senses.

To See and to Express

Curiosity is the key. I wonder sometimes if the curiosity which makes a man want to see clearer and clearer isn't related to the hunters' or trackers' alertness which might well have been the quality most needed for survival far back in the history of the race.

The state of mind that makes for objective description, like every state of mind in which you forget who you are, has a sort of primeval happiness about it. You look out at the world with a fresh eye as if it were the morning of the first day of creation.

There is a lucid little paragraph that has given me great pleasure in an English translation of William Harvey's *Circulation of the Blood.* Harvey by the way became a doctor of medicine in Padua at about the time this Academy of the Lynxes was first founded.

Let me read it to you:

> We have a small shrimp in these countries, which is taken in the Thames and in the sea, the whole of whose body is transparent; this creature, placed in a little water, has frequently afforded myself and particular friends an opportunity of observing the motions of the heart with the greatest distinctiveness, the extreme parts of the body presenting no obstacle to our view, but the heart being perceived as though it had been seen through a window.

The aim, the never quite attainable aim of the novelist or historian is to see men's private emotions and their movements in masses as clearly as William Harvey saw the heart of the shrimp and to express what they see as lucidly as Harvey did in the little paragraph I have just read. Undoubtedly this sort of seeing was what Galileo's friends had in mind when they called this academy the Academy of Lynxes.

To see clearly and to express clearly what he sees is still the writer's aim, but with all the narrative skill in the world, how hard it is to attain!

Notes

1. Juan Ruiz (see p. 47, n. 1).

An Interview with John Dos Passos

[While in Schenectady to give an address at Union College, Dos Passos on 16 October 1968 participated in an interview-discussion session conducted by Frank Gado, a teacher at Union College. The other participants were students and teachers at the college.]

FRANK GADO: Mr. Dos Passos, you've long been known as a chronicler of the disturbances of the twentieth century. May I begin by reading from an article written by a twenty-year-old student before going off to war? I would be most interested in your comment.

Has not the world today somehow got itself enslaved by this immense machine, the Industrial system? Millions of men perform labor narrowing and stultifying even under the best conditions, bound in the traces of mechanical industry, without ever a chance of self-expression, except in the hectic pleasures of suffocating life in cities. They grind their lives away on the wheels, producing, producing, producing. And of all the results of this degrading, never-ending labor, how little is really necessary to anyone; how much is actually destructive of the capacity of men for living, for the fathoming of life, for the expression of life.

. . . Are we so certain of the benefits of all this that the last hundred years has given us that there must be no discussion of the question? Most people are very certain; but most people are always certain. . . .

Still, there is discontent among us. In the light of the flames of burning . . . towns civilized men look at each other with a strange new horror. Is this what men have been striving for through the ages? Is this ponderous suicidal machine civilization?

DOS PASSOS: Where was that? I haven't seen it.

GADO: It appeared in a college literary magazine. The author is John R. Dos Passos, Jr. and the date is June 1916.

DOS PASSOS: Why that's amazing. I didn't recognize it at all. It's really pretty good.

GADO: The essay is entitled "A Humble Protest." Although you were quite young when you wrote it, to me it has always seemed the most seminal of your early works—in fact, the key to understanding the fundamental attitude underlying all your subsequent work.

DOS PASSOS: It's one I forgot. . . . A monthly editorial. . . .

Idol, 45 (Fall, 1969), 5–25. Reprinted in *First Person: Conversations on Writers and Writing*, ed. Frank Gado (Schenectady, N.Y.: Union College Press, 1973). The *First Person* republication corrected a few errors in the *Idol* text; these corrections are incorporated in the above republication.

GADO: Back in the days of the *Harvard Monthly*. Having sprung my one trap, I'll go on to ask whether you see similarities between the feelings of your college generation and those being expressed so volubly on campuses all over this country and, indeed, the world.

DOS PASSOS: Oh, yes, I see a great many. With one important difference, however: it seems to me that our ideas were really more constructive than those of the current generation. Naturally, we were reacting against the same thing, but now the reaction is one on a larger scale and more virulent. What we are witnessing now is a tantrum of spoiled children who really have had too much done for them. One of the most tragic things about the student revolution is its negativism, and here I'm not speaking about the Americans particularly. I did read quite a lot about the French students' revolt; despite all their cooking around, not one came out with a useful program. This is not to say that I can't understand what led to their rising up. The French universities are much more in need of reform than ours are—and I think that difference should be borne in mind. There has never been a society where education was finer or conducted on such a lavish scale than in ours, although of course a lot of it is rather mistaken in conception, I think, and the results are not always the best.

Initially, my generation was worried about matters similar to those which concern yours. We were strongly hit because we were brought up in a period when there hadn't been any wars for a long while. We believed that nineteenth century civilization had progressed to a point where wars were no longer needed. Then, suddenly, this fantastic series of massacres broke out in Europe. I was horrified by it all. The academic community became sold on the war. This was my first experience with the fantastic way people's minds became imprinted with slogans. Overnight, almost, men I'd known at Harvard who were quite respected—I won't mention their names—turned from extremely reasonable beings into fanatical Hun haters. (I'm afraid I was very much in the minority at that time, as I usually am.)

Today, we are seeing a similar turning away from reason. The whole operation of the SDS[1] presents a great potential danger. It seems to me it is leading people to something very much like the Nazi Youth. By itself, I don't think it has the power to get very far, particularly should their funds be removed, as I hope they will be.

Who among you has ideas on this subject? After all, it's all much closer to you than to me right now.

KEN KOBLAND: Last year, I was at Columbia visiting a friend who is very active in SDS. We had a long discussion one night and, in the light of your remarks about SDS, it's odd that he was saying almost exactly, in fact practically verbatim, what you said in "A Humble Protest." Really, the similarity is incredible.

DOS PASSOS: Except that they offer no solutions. So many things need attention in the modern world. Anybody with enthusiasm and a proclivity for self-sacrifice could dedicate himself to remedying a couple of dozen, seriatim. Our entire administration of justice in regard to criminals has become horribly misconceived, particularly the whole prison system. We started out in this country with a remarkably good system—that, after all, is what de Tocqueville came over to study: the excellence of American penal institutions. In that area alone, we need an immense amount of intelligent, self-sacrificing, dedicated work. But instead of setting such specific goals, the people making all this clamor seem to want just general revolution. All this accomplishes is a playing into the hands of the Communist regime, which, having the biggest propaganda organization in the world is happy to take advantage of the commotion.

KOBLAND: What structure could be proposed which, being different from what we have now, you wouldn't see as, in some way Communist. . . .

DOS PASSOS: Well, you certainly wouldn't want the events in Czechoslovakia to be enacted in this country, would you?[2]

KOBLAND: In some ways, we have them. . . .

DOS PASSOS: We don't at all. To try to claim that the system in the United States is equal to a police state is just insane. Really, it is just not true. Go live in a police state if you want to see. Look. There are plenty of them around. You can go to Cuba. . . .

ALFRED THIMM: . . . and hope they'll let you out again. . .

GADO: . . . or in again.

DOS PASSOS: We have gotten some distorted views of what happens in America. There is entirely too much encouragement of completely unregulated fuss and fury by television, by the media—although just why, I don't understand—looking for the sensational moment. They have lashed up the Negro thing to a point where we almost have a state of race war.

KOBLAND: Do you attribute this all to T.V.?

DOS PASSOS: It has a lot to do with it. Without television, the more moderate, sensible people would have retained control; it wouldn't have gotten out of their hands. We tend to forget that there are a lot of very sensible Negroes who are willing to live and let live and who realize that you don't get anywhere by rioting and some of the tactics now being used.

KOBLAND: Hasn't moderation just meant passing over the problems? One wonders whether, at this late date, we can afford to think in terms of moderation.

DOS PASSOS: Now you've got me because, I must confess, I was pretty immoderate when I was your age. Part of my lack of sympathy with the intentions of some of today's young people is due to my having just lived long enough to discover the results of our own immoderation. We were very hopeful about the Communist revolution, and then, of course, it turned out to be the most flagrant despotism ever imposed upon mankind.

WILLIAM DOUGHERTY: Had the media been, during the Communist revolution or the early states of World War I, what they are today, do you think that there would have been greater popular support in America. . . .

DOS PASSOS: No, because the establishment was so much against these events that it would have worked the other way.

The whole question of the effects of television needs a great deal of thought. Instead of giving the viewer the impression that he is part of the real world, it somehow transforms him into a spectator. Television feeds the spectator mentality. I am not all that satisfied with McLuhan,[3] but he does open up all sorts of things. I can't read much of him at one time because his writing is so repetitious, but occasionally he flashes out and throws light on some paradox that's stimulating to consider.

GADO: Many of us are in that same bag. I don't advocate McLuhan's thesis—in many ways his theory is riddled with holes and inconsistencies—yet I often find myself coming back to observations he has made. He is certainly not the first man to note the emergence of the "world village" or to forsee the awesome effects of electronic communication; nevertheless, he has brought such matters to public attention by dramatizing them.

DOS PASSOS: The trouble is, he jumbles his statements together—rather like a bag of eels in which you can't exactly see which are the heads and which are the tails.

THIMM: Of course, with someone who has fired off in as many directions as he has, probability dictates that, just at random, a few shots have to hit the target.

DOS PASSOS: Why, yes. In general, his books add up to much nonsense, but the phenomena he is dealing with are fascinating and demand careful scrutiny.

DOUGHERTY: In your day, such public questions as entry into the World War, the early strikes, and the formation of the IWW were pretty much cut and dry issues. Obviously, people were getting a bad deal and something had to be done. But today, with problems as ambiguous as the Viet Nam struggle, things are no longer cut and dry.

DOS PASSOS: Precisely. That's why these questions don't lend themselves to cut and dry solutions. The dynamics of a society are never simple matters. The IWW was a preparation for the CIO, and that, on the whole, was a good thing. The package of progress, though, does not contain just benefits. The problem with all social engineering is that when good accrues to one side, it is paid for with injury on the other. We have to be careful because sometimes the cure is worse than the disease.

PAUL BEALS: When you were in Russia in 1927–28, what was it you saw that disenchanted you?

DOS PASSOS: I had gotten a view of the revolution earlier in 'twenty-one and 'twenty-two in the Trans-Caucasus when the Red regime was just moving in. I got quite a feeling of the atmosphere of the Russian civil war. It wasn't pleasant, but I discounted it somewhat because all civil wars are pretty bloody and innocent people necessarily suffer. Then, when I was in Russia in 1928, that country was experiencing a moment of calm. Trotsky was in exile, but Stalin was not yet strong enough to persecute the Trotskyites.

What I wrote about Russia was rather careful. I did write a report of the Kronstadt massacre,[4] which has always horrified me. I didn't want to play up to the people who were all against the Russian Revolution because I thought that, at worst, it was an experiment—one which might produce interesting results and was therefore worth watching.

Along that line: the most fantastic thing about the Soviet Union today is that the results of their experiment are proving that a despotic hierarchical society fits the industrial picture better than does democracy. Practically. That's something that can't and shouldn't be laughed off. If democracy is to survive in this increasingly technical age, the challenge must be met in some way, and I don't think it is met by walking around with placards and attacking a harmless figurehead like President Kirk of Columbia.[5] Although I've always had something of an allergy towards college presidents, that poor fellow didn't deserve all that abuse. It was so overdone, and in the long run such actions invite worse than what they are attacking. The Wallace movement is backlash against all this sort of stuff.[6]

GADO: In one of the passages in *The Prospect Before Us*, you spoke of college presidents being the most accurate mirror of society.

DOS PASSOS: Did I say that seriously?

GADO: Yes. In fact, you repeated those comments in *The Theme is Freedom*. I have the passage here.

Institutions of learning eternally form the sacred ark in which the ruling dog-mas of any particular era are protected from the criticisms of the profane. Remember the Sorbonne in the great days of the canon law. A historian today could make out a very good case for sampling the opinions of college presidents as a way of uncovering the mentality of whatever ruling class is emerging. Since the business of a college president is to raise money, he has to be the type of man who will appeal to those who control the available funds. Forty years ago he had to be congenial with the individual capitalists of the day. Now the money, even when it has the names of individual fortunes still attached to it, is in the hands of institutions. So the college presidents of our day have to have the institutional mentality. How can they help feeling tender toward socialized institutions, whatever form these may take?

DOS PASSOS: Oh, yes, I will endorse that thoroughly.

GADO: What has struck me so during years of reading your many books is how accurate many of your observations are. They have an essential—dare I say poetic—rightness. Much of the current cant about alienation and anomie is vividly prefigured in such characters as Mac, G. H. Barrow, and Janey Williams of *U.S.A.* Two years ago, over BBC, I heard Galbraith delivering the lectures which became *The New Industrial State.* At one point, it hit me that he was saying something you had touched on in *The Prospect Before Us*—that at most levels there wasn't much difference between being employed by G.M. or by the soviet state.

DOS PASSOS: Except, of course, that you have much greater freedom of movement in G.M. and there isn't the risk of being killed or imprisoned.

GADO: To return to your answer in which you spoke of student agitation being counter-productive, you wrote something in *The Theme is Freedom* which is very apropos. I'm referring to earlier impressions of Russia which you reprinted in that book along with numerous glosses. You report of a conversation with a cab driver. . . .

DOS PASSOS: I remember that fellow quite well—an old fashioned cab driver with a big beard. My Russian was extremely bad at that time—it remains extremely bad—and we had to struggle to understand each other.

GADO: He had thought you were German; then you corrected him.

"Americans are civilized but Germans are more civilized," he said. "Here in Russia what we need is more Germans. Now we have too much liberty. Every bare-foot no-account in the village thinks he's as good as the next man. There is no discipline, too much liberty. With liberty everything goes to hell. Hindenburg, he's what we need. He's a great man. But the young men now they do nothing but talk about liberty. That will not make a great nation. To become a great nation Russia should have a great man to put every man in his place, a man like Hindenburg."

Then, to the reprinted passage, you appended, "'Now Stalin, Stalin is our man,' the cab driver added. To this day, I can't imagine why I left that out of the account." The parallel to our own situation is very strong and ominous, isn't it? This great liberalization, this great opening up of society, this turmoil, has in a sense permitted destructive men like Wallace, disguised as conservatives, to surface. We are nearing a polarization not unlike that found in the early stages of Communist countries.

DOS PASSOS: Yes. The destructiveness of the Wallaces has been bred by the thorough destructiveness of forces like those in SDS.

SCOTT SIEGLER: Your views about social change bring Blake to mind. I've been writing a thesis on Blake and I've been intrigued by his idea that in a revolution, one form of tyranny replaces another. Can change occur effectively on a large scale without one form of tyranny replacing another?

DOS PASSOS: I have never read Blake very carefully. He is exciting, full of sparks which he throws off in every direction. I'm glad you are working on him. Masses have been written about Blake, but there is certainly room for more: the whole thing hasn't been quite uncovered yet. I once had thought that someday I might try to do something with Blake, but I got involved in other problems.

BEALS: In regard to what Professor Gado said about your insight into certain institutions and the American scene: you were talking about your art during a speech made in accepting an award in Rome last January—

DOS PASSOS: I'll be reading that same paper again tonight. I think its point—that an artist has to be both engagé and disengagé—is still valid.

BEALS: You obviously believe that it is this which enables you to gain your insights.

DOS PASSOS: I wasn't talking particularly about me. I was describing what I think is a way writers advance on phenomena. As the experiences of life pour past, there has to be some method for using them. Personally, I am sort of a naturalist. In that paper, I was just describing the old naturalist method so wonderfully demonstrated in Darwin's *Journey of the Beagle*. All the good early naturalists—Bates' *Journey up the Amazon* is a good example—are full of this type of observation which to me is so important.[7]

In that same speech, I said that the great advantage youth has over age is undamaged senses which produce extraordinarily good perceptivity: the hearing, the eyes, keen smell, and the whole associative operation to the brain haven't lost the freshness of childhood. (I often think that the human brain is at its best at about eight or nine. It's amazing to watch how things come into the minds of children at that age.) How tragic for young men and women if they allow their minds to be stamped by one of these slogan factories! It will take them years to recover. The minute a slogan is imbedded in part of the brain and becomes an automatic response to any given stimulus, the perceptivity of that part of the brain is lost and you no longer can have a genuine reaction to that stimulus. Slogans, of course, should be examined, but they certainly have to be kept at arms length. That, I guess, is what I was really trying to say in that address.

GADO: Wasn't this rejection of hollow words one of the quickening factors among the writers right after the First World War?

DOS PASSOS: Yes, I think so. All the fellows about my age suddenly felt that we just had to examine life directly. But of course, all we had to combat was the comparatively mild slogan-forming operation of the daily newspapers. We didn't have to contend against the new peculiar types. Most of you kids were probably brought up watching T.V. The medium is much more indefinite in form and for that reason, the slogans may be harder to fight against. I just don't know what the real effects of that influence will be.

PETER WAGONER: When Professor Gado mentioned the writers' attitudes just after the first war, it set me to wondering whether this reaction to the hollowness of words might not have been tied up with their wanting to leave this country. Didn't they regard "patriotism" to be one of the hollow words?

DOS PASSOS: Among the people I knew, the pattern of the period was not at all one of anti-patriotism, though of course we were accused of it. It was actually a desire to get the ship of state back on its rails. Every ship of state has to be reorganized and gotten back on its rails every so often.—Now there's a mixed metaphor if there ever was one!

SIEGLER: You once said that the only excuse for a novelist is that he serves as a second-rate historian of the age in which he lives; he digs up the raw material which a scientist, an anthropologist, or an historian can later use to advantage.

DOS PASSOS: Having since talked to a good many contemporary historians in the universities, I no longer am as well disposed toward them as I was when I wrote that. They've come to think of history as a science, and as a result, it's become a pseudo-science. In the real sciences, a man can perform an experiment, gain certain results, and another man at the other end of the world can repeat the experiment and get the same results. Does that hold in history or sociology? History isn't a social science; it's an art—a great one. (Remember, Clio was one of the muses.) I would go so far as to say that history is the greatest of the literary arts. They run pretty close together, but I would rate a good historian higher than a novelist.

PETER FELDSTEIN: At the time you wrote *U.S.A.*, you seemed quite pessimistic about the future in this country because of the construction of American society and the influence of technology. Are you still of that opinion?

DOS PASSOS: It seems to me that the nature of the problem has changed. A wholly new, strange world has come into being. We see a good example of this in the space program—and I'm talking not primarily about the astronauts but about the army of technicians involved in all the tentacles of the operation. Many of these people, soon out of college, make $25,000 a year and live in luxurious surroundings. They lead a curious country club life. Now this, of course, has some advantages, but it also tends to keep them away from the ordinary problems experienced by the great mass of the population. They constitute an odd salaried class: they go to their jobs every day, but it's all on a very plush level. Except for some few G.M. engineers, that kind of world didn't exist in the twenties.

Other changes, too, have been remarkable. New institutions which were then just becoming popular are now losing their power. Like labor unions. The working class has become so prosperous that we have a new layer of bourgeoisie forming. The old notions about the proletariat really don't fit the picture we have now.

BEALS: After you wrote your social novels, Steinbeck started writing novels like *The Grapes of Wrath*. Do you think he picked some things up from you?

DOS PASSOS: No, no, I wouldn't accuse him of that.

He wrote one very good novel about a strike, something called *In Dubious Battle*. . . .

GADO: . . . the best he ever wrote.

DOS PASSOS: That's what I've always felt. It's truly excellent. But for some reason, it's never mentioned.

GADO: We've taught it for years at Union.

DOS PASSOS: It's really a little classic.

GADO: I haven't much taste for most of Steinbeck. So much meretricious sentimentalism. . . .

DOS PASSOS: I liked his *Sea of Cortez*, an account of his trip down the Gulf of California with his biologist friend. It's a good travel account.

GADO: One of the most remarkable features of *U.S.A.* is the Biographies. It's a form I think you originated and I don't know of anyone who has been able to copy you successfully. (In fact, for a writer acclaimed as one of the most experimental of our century, you have had incommensurately little influence, technically, on younger writers; I think this is due to your having so fully developed the innovation that its possibilities for others have been exhausted.) You had started advancing toward the multi-centered novel from the beginning. Certain elements of it were in *One Man's Initiation* and *Three Soldiers*; more were added in *Manhattan Transfer*; but it wasn't until *U.S.A.* that all the components of the formula found their place. Although there were small hints of the Biography device earlier, it was essentially a new element, and contributed mightily to the overall effect of the trilogy. What impelled you toward the Biography? What aesthetic concept was involved?

DOS PASSOS: It's rather hard to remember how one happens to hit on these things. The Newsreels were intended to give the clamor, the sound of daily life. In the Biographies, I tried to produce the pictures.

I have always paid a good deal of attention to painting. The period of art I was very much interested in at that time was the thirteenth and fourteenth centuries. Its tableaux with large figures of saints surrounded by a lot of little people just fascinated me. I tried to capture the same effect in words.

That was one of the ideas, but then a lot of things appear in books without the author knowing exactly how they got there. Also, I always had an interest in contrast, in the sort of montage Griffith and Eisenstein used in films. I was trying to put across a complex state of mind, an atmosphere, and I brought in these things partly for contrast and partly for getting a different dimension.

GADO: It has always seemed to me that the trilogy was very carefully thought out before it was ever begun. As I believe others have noted, in trying to achieve an amalgam, you were working on four levels: first, the Camera Eye, the personal experience of life in the twentieth century of the author himself; second, the narratives, mirroring the growth of this century, the emergence of this new beast U.S.A. following the Spanish-American War through which we became an imperial power—in fact—if not in name an empire; third, the Newsreels, the Greek chorus in this heroic, hubristic, tragic drama; fourth, the Biographies, the men who influenced or typified that age. All these various levels kept moving toward a point of union which occurs in the final novel. As in *Three Soldiers*, was it your conscious plan to go from stress on the commonly human experiences of youth to the rusting away of machinelike life at the end of the trilogy?

DOS PASSOS: Yes, I think it was. I started out to do it as one book. Then it became obvious the thing was going to be so long that it would be better to publish it in sections. But I did have a plan about the end particularly. Poe, you know, gives a very good maxim in one of his critical pieces: an author should always know what the end of a story is going to be before he starts the beginning.

GADO: Did any of these characters change in your own mind?

DOS PASSOS: Yes. They always do. They change enormously. If the character is going to come to life, he is going to have to take things into his own hands.

GADO: Did you intend at any point to have one character or set of characters somehow typify each of the volumes? It seemed to me that Mac was the central character in the first novel, Joe Williams and Dick Savage the twin stars of the middle novel, Charlie Anderson the central character in the last, and J. Ward Morehouse[8] perhaps the key figure of the whole trilogy.

DOS PASSOS: Yes, that's about right. I think I did have that in mind, although I'm not sure how much I knew when I *started* about who was going to turn out most important in the various novels.

WAGONER: In *1919* you had a Biography on a man namd Jack Reed. I was reading some critical material which discussed the emergence of "parajournalism" —writing which is half newspaper reporting, half personal reactions. It said that Mr. Reed had influenced such reporting . . .

DOS PASSOS: Jack Reed was a great character and, in addition, he wrote very well. His book on Mexico was excellent. And although it was not the most accurate, he gave us the most vivid account of the Bolshevik Revolution—

WAGONER: . . . in the newspaper vein . . .

DOS PASSOS: Oh, it was better than that. It was the tops of American reportorial writing, in the same line as Stephen Crane and that fellow from San Francisco —what was his name? He wrote short stories.

GADO: Bierce?

DOS PASSOS: Yes, of course, Ambrose Bierce. That was a great period in American journalism. We had awfully good writing in newspapers—which, unfortunately, you can hardly find today. Reporters then had much more freedom and there were a great many more newspapers. If writing according to your own tastes and standards lost you your job on one paper, you'd go on to another. Now we have journalistic monopolies and the business-like attitudes of the management are to some extent reflected in the reporters. The colorful styles, the flamboyance are largely gone.

SIEGLER: What influence did the expatriate movement have on your work during that period?

DOS PASSOS: Not very much. I was always opposed to it; I thought the whole idea was nonsense and I didn't spend very much time with any of those people. Hemingway was quite a good friend of mine and much of what I saw of all that was through him, although even he was not that much a part of that scene. Malcolm Cowley, whom I'd known ever since he turned up at Harvard, was more typical. He went on to popularize the expatriate thing, but he always had a genius for getting things wrong—just a little bit wrong, wrong enough to be not quite true.

DOUGHERTY: In *A Moveable Feast*, Hemingway struck out at a lot of people who had been friends. You were close to him, have you any ideas why he did that?

DOS PASSOS: The poor fellow was going into a psychotic state. There are still traces of talent in *A Moveable Feast*, but it certainly doesn't rank among his best books. He was in rather good shape the last time I saw him, in 1948. The last two chapters in Hotchner's book contain a marvelous description of his decline;[9] I've been trying to get psychiatrist friends of mine to read that book. It gives an excellent picture of a man entering—I don't know—you might call it schizophrenia or . . . well, the name doesn't matter. It seems to have been hereditary with him. His father apparently went into a similar state; he also killed himself—and at about the same age.

WAGONER: Could Hemingway's animosity have been due to his thinking he had been solely responsible for his success in writing and resenting others who tried to take some of the credit? That may have been the chief reason he turned on Gertrude Stein.

DOS PASSOS: To an extent. He was a very competitive man. He would try to ride a bicycle as fast as the professionals could. . . .

GADO: . . . part of his fascination with the six day bicycle races. He seemed to love the endurance they call for and the itinerant, hedonist way of life of the racers.

DOS PASSOS: Yes. He certainly made the six day races for me. Oh, he was a wonderful fellow to go around with—so enthusiastic and excited. He would point out all sorts of things you wouldn't have seen otherwise.

GADO: How would you rank your contemporaries, the men whom you are competing with?

DOS PASSOS: I don't know. I've never had much of a sense of competition. It may be a weakness in me.

GADO: Do you think of yourself as being above the battle?

DOS PASSOS: Outside of it—at least a little bit. I have always felt that way. Even in the period of the 'twenties, I always pretended that I wasn't going to be a writer, so I didn't feel as though I had to jockey for position. I had wanted to study architecture; I am a spoiled, frustrated architect.

THIMM: How much did you and Hemingway influence each other?

DOS PASSOS: Not at all, I think, although there were times when we were trying for the same things.

THIMM: Didn't you ever have discussions about style?

DOS PASSOS: He always used to bawl me out for including so much topical stuff. He always claimed that was a great mistake, that in fifty years nobody would understand. He may have been right; it's getting to be true.

At a certain moment, Hemingway produced some of the best short stories ever written in English. They hold up very well. Just as a stylist, he was awfully good. I used to claim that his style was a combination of cable-ese and the Holy Bible. He was a great reader of the Bible.

FELDSTEIN: Did you really get into architecture?

DOS PASSOS: No, not nearly as much as I once hoped to. I was always interested in objective painting, and I really did do more in painting than in architecture. By the time I got out of the war, I became involved in writing books about what I'd seen and felt over there. That changed my direction because I found that, having started writing books, I was always having to write one more to kind of make up for the deficiencies of the one I'd just completed.

BEALS: Was it as good a time for writers then as it is now?

DOS PASSOS: I think it was better. There were so many outlets. There must have been at least twenty, certainly fifteen, well-paying magazines in this country; if you couldn't sell something you'd written to one magazine, there was always the chance that another would buy it. Now the market has shrunk. Writers tend to fall back on teaching. Having the university as a patron may have advantages, but I think the disadvantages are greater.

GADO: I would agree. Most writers who find shelter in the university come to find that their work loses contact with the outside world. They begin to regard the university as an analogue to the universe. One sees this tendency magnified in the career of John Barth; to me it seems to have been injurious to the most dazzling of present talents.

DOS PASSOS: Barth's first novel was awfully impressive, but I've gotten rather discouraged with him.

GADO: Getting back to your connecting the nature of the magazine market and the nature of fiction which is produced: the peculiar properties of the American novel are to some degree due to our writers having served an apprenticeship as short story writers; could your departures from the mainstream of American fiction be partly attributed to your never having followed this traditional route?

DOS PASSOS: My "departures" were not due to my having rejected the short story, if that's what you mean. Rather you might say that the short story rejected me. I started a good many short stories, but they always got so involved, they turned into something else. Usually, they ended up as sections of some book. I never could write a short story.

GADO: So after "Honor of a Caliph"[10] and the other juvenalia, you let the form go.

DOS PASSOS: Yes. I found it just didn't work for me.

BEALS: Having told us why you gave up on the short story, could you tell us why you gave up poetry?

DOS PASSOS: My impulse for that sort of thing found an outlet in the novels, which do have poetic passages. That type of steam could be blown off in things like the Interludes in *Midcentury*. I got to a point where there was no particular reason for making separate little packages.

BEALS: Did you ever feel impelled to be a poet?

DOS PASSOS: Not exactly, no.

FELDSTEIN: When Allen Ginsberg was here last spring, he listed you along with Whitman as an important influence on his poetry. I think he had in mind the similarity to Whitman in the beginning and end of *U.S.A.* (the Vagabond part), but he might also have been referring to the relationship between the voice of the poet and the society he is commenting on.

DOS PASSOS: That's interesting. Some work I've been doing has sent me to my Whitman again; it's been a delight re-reading *Democratic Vistas*—I had forgotten how much insight there was there.

One of the things that strikes you about the great figures of that period is their ethics. At that time, people read the Bible and absorbed a body of tested wisdom about the conduct of life. Even when I was a boy, it was expected that children read the Bible, I remember my father seeing to it that I read chapters regularly. That's missing today and we're the poorer for it. No individual, no society can survive without ethics. I'm always very suspicious of the fellow who claims to have a personal morality; what he means is that he has no morality at all and feels free to do you dirt.

GARY ABRAMSON: Do you see any relationship between the decline in constructive attitudes among college youth that you mentioned earlier and a decline in contemporary fiction?

DOS PASSOS: I hesitate to say. I do think that the objective type of novel has now been run into the ground; it's become a means for exhibitionism in the technical sense, the psychiatric sense, of the word. It's become a bore for everybody.

STEPHEN GLANZROCK: Aside from Barth, are there any younger writers you have hopes for?

DOS PASSOS: I don't read many novels—so many other things which give me so much more pleasure cry out to be read—but I might mention John Updike. I haven't read any of his things since *Rabbit, Run*, but that book was full of talent; he described his people remarkably well.

GADO: If I may, I'd like to move into another area. After the Civil War, there seemed to be self-conscious concern with writing an American epic, a Great American Novel. In the works of various writers, this was manifested as an attempt to encompass the whole of our society. We got this in Frank Norris's projected trilogy and later in a number of other works as well. Somewhat modified, it is reflected in Wescott's *The Grandmothers*, in Sherwood Anderson's *Poor White*, in Gertrude Stein's *The Making of Americans*, even (to an extent) in the works of William Carlos Williams and the poetry of Vachel Lindsay. Certainly your own *U.S.A.* is a magnificent mural of a nation. How conscious was your generation of writers of striving for a panorama which would capture the essence of a nation?

DOS PASSOS: A good many people were pretty conscious of it. I think Scott Fitzgerald shows this in the one about the boot-legger—*The Great Gatsby*. It's his best work.

GADO: Perhaps the one Fitzgerald book which still stands up.

DOS PASSOS: I was very much taken with the last also—the fragment of *The Last Tycoon*. Had the fellow lived long enough, it might have turned out to be a wonderful book.

BEALS: You've said that in *The Last Tycoon*, Fitzgerald had created something new in the language. What was unique about it?

DOS PASSOS: It just struck me as being a well-rounded, Tolstoi-like picture of the things he was trying to describe. I mean Tolstoi at his best, not Tolstoi the propagandist.

BEALS: Hemingway felt that Fitzgerald whined in public in *The Crack-Up*. Didn't you upbraid Fitzgerald for the same thing?

DOS PASSOS: I didn't want him to publish *The Crack-Up*. I felt that he had so much more left to him and it wasn't the time to publish something like that. I think now that I was wrong. It really is a remarkable piece of work. He probably couldn't have done anything else.

BEALS: Talking about *The Crack-Up* brings to mind another writer who was involved in it—Glenway Wescott. When he was here in 1965, Wescott said he thought American writers went to Europe after the First World War, not so much because they wanted to flee from the artistic climate in America but because it was so much cheaper to live abroad. Would you agree?

DOS PASSOS: He gave a perfectly sound reason. Those were days when Americans had the advantage of a favorable currency exchange. But those writers did pay a price—after awhile, they tended to stew in their own juice. The world of the expatriate can become rather unreal, one in which the disengagé yet engagé thing I talked about earlier can disappear.

ABRAMSON: I'd like to ask you about a writer who is very engagé. Norman Mailer, especially in his *The Naked and the Dead*, has frequently been compared to Hemingway, but I think the parallel to your work is closer. The similarity in the way you both broke up your narratives is obvious, but beyond that, there is a resemblance in your rhythms, in the way the words fit together. I was especially conscious of this in re-reading the Charley Anderson sections of *U.S.A.* I believe I once read that Mailer admitted having your rhythms in mind when he wrote about the members of his platoon.

DOS PASSOS: Maybe that's why I liked *The Naked and the Dead*, although to be perfectly frank, I'd have to say I wasn't conscious of the resemblance. His account of the platoon as it goes on reconnaissance is really marvelous—awfully good naturalism—but some of the early passages and the end seem phony and make me uneasy.

THIMM: The Time Machine device, of course, was also derived from you. . . .

DOS PASSOS: Strange, I hadn't noticed that. In fact, I don't even remember it.

GADO: There is also a parallel between Mailer's career and yours in that he has become increasingly involved in social issues and, in a way, writing contemporary history much as you did and do. *On the Steps of the Pentagon*[11] bears some resemblance to the manner in which you reported the Harlan strike and the Sacco-Vanzetti case.

DOS PASSOS: That's an interesting parallel but a curious one because I've grown impatient with him. I don't think he makes for easy reading anymore.

SIEGLER: In 1930, you said that the heart of Broadway was in Hollywood; do you still think that's true?

DOS PASSOS: It was certainly true at the time I said it. Plays then were being written with an eye on Hollywood. I guess things haven't changed much. I keep getting encouraged about the new season when I read about it in the drama section of the newspapers, but when I actually go see the plays, I am very discouraged.

The situation in theater is tragic because we have such good producing organizations in this country—particularly in the small theaters—and a great many excellent actors. In all kinds of small theaters and in college theaters, I have occasionally seen first-rate acting, first-rate production, and truly imaginative scenic effects. Yet, for some reason, nobody seems to be able to breathe any life into the theater.

BEALS: You said Eisenstein and Griffith influenced *U.S.A.*; do you see any current relationship between cinema and fiction which might be producing something new?

DOS PASSOS: I haven't been following recent movies very much. I did see *2001* and was much taken with it. It's a very attractive, poetic piece of work—one of the few poetic things I've seen come out of Hollywood in a long while. It is, of course, reflective of a great mass of science fiction being written. I'm ashamed that I am not as up on science fiction as I might be, because that may be one form of writing where something quite good is being done. Some of Ray Bradbury's things, for instance, are really excellent.

GADO: The relationship between Eisenstein and Griffith and your work was one of technique . . .

DOS PASSOS: Entirely technique. It had nothing whatever to do with content.

GADO: Don't you see any connection between Godard, Truffaut, Polanski, and the rest of the cinematic avant-garde and the novel? Between the nouvelle vague and the mixture of comedy and tragedy, of farce and the real you get in writers like Barth and Vonnegut?

DOS PASSOS: I don't think so. There is now probably less interest by writers in cinema because we have become so accustomed to this medium that it is less exciting than when it was very new.

GADO: Before our time runs out, might we talk a bit about the Sacco-Vanzetti case? Being of Italian extraction, I've always felt what happened to those two men to be part of my heritage. Because of your intimate ties to that agony, I was wondering whether you have read Francis Russell's *Tragedy in Dedham*?

DOS PASSOS: Yes. It is very interesting, although I don't agree with it. I was very good friends with Carlo Tresca. . . .[12]

GADO: That's why I brought this up. Russell bases his conclusion that Sacco was guilty on two things: the ballistics test he ran at the time of writing his book and Carlo Tresca's off hand statement just before he died that although Vanzetti was innocent, Sacco wasn't.

DOS PASSOS: I wonder about his examination of the evidence because it was so long after the trial; and my report of what Tresca said would be different. As I remember it, Tresca was pointing out that there was no question but that Sacco and Vanzetti were both trying to protect members of the anarchist group. Carlo thought —and he knew more than he told about it—that his group had been involved with a professional criminal gang in some of these hold-ups.

GADO: You no longer think that Madeiros was involved in that crime?

DOS PASSOS: It's very hard to tell. He might have been. Tresca's view doesn't necessarily rule out Madeiros. Madeiros's reasons for saying what he did were, I thought, perfectly honest and above board. The way he put things sounded as if he knew what he was talking about.

GADO: How much similarity do you perceive between the agitation over Sacco-Vanzetti, which was something of a watershed dividing the "two nations" in America, and current agitation over Viet Nam and the race issue, which is also dividing us into two nations?

DOS PASSOS: To me, the Sacco-Vanzetti agitation was much more understandable. I had great sympathy for the Anarchist movement at that time, even though it was obvious the solutions they were suggesting were nonsensical. But it seemed to me that those attitudes served to freshen people's minds. It was also interesting because it was the last expression of the great Anarchist movement before it was finally crushed by the Soviet Union.

SIEGLER: But now there is renewed interest in anarchist theories. . . .

DOS PASSOS: We don't know exactly what these are. Incidentally, I think it will prove to be good for a lot of these kids to have this attitude for a while—as long as they don't get stuck in it.

We get back to your earlier question about one tyranny replacing another. With age, one discovers the way the human race works: in simple terms, top dog always gets to the top, no matter what the system is, and then top dog starts kicking bottom dog in the face. No change in ideology changes that basic fact. Fifty years of Soviet history magnificently exemplify it.

GADO: In reading your novels, one is hit by how often figures appear who are modeled in part on yourself. Very often you are quite unflattering to these people. Why do you expose yourself so? What makes you claw at such obvious *personae* as Ro Lancaster and Jed?[13]

DOS PASSOS: It's part of the search for objectivity. Any novelist gets a great deal of himself into all of his characters, although he usually starts by trying to describe something else and does get a great deal of other people mixed into these characters. Perhaps to say that he ends up describing himself would be an over-simplification. The blood and nerves of the characters have to come from the writer's emotions and frustrations. My system has always been to try to do it objectively. That's why I put the Camera Eye things in *U.S.A.*; it was a way of draining off the subjective by directly getting in little bits of my own experience.

GADO: For you, then, the author's relation to his novel is both that of the puppet master and puppet. You probably don't remember a chat we had seven years ago in which you mentioned the various influences on your work. One you mentioned was Thackeray in *Vanity Fair*. I took this to mean that you were intrigued by the tension between the man standing above his theater (like the Camera's Eye) and the characters on his stage (like the narratives.)

DOS PASSOS: No. What influenced me in Thackeray was that he tried to give a picture of society in *Vanity Fair* through primary and secondary figures. It's a marvelous job.

SIEGLER: Judging by that criterion, which of your books would you say are best?

DOS PASSOS: I haven't the faintest idea. It's up to the critics to fight that out.

GLANZROCK: How do you begin to write a novel?

DOS PASSOS: I get started somehow, and then one word just follows another. I have a fairly definite notion of what I am trying to do. I try to do it, then I rewrite. In the early stages particularly, I find things have to be rewritten a good many times. Then, later, I fall into the style I've created and the writing falls together more easily.

GADO: Someone reported, perhaps not accurately, that you were in the habit of filing away newspaper headlines in a drawer until, eventually, a novel suddenly emerged.

DOS PASSOS: I did keep a lot of them. That's how the Newsreel thing started. I kept cutting out little clippings that seemed amusing. I started doing that quite early in my career. In *Manhattan Transfer*, I didn't use them directly, but I introduced them to show that I knew more or less what was going on in the world in which my characters lived. It was important to know what these people were reading, seeing, thinking. Then some of these collections of bits started to look so good to me that I put them in intact. Later, I started searching for apt headlines and collecting what would fit the story.

WAGONER: Did you ever make them up?

DOS PASSOS: No. I didn't have to. It was a period in which the newspapers were rather amusing.

GADO: Although you talked earlier about how *U.S.A.* evolved, you've said nothing about the D.C. trilogy and the way it grew. When you began *Adventures of a Young Man*, Joyce seems to have been in the forefront of your mind; you were apparently trying to do something different from your earlier writing. In *Number One*, however, you went in the direction of the more conventional novel. Then, in *The Grand Design*, you returned to the same technical attack you had used in *U.S.A.*

DOS PASSOS: I was anxious not to go on imitating *U.S.A.* I felt I had to get on different terrain.

GADO: The three were such different novels; have you any thoughts as to which was the most successful?

DOS PASSOS: None. I haven't read them in such a long time.

BEALS: This morning another Harvard man pointed out that many important literary figures from Eliot and Cummings in your day to Mailer and Updike among the younger generation went to Harvard. You burgeoned as an artist at Harvard: do you believe there is anything about the place, now or in 1916 . . .

DOS PASSOS: For me, the main thing that was there was the afterglow of the great New Englanders. There were remnants of a kind of Emersonian Congregationalism that had turned out some awfully fine people. However, I fought against that quality all the time I was there. I stayed at Harvard only because my father wanted me to. He was getting quite old and I followed his wishes.

GADO: Wasn't there a lingering presence of Henry Adams?

DOS PASSOS: Not very noticeable. Santayana was very noticeable, though he had just left. There was an aesthetic atmosphere filtering through the place.

GADO: I was thinking about Adams's concern with the dynamo, with entropy, and your reaction to the machine and industrialism.

DOS PASSOS: Of those I knew, I was probably the only one interested in that.

BEALS: Although you are now citing your respect for the influences of the great New Englanders, didn't you satirize puritan ethics in your early novel *Streets of Night*?

DOS PASSOS: Yes, I think so. But my encounter with that atmosphere, as I look back on it, now seems to have been much more valuable than I was aware at the time.

GADO: Paul brought up *Streets of Night*. I have suspected that it, and not *One Man's Initiation*, was really your first novel, that you had begun it while an undergraduate.

DOS PASSOS: Strange, I don't remember. Yet, some notes I had made corroborate your impression. When I was writing *In Our Time* [*sic*],[14] I started looking back into some old notebooks. I went back to them again even more recently because people at Cornell had found unexpurgated proofs of *One Man's Initiation*, which somebody must have bought in England and donated to the Cornell Library. They had been there I don't know how long before they were fished out. Cornell was bringing out an edition of this unexpurgated version and they asked me to do a sort of preface. In writing it, I looked up some of the diaries of that time that I still have. There was one for 1917 which referred back to *Streets of Night* as something already started. So I must have started it when I was at Harvard, laid it aside, and then tried to bring it back to life after the war.

WAGONER: Were you in the practice of taking many notes in preparation for your writing?

DOS PASSOS: Yeah. A great bit. I wish I did as much of it now as I did then. Very useful to me. And it's wonderful to look back on these things because they sometimes contain most startling surprises.

GADO: Like "A Humble Protest." That brings us full circle. Thank you, Mr. Dos Passos.

Notes

1. Students for a Democratic Society, a New Left radical student organization of the late 1960s and early 1970s.

2. An allusion to the Russian suppression of the liberal Czechoslovakian government in 1968.

3. Marshall McLuhan's *The Gutenberg Galaxy* (1962) stressed the revolution in communications introduced by films and television.

4. The mutiny of Russian sailors at Kronstadt in 1921 was brutally put down by the Soviet government. Dos Passos comments on the event in *In All Countries* (1934).

5. President Grayson Kirk of Columbia University had been attacked for his role in the forceable removal of student protesters from Columbia buildings in the spring of 1968. He resigned in late August 1968.

6. Governor George Wallace of Alabama, an avowed racist, was a candidate for president on the American Independent party ticket in 1968.

7. Dos Passos refers to Darwin's *Journal of Researches during the Voyage of H. M. S. "Beagle"* (1839) and Henry W. Bates's *The Naturalist on the Amazon* (1863).

8. The correct spelling is *Moorehouse.*

9. A. E. Hotchner, *Papa Hemingway: A Personal Memoir* (1966).

10. Dos Passos' short story "The Honor of the Klepht" was published in the *Harvard Monthly,* 57 (Feb. 1914).

11. Gado means Mailer's *The Armies of the Night* (1968).

12. Tresca, an anarchist publisher, had advised Sacco and Vanzetti about their legal defense.

13. Roland Lancaster of *The Great Days* (1958) and Jed Morris of *Most Likely To Succeed* (1954); Morris, in fact, is modeled on John Howard Lawson rather than on Dos Passos himself.

14. An error for Dos Passos' autobiography, *The Best Times* (1966).

Portrait of a Man Reading

What did your family read to you as a child?

My father had a fine old eighteenth-century education—he had started with Gibbon, Macaulay and the great British historians. But the first thing he read to me was the Bible; and if I had to be marooned anywhere with a choice of only one book, it would still be the Bible.

What were the first books you read as a child?

God, this is the beginning of a long story. Naturally, the first was the Bible. Then, *Mr. Midshipman Easy* by Captain Marryat, and much of Dickens. And I began to read Gibbon's *Decline and Fall* when I was pretty young. By the time I was ten, I'd begun to read my way through the bookcases.

And in adolescence?

Well, I don't remember this period too well. When I was at school—it was the Choate School in Connecticut—I took up Dickens again, though I'd gotten disgusted with him several years before. Also, I began to read a good deal of poetry, mainly Shelley and Blake, but I didn't like Tennyson. Most of the time, though, I spent reading South Sea adventures. After reading Melville's *Typee*, I always wanted to go to sea.

What did you read in college? And what were your contemporaries reading?

In college I started to read the French writers in French, particularly Flaubert. I'd spoken French since I was a child. And, of course, everyone read Compton Mackenzie, especially *Sinister Street*. Though I doubt I'd read him now, I would have to say that Mackenzie was the biggest influence on college students in my time. But he was pushed out of the way pretty quickly once I'd gotten to D. H. Lawrence's *Sons and Lovers*, which was a first-rate book. I also read Conrad with great pleasure. And the Elizabethans, Shakespeare and Chaucer. I'd read Shakespeare under duress as a child, but it didn't catch on until later. But, basically, I've always had a tendency to read history over novels.

Joe Flaherty, *Washington Post*, 13 July 1969, Book World section, p. 2.

293

What did you read while you were in Europe as an ambulance driver in World War I?

Well, pretty copiously in Spanish and French. The Belgian poet Verhaeren was the first writer I'd run into who wrote poems of the modern cities. And Romain Rolland's series, "Jean-Christophe." We all saw ourselves in the role of the pacifist Christophe in those days. I also read Rimbaud's poetry with a great deal of enthusiasm. I was particularly interested in Pió Baroja. He was the first modern Spanish novelist to pick up again the picaresque narrative which had been developed in the seventeenth century. The sort of writers who influenced Henry Fielding. I mean Cervantes' *Exemplary Novels*, for instance. So I read Pió Baroja and the greatest Spanish poet of the nineteenth century, Antonio Machado. The personal influence of Unamuno, to whom I talked when I went to Spain, was important. In the winter of 1917 I went to Italy and began to read the Italians, the Futurists especially. I was definitely not interested in D'Annunzio, but the poems and stories of men like Ungaretti affected the style of *Manhattan Transfer*.

What sort of reading did you do in the Twenties and Thirties?

In the Twenties the new writers were reacting against the era, much as students today are reacting to the Establishment. In the Thirties, the Communists were trying to put over the proletarian novel. In fact, I was put down as a proletarian novelist, but they found some heresy in my work. Mike Gold's *Jews Without Money* was quite good, though it was heavily tinged with the influence of Gorki, who wrote by far the best of this genre.

Which of your contemporaries still stand up?

Scott Fitzgerald's *The Great Gatsby* is a classic, and I think *The Last Tycoon*, if he'd been able to finish it, would have been. Hemingway's first book, *In Our Time*, was terrific, and his short stories hold up very well. The characters in *The Sun Also Rises* weren't nearly as good as those in the short stories. But then, I was so familiar with the scene. However, Hemingway was a great stylist. An excellent example is "A Clean Well-Lighted Place."

What about Thomas Wolfe?

Wolfe? I think I like *Look Homeward, Angel* best, but there were marvelous passages in all his books. Unfortunately, his work got out of hand; he couldn't pull it together. And I read Sandburg and Sherwood Anderson with great pleasure, but I'm not crazy about Maugham.

Outside of fiction or history, what do you read for entertainment?

For entertainment, I read verse, Mark Twain and Walt Whitman, who was my mainstay during adolescence and in college.

Who do you think are the great novelists of the twentieth century?

I haven't yet finished the Russian Aleksandr Solzhenitsyn's *The First Circle*, but I did read *The Cancer Ward* and I suspect he might be as great as any of them. However, Faulkner comes very close with *As I Lay Dying, Intruder in the Dust*, and his last novel, *The Reivers*, a kind of recap of everything he had ever done. Certainly Faulkner in the U.S. No matter how idiotic his plots, his characters always are marvelous; and his humor is special. Of course, Joyce has been the great influence on everyone. And when speaking of great twentieth-century novelists, you can't leave out Proust. I also have a special affection for Dreiser, particularly *Sister Carrie* and *An American Tragedy*. I believe he had great influence on all of us.

What contemporary fiction writers do you admire?

This gets harder and harder. There are so many I haven't read; but I liked John Barth's *The Floating Opera* and *The End of the Road*, though I haven't been impressed with his later work. I liked the small-town effect John Updike brought to *Rabbit, Run*. Mailer seems to me the ruin of a great talent. There were marvelous things in *The Naked and the Dead*, especially the patrol scenes. I haven't read any of the Jewish writers, but I've heard many good things about them. Once again, however, my fiction reading is always secondary to reading history and documented works.

You once wrote Scott Fitzgerald that he should not have written The Crack-Up at a "time like this," which suggests the book had political overtones. Do you feel that the political novel is more important than a personal testament?

At that time, I guess I did. But I was wrong about *The Crack-Up*. On re-reading it, I thought it was one of Fitzgerald's very best books. But I don't like the writer as an exhibitionist—that's why I dislike Mailer. And with *The Crack-Up*, I was trying to keep Scott from exposing his heart. But it's so difficult with people you know. I just wished he'd work it into another *Gatsby*.

What are you reading now?

I'm afraid I haven't read anything in a very long time but the Portugal chronicles, and a very good Spanish novelist, Goytisolo.

What are your favorite books and why?

The arts are very fickle, like popular songs. But *The Great Gatsby* is a lasting classic. Also, Stephen Crane's *The Red Badge of Courage* and Tolstoy's *War and Peace*. I think *Catcher in the Rye* is going to stay—it's a real little classic, too.

What writers influenced your own work?

As I said, I was naturally influenced in college by Mackenzie. And I think, oddly enough, more by the excerpts from *Ulysses* than from a full reading. And Dreiser was very important in my development as a novelist. He opened the gate to writing naturalistic novels and persuaded the publishers to print the novels of the rest of us. He was a kind of old elephant.

Which of your own books do you like best?

I'd much rather avoid getting into that. You just turn them out and hope for the best. It's very painful to reread them.

What about black writers?

James Baldwin seems a very talented fellow. His essays show him as a man of real ability. And *A Man of the People* by the Nigerian, Achebe—now there is a human book! It's not full of all this hysterical hatred.

Did political writings help to shift your political philosophy from Left to Right?

No. After observing the Left in operation, I find it's been a complete disaster. The regimes of Kennedy and Johnson have proven this. Even Daniel Moynihan has begun to realize that their approach was wrong. There should be statues erected to public men who admit they were wrong.

Do you read contemporary political and social writers?

Most political and social writing is going down the drain.

Besides books, do you enjoy films or plays?

I like Pinter as a playwright; and I've just seen *1776*, but I don't know if that counts. As for films, I enjoyed *2001: A Space Odyssey* and wasn't *Yellow Submarine* a sheer delight?

On the Way to the Moon Shot

[Dos Passos visited Cape Kennedy in May 1969 to observe the
Apollo 10 rocket launch.]

There are dates when history turns a corner. December 24, 1968 was such a date. Ever since the discovery of atomic power men had been tortured by the fear that science had unleashed forces beyond human power to control. The success of the Apollo series of flights is proving that the achievements of scientific technology can be directed with undreamed of precision. Man is reaching for mastery over matter. On December 24, 1968 three men, cool at the controls, detached enough to make humorous cracks as they went along, proved they could command the intricate energies technology had placed at their disposal. Our thinking about the universe, about life on earth can never be the same since that moment when the astronauts of Apollo 8 orbiting the moon paused from their routine at the keyboards of the spaceship to look back tenderly over two hundred and forty thousand miles of emptiness at the tiny blue earth which was their home: "the only touch of color in the universe."

Their voices instantaneously reaching the earth, as clear as if heard from an adjoining room, shattered all preconceived notions of space and time. Mankind was on the threshold of a new beginning. The words they chose to express their emotion came from the beginnings of the civilization which had nurtured the minds that made the journey possible. Before blastoff Frank Borman had typed out the first chapter of Genesis on fireproof paper. Genesis means beginning. It is not often that a great moment in history finds the right words to express it. This time it did.

As they looked down on the steep craters and the brutal ranges and erratic zigzagging canyons on the moon's colorless face passing below them, there had come a moment of real apprehension. They were out of communication and behind the moon. Would the control systems set off the rockets at the right time that were to snap them out of the moon's orbit into their path toward the earth? No one had ever tried this before. They were confident but not quite sure. Would all systems go? They did. Just after midnight on Christmas morning, James Lovell's voice came into the Houston control center loud and clear: "Please be informed there is a Santa Claus."

The homespun phrase, echo of generations of innocent American childhoods, expressed the relief, the exultation, but also the humbleness of victory. The paramount problem of space travel: how to come back, was solved. A manned landing on the moon was assured.

National Review, 23 (9 Feb. 1971), 135–36. © by National Review, Inc. Reprinted by permission.

"What good will it do?" people ask. "Couldn't the money be better spent on earth? Is it worth all that expenditure and effort to coop a man up in a spacesuit so that he can take a few steps in that desert?"

The answer is not fame or fortune. The answer is not that men are impelled to the moon, like the first man to climb to the top of Everest, "Just because it is there." The answer is not: "We do this for national glory," or to prove that some system of political-economic organization works better than some other system. The answer is that by his very nature, man has to know.

In our century we have seen everything that is hideous in man come to the fore: obsessed leaders butchering helpless populations, the cowardice of the led, the shoddy self-interest, the easy hatreds that any buffoon can arouse who bellows out the slogans, public derision of everything mankind has learned through the centuries to consider decent and true; but now, all at once, like the blue and white stippled bright earth the astronauts saw rise above the rim of the moon's grisly skeleton, there emerges a fresh assertion of man's spirit.

We live in a time when scientism has been foisted as a non-religion on most of the human race. People have been taught to grovel before the word science. We musn't forget that science is just Latin for knowledge. The passion for knowledge constantly brushes aside the established dogmas of the day to seek the reality beyond. Each smallest addition to human knowledge makes it clear that nobody knows very much about anything. Your first cry when you studied a photograph of a lunar crater brought back by Apollo 10 was "I didn't know it was like that." The literary imagination has been pretty good in forecasting discoveries, but not all the science fiction in the paperbacks could have forecasted the astonishment, the awe, the feeling of your heart turning a somersault inside you, you felt when you first saw the photograph of the lovely living earth rising above the dead horizon of the moon.

We know a great deal about certain aspects of reality. About other aspects we know almost nothing. The most experienced astronomers' view of the universe is as full of gaps and mysteries as the medieval world maps where the engraver filled in the blank spaces with storm-lashed galleons and elegantly delineated sea monsters. Our present ignorance of the universe is intolerable to the best minds. There are many things we need to know about our own solar system. Some key to more precise knowledge may lie within the radius of the first faltering steps the astronauts of Apollo 11 will make on the lunar surface.

The most exhilarating thing about the moon flights is the hardly believable speed with which so much has been accomplished. Barely eight years have gone by since the Apollo program, at President Kennedy's request, was authorized by Congress. The repercussions of the Russian breakthrough with their first sputnik in 1957 had given a great boost to rocketry in America. The NASA program was set up soon after to put the American space program on a civilian basis.

President Kennedy lightheartedly named 1970 as a target date for a lunar landing but none of the experimenters with rocketry had the faintest idea of how it could be done. No spacecraft large enough for the trip had yet been developed. When it was invented how could the men aboard be kept alive? How could they be brought back? Time was lost in calculating the hazards of landing a whole rocket on some smooth place on the lunar surface. Then gradually, out of random sketches on blackboards, the idea developed of a lunar vehicle which would carry the men down to a landing and then rejoin a spacecraft in orbit. Pure conjecture. First, programs had to be arranged to test the possibility of rendezvous, the docking of one vehicle with another in the outer darkness.

Each program, as it turned out, stood on the shoulders of the last. The Vanguard experiments, the Explorer probes, the Mercury and Gemini manned orbital missions, brought answers to hundreds of questions. An artificial environment could be produced on a spacecraft in which men could live and function. In spite of the encumbrance of space suits they could perform the complicated maneuvers in the Gemini Agena program. Electronic guidance of space vehicles could be refined to an incredible degree. Crews could keep in touch with earth stations by voice and picture across astronomical distances and come back undamaged.

When the technicians reviewed the performance of the Apollo 8 flight in December 1968, they discovered that the combined booster rockets and spacecraft had attained 99.9999 per cent efficiency. Out of something like five million separate parts there were only five minor malfunctions. This hardly hoped for perfection speeded the program immensely. The Apollo 9 and 10 missions followed in quick succession, rehearsals to test the capabilities of men and machines to accomplish a descent to the moon's inhospitable face.

How was it possible to accomplish so much so soon?

Finding men willing to take a chance in space was no problem at all. Scores of test pilots and military and naval flyers were ready to volunteer. It was a question of picking the men who seemed physically and mentally best qualified and putting them into training. The astronaut turned out to be a rather special sort of man. Just to keep their spirits up, the Apollo 10 crew asked to be allowed to do as much stunt flying as they wanted during the week before the launching date. They said barrel rolls and the like would season their stomachs.

In producing the hardware needed for an enterprise that man had barely dreamed of up to that moment the planners could draw on the experience of the industrial coordination which had been the cornerstone of victory in World War II. Scores of committees argued out scores of problems, but these were not routine committees; the scientists who manned them were spurred on by a sort of racetrack enthusiasm. In the moon race American inventors were kept on their toes by the need to compete—this time, fortunately, in peaceful terms—with the industrial complex and the keen Russian brains at the Kremlin's command. Science is a sport as well as a discipline. Engineers, researchers in rare metals, computer programmers, welders, the seamstresses who cut out the spacesuits, the errand boys in the offices, caught fire from the notion of a race to the moon. People tended to do just a little more than was expected of them in the service of so rare an adventure.

American industry has reached a point where it can custom-build metals and plastics to almost any specifications. The innumerable varieties of novel materials the programs demanded, which were produced by thousands of different contractors in virtually every state in the Union, could never have been collected at the time or the place where they were needed without the refinement of management which computers made possible. The flight control and vehicle assembly complexes at Cape Kennedy had at their disposal the greatest potential for the storing and processing of data ever marshalled.

A new art, computers are the field for the young. The average age of the engineers engaged in computer work for the moon flight is twenty-three. Using methods improvised almost overnight an investigator can in an instant bring under his magnifying glass any event he needs to scrutinize in the chain of supply. In a matter of seconds the pedigree of a faulty valve can be tracked back to the lathe it was finished on and even to the ores that went into its manufacture. Management, from being a rule of thumb proposition, approaches an exact science.

Throughout history the human spirit has advanced unevenly. The best brains and the most ardent imaginations tend to face one challenge at a time, leaving other sectors to stagnation and degeneracy on the eternal battlefield where man struggles to dominate the evil within him and the impartial pressures of his material environment. The landing on the moon in the summer of 1969 may well inaugurate a period when the most fruitful human effort converges on space exploration. Already the technology developed for the accomplishment of the Apollo program can be seen as a permanent achievement available for the solution of a hundred different problems.

The most ignorant layman bussed through the installations at Cape Kennedy can't help but be stirred by the feeling that knowledge is being expanded dizzily fast all around him. After this the world, the universe will look different to him. Some astonished awareness of the great implications must account for the emotion people show on the packed viewing stands as they follow the countdown on each lunar flight. The families on the beaches, the groups with field glasses and telescopes along the shores of the Indian River wait tense with excitement as the minutes tick away. "This is like pioneering in the old days," fathers tell their children. "You are going to see something no man has ever seen before."

With each successive launching the tension has risen. Apollo 11 is the climax. All the rest were practice heats. Through the long apprehension of the countdown a myriad anxious eyes watch the gleaming white pencil wrapped in its dainty plume of steam on the launching pad miles away.

"Two minutes, thirty-six seconds and counting . . . all systems go." Ears throb in anticipation, hearts beat a tattoo. Suppose something went wrong. "Thirty seconds and counting." Now the fire. Red and yellow flames. The great white pencil lifts itself slowly out of its billow of brown smoke. That enormous rumbling roar fills the sky. Faster, higher. The flaming rocket curves into the clouds. Frantic throats answer the jet engines' roar only to be hushed when the quiet workday voices of the spaceship's crew take over the radio. Worldwide, uncounted millions of television viewers join in a prayer for the men in that golden bullet. In every one of them the need to know, the smoldering spirit of adventure, buried deep down under the routine of every day, flares for a moment like the rocket engine into soaring flame.

Index

Donald Pizer received his Ph.D. from the University of California, Los Angeles. Pierce Butler Professor of English, Tulane University, Professor Pizer has written many articles in scholarly journals and is the author of five books, most recently *Twentieth Century American Literary Naturalism: An Interpretation*. He has edited works of Hamlin Garland, Frank Norris, Stephen Crane, Jack London, and Theodore Dreiser.

The manuscript was prepared for publication by Michael K. Lane. The book was designed by Joanne Elkin Kinney. The cloth edition is printed on 55-lb Glatfelter text paper and is bound in Holliston Mills Roxite Linen.

Manufactured in the United States of America.